7th Cavalry Regiment

The Legacy of Custer's
7th U.S. CAVALRY
In Korea

TURNER PUBLISHING COMPANY

Publisher's Editor: Gardner Hatch
Writer: Edward L. Daily

Copyright © 1990
Turner Publishing Company

This book or any part thereof
may not be reproduced without
written consent of the publisher.
Library of Congress
Catalog Card No. 90-070004
ISBN: 978-1-681621-66-1

Limited Edition of 1,000 copies

Extra copies available from publisher

A platoon leader hurls a hand grenade at the enemy. (U.S. Army Photo)

Support artillery firing their 105-mm howitzers almost point blank into North Korean positions. (Courtesy of Bob Mauger)

Many bridges were destroyed along the Naktong River and within the Pusan Perimeter, 1950. (Courtesy of Bob Mauger)

Destroyed Russian T-34/85 tank - Waegan, South Korea, 1950. (Army)

A typical command post base as an infantry battalion detrucks near the frontline to assemble for action. (U.S. Army Photo)

Light .30 caliber machine gun position. (U.S. Army photo)

TABLE OF CONTENTS

Colonel John Wilson Callaway

This book is dedicated to Colonel (retired) John W. Callaway, Battalion Commander, 2nd Battalion, 7th Cavalry Regiment, 1st Cavalry Division, Korea 1950-51. And to the officers and troopers within his command during this particular time span who have endured the hardships of battle with unfailing devotion to duty, honor and country.

THE AUTHOR

Edward L. Daily

Edward L. Daily enlisted directly into the 1st Cavalry Division, in 1948. After completing Armored-Infantry basic training at Fort Knox, Kentucky, he was immediately sent to the Far East Command in Japan. Arriving in Tokyo, Japan in February 1949, he was assigned to Company H, 2nd Battalion, 7th Cavalry Regiment.

He soon found himself learning his new trade as a machine gunner in the 1st Platoon. But, at that particular time most of their training consisted of occupation duty that existed within the Eighth Army. A major influence soon appeared in his life and military career, which came from his company commander, Captain Melbourne C. Chandler. Captain Chandler attempted to instill in every trooper a dedicated effort to become a better soldier and he further emphasized the strict guidelines of the heritage and traditions of the famous GARRYOWEN regiment.

When the Korean War started, the 7th Cavalry Regiment departed Japan in July 1950, to fight against communist aggression from the North Korean Army. Fighting a savage enemy, the 2nd Battalion experienced many battle casualties during the early stages of combat. This created a very serious condition because there was a shortage of replacements and, in some instances, there were none at all! Because of this desperate situation, promotions within the ranks came to those capable survivors. From the recommendations of Lieutenant Robert M. Carroll, Captain Mel Chandler and Major Omar Hitchner, Commander, 2nd Battalion, he received a battlefield commission to temporary 2nd Lieutenant, on August 10, 1950.

Assuming leadership of the same 1st Platoon, it was a very proud time in his life and military career. However, two days later, on August 12, 1950, during a vicious battle on the Naktong River, the forward elements of his platoon were overrun and he could not evade capture.

With the grace of God, he managed to escape from the enemy on September 12, 1950 and was held captive only 32 days. Receiving the appropriate medical treatment, he volunteered to return to his previous unit and active duty on September 23, 1950. This time, conditions had greatly changed in favor of the United Nations Forces, because the United States Marines and the 7th Infantry Division had previously made an amphibious landing at Inchon, South Korea, thus, cutting-off the entire supply line of the North Korean Army.

Nonetheless, he would face many struggles and hardships as he remained in combat with the 7th Cavalry Regiment. On May 10, 1951, he returned to the United States. He was honorably discharged from the Army on May 27, 1952.

Among the medals awarded to him were: the Distinguished Service Cross; Silver Star Medal; Bronze Star Medal (V); Purple Heart w/2 oak leaf clusters; Army Commendation Medal; Korean Campaign Medal w/5 bronze battle stars; South Korean Presidential Unit Citation and the Combat Infantryman Badge. In June 1988, he was awarded the American Ex-Prisoner of War Medal by the Department of Defense.

He is a life member of the 1st Cavalry Division Association and the 7th U.S. Cavalry Association; and over the years he has maintained loyal and dedicated to both organizations. Currently, he is a member of the Board of Governors of the 1st Cavalry Division Association. The first Cavalry Division is stationed at Fort Hood, Texas.

PREFACE

Major General Charles D. Palmer, Commander, 1st Cavalry Division, presenting Silver Star Medal to Captain Crawford "Buck" Buchanan, 2nd Battalion, 7th Cavalry Regiment. To his left are Sergeants McMahan and Eddie Mohar. (Courtesy of Crawford Buchanan)

This book is but a small tribute from an ex-member of the 2nd Battalion, 7th Cavalry Regiment, 1st Cavalry Division, United States Eighth Army, to all fellow Korean War Veterans and ex-Prisoners of War all over the world. Especially to those who left their homelands to fight and did not return.

And this book does not pretend to be a technical work, but rather a story of an ordeal sustained by flesh and blood of United Nations soldiers, American soldiers, Republic of Korea soldiers, and least to mention, the innocent and defenseless refugees.

My story to tell is how they faced danger, pain and death, first on the ridge, and then on the blood-smeared litter. Also what they thought of their buddies, weapons, leaders, allies, and the enemy in this curious little war in Korea.

Fortunately, and with the grace of God; I managed to escape from the North Koreans and was captive only a brief thirty-two days. However, in this short time the traumatic experience in itself was horrible and unbelievable. To this day, it is still a mystery why the North Koreans did not move me northward to a prisoner of war camp. Why was I selected and retained to be continually moved within close distance of the battle front of the Pusan Perimeter? Was it for future propaganda reasons? As you read my story, maybe some of this mystery can be understood and possibly unraveled.

The North Korean atrocities perpetrated on South Korean refugees and Republic of Korea soldiers cannot be described in detail. However, mass killings which I witnessed executed in various groups (10-100) left an impression. Before being shot, many were inevitably forced to dig their own graves, which were trenches or open shallow pits. This grisly and ghastly killing of humans normally had their hands tied behind them and then bound to each other. Sometimes their pathetic bodies were never covered with dirt, but left exposed to the hot sun.

The writing of this book has come from two sources. The first was my personal garrison duty, prisoner of war experiences, and combat recollections. Those combat recollections of survivors who fought and served with the 2nd Battalion, 7th Cavalry Regiment, 1st Cavalry Division and who were kind enough as to grant me personal interviews or to correspond with me. The second was amassed during a period of almost three years. This included histories of Korea, military histories of Korean fighting, official unit histories, personal interviews as well as maps, photographs and other classified documents to which the Department of the Army generously though carefully granted me clearance and access. Professional monographs, citations, newspaper articles and magazine pieces were also used.

The Korean War, also called the "forgotten war" because today's generation knows so little about it, started as a military struggle fought on the Korean Peninsula. The current Collier's Encyclopedia, for instance, devotes only five paragraphs to the Korean War, twenty-six pages to World War II, fourteen pages to World War I, and five pages to the Spanish-American War.

It's a shame that a more active interest was not shown because it was one of very few successful actions taken to stop the spread of Communism. This would definitely suggest that the 72,500 men of the United Nations forces who were killed in Korea did not die in vain. In tribute to his men, General Matthew B. Ridgway said that he believed that history would someday record that:

"...the crest of the Communist wave of cold-blooded aggression was broken against the arms and will to fight of the United Nations battle team in Korea..."

As General John Wickman, Jr., Commander of the U. S. Forces in Korea, wrote at the end of an article in the October 1979 issue of Army magazine:

All Eighth Army soldiers and other members of the U. S. Forces in Korea do their jobs willingly in the knowledge that they contribute to keeping the peace on the Korean peninsula. Peace and stability linked to U. S. national security interest.

It is good to know that at least some people in the West have such a firm resolve. No doubt, those who fought for the principles of the United Nations in the Korean War must surely echo his sentiments.

BLAZON OF THE REGIMENTAL INSIGNIA
OF THE 7TH U.S. CAVALRY, U.S.A.

A cavalry horseshoe, or, heels upward, with crease, sabre and seven nail heads, white. Above and joining the heels of the shoe, a scroll, azure, bearing the words, "GARRYOWEN," or...

At the base and emerging from sinister side of the shoe, a dexter arm embowed, vested azure, the hand in the buckskin gauntlet, proper, grasping an old style U.S. Army sabre, or hilted, or blade extending to center or scroll gripe, sabre threaded or...

Explanation of Design

The horseshoe is symbolic of the Cavalry. Its color, gold (yellow in heraldic tincture), is the color of the old uniform facings of the United States Cavalry, in existence when the Regiment was organized and is still retained as the color of the Cavalry Arm.

The words, "GARRYOWEN," are the title of an old Scottish (sic) war song known and used as the Regimental song since the days of General Custer. Its rollicking air symbolizes the esprit de corps for which the Regiment is noted.

The arm, taken from the crest of the Regimental Coat of Arms, symbolizes the spirit of the Cavalry Charge. At the time of the organization of the Regiment this position of the arm and sabre was known as "Raise Sabre" and was taken at the command, "Charge." The sabre itself is of the old Cavalry type used in the Indian campaigns. The gauntlet is also symbolic of those times. The blue of the sleeve is the blue of the old Army uniform. The twisted emblem at toe of shoe is symbolic of Indian days.

*For many years the Regimental song was accepted as being of Scottish origin; however, it has been definitely established that the song is of Irish origin. It had been used by several Irish regiments as their quick march; the Fifth Royal Irish Lancers stationed in the suburb of Limerick called "GARRYOWEN," (the Gaelic word, meaning 'Owen's Garden') used it as their drinking song. The words can hardly be called elevating, but depict the rollicking nature of the Lancers while in town on pay day in search of their peculiar style of 'camaraderie.'**

Authority: Boosey: London: (no date, presumably about 1800) "Songs of Ireland."

THE SONG OF GARRYOWEN

It was an Irish quick marching or drinking song adopted by the 7th Cavalry Regiment in 1867. Its first introduction to war was at the Battle of Washita, on November 17, 1868. After that all 7th Cavalry troopers were known as GARRYOWENS.

We are the pride of the Army and a Regiment of great reknown
Our names in the pages of history from 66 on down
If you think we stop or falter while into the fray we're goin'
Just watch our step, with our heads erect when our band plays "GARRYOWEN"

Attorney General J. Howard McGrath, President Harry Truman and Defense Secretary Louis Johnson walk to the White House to discuss first Korean crisis on June 27, 1950.

The Korean War, also known as the "Forgotten War," started as a military struggle fought on the Korean Peninsula from June, 1950, to July, 1953. Begun as a Civil War between the democratic Republic of South Korea and the communist Democratic People's Republic of North Korea, the conflict swiftly developed into a limited international war involving these and eighteen other belligerent states. The Korean War, considered from a broad, general viewpoint, was one of the by-products of the post-World War II "cold war," the global political and diplomatic struggle between the democratic and communist systems; thus the original belligerents were internal components respectively of the two systems, as were their various allies. Specifically, the war (excluding its civil stage) resulted from a "police action" undertaken by the United Nations against communist aggression. There were no formal declarations of war, and the United Nations action was otherwise unique in history because, despite numerous earlier provocations, neither the United Nations nor its predecessor the League of Nations, had theretofore employed collective military measures to repel an aggressor.

Fighting began when, on 25 June, 1950, a Soviet-equipped North Korean army invaded South Korea. South Korean positions along the 38th parallel, demarcating the frontier between the two republics, were swiftly overrun, and the North Korean forces drove southward. The United Nations Security Council, with the Soviet delegate, voluntarily absent, invoked military sanctions against North Korea on 27 June, 1950, and called upon member states to aid the Republic of Korea. Almost simultaneously U.S. President Harry S. Truman ordered American military forces into action against the invaders. These forces, those of South Korea and (ultimately) contingents from Australia, Belgium, Luxemburg, Canada, Colombia, Ethiopia, France, Great Britain, Greece, Netherlands, New Zealand, Philippines, South Africa, Thailand and Turkey, were placed under a unified United Nations command headed by the U.S. Commander in Chief in the Far East, General of the Army, Douglas MacArthur. The participating ground forces of these nations, the United States, and South Korea were eventually grouped in the U.S. Eighth Army.

Seoul, the South Korean capital, fell to the North Koreans on 28 June, 1950. During July, 1950, the United Nations forces retired to and established the Pusan Perimeter-defense line about 50 miles north of Pusan, a leading seaport on the S.E. coast. An important sector of the perimeter was the Naktong River defense. Fierce North Korean attacks failed to dislodge them. On 15 September, 1950, the United Nations command launched a powerful offensive. Elements of the U.S. Army effected an amphibious landing at Inchon, on the west coast 200 miles above Pusan, cutting the lines of communication of the North Koreans. The Pusan defenders, breaking out the perimeter, drove toward Seoul. The South Korean capital was recaptured on 26 September 1950. The U.S. Forces then pressed across the 38th Parallel and captured the North Korean capital of Pyongyang, on 20 October 1950. In certain sectors, U.N. forces advanced to the Yalu River, the boundary between China and Korea. The North Korean army had ceased to exist as an effective fighting force, and the way seemed open to a speedy end of hostilities.

However, late in October, 1950, Chinese Communist forces crossed the Yalu and engaged forward elements of the U.N. Army. Undeterred, General MacArthur on 24 November, 1950, ordered an "end-the-war" offensive. The latter was almost immediately frustrated by a massive Chinese counter-offensive. The U.N. forces, over-extended, out-numbered, and ill-equipped to fight a fresh enemy in the bitter North Korean winter, were soon in general retreat. On 26 November, 1950, the Chinese cut the escape route of more than 200,000 U.N. soldiers and marines, who were later evacuated from the port of Hungnam, reoccupied Pyongyang on 5 December, 1950, and, sweeping into South Korea, recaptured Seoul on 4 January, 1951. The Chinese offensive was finally halted by the end of the month along a front substantially south of Seoul. On 22 February 1951, the U.N. command mounted the powerful counterattack known as "Operation Killer." Under pressure of superior firepower, the Chinese slowly withdrew from South Korea. The South Korean capital of Seoul fell to U.N. forces again on 14 March, 1951. By 22 April, 1951, U.N. forces had occupied positions slightly north of the 38th parallel along a line which, with minor variations, remained static for the rest of the war.

The war had assumed a new dimension, meanwhile, as U.N. bombers, hitherto virtually unopposed in strikes against communist rear positions, were challenged by increasing numbers of Soviet-built jet aircraft operating from bases in Manchuria. On the basis of this development and the Chinese intervention, General MacArthur concluded that victory could be achieved only by attacking Chinese bases in Manchuria. MacArthur's public advocacy of this strategy, which entailed the risk of a general war with China and the U.S.S.R., and which conflicted with policies established by his civilian and military superiors, resulted in his removal from command on 11 April, 1951. His successor, U.S. General Matthew Ridgway, pursued the limited objective of inflicting maximum personal loss upon the enemy along the fixed battle front and from the air. This strategy, while severely punishing the Chinese and the rehabilitated North Korean Army, could not drive them from the field. In the ensuing stalemate, the communists were unable to force the U.N. from North Korea and the U.N. was willing to pay the price necessary to drive the enemy into Manchuria.

Some of the most desperate battles of the war took place in the early and attritive phases of the conflict. The Pusan Perimeter and Naktong River defenses and in the area popularly known as the Iron Triangle and the hills called Old Baldy, Capital, Pork Chop, T-Bone and Heartbreak Ridge. The U.N. Air Force, retaining command of the skies despite strong opposition from enemy interceptors, devastated North Korean supply lines, railroad bridges, Hydroelectric plants, and industrial centers. North Korean coastal points were systematically pounded by U.N. naval units. The attritive phase of the war was marked also by bloody riots and demonstrations in the U.N. prisoner-of-war compounds, by communist charges (Never substantiated) that the United States had waged germ warfare against North Korea and China. With the exchange of sick and wounded prisoners of war, there were disclosures that the communist had been guilty of atrocities against captured U.N. personnel.

In June, 1951, as the positional-warfare pattern began to crystallize, the Soviet Union delegate to the United Nations formally proposed that the belligerents in Korea opened discussions for a cease-fire. On 10 July, 1951, following preparatory talks, representatives of the U.N. and communist commands began truce negotiations at Kaesong.

Though conducted in an atmosphere of mutual suspicion and recrimination, the negotiations finally resulted in settlement of all except one of the major issues. The chief obstacle to agreement was communist refusal to accept the principle, adhered to by the U.N., that prisoners-of-war should not be returned to their respective armies against their wills. Negotiations broke down in October, 1952, and were not resumed until April, 1953. In late spring the two sides agreed that prisoners-of-war unwilling to return to their own countries would be placed in the custody of a neutral commission for a period of ninety (90) days following the signature of the truce. It was additionally provided that during this period each side could attempt to persuade its nationals to return home. The two sides also agreed to hold a top level peace conference within three (3) months of the effective date of the armistice but effectuation of this provision was later postponed until April, 1954. On 27 July, 1953 the truce agreement was signed at Panmunjom.

Thus, the pending ultimate settlement at the projected peace conference, the Korean War was suspended after more than three (3) years of conflict. During the war, the United States suffered 54,235 killed in action; 103,000 wounded; 8,177 missing in action; 7,000 prisoners of war, of which only 3,450 returned alive. An appalling fifty-one percent (51%) died in prison camps and 389 prisoners of war were unaccounted for. South Korea sustained 1,312,836 military casualties, including 415,004 dead. Estimated communist casualties were in excess of 2 million.

The United States alone spent a total of $18 billion on the war. Almost all Korea, excepting the area in the Pusan Perimeter, was virtually laid waste. In South Korea more than 600,000 homes were destroyed, 2.5 million persons were made homeless, and an estimated 1,000,000 civilians killed. Damage in this section of the country was set at more than $1 billion. Adding to the South Korean casualties, 428,568 were wounded, while 469,264 were prisoners of war or missing in action. Other United Nations casualties totalled 17,214, of which 3,094 were dead, 11,297 wounded and 2,823 were prisoners of war or missing in action.

LEGACY OF THE 7TH CAVALRY

The westward surge of the American migration to the Great Plains in the 1850s symbolized the restless urge that gripped the entire nation. Spurred on by the pretending clouds of the Civil War between the States, the land-hungry hordes ignored the mounting unrest of the Indians. Marked with savageness, the Indians rose to block the ongoing tide that flooded their territories. The Indian warriors struck with impunity and remounted their attacks in blood-drenched orgies.

With this westward expansion and massive migration of settlers, the need for more soldiers to protect them soon developed. Under the Congress Act of July 28, 1866 (General Order 92), came the birth of the newly authorized 7th Cavalry Regiment and the beginning of a new chapter in the history of the Army.

The 7th Cavalry Regiment was organized at Fort Riley, Kansas, and its ranks were filled with a hardbitten crew of trappers, veterans from the Civil War and frontiersmen. Its prime field officers were Colonel Andrew J. Smith, Lt. Colonel (Brevet Major General) George Armstrong Custer and Major Alfred Gibbs.

Also the influx of Irish immigrants contributed a great share of the troopers within the Regiment, and the brawling, hot-tempered Irishmen found a ready outlet for their exuberant spirits in the campaigns against the Cheyennes. The influence of the Irish on the Regiment is particularly noted in the famous drinking song "GARRYOWEN," which the Regiment has adopted as its own.

When Custer organized the Regimental Band in 1867, he adopted the "GARRYOWEN" as the official song of the 7th Cavalry. On November 17, 1868, at the Battle of Washita, Custer had the Regimental Band play the "GARRYOWEN" as the 7th Cavalry engaged the village of Black Kettle to inspire his command during this battle. The scattered remnants of the Cheyennes were decisively defeated.

Until 1872, the Regiment rode out against the Sioux and Apaches. In 1874, the Regiment moved to the Black Hills of Dakota to afford protection for construction parties of the Northern Pacific Railroad. Hard on the heels of the newly-laid tracks came hordes of gold seekers and farmers, and this influx brought about new troubles with the Sioux. As the migration continued, the savageness of the Indians increased until 1876; the 7th Cavalry and its dashing, spectacular leader, Lt. Colonel (Brevet Major General) George Armstrong Custer, joined other Army units in a concerted drive to break once and for all the power of the Sioux tribes.

Fate was to pick the proud 7th Cavalry to play the leading role in a portrayal of devotion to duty, loyalty to country and honor to self that exemplifies the word "courage." Scouting patrols of Custer's forces were the first to locate the Sioux encampment on the Little Big Horn River on June 25, 1876. In all the months and years of matching tactical wits with the Sioux, Custer had never before faced such an opportunity for delivering a crushing defeat.

With the camp swarming with wives and children and their entire wealth, the Sioux warriors could not scatter and pick their battle ground. The slightest delay might mean the escape of the foe. Fulfilling his command responsibility, Custer made his decision. He split the Regiment into three units, sending two of them to his left under Major Reno and Captain Benteen with the mission of attacking the camp on line with the third unit under his own command. The soundness of this plan is, even today, the subject of heated discussion among military men.

Whether it could have succeeded will never be known, for Reno and Benteen met opposition to their progress, and the full might of an estimated 5,000 Sioux plunged head-on into the five companies under Custer. The determined stand of the valiant officers and men has been immortalized in story, song and picture. Fighting to the last man, they were finally overwhelmed by the masses of charging Indians. The next day when the delayed forces of Reno and Benteen reached the scene, there remained only a Cavalry charger named "Commanche," alive on the battlefield. It was Captain Keogh's horse!

In 1877, the Regiment returned to action against the wiliest of all Indian generals, Chief Joseph of the Nez Perces. During the bloody four-day battle, the might of the great chief was broken, and the defeated Indians were returned to their reservation.

By 1906, the Regiment had served two tours of duty in the Philippines and in 1916 joined the Mexican Punitive Expedition. It returned to Fort Bliss, Texas and remained there until it was assigned to the 1st Calvary Division in 1921.

In February 1943, and within the early stages of World War II, the Regiment was converted from horses to vehicles which was an exit of an era in military lore. It was passing of an age of chivalry in that had grown from the days of Knighthood and reached its peak in the great Cavalry charges of the Civil War.

The Regiment departed Camp Stoneman, California, in July, 1943, to their new home in Australia. At a location fifteen miles north of Brisbane, the Regiment - for the next six months - would engage itself in jungle and amphibious training. This specialized infantry preparation was for General MacArthur's strategic forces in the South Pacific. Even though it was now an infantry unit, Army standard operating procedures and sentiment of the 7th Cavalry Regiment, it was permitted to keep its old name and that was all.

The Regiment found itself fighting in several different Island Campaigns and eventually defeated the Japanese Imperial Army in the Philippines. These vicious, bloody battles fought in the extreme heat of the South Pacific jungles, were won at a cost to the Regiment of over 300 killed and 1,000 wounded.

On August 13, 1945, the 1st Cavalry Division - which included the Regiment - was selected by the Supreme Commander, General Douglas MacArthur, to accompany him to Tokyo, Japan, and be part of the Eighth Army Occupation Forces. In the early morning of September 8, 1945, the 7th Cavalry Regiment entered Tokyo, and - from that date until it sailed for Korea, it performed occupation duty in Japan.

The Regiment suffered drastically during the post-war demobilization of combat units throughout the entire Army. Performing its occupation duties effectively, it had difficulty, however, maintaining a combat readiness and capability. On June 25, 1950, the North Korean People's Army invaded the Republic of Korea, South Korea, with hordes of Communist soldiers. Being poorly prepared for combat, the 7th Cavalry Regiment was thrown into South Korea as an American infantry unit to temporarily halt the Communist tide.

During the Korean War, the Regiment fought many desperate battles within the Pusan Perimeter and throughout the endless mountains of South and North Korea. Amid the hot, stinking rice paddies to the sub zero frozen hills of Korea, the Regiment experienced some of the bloodiest fighting in its long history. By the time that the Armistice Agreement was signed on July 27, 1953, ending the Korean War, the 7th Cavalry Regiment had suffered more than 600 killed, 3,500 wounded, and 300 missing in action.

In a few short years to come, the 7th Cavalry would meet the call to an old, yet new conflict; the Vietnam War. A new concept in warfare and tactical doctrines in the use of helicopters opened the way to a bold, new role in combat for the Regiment.

These crack "Skytroopers," as a new Cavalry with an old spirit - but young at heart, would fight heroically with determination to destroy the Communist enemy in Vietnam. Many bitter and vicious battles were hard-fought and won, creating another new chapter in the history of the 7th Cavalry Regiment and the United States Army.

THE COMMANDERS

General Douglas MacArthur, Commander-in-Chief, United Nations Command, July 24, 1950-April 11, 1951 (U.S. Army Photo)

General Matthew Ridgway, Commander-in-Chief, United Nations Command, April 11, 1951 (U.S. Army Photo)

Major General Hobart Gay, 1st Cavalry Division Commander, Sept. 24, 1949-February 4, 1951 (U.S. Army Photo)

Major General Charles Palmer, 1st Cavalry Division Commander, February 5, 1951-July 16, 1951 (U.S. Army Photo)

Major General Thomas Harrold, 1st Cavalry Division Commander, July 11, 1951-July 4, 1952. (U.S. Army Photo)

Colonel William "Wild Bill" Harris ,Regimental Commander, 7th Cavalry Regiment, 1950-51 (U.S. Army Photo)

Lt. Colonel Melbourne C. Chandler, Executive Officer, 2nd Battalion, 1950-51. Commanding Officer of Co. H, 1949-50, 2nd Battalion Commander, July 1951.

GENERAL GEORGE A. CUSTER

Born on December 5, 1839
Birthplace: New Rumley, Ohio
Father: Emanuel Custer

General George A. Custer

Emanuel Custer had five children by his second marriage. They were; George Armstrong Custer, December 5, 1839, Nevin Johnson Custer, July 29, 1842, Thomas Ward Custer, March 15, 1845, Boston Custer, October 31, 1848, and Margaret Emma Custer, January 5, 1852. His father was born in Cryssoptown, Maryland in 1806. Leaving there, he settled in New Rumley, Ohio where he married Matilda Viers at the age of 22. She died 6 years later leaving him with 3 children.

In the early 1850s they moved out of New Rumley a few miles into Harrison County to live in a log cabin. They attended the Creal School a mile and a half North of Scio.

When George was 10 years old his half sister (By his father's 1st marriage), Lydia Custer, married David Reed of Monroe, Michigan, some 200 miles from their home in New Rumley, Ohio. At the age of 16, he taught school in Harrison County, Ohio at Beech Point, and later Locust Grove, and he attended McNeely Formal School (Hopedale College) in between school terms.

In March 1861 his father, Emanuel, purchased 120 acres of land in Wood County before moving to Monroe, Michigan several years later. George earned $26.00 a month plus board for teaching schools.

In the summer of 1857 he landed on the wharf of West Point, and he would be one of sixty-eight Plebes to be admitted there in July. At the time Custer went to West Point you were supposed to graduate in 5 years, but this was changed in April, 1861 to 4 years because of the Civil War. Custer was to have graduated that year in July, but in early June while on duty as Duty Officer he failed to stop a fight and was brought up on charges for failing to stop a riot. On July 15 he was brought to trial by court martial. He was found guilty and sentenced to be reprimanded in Orders.

In the meantime some of his friends who had graduated in April went to Washington on his behalf. He was summoned to Washington and there-by was given his first assignment. He was assigned to G Co., 2nd Cav. His 1st battle was at Bullrun, which turned into a defeat for the North.

Early in the Fall of 1861 Custer left his outfit and was attached to General Stoneman's outfit. He was sent home on sick leave, staying in Monroe, Michigan from October 1861 to February 1862. He was then assigned to the 5th Cav. (Army of the Potomac). In May of 1862 he was promoted to Captain and became General McClellans "Aide - De - Camp" (Temporary Rank).

He took command of A Company 4th Michigan Infantry. Most of these men were from Monroe, Michigan and many had gone to school with him at Stebbins Academy when he lived with his half sister.

About 2 weeks later he was promoted to 1st Lieutenant in the 5th Cav. On November 7 McClellans was put on waiting orders, so Custer went home to Monroe, Michigan. While there he met his wife to be, Elizabeth Libby Bacon.

In April of 1863 Custer was ordered to join his Co. opposite Fredericksburgh, Virginia. Once again Custer was a Lieutenant, and in June found himself as a captain and "Aide - De - Camp" to General Pleasonton. On June 29 Custer was promoted to the rank of Brigadier General and took command of the Michigan Cavalry Brigade and joined them in Hanover, Pennsylvania.

Custer and Elizabeth Libby Bacon were married on February 9, 1864 in the Presbyterian Church in Monroe, Michigan.

In October 1864 he was promoted to Major General of the Volunteers and placed in command of the 3rd Division which included his crack Michigan Brigade. On October 6 they were told to withdraw. Tom Custer was awarded the Medal of Honor twice. The only person in any branch of their service so honored. In May of 1865 the Civil War was over and Custer was ordered to Texas. In the early Spring of 1866 he was ordered back to Washington. The same month he was mustered out as a Major General of the volunteers and automatically reverted to his regular Army rank of Captain. He was paid $8,000.00 a year as a Major General and $2,000.00 a year as a Captain. At this time Custer was 27 years of age and returned to Monroe, Michigan for much earned rest.

In July he received his appointment as Lt. Colonel of the newly formed 7th Cavalry. In October he joined the 7th Cav. at Ft. Riley, Kansas. His brother Tom was appointed as a 1st Lieutenant in the regular Army on July 28, 1866. On August 27, 1867 General Grant ordered a general court martial at Ft. Levenworth, trying Custer for: 1. Absenting himself from his command without authority. 2. Using ambulances for personal business. 3. Ordering his officers to shoot deserters without a trial, among other things. The court convened on September 15, 1867, meeting for 4 weeks before reaching the verdict of guilty. He was sentenced to a suspension of rank and command and forfeiture to pay for one year.

Custer returned to Ft. Hayes, Kansas on September 30, 1868. In 1871 Custer took part of the Regt. to Elizabethtown, Kentucky. The rest of the Regt. was sent to South Carolina to break up the Klu Klux Klan and hunt down moonshiners.

In 1873 Custer and the 7th Regt. were assigned to Ft. Abraham Lincoln at Yankton, Dakota Territory. Margaret Custer, the General's only sister, married Lt. James Calhoun in 1871. He was killed at the battle of the Little Bighorn.

At the age of 35, Custer was 5'10" tall. He weighed 165 lbs, had clear blue eyes, and short wavy golden tint hair. Custer and his wife would spend his leave time whenever possible in Monroe, Michigan. Custer was also a great lover of literature. On June 27, 1876 Lt. Bradley and his scouting party returned with first hand information that Custer and all of his 225 officers and men were dead. There were no human survivors, but the horse, Comanche, belonging to Captain Myles Keough was found alive, but severely wounded. He was tenderly taken care of and nursed back to health.

Relatives of Custer who died with him at the battle of the Little Bighorn were: Brothers Capt. Tom W. Custer, age 31, Forager Boston Custer, age 25; brother-in-law Lt. James Calhoun; and nephew Harry Armstrong Reed from Monroe, Michigan age 18.

Comanche the horse was retired from all duty until his death at the age of 29 in 1891.

Things found out after Custer's death; 1. There were about three times the amount of Indians that the agent had reported. 2. The Indians had been supplied with Winchester repeating rifles and an abundance of ammunition for the purpose of hunting buffalo, while Custer and his men had single shot Springfield rifles.

General Custer adopted the song GARRYOWEN as a fighting song in 1867.

CAMPAIGNS FOUGHT BY THE 7TH U. S. CAVALRY

INDIAN WAR CAMPAIGNS

Comanches
Little Big Horn
Nez Perces
Pine Ridge
Montana 1873
Dakota 1874

MEXICAN EXPEDITION CAMPAIGNS

Mexico 1916-1917

WORLD WAR II CAMPAIGNS

New Guinea
Bismarck Archipelago
(With Arrowhead Device)
Leyte (With Arrowhead Device)
Luzon

KOREAN WAR CAMPAIGNS

UN Defensive
UN Offensive
CCF Intervention
First UN Counteroffensive
CCF Spring Offensive
UN Summer/Fall Offensive
Second Korean Winter
Third Korean Winter

VIETNAM CAMPAIGNS

Defense
Counteroffensive
Counteroffensive, Phase II
Counteroffensive, Phase III
TET Counteroffensive
Counteroffensive, Phase IV
Counteroffensive, Phase V
Counteroffensive, Phase VI

TET 69/Counteroffensive
Summer/Fall 1969
Winter/Spring 1970
Sanctuary Counteroffensicve
Counteroffensive Phase VII
Consolidation I
Consolidation II
Cease-fire

DECORATIONS OF THE 7TH U. S. CAVALRY

Presidential Unit Citation (Army), Streamer Embroidered <u>Antipolo, Luzon</u>
Philippine Presidential Unit Citation, Streamer Embroidered <u>17 October 1944 through 4 July 1945</u>
Presidential Unit Citation (Army), Streamer Embroidered <u>Yonchon, Korea</u>
Presidential Unit Citation (Army), Streamer Embroidered <u>Pusan, Korea</u>
Republic of Korea Presidential Unit Citation, Streamer Embroidered <u>Waegwan-Taegu</u>
Republic of Korea Presidential Unit Citation, Streamer Embroidered <u>Korea</u>
Chryssoun Arition Andrias (Bravery Gold Medal of Greece), Streamer Embroidered <u>Korea</u>
Presidential Unit Citation (Army), Streamer Embroidered <u>Pleiku Province</u>
Valorious Unit Award, Streamer Embroidered <u>Fish Hook</u>
Valorious Unit Award, Streamer Embroidered <u>Quang Tin Province</u>

CHAPTER I
WELCOME TO THE ARMY

The summer of 1948 was hot and dry, and my hometown community was still making minor adjustments from the post-war era of World War II. For some unknown reason I had the desire to join the military service, so one day I stopped by the local recruiting office to ask some questions. As I walked into the door, I was greeted by the Army Recruiting Sergeant, who had medals plastered all over his chest. He looked at me and said, "Well, boy, are you thinking about joining the Army?" "Uh! Oh, well I just want some information, if possible." He immediately replied and asked, "How old are you boy?" I answered with, "Seventeen, sir." "Oh, hell, boy, you're gonna need your parents consent, and they must sign their approval on the necessary induction papers. This is because you're too damn young, but if you were eighteen then there would be no problem." "That will be no problem, Sergeant, because my parents are divorced, and my mother will sign the papers for me." "Well boy, that's great, now bring her in here and the sooner the better."

He then asked me to sit down directly in front of his desk and asked me my name. I answered with, "Edward Daily." "Well, Daily, is there any particular job you would like to learn in the Army?" "Yes sir, maybe some type of specialty school, and I want to go overseas." "You know Daily, we have a couple of offers for two divisions," as he pointed to the wall which had two individual Army posters displayed. One had a large Army division patch which was yellow and black with a horse head on it. The other was a drab green Army division patch with a large red "1" in the center of it. One stated, "Enlist for Japan and serve with the 1st Cavalry Division," and the other said, "Enlist for Germany and serve with the 1st Infantry Division - one of the Army's oldest divisions." Both stated, however, "travel, excitement, adventure and serve with pride, prestige and honor." Strangely, my eyes kept focusing on that big yellow and black patch with the horse head on it. The Sergeant looked at me and said, "Daily, that's probably the largest division patch in the Army. And it was one of General MacArthur's favorite divisions during the South Pacific campaign in World War II." "OK, Sergeant, sign me up for the 1st Cavalry Division." As he prepared the paperwork he said, "Daily, you must get your mother in here soon to sign all the necessary papers."

That evening after my mother arrived home from work, I had the unpleasant task of asking her to sign for me to enter the United States Army. Well, after several hours of debating, she finally gave in and agreed to sign the Army induction papers for me. As unpleasant as it may have been for my

Col. John W. Callaway, prior to his retirement on April 30, 1971. He graduated from West Point in 1941.

mother, she never regretted her decision.

My orders for basic training, dated 5 October 1948, were received a couple of months later and indicated the 3rd Armored Division, Fort Knox, Kentucky. Next to my name on the same order was 1st Cavalry Division, Far East Command. The Army had kept their promise just as the recruiting Sergeant had specified. Then, of course, there was the unpleasantness and difficulty of saying goodbye to my mother. Being an only child really didn't help matters either. And there was my wonderful and loveable grandmother who was present also to say goodbye. Her words that day have echoed forever in my mind: "Eddie, never lose faith in God, and don't forget to pray everyday."

From a civilian to my new life in the Army was not a difficult change for me. After 10 weeks of Armoured-Infantry training and at graduation ceremonies, I would have the honor of receiving my first award in the Army. How proud I felt that day when they called out Recruit Edward Daily for having qualified best scores in the Company with the M-1 Rifle and M-1 Carbine. Company Commander, Captain S.B. Scott, pinned the Expert Badge on the left breast of my jacket, and I could feel the slight tears come into my eyes as we shook hands and then saluted. Orders were received the following day which indicated for me to report to Fort Lawton, Seattle, Washington, for future shipment to Japan.

My stay at Fort Lawton would be brief as I received orders for shipment to Japan and the 1st Cavalry Division. We departed from Fort Lawton to Navy Pier 90, where we boarded the large troop transport ship. Everyone was immediately informed that the name of the ship was "Daniel I Sultan."

We sailed for Japan late in the afternoon, however, little did we know at the time that

Lt. Col. John W. Callaway, Commander, 2nd Battalion, 7th Cavalry, discusses with Gen. of the Army Douglas MacArthur, about the tactical situation north of Chipyong, Korea, March 1951. Gen. MacArthur sent this photo personally to Lt. Col. Callaway-note MacArthur's signature at top center of photo. (U.S. Army Photo, courtesy of Col. Callaway).

a February typhoon would be in our future path of travel. After a very rough and miserable trip, we finally reached the Port City of Yokohama in one piece. There were a lot of sea sick GI's during the trip, including myself.

As we sailed within Yokohama Bay and approached the pier, I was in awe as I looked from the ship toward this strange foreign country of Japan. The I noticed the air had an uncommon odor, and one of the GI's made an unfamiliar comment. "Man, you can smell those 'honey buckets' all the way out here!" I quickly asked, "What in the hell is a 'honey bucket?" He then replied with an explanation of how the Japanese use human defecate in their vegetable gardens, which is transported in wooden buckets. I was starting to wonder how this country could be so different than the United States. The months ahead would bring many happy and enjoyable days of learning the customs and traditions that were much different from my way of life in America. I came to admire the Japanese and cherished their friendship.

CHAPTER II
PRELUDE TO WAR

The next 18 months in Japan would also bring forth a particular military influence while serving with Company H, 7th Cavalry Regiment. It didn't take long for our Platoon Sergeant, Bob Earley, to explain the heritage and traditions of the 7th Cavalry Regiment, and the true meaning of "<u>GARRYOWEN</u>." And he fed us some history how a Battalion of the 7th Cavalry under the command of Colonel George Armstrong Custer had been wiped out at the Battle of Little Big Horn.

"GARRYOWEN" is a four syllable word which all officers and enlisted men recognized and cherished. Everyone was informed that its origin was from the old Gaelic word meaning "Owen's Garden," and was first used as an old Irish drinking song, and then later used throughout the military as a marching tune. We also learned how Colonel George Armstrong Custer organized the Regimental band in 1867, and adopted the "GARRYOWEN" as the official song of the 7th Cavalry Regiment.

Then we were told that the Unit Crest of the 7th Cavalry Regiment showed the name of "GARRYOWEN," and was accepted and approved by the War Department in 1924. Many of us looked at one another, and I had the personal feeling of pride that I was now a part of Colonel Custer's heritage and the 7th Cavalry Regiment.

In late March, 1949, the long-established and traditional Cavalry might was abolished throughout the Army, and the Regiment was organized as an Infantry Regiment. Notwithstanding this organization, all units remained designated as "Cavalry" with Infantry in parentheses after the unit designation. Most of us were extremely happy that "Cavalry" remained the same, but we were informed that troops would be called companies and squadrons became battalions.

Our various jobs in garrison duty were to guard the Imperial Palace, 22nd Ordinance Center, Bank of Chosen, Takashiba Pier and the Tokyo Quartermaster Base Depot. We also furnished escort guards for the Sugamo Prison - where the Japanese war criminals were being held.

The summer heat of July 4th prevailed as the regiment participated in a parade and review on the Imperial Palace Plaza for the Supreme Commander of Allied Powers. Immediately after the parade, we began packing weapons and equipment for the move to Camp McNair for maneuvers. This base was located approximately 100 miles southwest of Tokyo.

Eighth Army maneuvers during this period lasted until the first of September. We did various fire and squad tactics, and conducted a field exercise using ball ammunition in the attack. This defensive exercise was conducted by all units of the regiment. I now had the feeling that I was becoming a better trained soldier.

Upon our return to Tokyo, we found damage to Judd Barracks which had been caused by typhoon "Kitty." The next several days was spent not only cleaning our equipment but repairing damage that had been done to our barracks. Company H was given the assignment of guarding the Bank of Japan, and this lasted for a couple of months.

As the year of 1949 was coming to a close and just prior to Christmas, the regiment celebrated its 83rd anniversary on December 22. The day was declared a holiday with various festivities throughout the regiment. A Christmas party was held for 500-600 Japanese children from a nearby school. I personally enjoyed this as it gave me the opportunity to escort a group of kids to see a Mickey Mouse movie. After the movie, we passed out gifts to them and surprisingly, many of the kids spoke fairly good broken English. In this one-day affair, I met a wonderful group of Japanese children as they enjoyed sharing some of our American traditions.

The new year of 1950 would bring changes within our regiment. All units were relieved of their occupation duties, which in the months ahead would help to strengthen our training. Squad, platoon and company problems were emphasized, and the regiment developed an alert exercise to maintain all units in a quick compact readiness. These exercises would prove very valuable in the coming months.

Also, another important factor that would prove valuable in the future months ahead was that Captain Chandler insisted that everyone in the company, even the cooks and clerks as well as riflemen, be qualified with every weapon on the firing range. Also our dapper, cocky mess Sergeant Bill Brown went out on the firing range. In a few short months to come, Sergeant First Class William Brown would distinguish himself in Korea.

In February, the entire 2nd Battalion moved all personnel, equipment, quarter-ton vehicles, three-days ration, and a basic load of ammunition by shuttling with six C-54 aircraft from Tokyo's Tachikawa airport to Sendai, Japan. Upon arrival at Sendai, the battalion conducted a short overnight defensive exercise and returned by shuttle movement in the same aircraft. This air mobility exercise would also prove to be very valuable in later months in Korea.

March brought forth a St. Patrick's Day party which many of the officers and enlisted men of the 7th Cavalry Regiment attended. Many also brought their wives to join in the festivities. Lieutenant Marvin

L to R: Korean Ambassador John Chang and Secretary General Trygve Lie, confirm that it is "war against the United Nations." (Acme) UPI

The North Korean soldier was tough, disciplined and experienced. (Eastfoto)

15

Squad Tents at Camp McNair - Note Mt. Fugi in the background. (Courtesy of Ed Daily)

The North Korean People's Army moved south to cross the 38th Parallel, 1950. (Eastfoto)

Goulding, with his wife and their two children, presented Captain Mel Chandler a large green shamrock. We all sang various songs of "GARRYOWEN" - and here was Lieutenant Goulding, a Jewish officer singing Irish songs the best of all. Little did he know at this particular time that in a few months he would sacrifice his life for the name of "GARRYOWEN."

At the end of March, my name appeared on the company bulletin board that I had been selected to attend a forthcoming Eighth Army leadership school in Tokyo. Several of us from Company H were selected by Captain Chandler, and I considered this an honor because I was only a Private First Class. However, at this particular time there was very little rank not only within the company, but the entire regiment.

I was starting to realize and understand even more that Captain Chandler and the military were trying to develop me into a better and more proficient soldier. Each day I tried to exemplify my very best as a soldier, and Captain Chandler recognized this fact. I admired and respected him not only as my company commander, but as an excellent officer and leader. He possessed a knack for inspiring people and had a remarkable skill in the art of motivation.

After my return from leadership school, the 2nd Battallion continued to drill and train to keep in top shape. However, many of us in Comapny H were starting to realize how challenging previous Eighth Army maneuvers had been to our regiment as we still had weapons and vehicles that were used on Leyte and Luzon during World War II. And here I was, a first gunner on an M1917A1, 30 caliber, heavy water cooled machine gun; a weapon that was also used in World War II. It had great fire power, but it was heavy and cumbersome to carry or transport. The difficulty of this weapon would prove itself in future months in the mountains of Korea.

Sunday morning, 25 June 1950, really seemed like an ordinary Sunday. After returning from church services, Sergeant Bob Earley was talking at the mess hall that approximately 60,000 North Korean soldiers had invaded South Korea at 0400 hours. However, none of us really took the so-called rumors seriously. For the next several days not much was said about the North Korean invasion.

On June 30, we were alerted that all furloughs and passes were immediately restricted or cancelled. Captain Mel Chandler told us that President Truman authorized Gen. MacArthur to commit U.S. ground forces in the Korean action. He did emphasize that it was a "police action" and not a war. A Task Force from the 24th Infantry Division would be used first, and some of our Cadre were being immediately transferred to build up their Division strength. For the next couple of days we would see approximately 168 non-commissioned officers leave the 7th Cavalry Regiment. As we said goodbye to numerous friends, those of us that were left, started to wonder how long it was going to be before the 1st Cavalry Division would be sent to South Korea.

We received some minor training of cargo net climbing on how to debark from ships. All of us now realized we were preparing for an eventual amphibious landing. After this very brief training exercise, we returned to McKnight Barracks in Tokyo.

Later that afternoon, several of us were looking at the Stars and Stripes newspaper, and it stated that the situation in South Korea was getting worse. Private First Class Gossett shouted to me and said: "Hey Daily, your name appears on the bulletin board, and you've been promoted to Corporal." "Oh boy! I get another pay raise and when is that promotion effective?" Gossett replied, "July 2." I didn't waste any time getting my corporal stripes sewn on my class A and fatigue uniforms.

The awaited news finally arrived on July 8, that the 1st Cavalry Division was being sent to South Korea. Captain Chandler told us that our Division Commander General Hobart Gay stated that we would be used for an amphibious landing somewhere in South Korea. And most of us were starting to wonder about the so-called "double talk." One statement is "police action" and the other would be "combat." Well, in any case, the reports we continued to hear about the 24th Infantry Division were not good or encouraging.

John Osborne, a senior correspondent for Life and Time, wrote from Korea that the war was brutalizing American troops. Fought the way the United States was doing it, it was beginning to "force upon our men in the fields acts and attitudes of the utmost savagery." This means not the usual inevitable savagery of combat in the field, but savagery in detail; the blotting out of villages where the enemy might be hiding; "the shooting and shelling refugees who may include North Koreans."

The next several days were spent checking weapons and equipment. Being that I was a first gunner on an M1917A1, 30 caliber, heavy water-cooled machine gun, I closely inspected the head space and packing around the barrel, which prevented water leaks. Everything looked perfect. And as we were issued ammunition, I immediately instructed all ammo bearer's to open each case and check every belt which contained 250 rounds each. This was to see if there was any damage to certain cartridges within the belt which could cause the weapon to become jammed.

On July 15th, the battalion was instructed to turn in all pillowcases, sheets, steel bunks and office furniture to supply storage. All personal items had to be put in our foot lockers, as they would also be left behind in storage. Only necessary military items needed in combat would be taken to South Korea.

The following day, July 16th, our entire battalion loaded up their trucks and equipment, (except 2-1/2 ton trucks) on the USNS Shanks, located in a Yokohama Pier. On July 17th, we departed McKnight Barracks in Tokyo, and as we left in convoy, the majority of us thought we would return in 30-90 days. Little did I know at this particular time, I would never see McKnight Barracks again.

Our battalion was finally aboard ship, and we pulled away from the pier late in the afternoon of July 17. As we waited in Yokohama Bay, it was almost dark as the USNS Shanks in a convoy with other ships, sailed for South Korea.

CHAPTER III
KOREA - "LAND OF THE MORNING CALM"

...And he smelleth the battle a far off, the thunder of the captains, and the shouting.
—Job 39:35

The 1st Cavalry Division lands in Pohang-dong, South Korea, July 18, 1950. First amphibious landing of the Korean War. (U.S. Army Photo)

As our ship convoy continued toward South Korea, we were notified that there were going to be rough seas because of approaching Typhoons: "Flossie", "Gracie," and "Helene." Now my thoughts returned to early 1949 when our transport ship from the United States Japan passed through a miserable typhoon. For the next couple of days, Company H was oriented on S-2 and S-3 communications and proper use and care of the radio sets. Also the seriousness of the Korean situation was stressed, and various pointers on combat were emphasized.

Most of us realized that our division was one-third understrength because we were lacking the third Battalion in each of the three infantry regiments. Also lacking were the third batteries in the division's four artillery battalions. However, at this particular time, the seriousness of previously losing 168 non-commissioned officers to the 24th Infantry Division in early July was not recognized. This would show up later in some of our first battles.

What were they like, these American soldiers? A rifleman with a poetic name like Robert Smith was perhaps representative. He could have come from a broken family and live in a run down, nondescript neighborhood in Chicago. The romance of military life probably seemed more exciting than the humdrum classes at school. At 17 he joined the Army. He was an irrepressible, voluble youth, filled with zest; and he was good-looking with dark hair. Now he was in Korea, fighting in a so-called "police action."

Being detained an extra three days by severe weather, on July 22, we finally reached the harbor of Pohang-dong and immediately began our debarking process. We were now part of the first amphibious landing in South Korea. As we reached the shore and dry land, we quickly assembled to move to a bivouac area several miles out of town. Captain Chandler issued orders to dig in for the night with a 50% alert. Nothing happened during the night except the slapping of mosquitoes and the sound of men cursing. Rumors were beginning to mount on how badly the 24th Infantry Division was taking casualties. Also, there were the tales of heroic deeds performed by brave soldiers. Our minds were curious as to what our futures would be.

The early morning of July 23, we were ordered to assemble and wait for orders for our move to the Kumchon-Taegu sector. At first we were informed of our move by truck then orders of our departure would actually be changed to rail transport. After a long delay, due to the lack of rail transportation, the 2nd Battalion was finally loaded and departed Pohang-dong late in the afternoon. During

1st Cavalry Division troopers loading into Landing Craft at Pohang-dong, July 18, 1950. (U.S. Army Photo)

this particular delay, all weapons were carefully checked by all personnel. Some expressed their eagerness for a taste of the so-called "police action."

As the train continued to move toward our destination of Kumchon, we could see various roads clogged with hundreds of refugees who were forced to flee their homes by the North Korean advance. Many of us were becoming apprehensive as to our future and conversations lulled to personal thoughts.

After approximately 20 hours, our train finally arrived with the 2nd Battalion. Immediately, word was received to prepare for combat because of a serious breakthrough on the right flank of the 5th Cavalry Regiment. Captain Chandler (with excitement in his voice) went on to explain why everyone must be extremely cautious of the refugees. "The damn North Koreans are dressing in native white clothing and are mingling with the innocent refugees to cause panic." It's

A typical Korean village prior to the Korean War, 1950.

17

A village house with a thatched roof and constructed of mud. Many contained only a dirt floor. Most of the cooking was done outside of the house over an open fire. Vicinity of Taegu, South Korea, 1951. Photo Courtesy of Paul (Bill) Fleming.

A village house made of mud wattle and thatched roof. Once on fire they burned smokily. The vicinity of Taegu, South Korea, 1951. Photo courtesy of Paul (Bill) Fleming.

General Walker, Eighth Army Commander, conferring with fire support officers July 16, 1950. (Wide World)

Floating pontoon bridge over the Naktong River at Waegwan, 1950. (U.S. Army Photo)

starting to be damn difficult to know where the enemy really is. Also, the 8th Combat Engineers are starting to use mine detectors on them which will help some, but they can't do it all. So, I want every refugee carefully screened and checked that might move through our sector. Now, let's move out on the double!"

We quickly moved into position for our first baptism of fire. Our location was very near the 7th Cavalry Regiment command post, which was a blocking position to the rear of the main forces. During the evening and the remainder of the night, we were ordered for 100% alert. Several enemy attempted to infiltrate our line, and we continued to fire at whatever moved throughout the night. Many of us were becoming "trigger happy," which really showed our inexperience in combat. The mosquitoes were eating us alive as the mosquito repellant didn't seem to work.

The morning of July 25, word was received that an officer was killed and an enlisted man was wounded during the night. Both were from Company E. No apparent heavy attacks were experienced in our sector. The temperature from the July heat, we

were told, would probably go over the 100 degree mark. This helped to make the rice paddies a humid, stinking pool of water. Then word was received from Lt. Bob Carroll, that we were moving out to give support to the 8th Cavalry Regiment. He emphasized to us that we should use extreme caution as enemy patrols were harassing our flanks and enemy soldiers posing as refugees were causing considerable casualties. With some delay, we finally moved out late in the afternoon.

Word was received that Division Headquarters issued orders for the immediate removal of all 1st Cavalry Division patches from our uniforms. We were told that the large yellow and black patch in some instances was an easy target for North Korean snipers. Also, the identifying red crosses on ambulances and other medical vehicles had to be removed. The enemy was deliberately firing at such vehicles as wounded were being evacuated from the front.

As the 2nd Battalion moved slowly toward the front, it became apparent that the road was too congested. Masses of refugees, Republic of Korea soldiers, 24th Infantry Division and our 7th Cavalry Regiment, were

all in this confusing and disorganized mess. Lt. Marvin Goulding informed us that he just had contact with Company H command post, and they were under enemy fire and an enemy Russion T-34 tank also passed them heading toward the rear of our position. However, we received no orders to withdraw, and all hell was starting to break loose as firing from everywhere along the road was directed at the 2nd Battalion. Everyone in our company was scattered along the roadside. During this chaos and panic situation, I became separated from my assistant gunner. Here I was, a first gunner with 53 pound tripod and no weapon to place on it. Needless to say, I still had my trusty M-1 rifle to defend myself with, but I had placed myself in a very embarrassing position in the face of the enemy. Nonetheless, I had to admit my mistakes along with my inexperience in combat. After this particular night, many of us in the 2nd Battalion would learn a great deal from our poor performance in this one, but very confusing combat ordeal.

It was after midnight as several of us continued to withdraw toward the rear as we received sporadic enemy fire. On down the road, we finally came in contact with our

Both the officer and his driver are from the 2nd Battalion, 7th Cavalry . Names are unknown. (Courtesy of Ed Daily)

Officer on left is Lt. Colonel John W. Callaway, Commander of the 2nd Battalion, 7th Cavalry Regiment. Officer on right is unknown. (Courtesy of Ed Daily)

Officer on right is Captain John B. Wadsworth, Commanding Officer of Company H, 2nd Battalion. Other two officers unknown. (Courtesy of Ed Daily)

1st Lt. John "Jack" Lippincott in front of jeep that belonged to Colonel William "Wild Bill" Harris, Commander, 7th Cavalry Regiment. Note saddle on hood. (Courtesy of Ed Daily)

2nd Lt. Edward L. Daily, 1st Platoon Leader, Company H, 2nd Battalion, 7th Cavalry Regiment. (Courtesy of Ed Daily)

Sharpshooter from the 2nd Battalion, 7th Cavalry. Name unknown. (Courtesy of Ed Daily)

company commander, Captain Chandler. He was directing men from the 2nd Battalion to a railroad where Company H command post was previously located. An enemy T-34 tank was now starting to fire down the road at us as we followed Captain Chandler and headed toward the railroad.

It was really starting to show how extremely difficult it was for company commanders and their platoon leaders to properly direct and lead their men. Not only were they hampered by a confusing mess, but they were lacking leadership experience by the non-commissioned officers in the squads and platoons. Not only the 2nd Battalion, but the 7th Cavalry Regiment was being plagued by the loss of many of its experienced unit leaders and specialists that were transferred to the 24th Infantry Division in early July.

Captain Chandler tried to assemble together as many troops as possible from the 2nd Battalion. His orders were to follow him down the railroad to an unspecified location. We had no radio communication with other units and the dark of the early morning made it more difficult to see friendly units. The enemy continued to fire at us with their tank as we made our withdrawal. After fight-

ing our way for approximately six or seven miles, our disorganized and exhausted groups were met by Major William Witherspoon of Regimental S-3. He directed us to an assembly area where Captain Chandler ordered all Company H personnel to regroup as soon as possible, "if not sooner!"

You could tell by the voice of Captain Chandler that he was not pleased with our performance. He said, I have very little time to express myself! But I will tell you this, from now on Company H will not become disorganized! "We came to Korea as a fighting unit and that's the way it will remain! From now on I want to hear 'GARRYOWEN' shouting from everyone's mouth."

Lt. Bob Carroll then notified me along with several others, that we had to return to the railroad and the road to investigate and try to recover lost weapons or equipment. He also emphasized extreme caution of the enemy and refugees. Several groups of us from the 2nd Battalion would depart with the use of jeeps, trucks and 3/4 ton weapon carrier vehicles.

It didn't take long for us to locate and find numerous weapons and equipment strewn along the road and railroad tracks. Strangely,

the enemy had not seen these lost weapons and equipment as we assumed they had pulled back prior to daybreak to possibly regroup. The only contact we had with the enemy was minor sporadic sniper fire.

Regarding this chaotic withdrawal of July 26, 2nd Battalion Headquarters reported the following was left behind: one switchboard, one emergency lighting unit, 14 machine guns, nine radios, 120 M-1 rifles, 26 carbines, seven BAR's and six 60-MM mortars. Included in those figures were my own M1917-A1 30 caliber, heavy duty water-cooled machine gun that my assistant gunner lost during the night. As far as I could tell at this particular time, it still looked in perfect working condition.

As we quickly tried to recover the weapons and equipment, Sergeant First Class Bill Brown notified us of radio contact with the 2nd Battalion. Orders were for us to rejoin our particular units which were now in defensive positions. Sergeant Brown, surprisingly, was our mess sergeant, but Captain Chandler had him assigned to our machine gun platoon. At this particular time, all company field mess equipment was in the extreme rear.

The following is a brief story of the withdrawal on July 25th-26th, 1950, from Sergeant First Class Harold Blanc, Communications Sergeant, Company H, 2nd Battalion, 7th Cavalry Regiment.

During the chaotic withdrawal of July 25th-26th, 1950, I was assigned within the communications section of Company H. We were ordered to proceed to Yongdong and relieve elements of the 8th Cavalry Regiment. However, the road to Yongdong was clogged with refugees and various units of the 24th Infantry Division and 1st Cavalry Division. There was no way for our unit to progress forward as ordered.

As darkness came, a Russian T-34 tank appeared in the distance and started firing directly into our positions. Within the darkness, the projectiles from the tank cannon looked like large tracers or balls of fire. The hundreds of refugees caused more confusion and panic as we attempted to withdraw to the rear. Our movement on the narrow dirt road was almost at a standstill.

PFC Bob Alicea and myself were actually the last two troopers to leave this location. Soon we came in contact with Captain Mel Chandler, and he directed the two of us to immediately locate some 81-mm H E mortar ammo for the 3rd Platoon. They were in extremely short supply. He also directed us to take a small road to a railroad track, then turn right and follow it to an assembly area.

We did what Captain Chandler ordered and we found the 81-mm ammo and delivered it to elements of the 3rd Platoon. Then we soon found Major Bill Witherspoon directing disorganized troopers of the 2nd Battalion to an assembly area, which was a dried-out river bed. This was adjacent to and very near the railroad track. All troopers were being grouped together by whatever company they were assigned with. We quickly discovered that many troopers had lost their equipment and weapons.

Needless to say, Captain Chandler was very displeased and angry over our poor combat performance during the withdrawal. He expressed to all troopers of Company H that he would not tolerate such poor conduct and performance in the future. I personally believe that after this one very confusing ordeal, every officer and trooper within the 2nd Battalion became a better and more proficient combat soldier.

The next couple of days would be of extensive patrols which engaged with enemy guerilla forces in nearby villages and various enemy patrols. On July 28, the 1st Battalion was moved and extended to the left of the 2nd Battalion. During the early morning the enemy attacked the extreme right flank of Company G. The enemy was following a pattern by using hundreds of refugees in front of their attack. Also, they concentrated on small forces and would try to overrun one unit at a time by massive overpowering use of men. With the support of Company E, the enemy was temporarily halted in this particular attack.

Also, the North Korean tactics would often vary from one attack to another. Sometimes the first wave not being fighters, but human pack animals, carrying ammunition and grenades. Then the second wave would arrive with the rifles and burp guns. The word burp gun (Russion 7.63-mm) was very respected by the GI, as the ammunition drum on the bottom held 75 rounds, and in less than a minute the damned thing was empty. It could not be aimed with an accuracy; however, a quick burst of fire would send a shower of slugs. In many North Korean units, every fourth man carried a burp gun. We would very soon learn that the North Koreans were well trained by Russians, and they had given them excellent equipment. In what we optimistically termed as a "police action," many of us in the 2nd Battalion completely under-estimated the enemy.

Destruction of the Kum River Bridge, July 1950. (U.S. Army Photo)

The decisive factor, the Air Force, bombing a North Korean railroad yard. (USAF, VIA-Wide World)

Papa-san in South Korea, 1950. They were highly respected for their age.

Captured American soldiers during the first few days of fighting in Korea, 1950. Many were from the 24th Infantry Division. (Eastfoto)

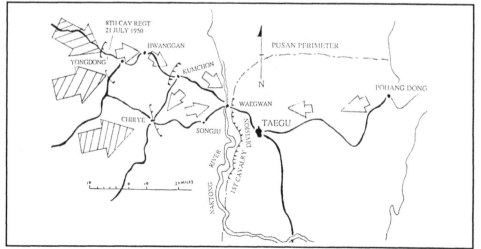

Landing and initial committment - After landing at Pohang-dong on 18 July 1950, the 1st Cavalry Division quickly took up blocking positions near Yongdong. The crushing North Korean offensive, however, forced United Nations defenders to pull back into the Pusan Perimeter, early in August.

An infantry squad captures and burns a Korean village. (U.S. Army Photo)

Litter bearers moving wounded trooper over rough terrain. (U.S. Army Photo)

Some roads were almost impassable. (U.S. Army Photo)

CHAPTER IV

WITHDRAWAL TO THE NAKTONG RIVER

It was very apparent that we would have to fight the North Koreans in ditches, small villages, and over endless mountain ridges. Some of the reports we thought were being exaggerated were that we might be outnumbered at times more than 20 to one, and needless to say, this didn't help our morale.

Sporadic enemy small arms fire was being received all along our positions as Captain Chandler notified us that the entire 2nd Battalion had orders to withdraw. The daybreak of July 29 was a couple of hours away as we made our way down a valley in total darkness. The enemy was firing at us from both sides with small arms and automatic weapons. Their artillery fire was landing near our column as the endless red, green and white signal flares lit up the sky. Then out of the darkness there would be an occasional shout for "medic," as a fallen trooper was wounded and needed medical attention.

Daybreak, and we were still moving back and searching for a new defensive position. As we passed a railroad station, I could see the name which read," Hwang-gan." The refugees contributed to the mass confusion as they staggered with their overloaded A-frames and clogged the road to the south. It was equally difficult to screen the refugees.

We took up our defensive position parallel to the road we had just left. The 2nd Battalion was notified that no friendly troops would be to our extreme front. I was very apprehensive to our position as we waited for the enemy to attack. However, a quick check of my machine gun revealed everything in order and Private First Class Ray Scarberry said; "We got plenty of ammo, Daily!" Then Lt. Bob Carroll came to our machine gun emplacement and said: "Congratulations, Daily, today you were promoted to the rank of Sergeant." "Oh boy, Lieutenant! Thank Captain Chandler when you see him because he fought for several promotions within our company. We are still lacking in rank"!

Lieutenant Carroll went on to say that he knew Captain Chandler was going to make some changes in the platoon as soon as we got back in reserve. He stated that he didn't know what squad I would have until then. However, I would very soon experience the task of not only leading a squad, but the continued duty as first gunner on the heavy machine gun. Our company was still extremely short of personnel.

During the night, a 100 percent alert was passed on to the Battalion as we waited for an apparent attack. Then word was received that two enemy tanks were seen down the road, and they were near the location of Company E. This information was sort of confusing because the sounds that we were hearing were supposed to be coming from

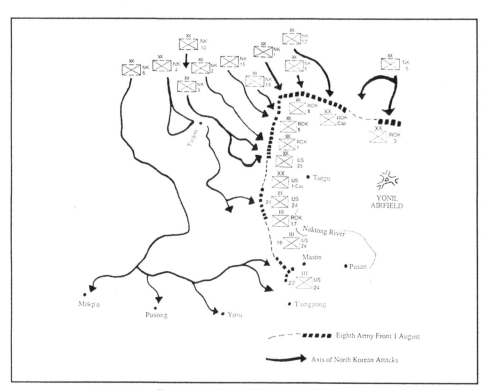

The front moves South , July 14 - August 1950

bulldozers from elements of the 8th Combat Engineers. Just prior to daybreak, the awaited enemy attack came as they started to hit our positions with heavy mortar fire. This was followed by their tanks firing directly into Company H command post and their heavy mortar platoon. A tank round burst in a tree killing Lieutenant Robert Wood, 3rd Platoon Leader - and which nearly wiped out the entire heavy mortar platoon. The early morning darkness carried the sounds of shouting and crying for "medic," from the wounded troopers of Company H.

The following is a brief story of the action on July 28th-29th, 1950, from Sergeant First Class Harold Blanc, Communications Sergeant, Company H, 2nd Battalion, 7th Cavalry Regiment.

In the evening of July 29th, we established positions for an apparent attack from the North Koreans. I shared a foxhole with P.F.C. Marvin Hoffman, which was very near the 3rd Platoon and Company H command post. This was the 81-mm mortar platoon and its leader was 2nd Lt. Robert Wood.

Actually two years prior, in 1948, at Fort Dix, New Jersey, I had met Robert Wood when he was a Corporal and a company clerk. He had recently attended Officer Candidate School (OCS) and graduated as a 2nd Lieutenant; he was then sent to Korea as a replacement officer.

Just prior to daybreak on July 29th, we heard the sounds of enemy tanks approaching. Since we had no communication with the 2nd Battalion command post, 2nd Lt. Wood directed me to proceed there and notify them of the enemy tanks. I moved out on the double and as fast as I could run. The tanks were now starting to fire on our positions.

It didn't take me very long to reach the 2nd Battalion command post, and I informed Major Omar Hitchner, Battalion Commander, that enemy tanks were firing on Company H defensive positions. I was ordered to return immediately to Company H and inform 2nd Lt. Wood that support was on its way.

Upon my return to Company H, I could see the fire belching out of the tubes of the 81-mm mortars as they fired on enemy positions. It was almost daylight, but I know the enemy could also see the fire from the tubes which exposed the location of the mortars. Also, the mortars were positioned on the forward slope of the hill.

Then, suddenly, an enemy tank round burst in a tree, sending a shower of shrapnel which killed 2nd Lt. Wood and nearly wiped out the entire 3rd Platoon of Company H. I ran to the foxhole that I shared with P.F.C. Hoffman and discovered that he had also been killed by the same tank round. Had I remained in the foxhole, I would have been killed also. God had looked out for me again.

Captain Chandler was shouting at the top of his lungs for a 3.5-inch rocket launcher team to immediately proceed forward and try to knock out the enemy tanks. Just a couple of days prior, our company was issued the new 3.5-inch rocket launcher along with the proper instructions on how to operate it. When we first arrived in Korea, we were still using the old 2.36-inch rocket launcher, which was used in World War II. This particular rocket launcher would not penetrate the armour of the Russian built T-34 tank. We welcomed the new 3.5-inch rocket launcher, which proved to be a very vital weapon.

The enemy tanks continued to fire into our position as confusion became apparent with wounded and killed personnel of Company H. The enemy infantry launched an attack between Company E and Company H, where I had my heavy machine gun emplacement. Further to my left and giving fire support to Company E was a heavy machine gun emplacement manned by Sergeant First Class William Brown. Sergeant Brown was our mess sergeant, and here he was operating a heavy machine gun in the midst of an enemy attack..

With our machine guns firing at their maximum potential of 450-600 rounds per minute, two waves of the enemy attack were repelled. However, a third was beginning to form as we looked at our ammunition supply which was almost exhausted. My heavy water-cooled machine gun was extremely hot and steam water vapor was starting to leak from the front barrel packing.

As I looked to my left, I then noticed Sergeant First Class Bill Brown and his assistant gunner Private George Vernon, charging down the hill with fixed bayonets and screaming, "GARRYOWEN" from the top of their lungs. Then suddenly, the enemy, being so surprised, dropped their weapons and started to run. They immediately picked up enemy grenades and threw them at the running enemy.

For this particular action, Sergeant First Class William Brown was awarded the Silver Star Medal and Private George Vernon, the Bronze Star Medal. Many of us, including myself, told Mess Sergeant Bill Brown that we would never complain of or about his food from this day forward. It was cocky Mess Sergeant Bill Brown who did all of the bitching and complaining in Japan when we were on maneuvers, and Captain Chandler insisted that all company personnel learn to operate and fire every weapon within our company.

The enemy had temporarily retreated along with their tanks, and all we were receiving was sporadic enemy small-arms fire. Captain Chandler was directing the evacuation of the wounded and dead of Company H. Shortly after this gruesome and horrible task, he ordered me and my squad to follow him to an adjacent small ridge. When we reached the peak of the ridge, we could see not only the original two enemy tanks from earlier in the morning, but three more enemy tanks moving slowly down the road to support another attack.

It was now late morning as Captain Chandler ordered us to immediately establish machine gun emplacements to give appropriate fire support. I then asked Captain Chandler why our 3.5-inch rocket launcher teams didn't attempt to knock out the two enemy tanks earlier in the morning. He replied, "Sergeant Daily, there was no way in hell those rocket launcher teams could get close enough for proper positions to fire because of the incoming enemy mortars. Now I want good fire support because I'm moving forward to locate a position to direct air, artillery and mortar support." Captain Chandler, with a field phone, moved to an exposed position as enemy fire became very heavy. From my machine gun emplacement, I was trying as much as possible to keep the enemy soldiers pinned down as they attempted to move forward.

For several hours, Captain Chandler directed air, artillery and mortar support from the exposed position. Air strikes from F-51 Mustang fighters dropped napalm bombs and strafed the enemy tanks and their infantry positions. The 77th Field Artillery with their 105-MM Howitzer guns, fired endless barrages at the enemy. Within every line company of the 2nd Battalion, their mortars belched projectiles upon the enemy.

Suddenly I saw Captain Chandler fall to his side and I thought he had been hit by the enemy fire. I immediately ran forward to his location, and then he was laying on his back with blood all over both legs of his fatigue uniform. I asked, "Captain Sir, have you been hit?" He looked at me and said, "There's nothing wrong with me, now get the hell out of here and back to your position." I answered, "Yes Sir!" I ran back to my position and squad.

The enemy finally retreated; they had suffered extremely heavy casualties. Four enemy tanks were destroyed, but somehow a fifth tank had managed to pull back without any serious damage. Countless enemy soldiers lay dead on the road, rice paddies and on the mountain ridges from the morning and afternoon battles.

Captain Chandler looked exhausted and he had definitely been slightly wounded earlier, but he continued to refuse medical treatment. Many of us felt battle weary as he ordered us to reorganize and prepare for a possible renewed enemy attack. Not helping matters was the continued heat of the day which sent temperatures well over the 100 degree mark.

As we attempted to reorganize, it gave me an opportunity to look at the many dead North Korean soldiers. This was the first time that I had a real good look at them. They wore mustard brown colored uniforms and

their hats had a large red star on the front. Several of the officers wore blue-breeched uniforms with high boots up to their knees. I noticed that many of them had stuck twigs in the netting on the back of their shirts and their cloth hats for camouflage purposes. This seemed to be very effective by blending with the branches and leaves. I was told that papers on one of the enemy officers by the roadside indicated that he was a tank platoon leader. Regardless, I was really starting to realize even more that the enemy was an excellent trained soldier. The extreme heat of the day was creating a dead body stench that was almost unbearable.

Many of us had a look at the Russian -built T-34 tank. All the tanks had three very large numbers painted in white on both sides of the turret. Captain Chandler told us these identifying numbers were originally painted on by the Russians during World War II. He also emphasized the fact that they were far superior to our M-24 Chaffee light tank.

During the night the 2nd Battalion received an extremely heavy barrage of enemy artillery and mortar fire. Warning orders were issued to the Battalion for a planned withdrawal to the rear. Enemy patrols were attacking us at all positions of our front. Lieutenant Marvin Goulding rushed to our position and ordered us to move the machine gun emplacement and for me and my squad to follow him on the double. It was now almost daybreak and the enemy artillery fire was getting heavier. Since our arrival in Korea, this was the most severe attack on the 2nd Battalion.

As we quickly moved forward I could see that our Battalion was suffering many casualties. Our Battalion Chaplain, Captain Emanuel Carlsen was directing evacuation of the wounded under heavy enemy mortar fire. Lieutenant Marvin Goulding was lead-

ing us toward the road when suddenly a mortar round hit very near us, which sent me tumbling over the top of him. As we arose from the dust and dirt, leaving both of us somewhat shaken up, he immediately asked, "Are you okay, Sergeant Daily?" I responded with a quick, "Yes, Sir!" However, as I looked to my rear I noticed that one of our ammo bearers had been seriously wounded from the mortar explosion. I immediately shouted for a medic! Then Lieutenant Goulding looked at me and said, "Daily, it's no use, he's already dead." I felt very strange about this young private; I didn't even remember his name, as he was a very recent replacement within our platoon.

Our squad continued to move forward as quickly as possible. As we approached the road I could see the enemy was determined to break through the road guard leading into the Battalion sector. Intense enemy mortar and machine gun fire made it extremely difficult to reach our objective. The cumbersome weight of a heavy machine gun made the task more of a burden.

Finally we came into contact with Lieutenant John C. Lippincott who was the 3rd platoon leader of Company F. He immediately explained to Lieutenant Goulding and my squad how certain enemy machine guns and two enemy tanks were playing havoc to his platoon near the road. The enemy tanks were firing from a railroad position which ran parallel to the road. To the right flank of Company F. Lieutenant Lippincott told us that he wanted us to give appropriate heavy machine gun support for a 3.5-inch rocket launcher team. The team had to move closer to a point that would be more advantageous, and within range of the enemy tanks and machine gun positions. He also emphasized the needed support when actual orders were received for our planned withdrawal.

The tragedy of combat - some would break down. (UPI)

Army nurse taking a breather- they had to work under very deplorable conditions. (Army photo)

He pointed to a small slope to the right of the road from where several of his riflemen were firing. He explained how he thought this would be a good position for our machine gun emplacement and eventual rocket launcher team.

Needless to say, it was very difficult just to make our way to the small slope because of the intense enemy rifles and machine gun fire. However, after we reached this objective, it revealed an excellent location for fire distribution. Not only did it offer enfilade fire in respect to the road, but plunging fire as well. In a few short minutes, I was giving the 3rd platoon of Company F their requested, and very appreciated machine gun support. However, the 3.5-inch rocket launcher team never reached this particular location. Rumors had it that there was a shortage of ammo and what was available was being saved for the enemy tanks.

The following account of the withdrawal of July 30-31, was given by Donald D. Down, a Browning Automatic Rifleman from the 3rd Platoon, Company F.

Co.mpany F was positioned to the right flank of the 2nd Battalion which had approximately 1,000 yards of rice paddies to our front. To the right of this location was a railroad. On past our frontal position of the rice paddies was a large area of trees. In that tree coverage were five or six enemy tanks which started firing on our position during the night. Also, we received heavy enemy artillery and mortar fire. I called this our "blood letting," because it was the most severe enemy shelling since our arrival in Korea. It was really our first chance to prove ourselves in heavy fighting.

At daybreak the enemy troop assault started with their attack of heavy mortar, machine gun, tanks, and small arms fire. All along the Battalion front the enemy attack of wave after wave was repelled. Then our fighter planes arrived to bomb and strife the enemy position and tanks. The old 5th Air Force pilots were really clobbering the enemy with their napalm and high explosive bombs. As one particular F-51 fighter plane was coming in, I noticed that it was wobbling as if it had been hit by enemy fire. However, I noticed that his bomb was hanging loose and looked as though it was heading straight for our platoon. Luckily, the bomb released in time and hit the hill located high above us. Needless to say, many men in our platoon had the hell scared out of them. Wounded during this action was our platoon sergeant, Sergeant Clark, and Corporal Neeley a squad leader. Killed was my friend, Private Pop Bohem, who played the harmonica for many of us in the platoon.

We made another withdrawal late at night to establish a better position. We were still to the right flank of the 2nd Battalion and very near the railroad. However, our position now also protected the road leading into the Battalion sector. At approximately 01:00 hours, squad leader Corporal Alfred Clair and assistant squad leader Corporal Ralph G. Bernotas, said they knew where two enemy tanks were causing havoc to Company F. They further told me that they intended to take a 3.5 "bazooka", rocket launcher and extra shells to go and knock out the tanks. They wanted me to go with my automatic rifle to give them fire support. Our Company sniper, Private Alzondo Berryman was ordered to go along also.

After leaving our platoon, the four of us went to the bottom of the hill next to our right flank and crossed the railroad and followed the tracks to a bridge culvert. There we stopped to organize our plan. We could see the enemy tanks at a distance of approximately 50 to 100 yards. Corporals Clair and Bernotas proceeded forward with the 3.5 (bazooka), rocket launcher and Berryman and myself remained in the culvert. At 03:45 hours we heard a large explosion and we could see that they had knocked out one of the enemy tanks because it was on fire. Suddenly, enemy automatic weapons fire was directed at our platoon position and some stray shots were bounding off the walls of the culvert that we were in. About fifteen minutes later we heard another large explosion as Berryman and I looked again to see another enemy tank knocked out of action.

As we waited for Corporals Clair and Bernotas to return, it was starting to become daybreak, and still no Clair or Bernotas. We then decided to go back down the tracks to return to our platoon position. However, we had forgotten the password, so being afraid of possibly being mistaken for the enemy, we stayed near a station house by the tracks until we heard voices from members of our platoon mortar squad. They were shouting range orders to their mortar crews to shell the station house near us. We took a chance and started shouting and they recognized us and we returned safely to our platoon.

We immediately informed our platoon leader, Lt. Lippincott on details of what had happened. Between 10:00-11:00 hours we heard someone blowing a whistle in front of our lines, and to our surprise it was Corporals Clair and Bernotas running like hell toward us waving their arms. They made it safely within our platoon sector.

Later on I heard rumors that Corporals Clair and Bernotas were recommended for the Silver Star for gallantry in action. Berryman and myself were recommended for the Bronze Star for valor, but somehow I never received the medal. If the others ever did, I don't know.

Also is the following account of July 30-31, from Corporal Ralph G. Bernotas, assistant squad leader, 3rd Platoon, Company F.

Squad leader Corporal Alfred Clair and myself took a 3.5 "bazooka", rocket launcher, and three shells to go T-34 tank hunting. Privates Don Down, a B.A.R. man, and Alzondo Barryman, a sniper, went along with us for fire support.

We quickly moved down the railroad tracts where I observed the muzzle flash from a couple of T-34 tanks, firing at Company F positions. From between the railroad tracts I prepared the 3.5 "bazooka" to be ready to fire at the closest muzzle flash in the early morning darkness. As I aimed the weapon and squeezed the trigger, it fired as the T-34 tank muzzle blast flashed off. However, the damn round hit short of the target and the tanks stopped firing for a brief period of time.

I elevated my sights and reloaded a second shell into the "bazooka," and waited for further firing from the tanks. When the tanks resumed firing, I squeezed off another round and this time it was right on the button. The enemy tank immediately exploded and continued to burn and further explode throughout the morning. All firing from

the enemy tanks stopped completely. The enemy knew we had a weapon that could knock out their tanks from ground personnel. Before the only reliable weapon against them was the support of our Air Force fighter planes.

As Corporal Clair and I moved through a culvert to return to our platoon sector, we could hear our mortar crew giving fire commands. On the other side of the railroad track we could also hear an enemy machine gun firing. We threw a hand grenade in that particular direction and it went quiet. It seemed that the enemy attack was more toward our left flank, which was Co. E.

The early morning fog was starting to lift, and we heard the enemy starting the engines in their tanks. A couple of them were heavily camouflaged with limbs of trees and bushes. One started back across a small creek and up along a road near a hillside. Corporal Clair and I started running toward that direction, but we stopped as the railroad tracks came together. Further ahead there was no cover. Corporal Clair gave me fire support with his B.A.R., as I reloaded the "bazooka" with the third and last shell. I reset the sights, took aim and squeezed off the last round. Of all damn things, I had set the sights too high and missed the sitting duck. I almost cried because it was such an easy target and shot. Well anyway, one enemy T-34 tank out of three shots wasn't too bad.

We immediately started to run, and we safely reached Company F and our platoon sector. Privates Don Down and Alzondo Berryman had given us fire support and alerted the mortar crew of our location. When we reached our platoon, Sergeant Lucas was really excited to see us. The following day, both Lucas and myself were wounded in action.

I understand that all four of us were recommended to receive Silver Stars, but to my knowledge not one of us was awarded such a medal. I suppose at that particular time too much happened too quickly to get written up.

The enemy suffering heavy loses finally

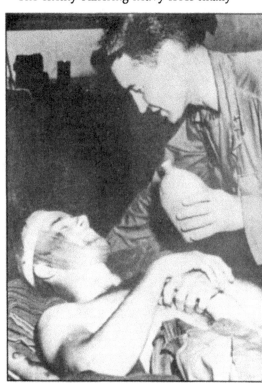

Chaplain helping a wounded trooper. (Army photo)

withdrew from the line. The 2nd Battalion, subjected at all their positions to massive enemy attacks, intense mortar and artillery fire, held their ground. Throughout the battalion were many acts of bravery and heroism during this particular phase of action.

Lieutenant John C. Lippincott, and his platoon from Company F held to their position and ground along the road leading into the battalion sector while subjected to intense enemy machine gun and mortar fire. Captain James T. Milan, Company Commander of Company E, accounted for 34 enemy dead in front of his position and personally led a patrol forward and destroyed an enemy machine gun and killed seven more enemy soldiers in the vicinity of his Company sector. Lieutenant John O. Potts of Company F rendered aid to a wounded soldier while under heavy fire and Private Willis Mornington, also of Company F, maintained communications by repairing broken wire throughout the entire action. Corporal Chester L. Harr of Headquarters Company, 2nd Battalion went to the rescue of a seriously wounded soldier, completely disregarding the hail of enemy rifle and machine gun fire.

How does one describe the loss of a close comrade, battle wounds or battle death? Wounds or death are not quiet. Men scream in the high-pitched shrills of women in labor, in the yip-yipping of run-over dogs, in stunned surprise. Men swear the earthiest expletives of their people, the coursest, foulest curses that they know. Some men cry, some whimper softly, only a few tumble quietly and do not move.

Nor is death clean and dignified. Shrapnel from a mortar or artillery explosion can rip filthy gashes in the body, or tear off a limb, leaving artery ends vibrating within a stump. Bullets can rip through a man's abdomen and turn his insides out.

I was quickly learning and experiencing that combat was not a romance. It was a profound and vicious ferocity. Captain Emanuel Carlsen, our Battalion Chaplain, tried to emphasize the importance of praying and keeping our faith in God.

Hanson W. Baldwin, the military critic of the New York Times, referred to a "stand or die" comment of July 29, made by Lieutenant General Walton H. Walker, commanding general of the United States Eighth Army. The "stand or die" order, as a well merited rebuke to the Pentagon, which has too often disseminated a soothing syrup of cheer and sweetness and light since the fighting began. It is clear that by the end of July, the reading public in the United States should have realized that the country was in doubt, and that many uncertainties lay ahead.

Orders were finally received in the early morning hours of August 1, that a strategic withdrawal would be taken for better defense purposes. However, the enemy did not pursue or follow this particular withdrawal and no enemy contact was made.

The early afternoon of August 2, the 7th Cavalry Regiment was assigned the task of protecting the withdrawal of the entire 1st Cavalry Division. The withdrawal movement would be from the Kumchon area to an undisclosed location north of Waegwan. Captain Chandler gave us orders for Company H to proceed to the main railroad line which traveled in a southeasterly direction from Kumchon to Waegwan then on into the city of Taegu. He told us that 1st Cavalry Division Headquarters would be established in Taegu.

As we attempted to arrange positions to defend our withdrawal from possible enemy flank attacks, refugees again caused confusion and panic. Orders were issued that no refugees would be permitted to come near or pass through our sector. Enemy small arms fire from various snipers was increasing. Suddenly from the rear of our position, five enemy soldiers dressed in native refugee clothing, had infiltrated our line and they immediately fired into us with rifles and burp guns. An enemy hand grenade ricocheted off the rail edge of the railroad and landed at my feet. Immediately, I kicked the grenade with my boot, which went forward and it detonated simultaneously. Luckily, it was only a concussion grenade and when the dust cleared, all I sustained was a minor concussion and a small metal fragment in my right hand. Fortunately, there were no other injuries to myself or others in my squad. Within a matter of minutes, four enemy soldiers were killed and one seriously wounded. I refused evacuation and went to the Battalion aid man, and then to the aid station for treatment. After my wounds were treated, I quickly returned to the Battalion, and we continued our withdrawal. Each time refugees attempted to proceed behind us, we would fire machine gun bursts over their heads to discourage them from following too close. We weren't taking any chances because of what we experienced an hour earlier.

I later developed a severe headache from the concussion caused by the exploding enemy grenade that happened several hours earlier. Lieutenant Bob Carroll ordered us to move to a road which briefly ran parallel to the railroad. He informed us that this road led to the town of Waegwan, and this is where we would assume our new positions.

It was very near dark, and our Company Commander Captain Chandler was waiting near the road. Captain Chandler called to me and said: "Sergeant Daily, that was a very brave act on your part this afternoon when, without hesitation, you picked up that enemy grenade and threw it; which kept it from exploding within your squad. You probably not only saved your own life, but others in your squad. By the way, how is your wounded hand?" I replied with, "I'm fine sir, thank you sir!" He said, "Regardless, you distinguished yourself and I'm recommending you for the Bronze Star." I quickly answered with, "thank you, sir!" We saluted each other as he turned and said, "Now, let's get our positions established because Company E of our Battalion and Company A of the 8th Cavalry Regiment are out in front of us, and we will probably protect their withdrawal through us."

The 2nd Battalion position now was guarding the Kumchon-Waegwan road, and our location was just north of Waegwan. The traffic was extremely heavy and various trucks and vehicles were causing large clouds of dust. Not only was it difficult to see, but very hard to breathe. Since my arrival in Korea, I was realizing more than ever that two important physical aspects that God had blessed me with were an excellent pair of lungs and legs.

Captain Chandler informed us that our next withdrawal would be across the Naktong River. The bridge crossing the river from Waegwan was dynamited and would be blown when the last elements of the 8th Cavalry Regiment were on the other side. During the night only sporadic enemy small arms fire was received in our company sector. As the morning of August 3 arrived, many thousands of refugees were now complicating our planned withdrawal. Company E of our Battalion had now reached us, which left Company A, 8th Cavalry Regiment as rear guard. To our extreme front, the Air Force was strafing and bombing the enemy advance. Our artillery continued to fire barrage after barrage into the enemy positions.

As we were informed by Captain Chandler to start our withdrawal to the Naktong River, many of us were wondering if we would make the bridge before it was blown. Down the road and near the town of Waegwan, I could see that many refugees were being stopped and not being permitted to progress any further. Traffic was still extremely slow and many refugees ignored the commands of the 545th Military Police Company, and our 2nd Battalion.

After we crossed the bridge, elements of Company A, 8th Cavalry Regiment experienced the difficult task of crossing as hundreds of refugees dashed madly for the bridge. Several times the refugees were informed that the bridge would be blown. However, this repeated maneuver was not successful and there was no way to keep the South Korean refugees from using the bridge.

It was now late afternoon and the North Korean enemy was closing. After the last elements of the 8th Cavalry Regiment cleared the bridge, orders were issued to "blow it." Hundreds of South Korean refugees went into the river with the bridge. As we looked in despair for possible survivors, the 2-1/2 ton trucks had now arrived to transport us to an undisclosed area of the Naktong River.

American Army casualties in Korea through July 31, 1950, totaled 6,003 men: 1,884 killed, 2,695 wounded, 523 missing and 901 reported captured. Almost 80 percent of these casualties occurred in the last half of the month. More than half the total battle losses were from the 24th Infantry Division.

During its first ten days of action in Korea, the 1st Cavalry Division had 916 battle casualties - 78 killed, 419 wounded, and 419 missing. The enemy had effectively and quickly driven the 1st Cavalry Division to the Naktong River.

CHAPTER V
THE NAKTONG RIVER DEFENSE

Once in a while you find yourself in an odd situation. You get into it by degrees and in the most natural way ,but when you are right in the midst of it, you are suddenly astonished and ask yourself how in the world it all came about...

Thor Heyerdahl, Kon-Tiki (1950)

From Waegwan we were trucked to an area overlooking the Naktong River, which was located approximately 12-14 miles southwest of Taegu. Captain Chandler immediately ordered us to arrange defensive positions as the evening darkness was very near. The extreme heat of the summer was also making things difficult. We were exhausted, covered with dirt from days without a shower and our sweat-soaked uniforms were giving off a foul odor.

The Pusan Perimeter of August 1950 was almost three quarters of the Naktong River. It flows south, and the Naktong is Korea's second river; it bends and folds its way between rice paddies and the hills running down to the water's edge. The Naktong River averages more than one-quarter mile in width, and more than six feet in depth. At low water, as during the hot, dry summer of 1950, large sandy beaches and bars appeared in the river. It is at all times formidable.

Directly behind the river to the east, the hills rise to 2,500 feet, and on its north, across the top of the Perimeter, they reach 3,000 or more feet. It was here, on the highest hills that the United States Forces, The Republic of Korea Armies and the United Nations Forces organized their defense.

I believe that every unit in Korea, either division or regiment, had its particular moments of desperation or moments of glory. What was happening in certain areas of the Naktong River defense was probably very much like what was happening in the next.

The 1st Battalion of the 7th Cavalry Regiment was placed in Division reserve which left our 2nd Battalion to guard approximately 30,000 yards of frontage along the Naktong River. Although the front was relatively quiet for the next five to six days, we continued to maintain our patrols night and day. Every night listening posts were established along the entire river. Even day and night patrols were sent across the Naktong River to search and maintain contact with the enemy because we knew from our intelligence reports that an attack was impending. During the day were the endless lines of refugees struggling to make their way south. Then there was still the difficult task of screening them.

Company H was assigned approximately 3000-3500 yards of frontage to defend along the river. Within this area was a strong outpost position near the partially destroyed steel and concrete bridge which previously crossed the river from the town of Toksan.

Other positions in our company were established on the higher ground of Hill 209. To our extreme right flank was Company G and on the extreme left flank was Company F.

In the early morning of August 9, I was told to report to the company command post because Captain Chandler wanted to see me. I immediately went there as ordered and was greeted by Captain Chandler when I arrived. He said, "Daily, the 1st Cavalry Division has been authorized by the Department of Defense to temporarily promote certain non-commissioned officers to the rank of Second Lieutenant. It is classified as a Battlefield Commission which is a temporary rank of Second Lieutenant; and it was used during World War II, with very much success. Our regiment is extremely short of officers and replacements aren't coming as fast as expected. You will remain with Company H, because of your heavy weapons experience. I have talked to Colonel Nist, our Regimental Commander and Major Hitchner, our Battalion Commander about this and I have their full approval."

As I looked at Captain Chandler, it seemed like minutes passed before I could speak or give him a reply. I finally answered with, "Sir, I don't know if I can really handle the commission or a platoon." He replied, "Listen, Sergeant Daily, if I didn't have confidence in you, I wouldn't have recommended your name to begin with. Furthermore, I'll be giving you all the necessary support and direction that you will need." I asked, "Okay, sir, what are the procedures to receive this so-called Field Commission?" He answered, "You and Sergeant Harold Blanc will be taken tomorrow morning to the Adjutant General Command at Division Headquarters." He then said, "By the way, Daily, don't mention this to no one!" We saluted each other, then I turned and left the command post tent.

After I returned to the platoon and my squad, I couldn't think properly because of my personal excitement and feelings. During the night many thoughts were running through my mind.

Also during the night, the enemy attempted several times to infiltrate our lines, which set off trip flares illiminating the sky. It was becoming difficult to replace the flares that were tripped because of short supply. Even our 60-mm mortar illuminating shells had deteriorated to such a degree that only 20 percent issued to the battalion were effective. Also the 155-mm howitzer illuminating shells were in short supply from the 82nd Field Artillery. Many of the enemy infiltrated our lines before the threatened area was actually illuminated. I had previously noticed in Japan and now in Korea that the majority of our ammunition cases were painted with markings of the year 1944.

The morning of August 10th, I didn't have much of an appetite even though we were served hot chow for breakfast. I was very apprehensive in going to Division Headquarters, and what the future military adjustment to officer would bring. I had just finished cleaning my mess kit when the com-

1st Cavalry Division Commander, Major General Hobart Gay. Heading for the front. (U.S. Army photo)

pany messenger notified me that the company clerk had orders to drive me in a jeep to Division Headquarters in Taegu.

I immediately went to the company clerk. When I arrived I didn't see Captain Chandler or Sergeant Harold Blanc. The clerk informed me that Captain Chandler went to a briefing at battalion headquarters. He then told me that Sergeant Harold Blanc wouldn't be going with me as previously arranged. I later found out that Sergeant Harold Blanc declined the field commission because Captain Chandler was going to transfer him to another company within the battalion. He wanted to remain with Company H.

On the way to Division Headquarters, the jeep bounced on the rough road, and we had to stop occasionally because the refugees were interfering and blocking the traffic south. The company clerk informed me that I had to report to an officer and his name was

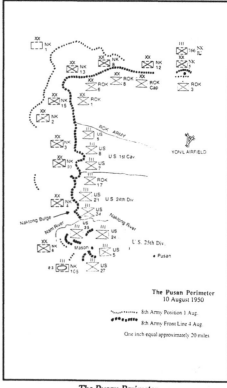

The Pusan Perimeter

on a letter which was in the pocket of his fatigue jacket.

When we arrived at Division Headquarters in Taegu, I could see that someone was still carrying on the 1st Cavalry Division traditions. The large yellow and black division patch was painted all over the place. At least I knew I wasn't lost. The company clerk handed me the letter from his jacket pocket as I looked down to see what officer's name was on it. From the letter I could see that I was to report to Lieutenant Colonel, J.A. Pongonis of the Adjutant General Command. I was starting to feel nervous and uncomfortable. Then the company clerk told me he had orders to wait for me as I walked toward the entrance of Division Headquarters. The company clerk called to me and asked, "Hey Daily, what in the hell is going on?" I answered, "I don't know, but I guess I'll soon find out!"

Once inside of the building I asked a sergeant where I could find Colonel Pongonis. He pointed down to the other end of the building where I could see four other soldiers standing in front of and near a table. When I reached the table where they were standing, I immediately asked one of them that where Colonel Pongonis was, and he replied was waiting be back in a minute. While I find out that we the Colonel to return, I did reason, to receive a ba all there for the same to Second Lieutenant. From field Commission Regiment was Sergeant Alvin A 5th Cavalry Master Sergeant "Hup" Mayo, and the n and two sergeants were from the 8th Cavalry regiment.

Shortly the Colonel returned as we all came to attention and saluted. He immediately started to explain how each of us should feel extremely proud of being recommended for temporary commission to officer. He went on to tell us that records indicated that we were all Regular Army soldiers. However, he told us that we would temporarily lose our Regular Army status, but it would be reinstated if we lost or were demoted to our highest non-commissioned officer rank held under a permanent status. I asked the Colonel what was my permanent rank and he immediately replied, "Sergeant First Class." Then he told us our serial numbers would also be changed to indicate we were officers. In a way I was starting to feel a little confused.

Within a few minutes the so-called ceremony was over as the Colonel picked up from the table the gold bars and gold crossed rifles to pin on our fatigue uniforms. The Colonel gave each of us a personal congratulation and best wishes on the promotion. Then a sergeant came to us with a concoction of yellow and brown paint he had mixed to paint the gold bar on our helmets. The so-called gold paint mixture didn't look that bad. We all thanked the sergeant for a job well done as he gave us a very snappy salute, which we all returned. After he walked a short distance, he turned and shouted, "Don't forget that paint is still wet." All of us shouted a reply, "Okay sergeant!"

After the five of us congratulated each other, we left on our separate ways and particular units. As I walked out of the Division Headquarters building, I had a tremendous amount of pride for individual accomplishment. When I reached the jeep that was waiting for me, the company clerk took one look at me and said, "Holy shit Daily, who did you brown nose to get a promotion to 2nd Lieutenant?" I replied with, "It's a long story and furthermore, I want to see you give me a salute from now on." He looked astonished at first, then he replied, "Yes, Sir!"

After that small incident, the company clerk had very little to say to me as we prepared to leave Taegu. As we drove down one of the streets, I noticed a South Korean merchant who was selling various leather holsters. I immediately had the company clerk stop the jeep. As I walked over to the merchant, I noticed a beautiful handcrafted leather shoulder holster which I fell in love with. The holster I was using was an Army issue which attached to my cartridge belt. Finally, I managed to understand that the merchant wanted several thousand Won, which amounted to approximately three dollars in military currency. I had no South Korean money so the merchant agreed to accept my military currency. After I put my new shoulder holster on, I told the company clerk to exit Taegu. Both sides of the road had an endless line of refugees, still making their way southward.

Upon our arrival at Company H, Command Post, I was greeted by Captain Chandler as we saluted each other, and he shook my hand and gave me his personal congratulations. We immediately went into the command post tent where he informed me that I would become Platoon Leader of the 1st Platoon and Lieutenant Bob Carroll would become our Company Executive Officer.

I looked at Captain Chandler and he seemed to have a very worried look on his face, as he explained the massive enemy troop buildup on the Naktong River. We briefly looked at a map, and he pointed to where the 1st Battalion was located. They had just recently come out of reserve, and he emphasized they were engaged in vicious enemy attacks for the past two days. Then he said an impending enemy onslaught was developing, but he didn't know where the initial attack would come from. He emphasized that we must hold our positions under all circumstances. This was because the partially destroyed bridge near our outpost could be repaired by the enemy and used as a rear door entrance to Taegu.

As I prepared to leave the command post tent and assume my new duties as platoon leader, Captain Chandler called to me and said, "Daily, here is a pair of field binoculars that I want you to have. And make sure you put them to good use!" I quickly answered, "Yes sir, I will!" We saluted each other, and I left the command post tent.

Everyone in the 1st Platoon congratulated me on my promotion, and they welcomed me as their new leader. However, this was the light and heavy machine gun platoon and many of us had already been together for the past 18 months so it wasn't like assuming a totally new unit. Surprisingly, I had the immediate respect from each and every man because many of us were the same age. I was 19, but I knew that many, including myself, were feeling a lot older from just a few weeks of combat experience. All of us were becoming a better fighting soldier.

The late afternoon of August 10, there was little enemy activity except for the exchanges of hand grenades and mortar fire. There was some sporadic small arms fire coming from various positions along the river. I looked through the field binoculars that Captain Chandler had given me earlier, and across the river in the distant hills. I could see the movement of many enemy soldiers as the Air Force was bombing and strafing their positions. The Air Force was doing a tremendous job of preventing the enemy from crossing the river during daylight hours with their soldiers, supplies and equipment.

Also, many enemy soldiers lay dead along the river bank, unable to be buried because of the constant fighter plane movement. From the extreme heat of the day their bloated

Destroyed bridge that spanned the Naktong River. Site of the 10th North Korean Division crossing and battles of August 12-14, 1950. (Courtesy of Bob Mauger)

Litter team with the difficult task of getting wounded off the hill. (U.S. Army photo)

Republic of Korea soldiers. They were tough and determined fighters. (U.S. Army photo)

bodies were giving off a stench that was almost unbearable at times. Flies were buzzing over the unburied corpses and were so thick in some areas that they actually blocked the sun.

During the night, listening posts were established along the river and orders given to shoot anything that moved in our direct front. I further issued orders not to fire our machine guns unless there was a massive or major attack. I had recently experienced that any fire from an automatic weapon would quickly bring the enemy upon its position to silence it. However, the night was relatively quiet and only an occasional trip flare lit up the dark night as the enemy attempted to infiltrate our lines.

On August 11, just prior to darkness, I was briefed by Captain Chandler that G-2 Intelligence had reported a massive enemy concentration across the river. However, at that time everyone thought a major attack would come further up ___ the river. He also emphasized the order to not fire any weapons unless it was absolutely necessary. This was to avoid the possibility of the enemy detecting our positions at night.

As Captain Chandler prepared to leave, a young officer arrived at our position. He briefly talked to Captain Chandler, and then he introduced the young officer to me. Captain Chandler said, "Lieutenant Daily, I want you to meet Lieutenant Cillary who is a Forward Observer for the 77th Field Artillery. "He will spend the night with your platoon." As we shook hands, I answered Captain Chandler with a, "Yes sir!" We both then saluted Captain Chandler and departed for my platoon.

Lieutenant Cillary was also carrying an SCR 300 radio on his back. This equipment was excellent for communication purposes with the artillery and command post. When we arrived at the outpost, I immediately introduced Lieutenant Cillary to Sergeant Millard Gray, a forward observer from our 81 mm mortar platoon, and Private First Class Harry Shappell, a radio operator. As we whispered in the evening darkness, each of us was very apprehensive as to an impending enemy attack. Even Lieutenant Cillary

commented that he thought something big was going to happen.

At 00:30 hours, I talked with Captain Chandler by radio and informed him that our flares were exposing enemy movement to our immediate front. Some of our listening posts were being driven back by enemy small arms fire. Again I had radio contact with Captain Chandler at 03:00 hours and told him of more enemy activity. This was to our immediate front and right flank. To our immediate right flank were two rifle squads from Company G. Captain Chandler ordered me to hold our positions and not fire because it might only be a small group of enemy soldiers that infiltrated our lines. During this radio contact I told Captain Chandler that I could really smell the enemy because of a different strange odor in the air.

At 05:30 hours, enemy activity continued, and all of our listening posts were driven back by small arms fire. I left our mortar observation post to converse with Privates First Class Norman Tinkler, J.P. "Smitty" Smith, and Ray Scarberry. All were gunners on our forward heavy machine gun positions, and I wanted to issue them instructions on the most certain enemy attack. As I moved from position to position in the pre-dawn darkness, everyone had the feeling of an immediate large scale enemy attack. We all noticed that the entire area had become very quiet from small arms fire.

As I left the machine gun position of Private First Class Ray Scarberry, I looked at my watch which indicated 06:00 hours. On my way back to our mortar observation post, an explosion came from that particular position. I started to run as fast as my legs could carry me to the position. Upon my arrival, I immediately saw that an enemy hand grenade had exploded between Sergeant Millard Gray and Private First Class Harry Shappell. Both had been severely wounded, and I quickly called for a "Medic." As I attempted to administer some medical aid, the combat aid man was quick to arrive with two litter bearers. In a few minutes, both wounded men were on their way to the company rear position.

All hell was starting to break loose now as

I attempted to use the radio which I soon discovered was inoperative due to the enemy hand grenade explosion. Then I realized that Lieutenant Cillary, the Forward Observer from the 77th Field Artillery, was missing.

Daylight was imminent, and I could see that the attack was coming from our immediate front, and near their partially destroyed bridge. The first wave consisted of white-clad refugees equipped with only crude spears or wooden clubs. Very few had been issued a rifle or any other type of military weapon. The second wave was well-armed North Korean soldiers using automatic weapons and hand grenades. Everywhere I looked the enemy had outflanked our company positions. Our machine gun positions were annihilating the refugees and enemy soldiers, but we were being overpowered by sheer numbers alone. I quickly threw the six hand grenades I was carrying. Then I put my old trusty M-1 rifle to good use. In my mind I estimated between 800-1000 refugees and North Korean soldiers in this particular enemy assault.

Things were happening extremely fast, and we had repelled four or five of the wave attacking enemy forces. Korean troops. I were well-trained North Korean troops. I could see that the looked to my left. Position of Private First Class machine gunkler was in trouble. I immediately Norman to the position and discovered that atel had been severely wounded. I ordered him to the company rear which he agreed to do, but with some hesitation. An ammunition bearer lay dead from a head wound just below the right eye. I then noticed one ammunition container of 250 rounds which I placed into the machine gun. The weapon was extremely hot from previous firing. I fired the weapon at the attacking enemy troops on my left flank and front until all ammunition was exhausted. I immediately made the weapon inoperative. I could see many wounded or dead enemy soldiers laying throughout the area.

I looked to my rear toward Hill 209, and I could see the enemy moving upward to secure the higher ground behind us. I knew our company command post was located near the rear of the hill; and I realized that all company positions had been overrun.

Again, I looked in desperation, and I knew I had lost control of my platoon as the enemy soldiers were closing in. Somewhere I had lost my old trusty M-1 rifle as I started to fire my 45 caliber pistol wildly at the enemy troops. One clip went very quickly as I put the extra one in the pistol. Then shortly all ammunition was exhausted, as I placed the enemy pistol back in my shoulder holster. I ran to a small gully in search of some type of weapon to fire at the enemy. As I approached the lower part of the gully, I came face to face with a North Korean soldier who jammed his rifle into the left side of my chest. He immediately made me put both hands on top of my helmet.

Suddenly a second North Korean soldier appeared as they both immediately fought over my 45 caliber pistol I was wearing. Evi-

Boots of trooper that was killed on a patrol. (U.S. Army photo)

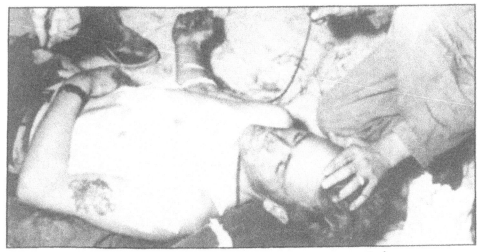
By wounded trooper receiving blood plasma at Aid Station. (U.S. Army photo)

dently the enemy soldier with the higher rank took the pistol. The other enemy soldier took my field binoculars, which Captain Chandler had given me a couple days prior. They removed my cartridge belt and then searched all of my pockets. My watch, compass and all other personal items were immediately taken.

Without hesitation they pushed me forward and shoved the end of the rifle barrell between my buttocks to make me move faster toward the Naktong River. We moved in a southwesterly direction near the river until we reached a collection point where other American soldiers were waiting. Most of them looked dazed or battle weary, and none of us were permitted to speak to one another. I didn't to recognize any of them. I felt as though I was in a dream, and this horrible nightmare would go away once I woke up. However, I was already losing my personal feelings of reality. For being captured, I was starting to feel guilty or ashamed of the situation. One thing I did realize was that I had been stripped of my dignity; and I wondered how in the hell it all came about.

The following is an account of the action on August 12, 13 and 14, from Corporal Donald D. Down, a Browning Automatic Rifle man from the 3rd Squad, 3rd Platoon of Company F.

Our Company was supporting the extreme left flank of the 2nd Battalion. Next to our Company right flank was Company H. The right flank of our Company, along with Company H, bore the brunt of the initial attack on August 12. There were numerous casualties from our Company, but Company H suffered almost 70 percent. A couple of my friends, Corporal Ralph Rathburn, a cook, and Private Vanhorn, a rifleman, were killed in action on August 12. Our Company was short of personnel and Company cooks were used as riflemen. Wounded in action on the same day was Corporal Paul J. Szezepanski, a cook and Private John Harcula, a rifleman.

I was on the extreme left flank of our Company with a 57 Recoilless Rifle Team, a .30 caliber light machine gun squad and myself a B.A.R. man. We were set up as a left flank outpost. There was supposed to be Republic of Korea soldiers on the hill farther down on our left. During the night there was only stray fire within the area.

However, at 07:00 hours, August 13, there was sporadic fire coming from our left flank which we thought the Republic of Korea soldiers were playing around testing their weapons. Shortly thereafter, I was crouched down when suddenly a bullet hit next to my foot. Then all hell broke loose as the North Korean soldiers had gotten in between us and the Republic of Korea soldiers. They had come up the back side of the hill we were on and then came in on us from the top

of the hill. We immediately had to reverse our weapon positions and fire on them as they came down on us. Needless to say, we were fighting like hell to get out of their leep-frogging, while working our way toward the bottom of the hill. Corporal Robert Conlon, our machine gunner, got hit in his upper leg and his assistant Corporal Eugene Cossich got hit in his right forearm. His arm actually twisted around like a spinning top, and I knew his forearm bone was severely broken.

The 57 Recoilless Rifle Team while attempting to change positions got cut down like trees. We regrouped at the bottom of the hill, and Sergeant Hillary Logue took charge of the situation. He sent us crawling along the ditches, rice paddies and road and told us to work our way toward our Ccmpany position. This was approximately 100 yards across open rice paddies. We tried to patch up our wounded the best we could as we took off running and sometimes crawling on our hands and knees and stomach. The main part of our company was laying down heavy fire power as we worked our way back to the Company sector. Late that day we finally got most of our wounded back under heavy enemy sniper and machine gun fire. Sergeant Hillery Logue was hit by a bullet in his right foot.

The North Koreans got the 57 Recoilless Rifle and .30 caliber light machine gun. However, they had no trouble using the light machine gun on us, but when they attempted to use the 57 Recoilless Rifle, the back pressure blast killed several of their own men. We discovered this when we retook the hill the following morning. This was accomplished with the support of Company D, 1st Battalion.

Some of my friends killed in action on August 13, were Private First Class Leonard Finlay, Corporal Clarence W. Deal, and Sergeant Glen W. Taturn.

The 2nd Battalion was strung out on the hills and along the road in front of our company position. We had a forward observer with us from the 77th Field Artillery. I believe between 04:00-05:00 hours of August 14, the North Korean soldiers hit Companies G and H with a massive attack. This vicious attack came in the lower and flatter terrain near the river and through the rice paddies and bean fields.

It was starting to get more daylight, and the North Koreans were really being exposed in the wide open territory. The forward observer with his binoculars was calling the enemy positions back to the 77th Field Artillery. Some of our tanks had moved into position and were firing their 76 mm weapons point blank at the enemy. We in Company F were not getting too much of the action until the North Koreans started to run to make it back across the river. Then, we started firing at them and they were taking one hell of a beating.

The artillery and tank crews were having a field day as the enemy was caught completely in the open. You could see the shell explosions hit a bunch of North Koreans as bodies were blown into pieces and they went flying through the air. Very few were making it back across the river and not many were trying to surrender.

Around noon everything was settled down and Company F was informed that since we didn't get in on the action, we would have to sweep the fields and rice paddies in front of the

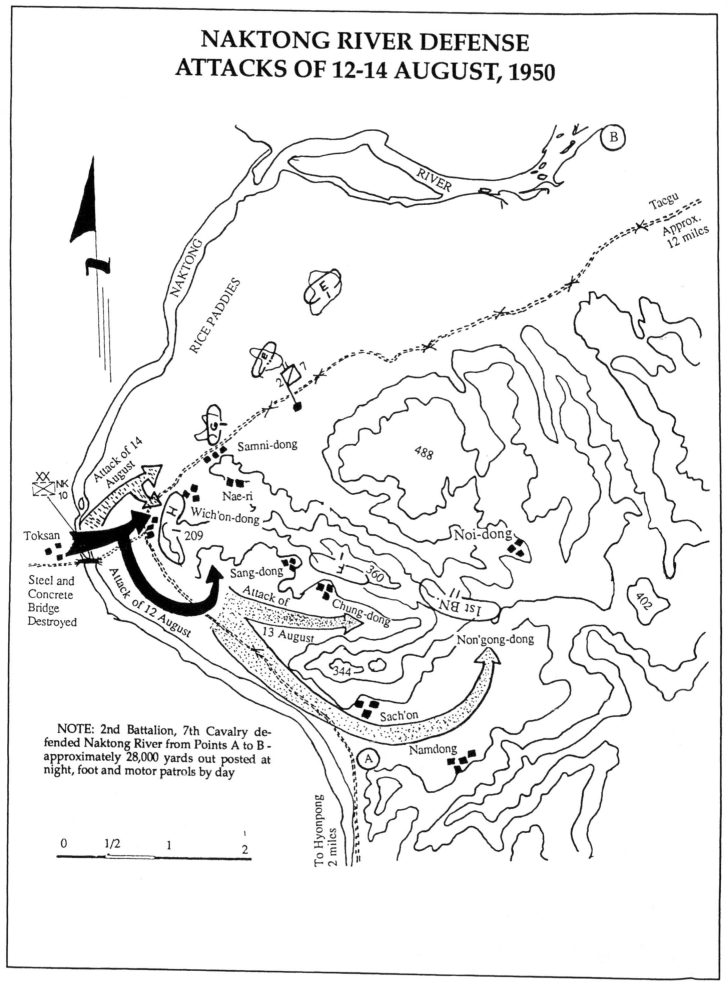

NAKTONG RIVER DEFENSE
ATTACKS OF 12-14 AUGUST, 1950

RIVER

NAKTONG

RICE PADDIES

B

Taegu
Approx.
12 miles

488

E
I

E

2   7

G

Samni-dong

Attack of 14
August

Nae-ri

Wich'on-dong

H

209

Noi-dong

XX
NK
10

Toksan

Steel and
Concrete
Bridge
Destroyed

Attack of 12 August

Sang-dong

Attack of

F

360

Chung-dong

1st BN

402

13 August

Non'gong-dong

344

Sach'on

NOTE: 2nd Battalion, 7th Cavalry defended Naktong River from Points A to B -
approximately 28,000 yards out posted at
night, foot and motor patrols by day

A

Namdong

To Hyonpong
2 miles

0   1/2   1   2

F-80 Shooting Star (note napalm bombs) Army

F-84 Thunderjet (note napalm bombs) Army

These endless trenches were heavily fortified by the enemy. "Old Baldy!" (U.S. Army Photo)

An infantry platoon under an enemy attack. (U.S. Army Photo)

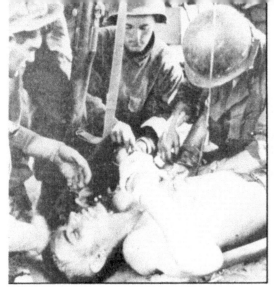

Combat "Medics" giving aid to a severly wounded trooper. (U.S. Army photo.)

Battalion position for stragglers. They brought up some 2-1/2 ton trucks and South Korea laborers to help us pick up the (enemy) dead and load them on the trucks. Their bodies were transported to the rear for identification and burial.

This victory was a morale booster because we had beaten the enemy head on. The enemy had lost a 2000-2500 men during this particular action. We had captured two prisoners with one being a Lieutenant and the other a Sergeant. They were questioned by two South Korean Interpreters for possible valuable information. The enemy officer finally admitted that they were told by their superiors that our Battalion consisted of green men and should have no trouble in beating us. But once they were across the river, they knew then that we were seasoned troops. Also, he called us "The Ghost Battalion," because their reports from previous actions against us, we were supposed to have been annihilated. Later on I heard the two prisoners were shot trying to escape. So ended another day on the Naktong River.

The following brief story is from Corporal Barton M. Smith, a First Gunner from the 4th Squad, 1st Platoon, Company H.

During the early stages of the Korean War, the majority of the infantry companies experienced heavy losses from casualties. The story from Barton M. Smith is an example of just how critical and desperate the situation became. But for the most part, the inexperienced replacements were expected and had to be accepted to fill the many vacancies. At the time, such was the way of operations within an infantry company. His story is as follows:

I entered the Army as an enlistment directly into the 1st Cavalry Division Band, which was stationed in Tokyo, Japan. At the time, there were no requirements for basic training, so the only needed ability for my future assignment was knowing how to play a trombone.

In Tokyo at the end of June 1950, word reached the 1st Cavalry Division Band about the Communist aggression by North Korea as they crossed the 38th Parallel and invaded South Korea. At first, we didn't think much about the news or even take it seriously. However, by the middle of July we were alerted and shipped out of the port city of Yokohama.

After sailing for several days in a typhoon, we reached the port city of Pohang-dong, South

Korea. We went over the side of the transport ship in cargo nets, and then into the awaiting LST's to be taken to shore. Our unit was quickly assembled and we moved out for the town of Yongchow. Once there, we were directed to guard a particular roadway and this lasted for two days. From there we were shifted to Waegwan to act as a rear guard for other units moving back to the vicinity of Taegu.

Then we were sent to an airfield for duty as perimeter guards for one night. The very next morning we moved out for the town of Taegu, where the 1st Cavalry Division Headquarters were established in a large school yard. The Division offices were in the school house building. Again, our duty was perimeter guards.

So far our unit had experienced only a couple of small skirmishes with so called guerrillas. It was small arms fire only, and our wounded were very minor.

In the early morning of August 10, 1950, John Maxwell, John Bensted, Ed Sbragia, McDermott, and myself were called out and told to immediately pack our gear. All of us had been transferred to the 2nd Battalion, 7th Cavalry Regiment. John Maxwell and I were assigned to Company H, and the others to Company G. Soon, a 2-1/2 ton truck arrived, and we were all on our way to the so called frontline.

Later on I heard that the entire Division Band was disbanded, and the men were sent to various companies of the three regiments of the 1st Cavalry Division. I never saw any of my friends again.

Upon my arrival at the command post of Company H, I was briefly introduced to the company commander, Captain Mel Chandler, and to my new platoon leader, 2nd Lt. Ed Daily. Then after Lt. Daily heard that I was a trombone player from the Division Band, he quickly shouted to Captain Chandler, "You know Captain that's all we need is a horn blower!" Then the Captain replied, "I'm sure ,Lt. Daily, that he will learn very fast how to operate a machine gun in your platoon!"

For some reason I personally felt that I wasn't wanted in Company H. But I knew they desperately needed men from the various rumors that prevailed. I would very soon learn that the rumors were very true indeed.

I left the command post tent with Lt. Daily and very shortly he introduced me to Sergeant Biege who was the 4th Squad Leader in the 1st Platoon. Before Lt. Daily departed ,he emphasized the strict orders that a 100 percent alert would continue throughout the company, day and night. He told us that a massive attack by the North Koreans might be forthcoming at any given time.

Our machine gun position was directly behind the village of Yong-po, and our company command post was located up the ravine about 50-75 yards behind us. To our right flank just across the dirt road was an apple orchard and Company G was located there. To my left flank was Hill 209, and Company H men were positioned there also. We had a commanding view of the Naktong River and the concrete-steel bridge which had been blown up. I believe we could actually see up and down the river to out across an open area of over 1000 yards. I estimate that Company H had approximately 3000 yards or more of river frontage to cover along the Naktong River.

During August 11th, the horrible stench of dead bodies filled the air of the hot summer day. Lots of flies during the day and plenty of mosquitos at night. Out across the river on the other side we could see various enemy soldiers moving around, but they weren't establishing any positions.

I was apprehensive to the overall situation as I attempted to learn more on how to disassemble and assemble a .30 caliber light air-cooled machine gun. I was eager to learn, and the overall operation of the weapon was coming to me fairly easy. But I still preferred my old trombone which I had to leave in Taegu. Then, I thought of Lt. Daily calling me a horn blower, and I started to wonder what in the hell I was doing in a machine gun platoon to begin with.

At 0600 hours in the morning of August 12th, it began with a lot of shouting and shooting. Our position was actually dug-in next to the Korean burial mound. As I looked out across the open space all I could see was swarms of refugees ,and North Korean soldiers running towards us shouting and shooting wildly. It seemed as though they were trying to make more noise than to actually hit a target.

We continued to fire the machine gun ,I had never seen anyone get shot or killed before. This was my very first experience in actual combat, and I could feel my body going into knots from the shock. Then a mortar round or a hand grenade exploded on the other side of the burial mound. The concussion stunned me but only momentarily.

I looked down toward the village and saw five North Korean soldiers coming up the ravine toward us. I started firing at them and immediately hit four, but the fifth one ran back into the village. Then a sergeant crawled over by me and told me and another soldier to slowly move down to the edge of the village with our rifles and shoot any refugee or North Korean soldier that we saw. The sergeant remained with the machine gun.

We crawled down to the village and stayed there until noon. However, we didn't see much but there was plenty of shooting all around us. The soldier with me said he was going back up the hill, and I told him that he had better remain in the village with me. As he stood up to leave, a bullet tore through his head, and he fell dead.

I remained in the village for another hour before I crawled back up to my original position. There were several dead and many wounded soldiers from Company H, laying within the area. However, the enemy had paid dearly in their morning attack as hundreds lay dead within the open area along by the Naktong River. Over 200 enemy were killed behind our company positions.

The artillery barrages had slowed down, but the air force continued to strafe and bomb near the Naktong River and the destroyed bridge site. By late afternoon ,things seemed to finally calm down as we prepared for a possible renewed attack by the enemy.

Many rumors now existed within Company H, as we received some communication that Captain Chandler was wounded during the day, and several other officers were either wounded or killed, and this included my platoon leader, Lt. Daily. I never saw the sergeant again who had given me orders earlier in the morning to crawl down to the village. It was very evident that a

A United States Fifth Air Force F-51 Mustang (SEXY SALLY), drops napalm jellied gasoline tanks on an industrial target in North Korea. (U.S. Air Force photo)

U.S. Navy F4U, leaving for bombing and strafing mission. At the time, it was a terrific fighter plane. (U.S. Navy photo)

critical shortage of officers and troopers definitely existed within Company H.

For the next two days, we continued to hold our defenses against the enemy attacks of August 13th-14th. New replacements arrived which helped to alleviate the problem of personnel shortages. We remained at this location until the end of August. However, within this same period, we would have to face yet another severe problem.

Extreme shortages of food and ammunition existed throughout the entire Eighth Army. All ammunition including M-1, machine gun, mortar, and hand grenades were short supply in our 2nd Battalion. We were supposed to eat only one food ration per day, and the water supply became critical. It was difficult to obtain artillery support because of their ammunition shortages. All of this put a very bad taste in my mouth.

From this location we moved to the vicinity of Hills 490 and 518. The I & R Platoon of the regiment reported numerous small enemy groups had crossed the Naktong River, and were reinforced with artillery pieces, tanks and heavy mortars.

Our first night was nasty, and it was pitch dark, and you couldn't tell who was who. Our positions were spread out very thin with some of them being 20 yards or more apart. The enemy harassed us all night long with their heavy 122-

mm mortars and artillery.

At 0600 hours in the morning the North Koreans attempted a series of attacks, and each consisting of five men each. Within each of their assaults, four enemy soldiers carried rifles, but the fifth one carried a burp gun. They failed in each attack, and many enemy soldiers were killed. Our light and heavy machine guns were firing effectively at ranges from 500-800 yards. We didn't waste any of our ammunition because it was a very precious item.

As dusk arrived, the North Koreans laid down a barrage on us with their 122-mm mortars and artillery. Then they attempted to infiltrate during the night and some units had to fight almost hand to hand. We continued to defend and hold our positions, and the enemy kept hitting us with everything they had.

At daybreak, all hell broke loose as the enemy had positioned a couple o Russian T-34 tanks, and they were trying to eliminate us with their direct cannon fire. This was followed by their heavy 122-mm mortars that seemed like an endless barrage into our positions. Nevertheless, I continued to fire my machine gun while Frank Maxwell was spotting the various enemy movement for me.

Suddenly, a mortar shell exploded directly behind us, and we were both wounded. After the

dirt and debris cleared, I discovered that I had a head wound and multiple shrapnel wounds over many parts of my back. Maxwell had lost his hearing, and for some reason I couldn't walk.

Through the confusion and pain, somehow Maxwell managed to carry me down to the aid station which was at the bottom of the hill. The "medics" shot us with some morphine, and we were both loaded on a 2-1/2 ton truck. From there we were transported to the 15th Medical Company in Taegu. Then I was put on a hospital train, which was an experience in itself, and ended up in Pusan. From Pusan, I was evacuated to Kobe General Hospital in Japan, and I never returned to Korea.

I never did find a horn in Company H, nor did I ever get the one back that I had left in Taegu. I did get the President Truman extension year, and I was transferred to GHQ (General Headquarters) in Tokyo. There I was given another trombone and assigned to General MacArthur's Band. I finally returned to the United States in December, 1951, and I was honorably discharged in January, 1952.

The following is a brief story of the action of August 12th-14th, 1950, from Sergeant First Class Harold Blanc, Communications Sergeant, Company H, 2nd Battalion, 7th Cavalry Regiment.

The three-day battle during August 12th-14th, were extremely furious as we continued to defend our positions as the destroyer concrete-steel bridge site and along the Naktong River.

During these attacks by the North Koreans, they somehow knew where all our forward machine gun positions were located. They even knew the exact location of our company command post, which was on the reverse slope of Hill 209. The G-2 Intelligence section of the 7th Cavalry Regiment had received some information that possibly a North Korean agent was working within Company H.

On August 15th, it was determined that valuable information about Company H was supplied to the North Korean Army, by a 15 year-old Korean boy by the name of Kim.. He worked within the company field mess, and he did various jobs for me in the communication section. After a brief interrogation of Kim by a South Korean interpreter, he actually admitted to giving information to the North Korean Army. Needless to say, he was quickly executed! He wasn't given an opportunity to appear and testify in the South Korean court. Sometimes the conditions of combat create ways that are very barbaric.

Among the enemy dead on August 14, were found the bodies of two colonels of the 10th North Korean Division. Also found were many enemy documents. One of these documents, dated August 13, said in part:

Kim Il Sung has directed that the war be carried out so that its final victory can be realized by August 15, fifth anniversary of the liberation of Korea.

Our victory lies before our eyes. Young Soldiers! You are fortunate in that you are able to participate in the battle for our final victory. Young soldiers, the capture of Taegu lies in the crossing of the Naktong River... The eyes of 30,000,000 people are fixed on the Naktong River crossing operation...

Pledge of all fighting men: We pledge with

our life, no matter what hardships and sacrifice lies before us, to bear it, and put forth our full effort to conclude the crossing of the Naktong River. Young Men! Let us protect our glorious pride by completely annihilating the enemy!!"

And throughout the entire 2nd Battalion there were many heroic and brave deeds by members in defense of their positions along the Naktong River during August 12-14.

Although being outnumbered by the enemy onslaught and severely wounded on August 12, Privates First Class Norman Tinkler, Louis Gossett, James "Buck" Buckley, Raymond Scarberry, and Private J.P. "Smitty" Smith, remained with their platoon leader 2nd Lt. Edward Daily and their forward machine gun positions. They continued to fire their weapons until all ammunition was exhausted or their weapons were made inoperative by enemy fire. Because of this extreme volume of fire placed upon the enemy, the first attacking enemy soldiers were forced to withdraw up Hill 209 where they regrouped and began attacking the 81-MM mortar positions and Company H command post. Extremely heavy casualties were suffered during the first hour of battle as all company positions were overrun.

Captain Chandler, seeing that the enemy was receiving reinforcements from the reverse side of Hill 209 and that his company would be cut in half, decided to make a bold move. He decided to attack the enemy to the rear of his company position where an estimated force of 125 were located on higher ground. He assembled a group of 25 men composed of wounded soldiers waiting to be evacuated to a rear medical aid station. Within the group was the company clerk, supply men, cooks and various drivers. One of the more seriously wounded was Lieutenant Bob Carroll where Captain Chandler had left him to direct any reinforcements he could find to fight.

As Captain Chandler started up the hill, he took one step, two broke into a trot and then into a run. He shouted "GARRYOWEN" from his throat as his followers shouted the old battle cry after him and charged the hill, firing their weapons as they ran.

The North Korean soldiers fell back, but regrouped at the top of the hill and pinned down the Company H troopers with a hail of fire, and hand grenades. Captain Chandler, observing his men from left to right, suddenly saw another figure charging up the hill throwing hand grenades and hollering the battle cry "GARRYOWEN" as he ran. He had formed his own fighting force of three stragglers and led them in a Fighting Seventh charge up the hill. The main group that had been pinned down on the hill was able to charge forward again. However, an enemy grenade hit Lieutenant Bob Carroll in the head and detonated simultaneously, causing his body to fall in face of the withering enemy fire. He seemed to have had his head practically blown off by the exploding grenade. Somehow and miraculously, Lieutenant Carroll survived his wounds and continued his military career with the United States Army.

The enemy seeking a soft spot, came pouring down with reinforcements. They found it at the junction between Companies G and H, as they prepared to counter-attack. Lieutenant Marvin Goulding saw what was happening as he turned to his platoon and shouted "Okay, men, follow me!" As he leapt to his feet, he began to shout the

battle cry "GARRYOWEN." But before he could finish the words from his lips, shrapnel from an enemy mortar round ripped through his body, and Lieutenant Goulding fell dead. For a moment his men couldn't believe their lieutenant was dead, the most popular officer in the battalion. Suddenly his men felt the anguish and rage and began cursing, screaming, and hollering "GARRYOWEN", as they charged into the enemy like wild men. Goulding's platoon pushed back the enemy which broke up the timing of their entire attack.

Being pinned-down by enemy fire and unable to progress any further up the hill, Captain Chandler and Private Thomas Palmer returned to the overrun 81-MM mortar positions. By taking all powder chargers from the rounds and elevating the tubes to a vertical position, fire was brought upon the enemy as close as 100 yards. This enabled the pinned-down troopers of Company H to disengage from the enemy and return to their original positions at the bottom of the hill and replenish their ammunition supply. This bold attack stopped the enemy in rear of Company H.

Also, to arrive with a force of support was Major Charles King who commanded 242 South Korean police, who were temporarily attached to the 7th Cavalry Regiment. Lieutenant Crawford "Buck" Buchanan leader of the Intelligence and Reconnaissance Platoon, along with 15 truck drivers, cooks, and supply personnel from the Regimental Service Company arrived to assist the beleaguered troopers of Company H. ("Buck" continued his military career with the United States Army and attained the rank of Full Colonel, prior to his retirement.)

Two platoons of Company F had been sent from the left flank to aid and assist Company H. Lieutenant John "Jack" Lippincott with a rifle platoon reached the high ground to give support to Lieutenant Thomas Stone's platoon. Lieutenant Lippincott stated at first he couldn't determine which direction to fire at the enemy. This was because Lieutenant Stone was exchanging so many hand grenades with the enemy that it looked like blackbirds flying in the air.

With the support of Company G on the right flank, the tide of battle was turned ,and the enemy retreated through the rice paddies toward the Naktong River. Artillery barrages and air strikes were brought forth upon the fleeing enemy, killing hundreds before they could recross the river.

During the action of August 12, 237 enemy killed were counted in the rear area of Company H, with the probability of many others. Enemy killed in front of Company H, with the support of other elements from the regiment, including the 77th Field Artillery and Air Force, were never accurately determined. It is known however, that an enemy battalion was destroyed and 35 prisoners were taken. Needless to say, the enemy suffered a severe blow from these devastating lossess and to their 25th Regiment, 10th North Korean Division. This failure ,however, would not end their efforts to cross the Naktong River.

The 7th Cavalry Regiment lost 15 killed and 60 wounded, the majority from Company H. Also, wounded at close range by an enemy hand grenade was Captain Chandler. This would required his evacuation to a rear aid station for proper medical treatment. Over 70% of the enlisted men of Company H became casualties during the day. Also, the following day on August 13, the regiment casualties amounted to 25 killed and 39 wounded.

On August 14, the 2nd Battalion consisted of Company E on the right, Company G in the center, Company H and Company F on the extreme left flank. The third attack to seize Taegu

began during the early morning hours of darkness in the area of Company G. An attacking enemy force of 700 succeeded in driving their outer perimeter defense to the rear. Again the enemy was determined to gain higher ground as they attacked the now scattered troops of Company G and H to obtain control of the back entrance into Taegu.

The enemy with 400-500 soldiers had penetrated as far as Yong Po by 06:20. Then by 06:35, the enemy penetration had reached Wichondong, and fighting in the understrength Company H and an area of Company G, had reached the hand-to-hand stage.

Lieutenant John B. Wadsworth, Jr., serving as intelligence officer for the 2nd Battalion, 7th Cavalry Regiment, voluntarily performed a duty not expected of him. He heard that one of his battalion companies had been overrun very near Yong-Po and was under heavy enemy attack. Securing a jeep and then mounting a 75-MM recoilless rifle on it, he voluntarily rushed to the battle area and took a position where he could bring fire upon the enemy. Despite hostile fire and with complete disregard for his own safety, he remained in his forward position and placed effective fire on the enemy to cover the company's withdrawal from its untenable position. Lieutenant Wadsworth was awarded the Bronze Star for heroism and within the few weeks to come, he would be promoted to the rank of Captain. Also in the future weeks ahead ,he would take command of Company H. (He continued his military career with the United States Army and attained the rank of full Colonel prior to his retirement).

The deepest enemy penetration reached Samuni-dong which was about a mile and a half from the blown bridge. By noon, large groups of enemy soldiers were trying to recross the Naktong River to the west side. Artillery and mortar fire on the retreating enemy caused heavy casualties. By dusk the 7th Cavalry Regiment had eliminated the enemy bridgehead at Yong-Po.

The 25th and 27th Regiments of the 10th North Korean Division suffered crippling losses. The young enemy soldiers never fulfilled their promise to secure and conclude the crossing of the Naktong River. Instead, the Naktong valley and surrounding hills were to hold countless graves of the North Korean soldiers. According to enemy prisoners taken on August 12-14, they had suffered in excess of 2,500 casualties; some units suffering as much as 50% of their soldiers.

In this river crossing battle, the only major one to take place along the Naktong River at a crossing site, the 2nd Battalion of the 7th Cavalry Regiment, distinguished itself. This was the same battalion that only three weeks earlier had performed in a highly unsatisfactory manner, east of Yongdong.

CHAPTER VI
PRIVATE HELL IN NORTH KOREAN HANDS

Of the thirty-six ways, escape is the best way...
—Chinese Proverb—

`This ferry crossing site on the Naktong River was captured from the North Koreans by elements of the 1st Battalion, 7th Cavalry Regiment and put to their own use in late September 1950. The enemy used this ferry operation to transport their wounded, supplies and equipment. (Photo courtesy of Reuben Kvidt)*

North Korean soldiers captured by elements of the 7th Cavalry Regiment, in September 1950. They are being processed by a clearing station of the 545th Military Police Company. (Photo courtesy of Reuben Kvidt)

Our small group of American prisoners was being retained in a partial washout and tree coverage very near the Naktong River. This was in a southwesterly direction from the area where I was captured. The artillery was still sending barrage after barrage into the enemy positions. The Air Force continued to strafe and bomb the enemy movement along the river. Later on I would learn that the massive enemy attack of this particular day that successfully overran our company forward positions were elements of the 25th Regiment, 10th North Korean Division. Now I was getting a good look at the enemy soldier, and I could see that he was well trained and disciplined.

For some unknown reason, I was being kept alone and separate from the other prisoners. Still no one was permitted to speak or talk as I continued to look around in search of prisoners who might be from my platoon or company. My mind wasn't functioning properly because of my own personal shock, and everyone appeared strangers. Then I saw two ammo bearers from my platoon, but I couldn't remember their names as they were very recent replacements within my platoon.

As I looked at these brave American prisoners, their eyes expressed sadness, fear, shock and disbelief. Then I briefly thought of Captain Chandler, Company H, and the battalion and wondered if they survived the massive enemy attack. I thought, if I get out of this mess how in the hell would I explain what went wrong to Captain Chandler, my company commander, who had put his personal trust and faith in me as a new platoon leader. I had the personal feelings of guilt and shame for losing control of my platoon and letting myself be captured. Again, I thought, maybe I'm in a dream, and I'll soon wake up from this horrible nightmare. None of us had ever received any military training on what to expect if ever captured by the enemy. The coming days, weeks and months that lay ahead for all of us would be traumatic and devastating .

It was now near dark, and I didn't hear the fighter planes overhead anymore. The artillery had slowed down their firing activity somewhat. Small arms fire was sporadic along the river and nearby hills. The evening still carried the heat from the day, and the mosquitos were now on the attack. The stench of dead bodies filled the air of the evening.

Time had slowly passed on, and I assumed it was now near midnight. The North Korean guards notified all of us to stand up,

and it was extremely dark as they motioned for us to walk toward the river. We reached the waters edge where suddenly a flare lit up the dark sky. I could see two lines of North Korean soldiers moving across the river toward us. However, I then noticed that one line was enemy soldiers and the other was refugees carrying various supplies on their heads. Suddenly heavy small arms fire started coming from a nearby hill directly behind us, as they forced us to enter the river. When the flare went out, the heavy small arms fire on the nearby hill became sporadic again. Company F of our Battalion had their defensive positions along those nearby hills.

The water of the river was sort of cool, and it was soothing to the body. As we carefully walked within the water, I discovered that the North Koreans had installed underwater ropes to help support the body from the river current. The water was now starting to reach my waist, then to the center of my chest. Near the middle of the river, another flare lit up the dark sky and I was starting to wonder if a forward observer might see us and send an artillery barrage into our location.

When we reached the other side of the

river, the North Korean soldiers were immediately regrouping us. Again I was kept separate from the rest of the American soldiers. Then I noticed that several American soldiers were missing their boots and were barefooted. We were moved along the edge of the river for a short distance, then through a ravine and up over a small hill. It was extremely dark, but the North Koreans seemed to know their way around. Once over the hill, we continued on down the reverse side toward an area that had the sound of tanks and other military vehicles.

To my amazement and surprise, I thought at first my eyes were deceiving me as we approached the road. North Korean soldiers were moving along both sides of the road, heading to an area I assumed near the river; or possibly I thought, they were going to cross the river while it was still dark. As we stood by the roadside, I counted as they passed; six T-34 tanks, ten supply trucks and two jeeps. However, one of the jeeps pulled over to the edge of the road and stopped near us. I could barely see that he was a high-ranking North Korean officer. As he talked to several of the guards, he kept pointing down the road which was an opposite direction from the river. One of the guards pointed at me as I started to wonder what in the hell was in store for me. The North Korean officer then walked over to me and said with very poor English, "All of you will be taken to a prisoner of war camp in Seoul." I quickly replied with a "Yes, sir!" He made no attempt to salute and he made no other comments. He walked back to his chauffeur-driven jeep which pulled away and headed toward the river. The North Korean soldiers were still moving in that same direction. Then I wondered how long it would take us to reach Seoul, the capital city of South Korea.

I estimated it took a couple of hours for the North Korean soldiers to pass. I thought to myself, "God there must be a full regiment staging at the river; or possibly, they were crossing the river this very morning in the darkness." Now I was starting to wonder if our Battalion would be ready and prepared for the future enemy assault.

The enemy soldiers then motioned for us to start moving onto the road as the morning daylight of August 13th approached. We walked down the center of the road for a brief distance, and then they directed us to start a dog trot toward a ravine behind a nearby hill.

It was starting to get daylight faster then they estimated or predicted. It was quite noticeable that some of the American soldiers were not in good physical shape as we rushed up the ravine. The North Koreans insisted on our rapid movement, and they could see that it was starting to take effect on certain American soldiers, particularly the ones that previously had their boots taken from them. A couple of them complained about their sore feet, but the only answer they got was a quick punch from an enemy rifle.

We finally reached an area that was hidden by a heavy growth of trees. Very near our location was an apple orchard. As I looked around, I could see approximately 40 to 50 seriously wounded enemy soldiers laying on thick thatch matting. In the group I counted three Americans soldiers that looked near death. Maybe they were already dead because their bodies were lifeless. I kept looking around, but I didn't see any other wounded Americans.

I assumed this was a medical aid station for the more seriously wounded North Korean soldiers. One North Korean doctor appeared to be caring for the entire group. He had the help of four (supposedly) aid men. You could easily see they were lacking medical supplies and equipment. Then I realized how damn barbaric the North Koreans were as I watched the doctor treat an enemy soldier's leg wound. The doctor took a small metal container which he sprinkled over the open wound. I closely watched as the small white worms moved within the wound. Then I realized the worms were actually maggots. I started to become nauseated as he covered the wound with a bandage. Was this the way the enemy doctor treated the more seriously wounded by using maggots to help fight infection? In my mind, I asked God to please get me out of this horrible nightmare.

I was thirsty and hungry, but after watching the North Korean doctor and looking at the severely wounded, my stomach was in a complete knot. I thought to myself and I realized by now that I had had no food or water for over 24 hours. After standing all this time, several enemy guards ordered us to sit down.

All of us were extremely exhausted and were covered with dirt, bruised and our fatigues were sweat-soaked. The heat of the Korean summer which constituted flies, fleas and lice, became constant irritants. The foul earthy smells filled the air along with the horrible stench of dead bodies. Some of the odor was coming from the wounded enemy soldiers, and I realized that some had died from their injuries. As the flies buzzed softly around to gorge on blood, I laid on my side and quickly dozed off to sleep.

Suddenly I was awakened by a North Korean soldier. I don't know how long I had been asleep. They were preparing to feed us, as I noticed the arrival of 12 more North Korean soldiers. One went directly to the doctor and whatever he was talking about caused him to become very displeased and emotional. He started shouting and everyone became motionless, and we all stared at him. He walked a short distance, stopped and bowed his head as he looked toward the ground. Nothing else was said by the doctor.

Three North Korean soldiers were distributing the food to each of us. A gummy ball of rice, a small apple and approximately three or four ounces of water. This was a lot different from the C-rations I was used to, such as beef stew, chicken and noodles, pork and beans, or hamburgers. However, I was hungry and it didn't make any difference just as long as it was some sort of food. I could see that their water supply was inadequate, so I sipped on what little I received. As I looked to my left, I noticed a couple of American soldiers become nauseated and gag as they attempted to eat. The horrible odor continued to get worse with the day. The smell of vomit and sweat also hung in the air.

Again there was shouting, but this time it was over four F-51 Mustangs of the American Air Force. They were strafing two North Korean trucks on the road which I had come from earlier in the morning. Both trucks were hit with rockets and each immediately exploded into a large ball of fire. Now I realized even more that this was the main reason why the North Koreans moved their men and equipment so much during the night. It was to avoid the constant strafing from fighter planes of the U.S. Navy and Air Force during the daylight hours.

What little food I received, I very quickly ate. For some reason, I had the strange feeling that the North Korean soldiers might attempt a reprisal for the recent loss of their two supply trucks. It did happen, and they stopped distributing the food, and only half of our group received something to eat. I thanked God for letting me be one of the fortunate American prisoners to be fed.

Not too long after eating, I signaled one of the guards that I had to urinate and defecate. He took me over to a small narrow trench, which was used as their toilet. This was identical to what we Americans used in our combat areas. However, I didn't appreciate the guard standing there watching me do my business. After I finished, I discovered there was no toilet paper. Now I was starting to realize that I was being gradually stripped of my dignity. I returned to our group and sat down again.

The hot summer air continued to carry the stench of dead bodies. The enemy squad of 12 that arrived earlier were grouped together. Several looked toward us as one pointed his finger toward our direction. Somehow I had the feeling we were going to be moved to another location. Several enemy guards motioned for us to stand up as they started to select various American prisoners. In a few minutes, 15 of us were ordered to move out with the enemy soldiers. Of the selection, most of us I believe, were previously fed. Of those remaining within the group to stay behind, were the American prisoners who had their boots taken from them. As we departed, I briefly looked back at those remaining and little did I realize at the time that I

North Korean Soldiers captured by elements of the 7th Cavalry Regiment, in September 1950. Many were stripped of their clothing due to the concealment of weapons and hand grenades. (Photo courtesy of Reuben Kvidt)

would never again see that particular group of American prisoners.

The enemy soldiers now prodded us to move along. We found ourselves being treated like cattle. For several hours, we endured the blazing sun and worst of all, the torture of thirst. We had moved farther away from the sound of artillery and small arms fire. From the location of the sun, I estimated that we were moving in a northwesterly direction. I then assumed that we were headed for the capital city of Seoul. At least that's what the North Korean officer had told me, that we would be taken to a prisoner of war camp there.

Some American prisoners stumbled and fell as we continued to move up and down various hills and mountains. Many could only make incoherent grunts to express themselves. I was in a dreamlike state, and my lips and tongue were swollen. The enemy soldiers still would not give us any water. Even time had lost all meaning. However, I was starting to realize that the enemy soldiers were of a different culture and lesser standards of humanity, and we were being treated accordingly. Also I realized that we had not been prepared for combat, and we had not been prepared to go into captivity.

Suddenly shouting came from the rear as the enemy soldiers quickly shoved and pushed us in some heavy thick bushes. We were ordered to lie flat and warned that we would be shot if we moved or talked. Then I heard the sound of a small airplane as I looked upward. Through the small branches of the trees, I could see that it was an L-5 liaison airplane used by our artillery. Shortly, the airplane disappeared, and we were ordered to start moving again.

It was late afternoon as we moved forward within a small village near the foot of a large mountain. Many white-clad farmers looked without smiling as they scooped up various pots outside of their home doors, or what was left of them. In some of the surrounding villages that we passed earlier, many homes were completely devastated by our Air Force. Their life was hard, and many who stayed and refused to go South with the refugees were old. The North Korean soldiers didn't make their life any easier.

The enemy soldiers moved us to an area very near several mud huts. There we were told to sit down, and what a relief that was to each of us! We were exhausted, dirty and our uniforms were sweat-soaked from the heat of the summer day. Still the enemy refused to give us water, and some quickly dozed off to sleep.

I thought of my mother, grandmother, and many of my loved ones. These thoughts helped to comfort me, at least for the moment, and I was at peace. Then I thought of God and the 23rd Psalm, but I couldn't remember it. For some unknown reason, all that I could remember was, "The Lord is my Shepherd, I shall not want." In the future days ahead I would constantly repeat these particular words as I put my faith in God.

It was still daylight and the North Korean soldiers had assembled a large group of South

North Korean soldiers captured by elements of the 7th Cavalry Regiment. Many were wearing the civilian clothing of South Korea, which made it difficult to distinguish them as the enemy. (Photo courtesy of Reuben Kvidt.)

Korean civilians. They were taken away in the direction we had come from earlier in the day. I assumed that these poor defenseless people would be used, no doubt, as a human battering ram in front of a future enemy attack. Maybe they were going to be used as common laborers to do various work or move supplies and equipment. Many discovered at the end of their burdensome work, their only reward was death. I would soon learn that the North Korean soldiers preferred to kill their captives to avoid the extra handling and feeding. Their food and water was in short supply and in the future weeks ahead, it would become extremely worse and critical.

The evening darkness was just about upon us as more enemy activity was heard within the village. I could hear the sound of not only trucks, but tanks as well. There seemed to be a lot of shouting coming from the enemy soldiers. I assumed that this area was an assembly point for a particular enemy division, or possibly divisions.

Just prior to darkness, we were split up in two separate groups. Each group had a small mud hut with a straw roof and dirt floor. I was placed in a corner, while seven others stayed on the opposite side of the room. Each of us had our boot laces tied together to prevent a possible escape. Again we had to continually slap mosquitos during the night. Now all of us were covered with body lice, which didn't help our morale. We went to sleep that evening without food or water. It was difficult to sleep during the night because of the large enemy activity with their troops, tanks and equipment. The early morning of August 14, would bring forth the shouting of words from an enemy soldier, which I couldn't understand.

Our boot laces were untied, and we were taken to a shady area outside and ordered to sit down. I noticed to my right a large group of refugees digging a large, long, wide and deep trench near the base of a large hill. As I looked at the other American soldiers, you could see the grim look on their faces. I immediately had the feeling of fear in my mind and body.

Many of us had to use the make shift toilets as the enemy soldiers watched every move we made. Several of the American soldiers had developed dysentery and still we weren't provided with toilet paper. A few had to defecate many times during the day and their rectums were starting to become swollen open and red. Their fatigue pants were soiled with feces, which attracted many flies. To make things even worse, they never received any medical attention or help from the enemy.

Suddenly three North Korean soldiers appeared with two South Korean soldiers. The enemy ordered them to take off their American fatigue uniforms, which left them only in their undershorts. As they were questioned by the enemy, there was no way that I could understand what was being asked in the interrogations. One of the enemy soldiers pulled his pistol as they made both South Korean soldiers get down on their knees. As we watched in horror and disbelief, the pistol shot rang out, which passed through the skull and exited at the right jaw bone. The body lay lifeless as the blood flowed on the ground. The other South Korean soldier started to shout and scream, but that was silenced by a second shot from the pistol. Very shortly, both lifeless bodies were dragged away and thrown inside of the long, wide, deep trench near the base of the hill. Now I realized the refugees were digging a future mass grave. Then I had thoughts of who would be next.

I looked at the faces of the American soldiers and some were just staring at the ground. Some shook their heads from side to side with the grim look of shock and disbelief. Why was the enemy deliberately trying to intimidate us by making us watch this type of ruthless and brutal killings? Nevertheless, in our minds and souls it was starting to take effect. Would possibly any one of us Americans be selected for future brutal slayings?

Then I looked toward heaven and closed my eyes as I prayed for help and guidance from God. After I completed a brief prayer, suddenly it came to me to look for the location of the sun. One thing the Army taught me in basic training was how to use the sun

South Korean civilians loading dead North Korean soldiers on a 2 1/2 ton truck, in September 1950. The one in foreground is an enemy officer. (Photo courtesy of Reuben Kvidt)

Sixty defenseless civilians bludgeoned to death in cold blood. Many times the enemy used civilians to move equipment and supplies and rewarded them with death. U.S. Army Photo)

for approximate location and time when there was no compass in our possession. Was God telling me to make use of the sun whenever possible? In the future weeks to come, the sun would become an important part of my personal life and the survival in captivity. I had the strangest feeling that I must survive no matter what the future circumstances might be.

It was another hot summer day and around noon time we finally received some food and water. The gummy ball of rice tasted good due to my hunger. My mouth was extremely dry from thirst which made it difficult to swallow the rice. Shortly an enemy soldier started to give each of us a few ounces of water which I gradually sipped on. Several of the American soldiers drank the water very quickly, but never touched their rice, particularly the ones with dysentery, because their bodies were becoming dehydrated.

You could see that morale was gone, and the necessary discipline with many Americans for the hope for survival went with it. The disciplines that hold men together in the face of fear, hunger, and danger are not natural. Stresses that go beyond fear and panic must be overlaid on men. A fragile discipline at best, is human decency. With the degradation of mind and spirit, men will lean the way the wind takes them as most men have since the beginning of time.

As darkness came, we were ordered back to the mud huts which we slept in the previous night. Again I was put in the corner and my boot laces tied together. The mosquitos started their attack and the biting pest of lice, had everyone slapping and scratching during the night. Again the enemy movement with their soldiers, tanks and equipment continued to interfere with our sleep.

Early morning would bring the sound of enemy activity within the village. Several enemy soldiers started to untie our boot laces and we were quickly moved outside to the shady area. Once there, we were ordered to sit down.

To my surprise there was approximately 100 South Korean soldiers being marched into our area. They were captured by the enemy, possibly during the night or over the past several days. The enemy immediately started to strip the American fatigue uniforms from their bodies and replace them with the civilian white-clad type clothing. Now it was difficult for me to distinguish them from the actual refugees. Then I started to think that possibly many of the younger refugees seen over the past few days could in fact have been South Korean soldiers. Once the South Korean soldiers were redressed in civilian clothes, the enemy very rapidly moved them within the group of refugees. The North Korean soldiers expressed an extreme hatred to all South Koreans, especially the soldiers. I looked at the sun and estimated the time at 0800 hours as the enemy brought us food and water. However, the gummy ball of rice was smaller and the water ration remained the same. Then an enemy soldier started to give each of us an apple from a basket he was carrying. I was hungry, and I quickly ate what little food I received. I looked around at the other American soldiers and their sad faces; several still didn't eat the food, and only drank the water. You could see their health was very rapidly deteriorating.

The summer heat continued as we sat in the shaded area where it was much cooler. The enemy soldiers that were guarding us kept a close eye on our movement, and no one dared to speak a word. Then five enemy soldiers with three female refugees started to walk toward our group, and I wondered if they were coming after me. Immediately the fright started to build up inside of me.

As they approached, the enemy soldier standing near me started to talk to them, and I had no idea what they were saying. I noticed the three female refugees were wearing black cloth jackets and blouses. From a small bag, one of the enemy soldiers handed each one of them two apples, which they secured within their jackets. After a few words, they left and walked over to the large group of refugees and disappeared.

A short distance away, several enemy soldiers carrying white bundles of clothing and what appeared to be American fatigue clothing, called to the five enemy soldiers. They immediately went to the enemy soldiers with the clothing. The five enemy soldiers started to strip from their particular uniforms and quickly replaced them with selected American fatigue uniforms. However, over top of the American uniform, they put on the white clad clothing of the refugees. I was now witnessing some of the North Korean tactics used in combat. As in my own personal combat experience in the previous weeks, this organized group would possibly pass through the American lines undetected as friendly South Korean refugees.

You could see that the North Korean infantryman was a rugged individual and accustomed to various hardships of combat. He had only one uniform, a weapon, little ammunition and very few personal effects in his possession. His shoes were made of canvas and rubber in which he could move with speed over the difficult terrain - mountains and rice paddies. He carried only small amounts of food, and various loose strings from the pockets in which they could tie twigs or leaves for camouflage purposes.

In the future weeks to come, I would see the enemy propaganda methods somehow work on the South Koreans. The many that remained in the towns and villages were cooperating with the enemy by doing whatever was instructed or ordered. Also I would see how the enemy made callous use of the defenseless civilians.

Eventually I dozed off to sleep, only to be awakened by an enemy soldier kicking at my back with his boot. He motioned for me to get up, which I did. Then he started to push me forward toward a particular village house. Again I felt the sudden fear and fright come within my body.

Upon arrival, I walked cautiously through the door and was greeted by three enemy soldiers. All were young, disciplined officers. They wore blue-breeched uniforms and high boots. One enemy officer quickly asked me in poor English for my name and rank. I immediately answered him as requested. Then one of the other officers handed him a piece of paper, which he momentarily looked at. When he lifted his head he asked, "Do you come from ghost battalion?" I replied, "I know nothing about a ghost battalion!" "You lie, because I know you come from 1st Cavalry Division, and soon it will be annihilated." "Very soon all Americans will be destroyed." "We make plans to send you to prisoner of war camp in Seoul." He said a few words which I couldn't understand, and the enemy guard proceeded to escort me back to the group.

As I walked, my body was still trembling from fright. The sun was extremely hot as I looked up to see its location. It was early afternoon because it was already past the high noon position. There seemed to be a foul stench in the air, which I recognized as that of dead bodies. Maybe it was coming from the two South Korean soldiers that were murdered yesterday morning. Nevertheless, I didn't even want to think about that horrible incident or the long, wide and deep trench at the base of the hill. When I got back to the rest of the Americans, everyone that was awake looked at me. You could see from the facial expressions that there was a sigh of relief that nothing happened to me during interrogation. If I could only speak to them, I know that I would feel a little more comfortable, and maybe they would too, but we dared not speak a word.

I started to think of the days in captivity and estimated the day to be August 15. Then it hit me like a ton of bricks, and I quickly started to count total heads. Something didn't seem right since I returned to our group. I counted 12 heads. and we had originally 15 when we arrived here. Where in the hell did the other three go while I was gone? I know I couldn't question the enemy soldiers for fear of my life. I tried to observe which ones were gone, and it appeared that the more seriously sick with dysentery were missing. Maybe a North Korean doctor was giving them the proper medication and treatment. Nevertheless, I would never see the three American soldiers again.

Late afternoon we received our second meal of the day. This time the small gummy ball of rice was wrapped in a green leaf. I never experienced eating the leaf before, so this was something different. I was hungry so the leaf tasted pretty good. Then an enemy soldier with a bag of pears gave each of us one which was not a bad meal; and surprisingly we were fed two times that day. Maybe it was because there were high-ranking officers in the village. However, the water ration was still only a few ounces.

Evening darkness was near, and I was thinking about the afternoon interrogation from the enemy officers. What were they talking about when I was asked about a "Ghost Battalion"? Maybe our battalion was wiped out the day of my capture. They knew exactly what division I was from! Then I wondered if they could really destroy all Americans. Possibly he could be right, I thought. Then I had the feeling that we might be moved tonight to the prisoner of war camp in Seoul.

The enemy soldiers motioned for all of us to move toward the same two mud huts we had been using to sleep in. Again I was put in

the corner, but for some unknown reason they never tied our shoe laces together. This gave me the impression that we would be moved toward Seoul tonight.

During the night, enemy activity and movement of vehicles was not as heavy as the past several nights. This finally gave me the opportunity to sleep somewhat better. However, the pesty little irritants of mosquitos and lice continued to work on my body.

The morning of August 16 came very rapidly, and the enemy soldiers didn't waste any time moving us to the outside. The sun was bright, and it looked as though it was going to be another hot day.

They quickly arranged to feed us and I couldn't understand why. Possibly we were going to be moved to Seoul during the daylight hours. Then I thought of the enemy high-ranking officers. Even though I didn't see them, maybe they were still here in the village. Could these enemy soldiers be trying to impress their superiors?

Late morning brought the sounds of airplanes in the distant sky. I looked at the sun, and it was almost high noon as the airplanes appeared to the northeast of our location. As I continued to look, so did the enemy soldiers and refugees. Were my eyes deceiving me or was it factual to what I as looking at? I estimated there were 100 B-29 bombers in this particular air raid. In my life time, I thought, at no time had I ever seen this many airplanes in one group. Even though we were some distance from the target site, the sounds of the bomber engines, the falling bombs, the bomb explosions, and the trembling earth, really started to build up my enthusiasm. Was this the beginning of a large American attack to crush the enemy army? Only time would tell and my hopes were high.

The bomber attack seemed to last almost one-half hour. Smoke and dust from the bomb explosions appeared high in the sky. It could be seen for miles. Many of the enemy soldiers and refugees looked in awe. I knew they had never seen anything like this before.

Then it happened in the afternoon between 1500 and 1600 hours. We would witness the most barbaric and ruthless savagery of mankind. The enemy soldiers brought in 75 to 100 refugees, and they took them to the edge of the long, wide trench at the base of the hill. Many of the refugees appeared to be young and possibly they could be South Korean soldiers. There was no way to tell. They were spread out with the width of the trench and directly in front of it. Fifteen to 20 enemy soldiers in the firing squad with Russian burp machine guns and rifles started shooting at the defenseless human beings as their bodies began to topple and fall within the open trench. Strangely, not one attempted to run.

Many cries of agony and pain came from the open trench. The ones who lay near the edge were kicked into the trench as the enemy soldiers walked by. They continued to fire their weapons down into the refugees as many lay moaning inside of the open trench. No doubt, many of these slaughtered refugees had previously helped to dig this particular trench. Not knowing at the time what the future would bring, they had actually dug their own graves.

I looked at the other American prisoners, and again you could see the grim looks of shock and disbelief. Why did the enemy decide to murder these defenseless civilians, and possibly South Korean soldiers? However, in my mind, there was no reason for this type of atrocity. Then I wondered if it was in direct retaliation of the earlier American bombing, or was there some other reason? I know all of us Americans had fear in our minds and wondered if we might be the next victims. As I had done many times before, I prayed to God for his support and guidance. I myself repeated the words. "The Lord is my shepherd, I shall not want."

That evening the enemy made no attempt to feed us. I really wasn't that hungry because in my mind there were reflections of the afternoon enemy atrocities. The mild evening breeze seemed to carry the echoes of screams and cries from the trench - or was my mind just playing tricks on me?

During the night it was difficult to sleep because two American soldiers with severe dysentery had to keep getting up to defecate.

The thousands of refugees always presented a problem on the narrow dirt roads. (U.S. Army photo)

Their pants were all covered with feces, which was giving off a very foul odor. In the dim candle light of the mud hut, you could see their bodies were suffering from malnutrition. Their stomaches were swollen, and their condition was worsening with each day. Still not one of us had seen a doctor or received any medical attention. The enemy soldier watching over us was really complaining, but I had no idea what he was saying.

The morning of August 17, brought the usual shouting from the enemy as we were escorted outside to our normal setting area. It looked as though it was going to be another hot day. For the next several days it was almost routine with the enemy soldiers. This village seemed to be unaffected by the war and particularly our fighter planes. The enemy had definitely selected an area that was excellent for the movement of troops, equipment and supplies. It was a great collecting point for the many hundreds of defenseless refugees, and I still couldn't understand why we were being retained in this village and not moved to the prisoner of war camp in Seoul.

On the morning of August 23, we were fed a brief meal of rice with a little water. The two Americans with severe dysentery were so weak now, the enemy had to take them away on stretchers. I assumed they were taken to a North Korean doctor at a medical aid station. We were now down to ten Americans left in our group. I looked at another starving American with dysentery in the group, and I knew it would be only a matter of time before the enemy would take him away also.

The horrible stench of dead bodies filled the air of the hot summer day. Thousands of flies buzzed around the open trench where the refugees had been slaughtered several days prior. I had noticed in the past several days hundreds of refugees or possibly South Korean soldiers being taken and escorted toward the battle front. Again, only to be used and treated as slave laborers. The North Korean soldiers continued to show a complete disregard for human life.

Five enemy soldiers arrived with four of them carrying rifles and one with a Russian burp gun. I quickly wondered what was going on as five Americans were selected to follow their group. Again fear and fright started within my body. We were taken to an area just north of the village where I noticed large amounts of supplies stacked up neatly and two large supply trucks parked nearby. As we got closer, I could see the Russian markings on the cases of ammunition and 85-mm tank shells.

There were 12 refugees standing near the trucks as we walked up to the supplies. The enemy soldiers motioned for us to help the refugees load the two supply trucks. The refugees looked young, and I thought to myself, could they possibly be South Korean soldiers. Again, there was no way to tell. It didn't take us that long to load up the two supply trucks. However, my fatigue uniform was sweat-soaked from the hot summer afternoon. My body and clothing were

giving off a foul odor because of no shower and clean clothing since my capture. My teeth were covered with a light film due to no brushing, and I felt like a garbage mouth.

The enemy soldiers moved us with the refugees to an area where the earth was recently dug in the shape of a shallow pit. The refugees were then taken from our group and placed in the center of the pit. My body started to tremble as my thoughts and prayers to God to please not let the enemy shoot and kill the refugees and us. Our bodies seemed to jump as the rifle and Russian burp gun shots rang out. Within seconds the refugees lay lifeless on the ground. Several had incoherent sounds of grunts and moans; and as before, not one attempted to run.

I know that each American prisoner dreaded to watch this kind of barbaric and ruthless treatment of human beings. In our minds was the constant fear that anytime it could possibly be us that would be lined up and shot down in cold blood.

As the enemy soldiers prodded us to move along, I took a quick glance back at the dead refugees in the shallow pit. I could easily see that the enemy soldiers made no attempt to cover the dead bodies with dirt. They were left exposed to the hot summer sun.

When we arrived at the village, the enemy soldiers put us back with the other five Americans. The hot summer air was filled with nauseating stench and odor of dead bodies. It was not only coming from the open trench, but it seemed the air in general carried the foul odor of death. I was extremely thirsty, but the enemy still ignored our signals and refused to serve us water. Within a few minutes, I dozed off to sleep; and even the flies and lice didn't bother me.

I was awakened by an enemy soldier prodding at my ribs with the barrel of his rifle. It was now late afternoon, and I could see they were preparing to feed us. My mouth was so dry and swollen that I could hardly swallow. I sipped on what little water I received, and the rice allowance seemed smaller than before.

Shortly after eating, (yet we were all still hungry), five enemy soldiers arrived with a very young officer. I had not seen these particular enemy soldiers or officer before. The enemy officer immediately told us in broken English that was understandable, that we were going to be taken to the town of Kumchon. Then from there, we would be transported to the prisoner of war camp in Seoul. The town of Kumchon rang a bell with me because we made had our withdrawal through there on our way to the Naktong River.

As we prepared to leave the village, we only had a few hours of daylight left before dark. The enemy officer went to the one American soldier who could hardly stand up because of his extreme weakness from dysentery. He shouted words that brought an enemy soldier running. The two exchanged a few words, and the enemy soldier escorted the sick American away from our group. We left the village with only nine American soldiers remaining in our group

on August 23. I prayed to God for his support, guidance and to give each of us individual strength to endure our future hardships.

For the next several days we would travel in the late afternoons and nights. According to my estimation, we were moving in a north and northwest direction. During the daylight hours we stayed in various villages to avoid being seen by American airplanes. The mud huts in the villages were infested with all types of insects, and my body felt as though it was being eaten alive.

The enemy showed an extreme fright toward the American airplanes. In this particular area during the daylight hours, American fighter planes flew constant missions overhead. Many times they flew at very low levels trying to spot enemy activity and movement.

Also as the enemy moved us from village to village, it gave me the opportunity to see how much devastation had been done by the American Air Force. Even during the night when we moved along the center of the roads, many tanks, trucks and other equipment lay about completely destroyed. I now realized more than ever how important it was to have appropriate air support.

Strangely, the young enemy officer that directed our movement seemed to express a certain amount of sympathy toward us Americans. You could see that the enemy rations were very low, but he made an attempt to give us a little food and water each day. Several times during our movement, he started to criticize the American Air Force and the way we prisoners slowed down his objective. But he always cut himself short of further words. He never attempted to start a conversation with us.

At daybreak, on the morning of August 27, we arrived in the town of Kumchon. Our Air Force had done severe damage to many of the buildings within the town. However, I would soon discover that through all of this mass destruction, the town jail was still intact. The jail itself had numerous cells in which some were occupied by South Korean soldiers and civilians. I assumed the civilians were political prisoners.

The nine of us Americans were placed in a separate cell together. We were exhausted, hungry and thirsty for water. As before, I was put in the corner by myself. Soon to arrive back at our cell was the young enemy officer who had brought us here. In broken English he said; "The war is over for you American running dogs and soon you will be taken to a prisoner of war camp in Seoul. From there you will be transported to North Korea."

A couple of the Americans started to speak to one another, only to be shut up and reprimanded by an enemy soldier. We still weren't permitted to talk. You could see in the faces of the Americans that their morale and discipline to live was gone. Now we were just called American running dogs and told we would eventually be transported to North Korea. Yes, I thought to myself, maybe the war is over for us, and possibly life itself.

Then the words came to me again, "The Lord is my shepherd, I shall not want."

Late in the afternoon we finally received a little food and water. Each of us received an apple which surprised me in a way. In the future days ahead, we would be served only one meal a day. There was no question in my mind about the enemy being short of food, water and supplies. As long as there was no overcast in the sky, our Air Force made sure nothing was transported by the enemy during daylight hours. With the enemy activity around or near this jail, there was always that possibility that our Air Force might see it and strafe and bomb us by mistake.

During the night no candles were permitted throughout the jail. It was extremely dark, and everything seemed quiet within the building. In the distance, you could hear the sounds of the enemy artillery. The flashes from the firing lit up the dark cells. They fired their artillery weapons the entire night. I assumed they were preparing for another large assault on our American or possibly South Korean troops. I seemed to fall asleep for a brief time, only to wake up from the constant sounds of enemy artillery.

The morning of August 28, would bring several enemy soldiers to our cell. They opened the door, and one of them walked directly over to me. He motioned for me to go with him and as I walked out of the cell, fear entered my mind and body. I didn't know what to expect. Outside of the jail, there was a Russian jeep waiting with a driver and one other enemy soldier standing beside it. They motioned for me to get into the jeep, which I did without hesitation. The four of us immediately drove away from the jail.

I couldn't tell what direction we were going due to the overcast and slight drizzle. The enemy was taking advantage of the overcast weather by driving a vehicle down an open road. If there had been sunshine, I know they wouldn't have attempted this type of chance.

The area where I was taken to looked like a shrine temple with other buildings very near it. I soon discovered that it was a large North Korean Operations Post, and our Air Force had hardly touched the place. Only various holes from the machine guns of our fighter planes had actually hit the buildings.

All around enemy soldiers in their mustard-colored cotton uniforms were moving in the wet, early morning murkiness. With the overcast, the enemy didn't have to worry about a sudden attack from our fighter planes. Then suddenly a sound of the start up from a T-34 tank sent the fumes of diesel fuel within the wet morning breeze. It was starting to drizzle heavier along the dark hills that framed the location.

The building I was taken into had a large North Korean flag displayed on one wall. I met the eyes of the booted and blue-breeched officers standing about. They were all young, and they looked extremely well trained and disciplined. I also realized they were the highest-ranking enemy officers I had seen since my capture.

I was asked my name, rank and what regiment or division I was assigned with at the time of my capture. I quickly answered with my name and rank. However, I told them I was a new replacement and couldn't remember the regiment or division. One enemy officer instantly replied in broken english, "You lie, you American running dog"! He rushed over to me and grabbed the left sleeve of my fatigue jacket and pointed to the darker area where my division patch had been sewn on previously. We had removed the large yellow and black 1st Cavalry Division patch from our fatigue jacket on July 25.

Now my body was starting to tremble and my lips began quivering. All eyes were on me as the enemy officer continued to talk in broken English. He stood back from me and again pointed at my left sleeve and said, "You come from horse division and ghost battalion!" I couldn't say anything as I wondered what in the hell he was talking about. I remembered the enemy officer the other day asking me about a ghost battalion. I didn't have an answer.

The enemy officer now waved a sheet of paper at me and said, "We have a complete report on you and it does not lie!" He took a pencil and a piece of paper and outlined a simple drawing of the 1st Cavalry Division patch with the horse head on it. Then some of the other officers started laughing and I wondered why. Maybe I thought, it was because of the remarks made about our horse division, and we had no horses. Nevertheless, I was speechless, and my complete body was trembling with fear. My teeth were clattering in an out-of-control motion.

This young enemy officer perhaps knew more about me than I anticipated. He was doing an excellent job of interrogation in the appearance of his superior officers. He asked me if I graduated from West Point? I moved my head in a motion of no. Then he asked me about Officers Candidate School and Virginia Military Institute? Again I moved my head in a motion of no. He started to become emotional and began to shout: "You lie, you American running dog!" He punched my stomach, slapped my face and shouted again, "Soon all American running dogs die in ocean!" One of the senior officers interrupted, and the interrogation stopped. I seemed to be in a state of semi-shock as my body trembled out of control. In my mind I prayed to God to please help me out of this horrible mess and situation.

I was taken over to a wall and was told to sit down with my back resting against it. Shortly, another American prisoner was brought in the room, and they started to interrogate him. I had not seen this American before, but I soon discovered that his name was Douglass Blalock, and he was a lieutenant.

As they had named me, they also called him an American running dog. Evidently each American prisoner was nicknamed such by the North Korean officers. Maybe the enemy thought these comments would perhaps work psychologically on our minds. Lieutenant Blalock was no doubt surprised to hear of the information that the enemy

had on him. The paper on him contained a lot of information, but there was no mention of a ghost battalion. This still plagued my mind.

While sitting there with my back against the wall, it gave me a chance to get myself and my nerves a little under control. It also gave me the opportunity to carefully observe the North Korean officers. The one senior officer appeared to be no more than 30 years old. However, every one of the officers were much younger when compared to our American officers of the same rank. Then I thought, "How in the hell did these young officers obtain their high rank?" Regardless, you could easily see they were extremely well trained and disciplined.

After the interrogation of Lt. Blalock, I was told to stand up. The senior officer finally started to talk in broken English and said; "You American officers must understand the war will soon be won by the North Korean Peoples Army. All American and United Nations soldiers will soon be annihilated in South Korea. This is not your war and you Americans do not belong here. You should be with your loved ones in America. Soon you will be taken to a prisoner of war camp in North Korea". Then words were spoken that I couldn't understand as several of the enemy officers briefly talked. An enemy soldier then came forward, and he escorted Lt. Blalock from the building. After they left, I never saw Lt. Blalock again. (However, many years later I was informed that he survived the Pyongyong atrocities in North Korea on October 21, 1950.)

As I stood there watching the enemy officers talk, I was wondering why I was kept there myself. The talking stopped, and everything seemed quiet except for the noise of the enemy activity outside. The senior enemy officer then asked me in broken English, "What state are you from in America"? I hesitated for a moment before I replied with, "Kentucky, sir!" He quickly replied; "Oh, Kentucky, it has many horses and tobacco." I answered, "Yes, sir!" Then as he started to talk with the other enemy officers, I wondered how in the hell did he know so much about America. Then he told me I would be given food before my departure. Not knowing it at this particular time, but in the future weeks ahead, I would again see this senior enemy officer in the town of Taegu.

Shortly I was taken outside by an enemy soldier. My hair and fatigue clothing had somewhat dried from being wet earlier in the morning. Now I was really starting to get rain soaked again because of the steady drizzle. A few minutes passed, and they placed me under a roof edge of a building where momentarily I was out of the rain. I was told to sit down on the wet ground with my back to the building.

Very near me several enemy soldiers were cooking some sort of soup or food in a large metal pot suspended over an open fire. The smell from the pot carried a foul odor. Within a short time, I was served a large bowl of soup which had chunks of meat and cabbage in it. Before I attempted to taste the meat I wondered what kind of animal did it come from. However, I was hungry, and this was my first hot meal since my capture. Even though the soup had a foul odor, it actually didn't taste that bad. I drank the soup from the bowl and used my fingers to pick out the odd pieces of meat and cabbage.

While I ate the soup, enemy activity was extremely heavy. They were really taking advantage of the overcast sky. Numerous trucks and tanks headed for what I assumed was their frontline. Suddenly, not too far in the distance, enemy artillery started to fire again. It seemed to come from the same area that I heard throughout the night and early morning. Hundreds of enemy soldiers passed by, and their officers shouted many commands to them as they rapidly moved without hesitation. From what I could see, I assumed that the enemy was preparing for a massive attack. I quickly finished off the soup and layed down the bowl.

I looked around to see if there were any other American prisoners. Then I wondered what happened to Lt. Douglas Blalock, as I thought there must also be other American prisoners in the area. I continued to look, but I never saw any other American prisoners mixed within the enemy activity.

The rain was coming down a little heavier than before, and the air carried the heavy odor of gas and diesel fumes. At least for the time being, the smell was better than that of dead corpses. Then for some reason I looked up at the sky and started to become very emotional because I couldn't see the sun. I felt lost and forsaken for not seeing the sun, and I didn't know what approximate time of day that it was. In my mind, I wondered what in the hell was wrong with me for being so upset and emotional over the sun. However, my personal thoughts were interrupted by the enemy soldier who was standing guard near me.

I was suffering from one of my periodic spasms of trembling. The enemy guard just stared at me for a moment, then he shouted words to his fellow enemy soldiers who were standing near the fire and metal soup pot. One other enemy soldier came over and then both looked at me as they spoke a few words of their native language. Then one took off running and shortly returned with a very young enemy officer. The officer looked at me and then replied; "You okay GI?" I shook my head in a motion of yes!

The enemy officer left, and it didn't take long thereafter for a Russian jeep to arrive with two enemy soldiers in it. The driver of the jeep was the same one from the morning trip. However, the other enemy soldier appeared to be much older, and his age somewhat surprised me. In the future days, I would discover that this older enemy soldier would remain with me as I was moved about in various holding compounds.

As we drove back to what I assumed was Kumchon and the jail, the rain had slacked off to a drizzle. My emotions were getting under control, but my body was extremely soaked from the rain. Travel on the road was extremely difficult because the enemy was moving soldiers, equipment and supplies to

their frontline. At times, we were at a standstill, and I couldn't believe what my eyes were seeing. It looked as though the whole North Korean Army was heading for the Naktong River.

Finally we reached the Kumchon jail, and the jeep and its driver immediately departed. However, the older enemy soldiers remained with me and escorted me into the jail where we met the enemy cell guards.

My fatigue uniform, boots and body were rain soaked as they put me back in the same cell that I was in previously. Again, I would be placed in the corner by myself, and I dared not speak a word for fear of my life. Then as I looked across the cell I could easily see that there were only three American prisoners sitting with their backs against the wall. Numbers came quickly to my mind that five Americans were missing from our original group of nine. In my mind, I thought maybe they were taken on a work detail or possibly to be interrogated by the enemy. Or were they like the others that were taken away by the enemy never to be seen again. In a few days it would prove true that my latter thoughts were right.

We didn't receive any food or water that evening, but I really wasn't that hungry anyway. There was some commotion in the cell holding the South Koreans, as they brought 10 or 12 more which were added with the others. They were all young looking, and I thought perhaps they could be South Korean soldiers.

As darkness came, there were no candles used and everything remained dark. I felt extremely exhausted, and I had very little trouble sleeping on the dirt floor of the cell. Just prior to my falling asleep, a low flying single engine airplane flew overhead. Could it be an American fighter plane lost and seeking a place to land? Not too far in the distance I heard several explosions and shortly the airplane flew overhead again. Then the sound of the airplane disappeared in the night darkness. I couldn't understand why he was flying so close to the ground, and was it a North Korean airplane? I dozed off to sleep.

I was awakened in the early morning of August 29 by large sounds of shouting coming from the South Korean cell. It didn't take long for the enemy soldiers to move toward the cell. The door was rapidly opened as the enemy soldiers equipped with Russian burp guns moved inside the cell to single out certain South Koreans. They quickly escorted them outside of the jail. Suddenly the door to our cell was opened and the four of us Americans were also taken outside.

Once outside, they lined up the four of us with our backs against one side of the jail wall. The 15 South Koreans taken outside previously were lined up in the small dirt street. The sounds of shots rang out from the Russian burp guns as we watched in horror the barbaric murder of these defenseless South Koreans. One of the Americans fell to the ground crying. An enemy soldier came over and lifted the weeping American by his hair. The brave American prisoner was taken

away, never to be seen again. As before, the slain South Koreans were all young, and no doubt they were brave soldiers from the South Korean Army.

The three of us American prisoners remained standing for a brief period of time. We continued to watch as numerous old men from the town were ordered to remove the bodies of the slain South Koreans. In my mind I thought, "Oh God, please help me!" as I felt in a daze and only half realized what was really going on. I found myself not surprised at the existing conditions, and in fact, I had subconsciously expected and prepared for it.

Sometime during the night, the rain had stopped, but the sky was still overcast. In my mind, I prayed to God for sunshine and to end this outrageous and ruthless slaughter of human beings.

Shortly, the bodies of the slain South Koreans were removed from the dirt street. We three Americans were finally taken back inside of the jail. I noticed that the older aged guard who returned with me yesterday had not participated in the morning enemy atrocities. He seemed to have a strange look on his face. Maybe I thought, an expression of sadness as he placed us back in the cell.

I continued to feel somewhat in a daze as we received an apple and a little water in the late afternoon. I had the personal feeling that our food ration was going to be little or nothing. As I thought, it seemed very strange that during my capture so far, I had seen very little food supplies being moved by the enemy with their various trucks or soldiers.

Finally the sun appeared outside and to a degree it brightened up the inside of the cell. I felt as though God was answering my prayers, and I even heard our fighter planes in the distance as they strafed and bombed enemy positions. I knew this would slow down the enemy movement and activity. I easily recognized the fact that the American Air Force was a decisive factor in our efforts to win this so-called "police action."

Just prior to darkness, several enemy soldiers brought in a battery-powered radio and placed it very near our cell door. They had turned the volume of sound to a high level, and a woman's voice was speaking in her native language. Then she started speaking in a very fluent English and said she was speaking from the city of Seoul and on behalf of the North Korean People's Army. She mentioned the 1st Cavalry Division on the Naktong River and the United Nations Forces in general; and that we were losing the war. As I listened, I wondered how much truth there was to her comments. Particularly, when she said the war would soon be over. Then suddenly I remembered, I had heard this woman's voice before on a radio at our Company Command Post. She was a North Korean propagandist and was nicknamed "Seoul City Sue". Shortly a young enemy officer arrived and had the radio removed. I had heard enough of her ridiculous comments anyway.

Again there were no candles and everything inside the cell remained dark. Then the same thing happened as the night before. A low flying single engine airplane flew overhead. In the distance, I heard several explosions and shortly it returned and passed overhead. In the weeks ahead I would learn that this particular airplane and its pilot were nicknamed "Bed Check Charlie." The various reports were that it was a modified World War II, Russian Yak fighter airplane, and the pilot would fly low and drop mortar shells from the cockpit. Reports indicated that little or no damage was done to the American or United Nation Forces from this type of enemy bombing. Rumors had it that many humorous gestures or comments came from those soldiers who experienced "ole Charlie."

The night went fast and in the early morning of August 30, I was awakened by the cell door being opened by the enemy. To my surprise, it was a young blonde-haired American prisoner who was brought to our cell. For some unknown reason, I asked him what outfit he was from. He immediately replied; "1st Cavalry Division!" I said, "Great, so am I!" Then I realized what I had done because I should have known better than to speak at all. The older enemy guard looked at me but he didn't say anything. The other enemy guard was at the outer door and fortunately he didn't hear our comments. Then the older enemy guard looked at me and said; "No talk!" I thought perhaps I could maybe try to talk with this older enemy guard and, he seemed to understand a little English.

As the older enemy guard was away from the cell door, I took a chance and called to him. "Can we please get more food?" Well, this was a mistake because two other enemy guards overheard my comments. They said a few words to the older enemy guard in their native language. The two enemy guards opened the cell door and removed me from the cell and then they took me outside to the other end of the jail. To my surprise, there was a 4' x 4' x 4' bamboo cage sitting up off of the ground. They quickly placed me inside of it.

For the next four days I would be placed in the bamboo cage during the daytime and then put back in the jail at evening time. Now I had to tolerate a new monstrosity from the enemy. Very little food or water, and it was extremely difficult on the back and legs. Cramps persisted throughout my body and the daytime seemed to be longer than usual. Occasionally an old man or lady would appear, and they would stare at me for a certain length of time. At times, I was frightened because I felt as though they were going to pick up a stone and throw it at me. However, the numerous enemy soldiers would stop and then start laughing out loud. The words they were saying I couldn't understand but somehow some had learned to say in broken English; "American running dog!"

In this ridiculous cage, time seemed to linger somewhat. It was more time to think of my mother and the loved ones at home. But I had to keep these particular thoughts out of my mind as much as possible because at times, I would become very emotional. I had discovered that certain emotions shared too many weaknesses to the mind and soul.

As I sat in the cramped position, I noticed the skin of my body had become worse. Many infected areas appeared from subsequent scratching of the lice, fleas and mosquitos. However, the cooler nights were keeping the attacking mosquitos to a minimum. Weeks without a shower or bath, and my fatigue uniform was starting to rot on my body. I could hardly stand the odor from my own body and clothing.

I would learn in the weeks ahead from Military Intelligence of the South Korean Army that this type of bamboo cage was used for the purpose of exhibiting certain town drunks. They never told me just how effective this method was for controlling drunks; however, I didn't care to know.

During the late afternoon of September 3, several enemy guards arrived at the bamboo cage to remove me. I had the personal feeling that something was wrong as they took me around to the front door of the jail. Waiting near the door were two more enemy guards and six South Korean soldiers. From their appearance, I presumed these six South Korean soldiers were all officers, and they still had their American fatigue uniforms on.

The late day sun was still hot as they rapidly moved us in an easterly direction of the town. To my surprise, the older enemy guard was with our group, and all the enemy eyes were watching the sky for possible American fighter planes overhead. As we reached a particular section of town, there were approximately 20 to 25 refugees waiting there with several enemy soldiers. These particular refugees were then moved with our group as we continued to move toward the east.

I thought of the other four Americans that were left behind at the jail, and the blond-haired soldier who recently was put in the jail and said he was from the 1st Cavalry Division. I never had the opportunity to learn his name or what particular regiment and company he was from. I never learned the names of the other three Americans who had been with me since August 12. Nevertheless, I would never see those particular brave American soldiers again.

Then I thought, why am I being taken toward the enemy frontline with these South Korean soldiers? Ever since my capture, the enemy had told me that I would be taken to a prisoner of war camp in Seoul. From there I would be taken to North Korea. It was very evident that for some reason, plans had been changed in my particular case. In my mind and as I had done so many times before, I prayed to God for his support and care.

As we moved down the center of the road, many enemy tanks and equipment lay on both sides, completely destroyed. The American Air Force was doing an excellent job in keeping enemy activity and movement at a complete minimum during daytime hours. Dusk was very near and the days were not as long as they were previously, and the nights were becoming cooler. Enemy activity this evening was increasing somewhat, but I had not seen any massive movement since August 28. Something drastic was happening within the enemy army and you could easily see it. Some enemy soldiers were looking very dirty, hungry and their uniforms were in rags. The further eastward we traveled, the worse they seemed to look. Up ahead in the distance, I could see a small village, and there seemed to be enemy activity.

When we arrived at the small village, the refugees were taken to where supplies and ammunition were neatly stacked. Each was instructed to carry a particular case or box. We were given an apple and a few ounces of water, and we were receiving only one meal a day which was practically nothing. After a brief rest, the group of us were on the move again. Darkness had arrived, but the enemy seemed to know their way and where they were going. Sounds of the distant artillery continued to become louder.

Also in the far distance I could see flashes of exploding artillery and hear what sounded like fierce battle engagements of the enemy and United Nations Forces. It appeared to be over a long wide area, and it sort of gave a panoramic view in the dark night. Then without any warning it started raining extremely hard, and it had a chilling effect on my body. I quickly looked up to catch the rain in my mouth, in hopes of quenching my thirst. For some reason, the enemy really wanted us to rapidly move along. We stopped once to rest briefly, but there was no water for my thirst. As I looked at the older guard, somehow I felt that he really wanted to help me. But no doubt, he was afraid of his fellow enemy soldiers. For a moment, I thought he was going to give me a drink of water from his canteen. However, shouting started, and we were on the move again.

Sometime during the early morning of September 4, we arrived at a small village or what appeared to be one in the darkness. The six South Korean soldiers and myself were placed in a small mud hut. I was put in the corner by myself, and they were put on the opposite side of the room. Surprisingly, one of the enemy guards lit a small candle which gave us some light. The older enemy guard and one other enemy soldier with a Russian burp gun remained in the room with us. I was so exhausted that I quickly dozed off to sleep. Even with my rain soaked fatigue uniform covering my body, I had no trouble sleeping.

I felt something hitting my leg as I awakened to see an enemy guard standing above me with a dark blue cloth in his hands. He bent down and opened the cloth which contained a ball of gummy rice. He broke a piece off the edge and handed it to me as I quickly put it in my mouth. It wasn't much to eat, but it was better than nothing at all. The older enemy guard then gave me a few ounces of water. As we looked at one another, I thought he was going to try and talk with me. However, his only comment was, "No talk!" I didn't say a word as he walked toward the door of the hut.

From the doorway I could see that the sun was shining very bright. The rain must have stopped while I was asleep. Suddenly overhead and very near our location, I could hear American fighter planes strafing and bombing enemy positions. I started to become frightened somewhat as I thought of the possibility of this location being within their attack. This attack lasted for what I assumed was approximately ten minutes, and the sounds disappeared. However, the distant sounds of artillery and fierce battles between the enemy and United Nations Forces continued on.

I still couldn't understand why the enemy had brought me back here to their front line, instead of taking me to a prisoner of war camp. I looked across at the six South Korean Army officers who were sitting opposite the room from me. Why were they brought here also? I knew the enemy had something planned, but what?

In the afternoon, a heavy rain started as the enemy guards came in the mud hut and instructed all of us to move outside. Once outside it didn't take long for the steady rain to make my fatigue soaked with water. I tried to look around the village as far as I could see to possibly spot something that looked familiar. I attempted to look upward to catch rain drops in my mouth to quench my thirst.

Above the clouds, I could hear the sounds of American fighter planes trying to find a break in the weather. With this kind of overcast there was no way they could give any air support. I was starting to become a little emotional because I couldn't see the sun, and I didn't know what was the approximate time or what direction we were going to head in.

After a brief waiting period, some enemy guards brought forth the refugees and many were carrying ammunition. There was approximately 30 to 40 in the group. Finally the enemy guards motioned for all of us to move out of the village. From the previously estimated position of the sun during the morning hours, I assumed we were moving in an easterly direction.

It didn't take long for us to move from the village to a nearby ridge which we crossed without any difficulty. However, to my amazement I could see from this position a large river not too far in the distance. I thought to myself, could that be the Naktong River? With the steady pour of rain, we moved on down off of the ridge toward the river.

The bottoms of my feet were becoming very sore from the extreme moisture from the rain and my water-logged boots. I couldn't even remember the last time that I had my boots off. I only realized that it had been a very long time.

As we approached the river, the stench of dead corpses lay heavy in the air. To my surprise, I could see three ferries working back and forth across the river. But as we moved closer, I was starting to get a glimpse of what looked like wounded enemy soldiers laying on the sandy area near the waters edge. Not too far from the sandy area were three enemy supply trucks and numerous oxen and ox carts.

From the opposite side, each ferry was carrying a load of wounded enemy soldiers. As they were unloaded, each soldier was being placed within the sandy area near the water's edge. Enemy wounded soldiers were spread out all over the area as refugees and other enemy soldiers were rapidly selecting one at a time. Once the selection was made, the wounded enemy soldier was quickly moved and then loaded onto one of the three waiting enemy supply trucks. The not-too severely wounded enemy soldiers I noticed were loaded onto the ox carts and probably taken to a medical aid station, which I assumed was located within the immediate vicinity.

The moaning and crying from pain was an eerie sound to hear as the rain continued to pour down. Their medical display was barbaric and cruel because I knew they didn't have any medical supplies to alleviate the pain. Also the sight was gruesome because many were missing their arms, legs, hands, and feet. I felt sorry to a certain extent, but more, I felt uncomfortable and wanted to get to where we were going.

Finally we were instructed to board a particular ferry. The refugees had almost finished loading supplies and ammunition to where there was very little room left. It didn't take us long to reach the other side of the river; and the river, in a way, still looked very familiar.

Before we reached the other side, I could see the large and massive group of wounded enemy soldiers just laying there waiting to be ferried across the river. During my capture, I had never seen a sight like this before. Many of the wounded seemed lifeless and the rain had completely saturated their bodies. I estimated the total wounded in excess of several hundred.

Once on the shore, we were then ordered off of the ferry. I followed the six South Korean Army officers off, and we were grouped togethe; and then moved from the river to a nearby road. This particular road seemed to run parallel to the river. It was too difficult to know what direction we were heading, but the river continued to appear to our immediate right.

The rain was still coming down at a steady pace, and my feet were hurting so badly that I could hardly walk on them. All of the rain made my boots extremely water logged. I really didn't know if I was going to make the trip to wherever we were being taken. Nevertheless, I knew that I would have to remove my boots before too long. There was constant fear that the enemy soldiers might attempt to steal my boots if I were to remove them from my feet. This was the prime reason I did not remove my boots periodically.

For some unknown reason, the older enemy soldier still remained with our group as a guard. I still had the personal feeling that he had some compassion within his soul for us prisoners. However, his personal fear of his fellow enemy comrades prevented him from expressing his individual feelings or thoughts.

One of the enemy guards prodded me with his rifle to move a little faster down the center of the road. My feet were killing me. Scattered on both sides of the road were several enemy tanks, trucks and other military equipment. The gray overcast and rain made the area look like a defeated enemy battlefield. But in my mind, I felt as though the North Koreans were a long way off from being beaten and defeated.

Suddenly not too far on my left, enemy artillery started firing barrages at the United Nations Forces. Our bodies seemed to jump from the sounds of each volley. The moist air from the rain was now carrying a mixed odor of gun powder and the stench of dead bodies.

When we reached a certain location of the road, I could see at a short distance to my

Atrocities committed by North Korean soldiers in September 1950. The long trench is filled with South Korean civilians that were shot and bludgeoned to death in cold blood. Many civilians were forced to dig these trenches which were actually their own graves. (Photo courtesy of Reuben Kvildt)

right a couple of destroyed bridges that once spanned the river. Then looking further ahead I could see a fairly large town. On my left was a large mountain which extended upward and actually overlooked the entire area.

Further on down the road it all started to come back to me. I knew that I had been in this area previously. Remembering our withdrawal at the end of July and the destroyed bridges, the town could only be Waegwan. But this particular location was sort of confusing in a way, and I thought maybe I was mixed up with another town. However, I knew that I had to be correct in my thinking because the large stream on my right could be no other than the Naktong River.

We were moved southeast of what was left of the town of Waegwan. From what I could see, the town was pretty well devastated by the American Air Force. From there we headed for the hilly terrain outside of the city.

After passing through the hilly terrain, we then proceeded to the location of the enemy encampment. Within the location was a very large apple orchard which seemed to be in an isolated valley; and actually made its way near the base of several surrounding hills. It was from this particular location that God gave me the wisdom and fortitude to attempt an escape.

It was now late afternoon, and it was still raining hard. I was exhausted, hungry and my feet were extremely sore. Along the way, however, I had kept tilting my head back in an attempt to catch rain in my mouth. It had helped quench my thirst to a degree.

There were several mud huts in this particular location. The six South Korean Army officers were taken to a separate mud hut. I was taken to a very small mud hut with a large hole in the straw roof; and the rain passed through the opening. Once inside I was very surprised to see two other American prisoners sitting with their backs against the wall. The one American with blonde hair had a leg wound in the calf of his right leg. I would soon discover that the North Korean medic was treating the leg wound with maggots. The other American had black hair and seemed to be suffering from dysentery.

I quickly asked permission from the older enemy guard to remove my boots. Surprisingly, he immediately shook his head yes and replied with an, "Okay!" As I removed my boots, pieces of my socks fell out also. Actually the socks had deteriorated or rotted off of my feet. The skin on the bottom of each foot had peeled off; and they were red and raw. What a relief to have them off.

Shortly, the older enemy guard returned with a white cloth shirt which I believe had belonged to a refugee. He quickly tore it into a couple of pieces, and then he showed me how to wrap up my feet with these particular pieces of cloth. Why was this older enemy guard trying to help? He had placed himself in a very serious position. However, there were no other enemy guards in our particular mud hut to see what actually was going on.

The evening darkness came quickly, and the days were becoming shorter. The air now had a chilling effect to it as the rain continued to come down. The enemy artillery had never stopped firing volley after volley at the United Nations Forces. In the not too far distance, incoming artillery from the United Nations Forces were exploding, hopefully, in the midst of enemy positions. Also in the distance, I could hear savage fighting between the enemy and United Nations Forces.

We three Americans never received any food or water that evening. Within the coming week, I would soon discover that the enemy possibly intended to starve us to death. I knew the enemy was lacking in food supplies themselves. I could easily see that something serious was going wrong in their effort. Some of the enemy soldiers were looking tired, hungry and their uniforms were very dirty. Also, within the coming weeks, I continued to pray to God more than ever and kept my faith for an answer.

The rain had stopped during the night, and the morning dawn of September 6, also brought the sunshine. Then came the sounds of American fighter planes flying overhead. I was starting to feel better already. It didn't take very long to hear in the distance, air strike explosions as they hit enemy positions. Air assault continued all day long as the Air Force flew missions relentlessly. I now realized more than ever that the Air Force would be a major and decisive factor in defeating the North Korean Army.

By now I was able to place my boots on the mud floor where the sun was shining through the hole in the roof. It didn't take long for my boots and myself to dry out thoroughly from the sun. Outside there seemed to be very little activity according to the sounds.

The older enemy guard arrived and relieved the other guard. He had brought three apples, one for each of us to eat. I hadn't seen him since the previous afternoon, but we sure welcomed the sight of him and the little food that he brought for us. He also gave each of us a few ounces of water from his canteen. That evening when I prayed to God, I had a special prayer for the older enemy guard. What little food and water he gave us, helped to keep us alive.

Actually, enemy activity and movement in this particular compound remained relatively the same for the next several days. However, in the early evening on September 9th, an extremely large movement of troops came into the area.

The large enemy troop build-up continued for the next couple of days. Not too far from our mud huts, three enemy tanks were brought in which were heavily camouflaged with tree branches. As usual, most of their movement and activity was accomplished during darkness. This again was to avoid the Air Force fighter planes during daylight hours.

These particular enemy troops looked battle weary and their uniforms looked dirty and ragged. However, there seemed to be a few very young enemy soldiers with cleaner looking uniforms that were mixed in with the others. They were, no doubt, very recent replacements.

On the morning of September 10, we were awakened and moved to the front of the mud hut which contained the six South Korean Army officers. They were also removed from their mud hut and the nine of us were escorted to an area where five enemy officers were waiting. I had a strange feeling that possibly our time had run out, and we were being taken to our future execution.

The five enemy officers and their staff command post was located in a heavy tree growth which was on the edge of an apple orchard. As I looked at these five enemy officers, several appeared familiar in a way and I thought that maybe I had seen them before on August 28, in the town of Kumchon. I continued to observe them closely, and then I realized that I had seen a couple of them previously. Astonishingly enough, their appearance had changed, and they looked tired, and their uniforms were dirty and dusty.

Again the enemy would commit atrocities, and we three American prisoners would have to witness the brutal and ruthless murder of these defenseless South Korean Army officers. Each one was interrogated about certain maps and paper documents. Of course, I couldn't understand their language. After their individual interrogation, the six of them were taken near an open trench and shot down in cold blood. Their lifeless bodies were thrown into the trench and another unmarked grave site. This outrageous intimidation was agonizing to the mind and soul.

Without any warnings, American fighter planes arrived very near our location, and I could see a glimpse that they were F-51 Mustangs. A couple of the enemy officers started shouting and a couple of guards quickly had us dog trot back to the mud hut. The other two American prisoners had to move slower as their condition and health weren't very good. Surprisingly, my feet didn't hurt that bad and they had healed better than what I thought.

In the afternoon, a medic arrived at our mud hut and he examined the right leg wound of the blonde haired American prisoner. As he changed the bandage, I could easily see the maggots moving inside of the wound; and a partial infection still existed. However, the medic never attempted to examine the black haired American prisoner or myself. It looked as though the bandage was made from the white-clad clothing that the refugees wore traditionally.

When darkness came, I prayed to God in my mind and thanked him for sparing our lives from the early morning enemy atrocities. I asked him for a quick solution to getting out of this horrible and confusing ordeal. Another day passed without any food or water.

On the morning of September 12, we were awakened by the older enemy guard, and he instructed us to move outside. I was somewhat tired because it had been difficult to sleep during the night because of heavy movement of enemy troops and equipment.

It was a beautiful morning as the sun was starting to come up over the mountains in the east. The morning breeze was sort of cool as the older enemy guard took us to the edge of a tree growth where he told us to sit down.

In a way, I was apprehensive and I had the personal feeling that something was going to happen. I really couldn't believe my eyes as I looked around within the surrounding and adjacent area. Enemy soldiers, equipment and supplies were all over the place. Many of the enemy soldiers had twigs and small tree branches tied to their uniforms for camouflage purposes. I assumed they were either ready or prepared for a future attack on a particular unit of the United Nations Forces.

Not too far from us I could see the three enemy T-34 tanks. They were still heavily camouflaged with tree limbs and branches. An enemy officer was instructing his particular men in front of the tanks, and I assumed he was the tank commander. Within a few minutes, the enemy officer walked toward our location, and he was carrying a small box. Upon his arrival I noticed that the box he had with him was actually American C-4 food rations. Then I wondered how in the hell did he obtain the box of rations. I could only assume that they were confiscated when they overran a particular position of the United Nations Forces.

The enemy officer handed the older enemy guard three cans from the box. They exchanged a few words in their native language, and the enemy officer left and returned to the tank crew. I was really puzzled as to why the enemy officer decided to give away the American rations—especially to us, the American prisoners! Then I thought, maybe we were going to be moved again to another area or compound.

I looked at the older enemy guard as he attempted to open the ration cans. He passed to the other two American prisoners a can of beans and franks for them to share. I was given a can of sliced peaches, and did they ever taste good! The older enemy guard put the other can into the pocket of his uniform.

We had just finished eating when suddenly several enemy soldiers started shouting. A small American L-5 airplane appeared almost directly overhead as several enemy soldiers started firing their rifles at the small target. The enemy officer became emotional and almost hysterical as he shouted commands to his tank crew. From what I could understand, he didn't want them to expose their location. As quickly as it appeared, the small aircraft disappeared within the mountain terrain.

However, the small airplane caused some panic and lots of conversation with the enemy soldiers. Everyone was caught by surprise because I never heard the airplane engine until it was almost directly overhead. Nevertheless, the American L-5 airplane was on a reconnaissance flight, and I was now wondering if it had spotted any enemy activity at this particular location.

Within 20 minutes or so, my thoughts of wondering were answered as incoming rounds from American artillery passed closely overhead and landed near the town of Waegwan. At first the enemy didn't get that excited from the artillery barrage. Then things started to change drastically as a walk back of the artillery barrage continued to come in our direction. The enemy officer was running and shouting commands to his crew as they started up the engines of the enemy T-34 tanks. Enemy soldiers were shouting various commands and were running all over the place, trying to move equipment and supplies. I really couldn't believe my eyes as everything seemed to turn in to confusion and utter chaos.

I was starting to become frightened as the earth began to shake and tremble under my feet. In knew from the explosions that this type of artillery projectile could be no other than a 155-mm, and it was capable of doing severe and extensive damage. But for the moment, I was hesitant to do something because of my own personal fright.

Then words were shouted from two enemy soldiers to the older enemy guard who was standing very near me. Suddenly and to my surprise, the older enemy guard took off running with the two enemy soldiers. I had to do something quickly, and this was the appropriate and opportune time to do it.

I looked at the blonde haired American prisoner and told him, "Let's get the hell out of here!" This was the first time that I had spoken to him since our first meeting on September 5. He immediately replied, "We'll be shot in the back!" I then told him, "If we don't try to make a run for it now we're going to be blown up anyway!"

Without hesitation I started to run as fast as my legs would carry me. I ran between the two mud huts and then up a ridge. From the location of the sun, I knew in what direction to move. For some unknown reason, I stopped for a moment on the ridge. I quickly turned and saw the other two American prisoners attempting to escape also. Then I didn't know whether or not to return and give them help and assistance. As if God was telling me, I returned to help the other two American prisoners escape.

I found it extremely difficult to carry the blonde haired American prisoner on my back. But there was no other choice because of his severe leg wound. The other American prisoner was suffering from dysentery and was very weak. Our movement and journey was burdensome as we made our way from the ridge and to the saddle of a nearby mountain.

We stopped briefly and turned to see that the American artillery barrage was now on direct target of the enemy compound from which we had just escaped. We had left there just in time. The massive bombardment continued, and I definitely knew that it had to be devastating to the enemy. For a moment, I thought of the older enemy guard that tried to show his kindness and help; and I wondered if he had possibly survived the shattering barrage. God would only know.

Moving over the saddle of the mountain became extremely dangerous as sniper fire seemed to be coming from several angles. As we moved along, some of the bullets were hitting very near us and occasionally at our boots. Periodically, we had to stop to rest, but we knew there was no turning back. We acknowledged the fact that if we were recaptured by the North Koreans we would immediately be executed.

I noticed from our position that a small narrow secondary dirt road was on down to our front and right. Rice paddies extended on both sides and parallel to the road. There were numerous enemy vehicles and equipment that were previously destroyed by the American Air Force. Again it resembled a battlefield of a defeated enemy army.

However, we contemplated the possibility of going directly into the hands of the North Koreans. We then agreed that there was no turning back or other choice but to take the chance. As we moved downward from the mountain, the horrible stench of dead bodies filled the air. Very shortly we came across the numerous decomposed corpses of North Korean soldiers. Then to our surprise, at the base of the mountain we observed several decomposed corpses of American soldiers. We didn't stop to investigate, because the stench was almost unbearable.

When we reached the rice paddies, enemy automatic weapons fire started to hit all around us. We quickly ducked for cover behind the rice paddy dikes. I almost fell in the rice paddy with the blonde haired American soldier with me. My heart was beating hard and fast as we worked our way toward the sloping edge of the road. Suddenly, the enemy firing stopped, and each of us paused to catch our breath.

From the direction of the sun, I knew the road went in a southeasterly direction. This was my only hope of finding friendly lines. We finally made our way to the bottom of the sloping edge of the road which was really a small ditch that ran parallel to the road. To avoid enemy fire, we worked our way through the ditch mostly on our hands and knees. Enemy sniper and automatic weapons fire continued to hit very near us.

The enemy firing finally ceased and after a certain length of time, we started to receive sporadic fire from our front. We stopped briefly and let our backs lay against the sloping edge of the ditch. Each of us looked at one another and questioned the possibility that the firing might be coming from American positions. Then, of course, there was the horrible thought that it could be the enemy. In my mind, I asked God to please help us.

Suddenly, the dark haired American soldier started shouting, "We are Americans! We are Americans!" Then he attempted to go up and stand by the edge of the road. Several shots rang out which knocked small stones from the road as the bullets ricocheted very near us. I quickly grabbed his one leg and pulled him back to me.

Then astounding words were heard from a voice that said, "Put your hands on your heads and come out and be recognized!" The three of us looked at one another and won-

Dead South Korean civilians in shallow grave - several were buried alive up to their neck and then left to die. These atrocities were committed by North Korean soldiers in September 1950. The two American troopers are from the 7th Cavalry Regiment. (Courtesy of Reuben Kvidt)

A Chaplain administers last rites for atrocity victims, from Company H, 5th Cavalry Regiment. They had their hands tied behind their backs and then were killed in cold blood. This was on August 17, 1950, just northeast of Waegwan, South Korea. (Stanley Tretick-UPI)

dered if it could be an excellent speaking North Korean. However, the voice seemed to have a peculiar southern accent to it. Again the voice repeated "Put your hands on your heads and come out and be recognized!" Very carefully, but with some reluctance, each of us stood up on the edge of the road with our hands on top of our heads; and with fear in my mind that we might be shot at any given moment.

Suddenly a Captain appeared and he closely looked at us momentarily before he said, "Looks like you soldiers need some medical attention, right away!" Then he quickly shouted to a nearby soldier, "Go tell the radio operator to call company headquarters and send me a jeep or weapons carrier up here immediately!" The soldier replied, "Yes sir"; and then he took off running. Then the Captain said, "Now let's get off the road before the damn North Koreans see us."

Once off the road, the Captain asked me what division I was from. I replied, "Captain, I'm from Company H, 2nd Battalion, 7th Cavalry Regiment". The Captain said, "My God soldier, do you realize that you are now in the hands of Company A, 5th Cavalry Regiment?" For a moment, I was dumbfounded from what I had just heard. I was speechless as I thought how strange and bizarre all this really seems. Of all possibilities of actually reaching friendly lines, I had miraculously found my way back to my own division, the 1st Cavalry Division.

A familiar sound caused all of us too look down the road to see a cloud of dust and the sight of an approaching vehicle. Upon our arrival, I noticed that it was a Dodge 3/4 ton weapons carrier. The Captain told the driver to get us to the medical aid station for treatnext to the driver, but he immediately informed me to sit in the back with the other

two American soldiers. In a way, it was understandable because of my personal appearance and very foul body odor.

The Captain said to the driver, "Now get this damn vehicle turned around and the hell out of here!" The driver replied, "Yes sir!" As he was turning the vehicle around, the Captain called to us, "The best of luck to you soldiers and be damn certain that you tell G-2 Intelligence everything that you know; I'll be looking forward to their report."

As the vehicle roared down the narrow dirt road, we were becoming choked on the clouds of dust. But for the moment, I started to reminisce somewhat, as we bounced around in our seats. Again, I thought of and thanked God for his help and support throughout the horrible ordeal; and how maybe the repeated words in my mind, "The Lord is my shepherd I shall not want." Could this have helped me to survive? Nevertheless, I was satisfied and believed the fact that God had definitely helped me, and this made my personal feelings even more strong.

Then I thought of the Captain that we had just left, and I didn't even know his name. However, that thought was put to an end as our vehicle slowed down and came to a stop. Two military police soldiers walked up to the vehicle and told the three of us to get out. I got out first, and then I helped the other two soldiers step down from the vehicle. They told the driver to report back to his company, and within a minute the vehicle disappeared in a cloud of dust.

I immediately asked them what was going on and whether this was an aid station. The one replied, "That's right, this is a clearing station for the 545 Military Police Company. We have orders from the Provost Marshall's office to process you three former prisoners before you go to the aid station." For some

unknown reason, I became infuriated over the orders. I started to shout; "What in the hell are you two talking about processing us through your office, I think it's a bunch of bull shit. Can't you see that we need a shower, something to eat and medical attention." Then the one soldier said; "I'm sorry, I can see what you guys have been through, but I've got my orders and it won't take that long."

As we entered the clearing station tent my irritation began to subside. It was very apparent that no one wanted to get near me. They took me to a separate desk where I had to give them my name, rank, serial number, regiment, battalion and company. At least they were right, because it really didn't take that long. We were hustled outside and put in another Dodge 3/4 ton weapons carrier, and we were then on our way to the medical aid station.

Soon we arrived at the aid station and the military police soldier who drove us there went inside of the tent with us. He told the medical Lieutenant that shortly he would return with orders from the Provost Marshal's office for the three of us. As strange and unbelievable as it may seem, I received a copy of those particular orders and other medical records, dated September 12, 1950. However, when I received them, I had already been honorably discharged from the Army. The envelope was from the War Department; Far East Command; Personal Effects Depot; 8083ED Army Unit; APO 43; c/o Postmaster, San Francisco, California. It was dated January 2, 1953, some 28 months later, but it must be remembered that the military police soldier did say that orders would be forthcoming.

The medical Lieutenant had us go outside to the back of the tent, where a temporary shower was installed. But first we had to strip down to our bare skin, and throw our fatigue uniforms in a pile to be burned. This was the first time that I had removed my fatigue uniform in approximately 40 to 50 days. It felt so good to have it off, but I looked at my body and it was completely covered with infected sores from various insect bites. The majority were from body lice.

The other two soldiers were told they would have to wait for a while. The calf of the right leg of the one soldier looked horrible from infection. I believe it still contained maggots. Another medical soldier handed me a cloth to cover my face with and then he started to spray my body with DDT, a chemical solution. The solution was cool and soothing to the skin, but in a short time it started to make a burning sensation. After completion, I had to wait for a specified time before entering the shower. I noticed a piece of equipment near the shower with the markings of 15th Quartermaster. It was a great feeling to be back with the 1st Cavalry Division.

Once in the shower, the soap and water felt terrific on my skin and body. I wanted to stay longer, but I knew that I couldn't because the other two soldiers were waiting for their turn. I was handed a towel, but due to the sores on my skin, I had to carefully pat my body dry. Then I was given a can of lice powder which I applied over my entire body. They gave me a complete fatigue uniform, but both the jacket and pants were too large. However, the hat seemed to fit, but the partially new boots hurt my feet.

I asked for some water and something to eat, but the medical Lieutenant said a jeep was going to take me to the 15th Medical Company in Taegu. There I would have to go through a series of tests and that I would be fed there. However, he did give me a little water in a canteen cup to quench my thirst.

As soon as I finished the water, I was told that the jeep was ready to leave for Taegu. I was really anxious to get there and get a good hot meal. Things were happening so fast as I went outside to get into the waiting jeep. We pulled away from the tent, and at the time I never gave much thought to the other two soldiers. I never got their names or what particular division they were from. I only assumed they were members of the 1st Cavalry Division, and I would no doubt see them in Taegu. However, at this particular time I never realized that I would never see those two brave soldiers again.

After a brief dusty and bumpy trip, we arrived at the 15th Medical Company in Taegu. They were extremely busy attending to numerous wounded personnel. Some of the soldiers looked in extremely critical condition. They didn't waste any time with me as an officer nurse immediately took blood samples from my arm. After I gave them a urine sample, she told me that starting immediately, I would be given heavy doses of penicillin each day. She said this antibiotic would help fight against my skin infection.

I asked for something to eat, and she said I would receive a little food and water soon. Since I was underweight I would be re-stricted to a mild diet at first. Also my stomach had shrunk to a certain degree, and this would be carefully watched. She instructed me to give her a stool sample once I had to defecate. This she said was to see if there were any signs of worms.

Well, I remained there for the next 11 days and experienced the professional care of the 15th Medical Company. I discovered within the first eight days an almost complete cure of my skin infection. The mild diet had my weight adjusted and was improving with each day. I remained in a building where several soldiers and officers were being treated for battle weary or fatigue.

I would experience several visits from fellow officers of the 2nd Battalion, 7th Cavalry Regiment, with encouragement to return to Company H. There were rumors of the imminent defeat of the North Korean Army which was also very encouraging. Along this line would be the United States Marine Corp invasion of Inchon on September 15-16, and the recapture of Seoul, the South Korean capital.

Then there was the never ending debriefing from G-2 Intelligence and the 683 Military Intelligence; and the army officers and their interpreters from the 1st and 6th Republic of Korea Divisions. It was possibly assumed that some of the refugees that I witnessed slaughtered may have been soldiers from the two respective divisions. In my mind, I knew that really God had the actual answer.

There was one order that disturbed me to a certain degree. That order was directed particularly to news correspondents. Any information concerning my brief capture was to be given to authorized personnel only.

During a brief visit, the most encouragement I would receive for me to return to my platoon and company came from Captain Mel Chandler. It was sort of emotional feelings for both of us because I had previously thought that maybe he didn't survive the battle of August 12, the day I was captured. He was previously the commander of Company H, which was my company. However, he was now Executive Officer of the 2nd Battalion, 7th Cavalry Regiment.

He told me to put the circumstances concerning my capture behind me. He said that a lot of brave and heroic deeds were done by many within the 2nd Battalion during the battles of August 12, 13 and 14. He also told me that he was going to prepare a citation on by behalf for my bravery of August 12; and for extraordinary heroism concerning my escape from the North Koreans on September 12. He quickly replied, "I understand that you also assisted in saving the lives of two other soldiers."

Captain Chandler went on to tell me that Major Omar Hitchner, our 2nd Battalion Commander was killed on September 6. Also killed the same day were Captain James Milam, 2nd Battalion, S-3. Captain Milam was previously commander of Company E. He also told me that we had a new 2nd Battalion Commander by the name of Major John Callaway. He had come from the 2nd Battalion, 5th Cavalry Regiment and has brought forth a fighting spirit.

Captain Chandler went on to say how the war was over for the North Koreans. Also he expected all of us to be in a large parade in Tokyo by Thanksgiving or no later than Christmas. However, we would soon discover in the weeks ahead that the reality of that dream would be eliminated by the Chinese Communists.

Early in the morning of September 21, I was notified by a Captain and a Lieutenant from G-2 Intelligence, that they were taking me to 1st Cavalry Division Headquarters. As I was putting on my new field jacket and steel helmet, I asked them what was really going on. The Captain answered that a high-ranking North Korean officer surrendered at daybreak to the 8th Cavalry Regiment. They think that you might be able to identify him as one of the enemy officers that interrogated you during your capture.

When the jeep pulled up to 1st Cavalry Division Headquarters, I noticed that it hadn't changed since I was here for my battlefield commission on August 10. However, there seemed to be more Division patches painted in conspicuous places on the building. There seemed to be more military police guards than before from the 545 Military Police Company.

As we entered the inside of the building, I quickly noticed on my left a North Korean officer sitting at a table, wearing a dark blue-breeched uniform and high knee boots. I noticed that his uniform and boots were extremely dusty. He was being interrogated by a South Korean army officer. Then to my immediate right were numerous intelligence officers sitting at various tables.

I was told to sit down at a table directly across the floor from the North Korean officer. He was told by a South Korean army officer to remove his hat, which he complied. My eyes focused on him and then I realized that I had seen and met this officer before.

A South Korean army officer told him to stand up, which he did. An American Colonel from intelligence then said, "You are now looking at Senior Colonel Lee Hak Ku, Chief of Staff, 13th North Korean Division. He surrendered early this morning to an outpost guard of the 8th Cavalry Regiment." He continued to say, "Lieutenant Daily, have you ever seen or were you ever interrogated by this officer at any time while you were a North Korean captive?" I replied, "Yes, sir!" Then he asked, "Where?" Again I replied, "Sir, I believe it was near the end of August at their Headquarters near the town of Kumchon." He asked, "How was your treatment from him?" I replied, "It was okay and I was given my first hot meal that day, which was a bowl of watered down soup." He then asked, "This question is very important because of the various enemy atrocities reported by you; did you ever see this particular enemy officer commit or possibly involved in any of these particular atrocities?" I replied, "No sir!"

The questioning didn't take that long, and shortly I was informed that I could leave. I saluted the group of intelligence officers as I departed the room. The Captain remained there and only the Lieutenant from intelligence returned with me. I got in the jeep, and the Lieutenant drove me back to the 15th Medical Company.

I would never again see Senior Colonel, Lee Hak Ku. No other enemy officers or soldiers were ever brought forth for me to possibly identify for their particular atrocities or war crimes. When the so-called Korean Conflict began, the military had no experience in the handling of hostile prisoners of war. It had developed no real doctrine or specifically trained personnel. Worst of all, the United States Army understood Asians imperfectly, and Communists not at all.

Many things seemed to happen on September 21. I was told that Colonel Cecil Nist, our regimental commander of the 7th Cavalry Regiment was relieved of his duty, and replaced by Colonel William A. Harris, who previously commanded the 77th Field Artillery. I briefly thought, how in the hell is an artillery officer going to command an infantry unit?

However, in the days, weeks and months ahead, I would personally experience the leadership qualities of Colonel William A. Harris. He would bring forth a new fighting spirit within the ranks of "GARRYOWEN." He would become highly respected by all officers and men in the regiment. In the near future, a new name would arise, and he would be nicknamed Colonel "Wild Bill" Harris. This expression would come for his future combat exploits, and that he had a horse saddle mounted on the hood of his jeep.

The G-2 Intelligence Section had me classified under the Status of Recovered Allied Personnel; which in a way prevented me from returning to my unit. Captain Chandler, my previous company commander, didn't particularly like the respected orders, and he argued that they should be changed. He emphasized to them of my own decision if I so desired to return to my previous unit.

After a brief argument with a Major from intelligence, Captain Chandler won his way. He always had a creative way of winning arguments, but he also possessed a knack for inspiring people and a remarkable skill in the art of motivation.

On the morning of September 23, I was given a complete physical and released to the 15th Replacement Company. I was taken there by a 2-1/2 ton truck from the 15th Medical Company which was on its way for supplies.

From the 15th Replacement Company, I was actually on my own to find transportation to the 2nd Battalion Headquarters of the 7th Cavalry Regiment. After a couple hours of hitchhiking, I finally arrived at battalion headquarters. Both Major Callaway and Captain Chandler were gone at the time. I was given a quick ride by jeep to Company H, where I would soon discover many new faces and friendships. I received a whole-hearted welcome from the few old friends that somehow had survived the many hardships of combat.

After all these years and to this day, my wonderful mother still says, "Eddie, why did you return to that horrible war, you should have come home as they wanted you to?" Then, of course, my only answer, "I'm sorry, Mom, please don't question it because it was God's will!"

Atrocities committed by North Korean Soldiers . (Photo courtesy of Reuben Kvildt)

Hill 303 atrocity victims gathered for identification and burial. (U.S. Army photo)

Senior Colonel Lee Hak Ku, Chief of Staff, 13th North Korean Division. He is being interrogated at the 1st Cavalry Division Headquarters in Taegu, South Korea, on September 21, 1950. During the night, he had surrendered to a couple of troopers of the 8th Cavalry Regiment who were sleeping on an outpost guard. (Wide World)

Corporal Richard Dowell, Company B, 1st Bn., 7th Cavalry Regiment, playing cards at Camp McGee reserve area on August 11, 1950. This camp was located two miles north of Taegu, South Korea. It was named in honor of Lieutenant Charles F. McGee, who was killed in action on Triangle Hill on August 10, 1950.

CHAPTER VII
THE NAKTONG RIVER BREAKOUT

Attack when he is unprepared; sally out when he does not expect you.

—Sun Tzu, The Art of War
(C. 400-320 B.C.)

To emphasize to the reader the many furious battles which took place during my capture of August 12, to September 12, they can be described as extremely relentless pressure exerted by the enemy during this particular period. This critical period along the Naktong River and better known as the Pusan Perimeter, had experienced some of the toughest fighting battles of the Korean War. The North Korean Army had failed in its desperate attempt to break through the United Nations and Republic of South Korea defenses and seize the town of Taegu.

The following is an account of the withdrawal action on September 6-7, from Sergeant Donald D. Down, assistant squad leader from the 3rd Platoon of Company F.

I remember the 2nd Battalion withdrawal action on September 6-7, 1950, and our critical situation at that time. Our battalion was completely cut-off by the North Koreans in the vicinity of Hills 380 and 464. Our platoon under the leadership of Lieutenant Pennel "Joe" Hickey, ordered our unit to move along steep ridge toward Hill 380. We were actually separated from the main group, and as we moved down the slope of the ridge our lead squad came into contact with the enemy. At first we thought they were ROK soldiers of the South Korean Army, but we immediately discovered they were North Koreans. We fired into the enemy group and killed most of them as they attempted to scatter along the hillside.

As we continued to move toward Hill 380, we received sporadic enemy sniper fire. Near the crest of the hill, we were suddenly pinned down by heavy automatic weapons fire. For a while we could not move and we could not see the enemy concealed positions on the peak of the hill. A Major approached our location and ordered that a machine gun be set up to fire on the enemy positions. The Major stood up and pointed his .45 caliber pistol to fire at a particular enemy position. Suddenly a sniper bullet from an anti-tank rifle tore through his skull. The Major was dead when he hit the ground. I would learn later on that he was Major Omar Hitchner, our 2nd Battalion Commander.

The enemy continued to hit our positions with mortar and artillery barrages. When darkness came, Lt. Hickey informed us that he was going to lead us back to friendly lines. However, there was no radio contact with other elements of our battalion, and we were actually surrounded by enemy forces. Myself, along with many others, prayed that Lt. Hickey would lead us in the proper direction, and not into the hands of the North Koreans. All of us were tired and exhausted because of no sleep, no food or water. Also, our supply of ammunition was getting low.

To avoid an ambush by enemy forces, our progress was slow in the valley. At times we crawled through rice paddies and within whispering distance of enemy troops. Approximately 36 hours later, on September 7, our disorganized group finally reached friendly lines of the 5th Cavalry Regiment. Our scattered units began to assemble and we were transported to an area where we were fed and reclothed, and then placed in Division reserve.

I would learn later on from my father that he was notified by telegram from the Department of the Army that I was listed as Missing in Action during this particular withdrawal action. The 7th Cavalry Regiment had given the entire 2nd Battalion up for lost and sadly reported the tragic news to Army Headquarters and the correspondents.

Also during this chaotic withdrawal, my good friend Private First Class Daniel Brumagen was killed by an exploding mortar round. He was a member of the light machine gun squad. Just a couple of days prior, he had returned to our platoon from the hospital. He had very recently recovered from wounds that he had received in a previous battle. Needless to say, after experiencing the previous two day withdrawal, it felt great to be put in Division reserve.

When the 2nd Battalion Commander, Major Omar Hitchner was killed on September 6th, Captain Melbourne C. Chandler then battalion executive officer, assumed command of the disorganized group for the remainder of the withdrawal. Surrender was out of the question as Chandler undertook to lead the exhausted 2nd Battalion troopers to safety. Even an enemy bullet knocked the heel off one of Chandler's boots as he attempted to run at full speed through the rice paddies. In order to walk he had to remove the shot-up boot. Then trying to run with one boot on and one boot off proved difficult, so he took off the other.

Finally, after almost 36 hours of running, dodging and slithering through rice paddies, Captain Chandler led the remnants of the 2nd Battalion into friendly lines on September 7th. However, being barefooted and covered with mud from head to toe, he was almost shot by the friendly troops because he just didn't look like an American battalion commander.

Also, on the afternoon of September 7th, the 2nd Battalion was reclothed and reorganized under its new commander, Major John W. Callaway. Coming from a previous command of the 5th Cavalry Regiment, Major Callaway understood the spirit of the officers and troopers of the 2nd Battalion the true meaning of "GARRYOWEN" and the Fighting 7th Cavalry Regiment. His excellent leadership was immediately recognized and he gained the respect and admiration of all officers and enlisted men within the battalion and regiment.

ENEMY FORCES

Enemy forces which began crossing the Naktong River to assault the United Nations forces in the Pusan Perimeter were estimated in strength by major units to be as follows:

Unit	Strength
1st Infantry Division	5,000
2nd Infantry Division	7,500
3rd Infantry Division	7,000
4th Infantry Division	7,500
5th Infantry Division	7,000
6th Infantry Division	10,000
7th Infantry Division	9,000
8th Infantry Division	8,000
9th Infantry Division	9,350
10th Infantry Division	7,500
12th Infantry Division	6,000
13th Infantry Division	9,500
15th Infantry Division	7,000
104th Infantry Division	2,000
105th Armored Div. (40 tanks)	3,000
16th Armored Brigade	500
17th Armored Brigade	500
83rd Motorized Regiment (detached from the 105th Armored Division)	1,000
766th Independent Infantry Reg.	1,500
	108,850

The following is the Mid-September United Nations Pusan Perimeter strength of the U.S. Eighth Army:

Unit	Strength
U.S. I. Corps.	7,475
(plus attached Koreans, 1,110)	
	13,904
U.S. 1st Cavalry Division	13,904
(plus attached Koreans, 2,338)	
U.S. 24th Infantry Division	16,356
(plus attached Koreans, 2,786)	
U.S. 25th Infantry Division	15,334
(plus attached Koreans, 2,447)	
U.S. 2nd Infantry Division	15,191
(plus attached Koreans, 1,821)	
British 27th Infantry Brigade	1,693
	80,455
ROK Army (Republic of Korea)	72,730
TOTAL	153,185

Upon my return to Company H, on September 23, I found myself extremely apprehensive to the overall surroundings within the company. I was introduced to our new company commander, 1st Lt. Crawford "Buck" Buchanan, who was previously the platoon leader of the Regimental I & R Platoon. During the previous eighteen months, 1st Lt. Buchanan had held several positions within Company H and the 2nd Battalion. He was respected as an excellent officer and leader. However, before the end of the week, we would welcome another new company commander by the name of Captain John B. Wadsworth.

Then there was the underlying fact of seeing so many new faces in the ranks of our enlisted men. However, I had to acknowledge the fact that we had lost 70% of Company H the day I was captured on August 12. Even though I had been with this same company since February 1949, I now realized that it was almost like arriving in a totally different unit. Eventually, I would find myself very reluctant to make close friendships within my platoon. I felt as though my self-confidence was high and I was determined to prove not only to myself, but to my superiors and subordinates that I could be an excellent officer and platoon leader.

They had integrated more South Korean soldiers (ROK's) into our company and many had fired an M-1 rifle only a few times. It was difficult at times to translate because of the language barrier. However, many proved to have the ability to withstand the climate and tough terrain by natural instinct. They had a definite desire for independence and victory and proved themselves in combat conditions. Many were used in carrying ammunition and supplies and in the dangerous role of litter bearers assisting in the evacuation of wounded. Many Americans owe their lives to these brave and rugged South Koreans.

Since my return to Company H, many of the enlisted men thought of me as a hero for escaping from the North Koreans. Some of them had even started rumors that I had gone behind enemy lines for G-2 Intelligence. However, they didn't realize the inner feelings that plagued my body; and little did they realize the horrible memories within my mind and soul.

Captain Chandler, my previous company commander who was now our 2nd Battalion Executive Officer, tried to emphasize encouragement to me. He said; "Lieutenant Daily, remember good leaders develop excellent followers and they must build an allegiance to themselves and to one another within the organization. Also, I want to see medals issued to all those who deserve recognition for their heroic deeds."

Also, Captain Chandler still possessed a remarkable way for inspiring and the art of motivation. He continued to make comments on the so-called conflict and that it would be over soon. In my own mind, I was totally convinced of this fact because of the various reports and rumors being circulated within the 2nd Battalion. Also, I definitely wanted to be a part of the future assault plans and operations that would eventually annihilate the entire North Korean Army.

The 1st Cavalry Division had been assigned part of I Corps on September 15th to correlate with the scheme maneuver of the amphibious landing made on the same day by the 1st Marine Division and the 7th Infantry Division of the X Corps. This amphibious landing took place at the port city of Inchon, South Korea. Also, the 1st Cavalry Division was ordered to make a sweeping movement from its existing positions toward the Naktong River and the Waegwan-Taegu road.

On September 16, at 1100 hours, the 2nd Battalion of the 7th Cavalry Regiment was ordered to move in the vicinity of Hill 246. This actually marked the beginning of the Pusan Perimeter breakout and the historic drive northward to within 35 miles of the Yalu River on the Manchurian border.

The 2nd Battalion on September 17 at 0700 hours, began its attack toward hill masses 100, 105, 184, 188 and 300. The Battalion continued its attack on September 18-19, and defeated a strong enemy force in heavily

dug-in positions and various emplacements. This particular 3-day attack was made over a distance of 8,000 yards across rice paddies and open terrain, and there were no roads to support the attack. The North Koreans suffered more than 400 casualties with an estimated 200 killed.

However, this objective and accomplished victory did not come cheap, as the 2nd Battalion suffered 28 killed, 202 wounded and 4 missing in action. Also, 2 company commanders, and 1 company executive officer were wounded, and Captain Fred DePalma, commanding Company G, was killed. Of the South Korean troops assigned to the battalion, an additional 6 were killed, 27 wounded, and 1 missing in action.

The following is an account of the action of the Naktong River Breakout during September 17-19, from Colonel (then Major) John W. Callaway, Battalion Commander, 2nd Battalion, 7th Cavalry Regiment. Colonel Callaway was the 2nd Battalion Commander from September 6, 1950 to July, 1951.

As the old saying goes, blind people have different ideas of how an elephant looks. The same is true in war. The battalion commander, company commanders and front line troops see a battle differently. The battle I shall attempt to describe is my best recollection of my actions and thoughts almost forty years after the event.

To lead up to this battle, let me begin on September 6, 1950. After three days of heavy fighting, the North Koreans had forced the 5th Cavalry Regiment of which I was a member to withdraw some four miles south of the Naktong River. At the time I was a Major and executive officer of the 2d Battalion of the 5th Cavalry Regiment. I had arrived in Korea some three weeks before as a casual officer. As we were preparing our defensive positions, word came for me to report to the 7th Cavalry Regimental Headquarters and assume command of the 2d Battalion of that regiment. The Regimental Commander explained to me that the battalion had been overrun and the battalion commander killed. He fur-

ther advised that stragglers would be walking south along a dry stream bed about a mile from his headquarters. These men were members of the 2d Battalion.

Not long after reaching this position, stragglers began to appear with their individual weapons and little more. They were sorted out by companies and advised to take it easy. By nightfall most of the stragglers had shown up. The next day or so, in a reserve position, the battalion began to receive additional stragglers, replacements and equipment since all equipment that could not be carried by a fighting soldier on foot had been lost.

The battalion spent the next week reorganizing and re-equipping. This, of course, was a major undertaking since there had been considerable casualties, both officer and enlisted.

On the afternoon of September 16, orders were received to go by convoy to an assembly area on the Waegwan-Taegu Road south of Hill 188. The battalion arrived in position around 1600 hours and dismounted in an assembly area awaiting further orders. The Division Commander, General Hap Gay, appeared on the scene and was furious that the battalion was not attacking to the North. Unfortunately, communications had broken down between his headquarters and mine. I convinced him that we could do a better job by attacking the following morning. Reluctantly, he approved.

The 2d Battalion, 7th Cavalry had been attached to the 5th Cavalry Regiment and would make the main attack from the south along the Taegu-Waegwan Road with the objective, Hill 300, which dominated the Taegu-Waegwan Road and the crossing of the Naktong River at Waegwan.

In studying the terrain, it became obvious that the key hill other than 300 was Hill 184 which dominated the rice paddies over which our troops must pass. The first order of business was to seize Hill 184 and then bypass to the south of it. Company E was assigned the mission of seizing Hill 184 and support the attack of Companies F and G toward Hill 300. I also decided to send a

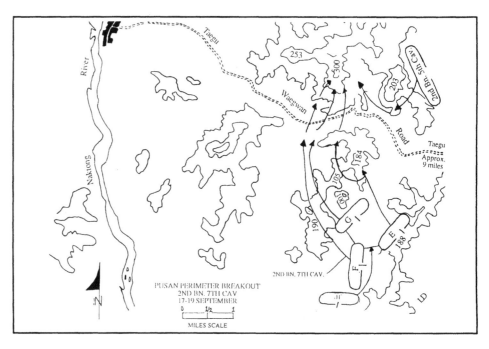

PUSAN PERIMETER BREAKOUT
2ND BN. 7TH CAV
17-19 SEPTEMBER

0   1/2   1

MILES SCALE

North Korean prisoners of war being taken to clearing station. (Courtesy of Bob Mauger)

North Korean soldiers, not so lucky, defending their positions. (Courtesy of Bob Mauger)

This North Korean soldier is waiting for burial. (Courtesy of Bob Mauger)

platoon that evening to reconnoiter Hill 184 to see if the enemy occupied it. If not, the platoon was to remain there until E Company arrived. By 2300 hours the reconnaissance platoon reported that it was on Hill 184 and there was no enemy. This knowledge gave me some relief, so I slept soundly.

By daylight the battalion was getting breakfast and moving toward the line of departure. For some this would be their last meal; for others, their last battle and for all members of the battalion, the most important battle they would fight in Korea. This battalion had been selected to open the hole for the breakout of the Naktong Perimeter and the final destruction of the North Korean forces.

As the companies started in an approach march formation across the one and one-half miles of open rice paddies, heavy enemy 4.2 mortar fire began to rain on them. From my Observation Post, I began to search with my binoculars for the platoon which was supposedly on Hill 184. Unfortunately, the platoon had gone to another hill one-half mile southwest of Hill 184. Convinced that Hill 184 was the enemy OP, I ordered our artillery to take the hill under fire. In the meantime Company E continued to move toward Hill 184. The enemy fire continued and Company E met stiff resistance as it attempted to seize Hill 184. Companies F and G were ordered to bypass Hill 184 and cross the Taegu-Waegwan Road toward Hill 300, the final objective.

By evening Hill 184 had been seized, but Companies F and G had run into heavy enemy resistance on the high ground across the road. Enemy mortars and machine guns as well as several tanks had been overrun; however, the enemy resistance became stronger. As a result, the companies withdrew south of the road for the remainder of the night.

The following day the battalion began its attack toward Hill 300, which was about a mile from the road. The going was rough as the enemy defended every foot from dominating terrain. Despite the enemy's stubborn resistance, the gallant men of the 2nd Battalion seized their objective and opened the hole for the breakthrough to the North. It was a great thrill to sit on top of Hill 300 and watch the miles of US 2-1/2 ton trucks and jeeps wind their way to the north.

The enemy had suffered over 400 casualties with approximately 200 killed. At least 8 enemy mortars had been captured and a number of tanks and flat trajectory weapons had been destroyed.

This victory was costly to the 2d Battalion with 28 killed, 202 wounded and four missing in action. In addition, six South Korean troops assigned to the battalion were killed, 27 wounded and one missing.

In my view this was the most significant battle the 2d Battalion fought during the year I served in Korea. Unfortunately, because the battalion was attached to another regiment, very little has been said or written about this great event. Those who were there know of the outstanding victory that was achieved and the great sacrifices that were made by those brave soldiers of the 2d Battalion, 7th Cavalry Regiment, GARRYOWEN!

Most experiences in combat are not pleasant; however, occasionally an amusing incident does occur. One that I have always enjoyed happened after our battalion opened the hole in the North

Korean defenses along the Naktong River on September 19, 1950. Because of our severe casualties, we were ordered to quiet sector along the Naktong River where we relieved the 27th British Mechanized Brigade which went north with the 1st Cavalry Division. During the relief the Brigade Commander advised me of his policy regarding the North Koreans which was to "live and let live". I accepted his advice, and other than sending a night patrol along our side of the river to rescue a British Landrover vehicle and two jeeps which we needed desperately, both sides remained quiet. By this time we had reverted to the command of Headquarters Eight Army Rear since most other major combat headquarters had gone through the hole to link up with X Corps units 160 miles away, just south of Seoul. The G-2 staff of Eight Army came up with an idea of sending a 2-1/2 ton sound truck with a person who could speak the Korean language to one of our line companies to advise the North Korean troops across the river that they had lost the battle and should surrender.

While I was not happy with the idea, I saw no harm since our front line company was well dug in and would probably suffer no casualties. My front line company commander was not so optimistic so I had to insist that he go along with the idea.

The 2-1/2 ton truck arrived shortly after dark with its blackout lights. I instructed the driver to continue up the road about 600 yards, and our front line company commander would show him where to set up. I remained beside the road to see the action.

The loud speaker sounded off for about 30 seconds when I heard the enemy mortar shells beginning to land in the area. It was quite a concentration of mortar fire. I next heard a vehicle coming down the road from the front line company. It was traveling about 20 miles per hour with only its black out lights. I tried to stop the truck but to no avail.

I called the company commander and he assured me that there were no casualties. We had a good laugh since it was apparent that the North Korean troops across the river had not heard that they had lost the war.

Several days later I received a call from the Eight Army G-2 Section asking what had happened to their sound truck and troops they had sent up. I told them about the truck passing me headed south about 20 miles per hour and would not stop. I suggested that they try looking down around Pusan, the US supply seaport, about 80 miles to the south.

The following is an account of the action of the Naktong River Breakout during September 17th-19th, by Captain John C. Rourke, Battalion Surgeon for the 2nd Battalion, 7th Cavalry Regiment. Captain Rourke served as the 2nd Battalion Surgeon from the end of July, 1950 to February 10, 1951.

At the time I had been assigned with the medical unit of the 2nd Battalion for approximately six weeks. I was well supported by the recent appointment of Major Richton who was a medical service administration officer. He was recently assigned to replace the previous assistant surgeon who had been wounded.

From my outstanding recollections, this was the first true attack in which the 2nd Battalion

Artillery fire from 105-mm Howitzers. (Courtesy of Bob Mauger)

1st Cavalry Division troopers riding their future meal. (Courtesy of Bob Mauger)

Destroyed Russian tank with SU-76mm self-propelled gun, vicinity of Waegwan, South Korea, September 1950. (Army)

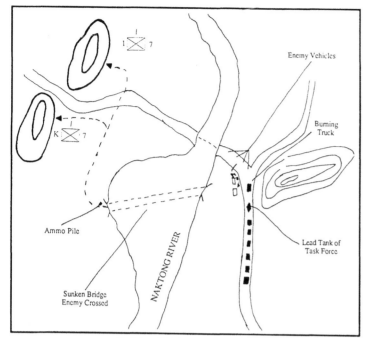

Task Force 777 September 22, 1950

Task Force 777 September 22-27, 1950

had been engaged in since my assignment to the medical unit. Secondly, it was an extremely difficult and bloody battle because the troops had to fight on foot across 8000 yards of open rice paddies and rough terrain.

Their first objective was to secure three small hills just south of the Taegu-Waegwan road. The road actually crossed between the line of battle and the final objective to secure several larger hills just north of the road. One objective was Hill 300, which was strongly dug-in and heavily defended by the North Korean soldiers. It was solid rock at the top of the hill and the enemy took advantage of this to build shelters over top of their positions. They were heavily supported by machine guns, mortars and artillery.

The forward medical aid station was established at the line of departure for the attack and it was commanded by Major Richton. He had the difficult task of directly supervising the arduous job of the litter teams. They followed the troops into battle, but once a trooper was wounded it required them to carry and walk that wounded trooper a long distance back to a point where they could be safely carried further to the rear.

Major Richton, and the litter teams under his command, performed bravely and diligently during the extremely difficult conditions of battle. The line was long in getting the wounded back to safety.

After the wounded were brought back to a transport point, they were either moved to my aid station or some went to the bypass medical aid station of the 5th Cavalry Regiment, which was located a short distance to our rear. At this particular time, our 2nd Battalion was attached to the 5th Cavalry Regiment during this phase of battle operation.

With the large number of casualties, we ran out of supplies, particularly, litter bearers and the Thomas Leg Splints which were used to transport wounded with broken thighs. It became extremely difficult to draw medical resupplies from the 5th Cavalry Regiment sources. This was due to their own shortages of medical supplies, because they had suffered heavy casualties themselves.

There may have been some misunderstanding on the part of the 5th Cavalry unit, that we had been ordered to draw medical supplies from. It left me with the impression that when a fighting unit is attached to another organization, and in spite of the plans and intentions, they can still find themselves in the status of an orphan.

One time during the final day, the backup supplies became so critical that I personally journeyed back to the supporting 5th Cavalry medical unit. There I found that they also were lacking in medical supplies and were unable to help. Then I journeyed several miles further to the rear to the Medical Company of the 7th Cavalry Regiment. However, they were all loaded up and ready to move and support the attacking elements to the north. This was the actual start of the historical attack and drive through enemy-held territory to eventually link up with the 31st Infantry Regiment, 7th Infantry Division. It was better known as Task Force "777", which actually covered a distance of 196 road miles and marked the longest drive in the history of the American Army through enemy-held territory.

They were unable to help me, which was somewhat of a disappointment. Not knowing what to do, I sought out the assistance from Captain McCoulough, who was the Catholic Chaplain in the 2nd Battalion. He had become a close friend during the long days of battle in the Naktong River Defense and Perimeter.

I said, "Father sir, your old friends in the 2nd Battalion are bleeding badly and need help." He listened and then quickly set off on his own plan of relief to help the situation. Within thirty minutes after my arrival back at the aid station, he came forward with large amounts of supplies that I had requested. He definitely was a true friend in need.

I remember this period very vividly. I must say that I never did have the opportunity to observe or visualize the actual field of action. My location was just south of the battle where a close view could not be obtained. Captain Mel Chandler, our 2nd Battalion Executive Officer, kept in close contact with what was going on within the battle..

In Mel Chandler's book, "Of GARRYOWEN In Glory," he states that during this particular battle and within the 2nd Battalion, there were 28 killed, 202 wounded and four missing in action. However, I do know that the number of killed in action increased somewhat because of the subsequent death of some of the wounded after they were taken from the battle area.

I would like to recall three separate individuals of these particular wounded that I know subsequently died. The first was a young rifleman, whose name I do not remember, who was about twenty years old. He was brought into my aid station in a state of irreversible shock and he was remarkably elusive. However, he could clearly relate what actually happened to him. Two days prior to his arrival at my aid station, he had been wounded in the thigh and was immobilized on the ground. This was during an attack and then a quick withdrawal, which caused him to be left behind and without proper medical treatment.

The North Koreans had retaken that same area and an enemy patrol had discovered him laying there quietly on the ground. One of the enemy soldiers walked up to where he lay and stood over him with a Russian Burp gun in his hands. At that time the enemy soldier took the automatic weapon and sprayed the chest and abdomen of the wounded American soldier. He had approximately eight or nine small caliber wounds in both of those particular areas.

He was so clear and coherent in explaining or recalling what the North Korean soldier had done to him. He was so eager to relate his personal feelings of outrage concerning the conduct of the enemy soldier. I'm positive that this young soldier did not survive his wounds even after he arrived at the MASH (Mobile Army Surgical Hospital), which was located in the town of Taegu.

Another wounded individual that I remember was Captain Herschel "Ug" Fuson, who was a very colorful officer. "Ug" as he was known to all of his men, was somewhat of a celebrity because he was a tall and heavy ex-football player. He had been a star performer at West Point while attend-

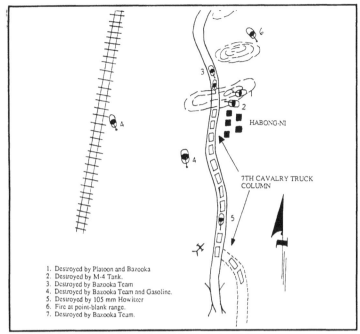

Tank fight at Habong-Ni September 26, 1950

1. Destroyed by Platoon and Bazooka
2. Destroyed by M-4 Tank.
3. Destroyed by Bazooka Team
4. Destroyed by Bazooka Team and Gasoline.
5. Destroyed by 105 mm Howitzer.
6. Fire at point-blank range.
7. Destroyed by Bazooka Team.

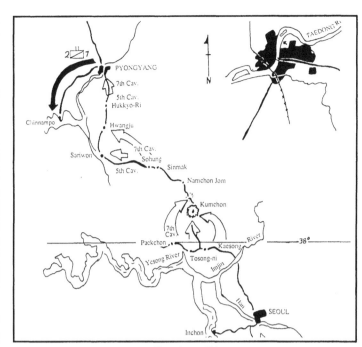

Above the parallel.

ing the United States Military Academy. Also, he had played football during the glory days of 1944-45. Further, he had been a lineman who played with such legendaries as Doc Blanchard, (Mr. Inside), and Glenn Davis, (Mr. Outside).

"Ug" was a pleasant and quiet person. We talked in brief statements after he was brought into my aid station. He had a bullet wound that went through his right arm pit and into the area where the neck and shoulder join. He didn't seem to be too uncomfortable, only that he was very hungry. His enormous appetite was one of his remarkable attributes.

He was oozing blood from the wounded area, which was difficult to control because of the many important blood vessels that were damaged. I can remember taking a tight wadded bandage and jamming it up into the arm pit and then bringing his right arm down against the side of his chest. I attempted to bind the arm there to keep the pressure on the breathing points.

All during this time "Ug" was not particularly attentive to what I was doing, but was surveying the situation. Suddenly he spotted, by accident, a young soldier from one of the mess halls walking around with a large carton of donuts. These donuts were being distributed to wounded personnel who needed food.

"Ug" called the donut giver over to him and with his large left hand open, he reached into the carton of donuts. Somehow he managed to grasp seven or eight donuts and which he then proceeded to heavily consume with his enormous appetite. In view of a very serious wound, I was amazed at how quickly the donuts disappeared. Needless to say, of those that knew "Ug" said that was the way he was.

About one month later I received the most unfortunate word that "Ug" had died in a hospital in Tokyo from delayed complications of his particular wound. However, I would learn many years later from a newspaper article that "Ug" had died the following year in June 1951, from complications that were attributed to a heart ailment.

My third memory of a wounded individual is that of Lieutenant Radcliff, who was the Commanding Officer of Company E. He was wounded seriously the last day of battle. Also, the 2nd Battalion troopers had almost completed their objective in securing Hill 300.

I got to know Lt. Radcliff prior to his serious wound when I treated him for minor scratches and scrapes. I had joked with him at that time that he was like a cat with nine lives. It seemed that in the midst of serious wounded personnel he had received only a few minor scratches. However, this time he was very seriously wounded with multiple bullet wounds of the abdomen.

Arrangements were immediately made to send him to the MASH unit located to the rear. This Mobile Army Surgical Hospital was established in a school house within the town of Taegu. Also, the Eighth Army Headquarters was located in this town. I was able to visit him there two days later and I'll never forget the scene which I saw.

The incoming unit for the wounded was established in a huge wide open area that looked like the combination assembly area and cafeteria of the school. Every square foot of space was utilized and occupied with cots. Many wounded were being treated for shock and every effort was put forth to keep them stabilized. This was to prepare them for emergency surgery which was being performed by five separate teams on a twenty-four hour basis. This was due to the large influx of casualties.

When I visited Lt. Radcliff, I discovered that he was extremely ill. Although he was heavily sedated, he did arouse enough to recognize me and say a few words. It was at this particular time that he gave me his report. His comments were, "Doc, they were looking down our throats"! This was in reference to the difficulty of fighting a battle up hill and against a heavily armed and entrenched enemy. Unfortunately, Lt. Radcliff died one week later at the MASH unit, from direct results of his wounds.

This visit to the MASH unit to see Lt. Radcliff, has always remained in my memory. It gave me the opportunity to see the grim determination and dedicated effort of the very talented medical personnel, performing under the most difficult circumstances. They attempted to provide the best possible treatment to the very large number of casualties. It was not, however, a happy or laughing situation as portrayed on the television series, MASH. I have always resented this particular television program for its casual, trivial and demeaning presentation of a very serious and important aspect of the wounded soldier during the Korean War.

We veterans of the Korean War remember the many deeds and sacrifices of the combat soldier, as they were. Unfortunately, I think the television series MASH has contributed to an overly casual and easily forgotten attitude of the younger generation toward the Korean War.

The following is an account of the assault action on September 19, 1950, from 1st Lieutenant Pennel "Joe" Hickey, 3rd Platoon Leader, Company F, 2nd Battalion, 7th Cavalry Regiment.

As I recall, we jumped off at 0800 hours to attack up one finger of the ridge with Company F. Company G was to advance up another finger of the ridge, with the two companies in a coordinated assault when we neared the enemy held ridgeline.

My platoon led the attack, but we didn't encounter any enemy as we secured over one half of the finger of the ridge. Suddenly, we started to encounter enemy foxholes and bunkers. One of my B.A.R. men, Corporal James Dady from Texas, did himself proud. The first 3-4 foxholes we encountered he made a one man dash up the finger of the ridge and fired a burst into the foxholes and then ran back to our lead elements and flopped down. There were no enemy in those foxholes, but that takes nothing away from the courage that Corporal Dady displayed.

The enemy obviously had pulled back to positions higher up the ridge. About this time we started receiving small arms and automatic weapons fire. It must have been between 1000-1100 hours, as Corporal Dady made one more dash up the finger of the ridge blasting everything in sight with his automatic rifle. Upon his return, he fell

Heavy artillery support fire at night. (U.S. photo)

187th Regimental Combat Team jumping from C-119's. (U.S. Army photo)

to the ground to my left, which was about 10 yards away. I moved over to him and as I got up in a prone position to tell him a "good job" on his behalf, a shot rang out and took a nip out of the top edge of his right ear. Corporal Dady turned white as a ghost, but he wasn't really hurt.

Feeling that Dady was putting us all to shame, I decided to rush the next foxhole. I ran up about 20 yards with carbine in my hands and set on full automatic, with a banana clip. I stood over the foxhole and pulled the trigger, when suddenly the carbine fell into two pieces in my hands. (I hadn't set a retaining clip). I couldn't help but laugh to myself at the foolishness of the situation, so I high-tailed it back to our troops in a hurry.

Shortly after this Captain William L. Webb, commanding Company F, was wounded while individually attacking an enemy machine gun position. He got shot through his leg a little above the knee. He gave me his map and told me to take command and continue the attack. I envied him somewhat as he fell back down the hill with a "great" wound.

We kept advancing against increasingly heavy fire, and shortly thereafter we were pinned down again. Talking by radio with the battalion, we found the situation was the same with Company G. We stayed in position because the ground provided good cover from direct fire. Now we attempted to regroup and count noses. Surprisingly, we could find only 35 of our platoon and attachments. The others were far down below us.

After 30-90 minutes in this position, word was received from the battalion that both Companies F & G would continue the attack. We jumped off together for the so-called "one inch movement." We had progressed only 10 yards when we were pinned down again. Hill 300 was definitely heavily defended by the enemy. To move forward any further would have been difficult because of the open and exposed ridgeline. Actually, we moved back to where we had been before and eventually we got relieved by a unit from the 8th Cavalry Regiment at approximately 1600 hours.

Lieutenant Pennel "Joe" Hickey remained in the Army and retired a full Colonel in 1975. Also, "Joe" Hickey graduated from West Point, the Class of '49.

In the meantime, Lt. Colonel William A. Harris, the new Commander of the 7th Cavalry Regiment, would institute a forthcoming plan called Task Force 777. When he assumed his new command at 2300 hours on September 20, he immediately assembled staff personnel, unit representatives and battalion commanders to plan for this future operation. The name was derived because it consisted of the 7th Cavalry Regiment, the 77th Field Artillery Battalion, and Company C, 70th Tank Battalion. Task Force 777 was organized as follows:

Task Force Lynch (3rd Battalion), commanded by Lt. Colonel James H. Lynch, which contained: 3rd Battalion, 7th Cavalry Regiment; Battery C, 77th Field Artillery Battalion; 2nd and 3rd Platoons, Company C, 70th Tank Battalion; 3rd Platoon, Heavy Mortar Company; Regimental I & R Platoon; 2nd Platoon, Company B, 8th Engineers; Medical Platoon Collecting Company; Forward Observer Party, 77th Field Artillery Battalion; Tactical Air Control Party; SCR 399 Radio Team, 13th Signal Company; Regimental Command Group.

Task Force Witherspoon (1st Battalion), commanded by Major William O. Witherspoon, which contained: 1st Battalion, 7th Cavalry Regiment; 77th Field Artillery Battalion (less Battery C); Company C, 70th Tank Battalion (minus); Company B, 8th Engineers (minus); 1st Platoon, Heavy Mortar Company; Medical Platoon, Collecting Company.

The 2nd Battalion, 7th Cavalry Regiment and the 2nd Platoon, Heavy Mortar Company would remain in Eighth Army reserves, southwest of Taegu. From this location, daily patrols and skirmishes were employed to seek and destroy die-hard enemy troops which had been cut off from their retreat northward.

On September 27 at daybreak hours, 1st Lt. Crawford "Buck" Buchanan notified all Company H personnel of the successful accomplished mission of Task Force 777. The entire company was overjoyed with the news and we knew that the enemy was on the verge or brink of total collapse. We all knew that forthcoming orders would soon alert us to proceed northward to rejoin the 7th Cavalry Regiment. However, at this particular time none of us realized what future mode of transportation would be used for our eventual troop movement.

The Task Force 777 mission was actually accomplished at 0826 hours on September 27, when contact was made with Company H, 31st Infantry Regiment, 7th Infantry Division. The contacting unit from the 1st Cavalry Division was Company L, 7th Cavalry Regiment. They met in the town of Yongjon-ni, very near Osan, South Korea. Task Force 777 sent a message to the 1st Cavalry Division at 0855 hours, which read as follows:

"Mission accomplished. Contact between Company H, 31st Infantry Regiment and forward elements of TF 777 accomplished at 0826 hours. Our contacting unit was Company L. We are jointly reducing enemy positions east and west of Osan with 7th Division elements under Air Force and Navy fighter strikes. This is unification."

However, at 0300 hours, a prior message had been sent from Lt. Colonel William Harris to Major General Hobart R. Gay, referring to the Commanding General's earlier offer to provide a bottle of champagne for each tank knocked out by ground forces. It read as follows:

"... FM TF 777 - Send 7 bottles of Champagne to CO TF 777. Put 3 more on ice. I'll get them later. Will continue on mission."

Also, on September 27 at 1500 hours, the Commanding General and the assistant General of the 1st Cavalry Division, arrived in Osan and personally congratulated Task Force 777.

The 1st Cavalry Division extremely proud

of its accomplishments, erected a sign on the north side of Osan, and it read as follows:

"Osan, Korea

At 0826 hours on 27 September, 1950, forward elements of Company L, 7th Cavalry Regiment, 1st Cavalry Division made firm contact with Company H, 31st Infantry Regiment, 7th Infantry Division at this location thereby making a solid United Nations front from Pusan to Seoul.

This drive from Taegu to Osan, a distance of 196 road miles and 116 air miles, marked the longest advance in the history of the American Army through enemy-held territory - GARRYOWEN".

The I & R Platoon of Task Force 777, commanded by Lt. Robert W. Baker, with three Sherman tanks and three jeeps raced up the highway to link up with the 7th Division. In eleven hours Baker covered 106.4 miles through enemy held territory to Osan. His gunners popped away at North Korean soldiers on the roadway, with one of them keeping a lively log: "9:05 PM - two more; two more; seven more; 9:35 PM - 3 Reds; two carts; two more; two mule carts full of Reds; one jeep; six more....." "GARRYOWEN."

Major General Hobart Gay, the 1st Cavalry Division Commander, issued a commendation to all members of the Division which read in part as follows:

"By your dogged defense, your encirclement of three enemy divisions in the Taegu, Waegwan, Tabu-dong and Sangju areas, and by your breakthrough to Osan — the most rapid advance ever made in the history of American arms — you have added a new and glorious chapter to our national military history. Therefore, I extend my hearty thanks and commend all . . ."

And from within the 2nd Battalion there were various reports about "Ole Charlie." It seems there was a charred object a few yards off the road. Close inspection revealed that a Napalm bomb had literally incinerated a North Korean soldier on his feet. He was still standing there, rifle at his feet. Some "GARRYOWEN" troopers had nicknamed him "Ole Charlie."

On October 2, the 2nd Battalion, being held in Eighth Army reserve, was finally released to rejoin the rest of the 7th Cavalry Regiment. Captain John B. Wadsworth, our new company commander, notified us that we would be trucked to Taegu Airport, and then air transported to an airstrip in the town of Suwon. He also told us that this air transport maneuver would be accomplished on C-119 aircraft, which many of us knew by the term of "flying box car."

Now my personal thoughts went back to the past February when the entire 2nd Battalion was shuttled by C-54 aircraft from Tokyo to Sendai, Japan, for a short overnight defensive exercise. However, very few men now remained in our battalion who participated in that particular maneuver. Nevertheless, that previous air mobility exercise proved itself to be very valuable in our approximately 120 air mile trip.

Many of the men in my platoon were very apprehensive about flying, but the air flight to Suwon proved to be successful. Looking down from the airplane at the various landscaping below, things actually appeared peaceful and quiet. Needless to say, we all knew that down below there were vicious battles being fought between the North Korean Army and the United Nations Forces.

After landing at an airstrip southwest of Suwon, we were quickly trucked to an assembly area near Osan where we would rejoin the rest of the 7th Cavalry Regiment. Since its arrival in Korea, our company was now at its highest strength. Our morale was very high at this time, and a successful end to the war seemed in sight.

Division orders were received and the 2nd Battalion departed Osan and proceeded northward to an area near the Imjin River. Original orders were to cross the river and seize the town of Kaesong, which was heavily defended by enemy troops. However, orders were changed and the 2nd Battalion was given the difficult task and assignment to proceed westward to the Yesong River. This sweeping movement was to search for river crossing sites and clear enemy troops from the area southwest of Kaesong.

Upon reaching the Yesong River, contact was made with the I & R Platoon of the 7th Cavalry Regiment. They had discovered that the river wasn't fordable within the immediate area of the regiment. However, a partially destroyed combination road and rail bridge did span the river. Although damaged and weakened, it was determined that the 800 yard bridge could support only foot troops. The I & R Platoon also reported that the bridge was heavily defended from the west side of the river by fanatical enemy forces. The road on the other side of the river was the main route northward to the town of Paekch'on.

At noon on October 9, the 77th Field Artillery started a preparatory artillery fire against enemy positions on the west bank of the river. This devastating barrage lasted for approximately three hours. Shortly after 1500 hours, Company C, 1st Battalion was ordered to lead the initial attack across the bridge. Once on the bridge, the enemy sent an overwhelming barrage of small arms, automatic weapons and mortar fire upon the advance column.

Then Company B followed behind Company C, and was pinned down by heavy concentrations of fire on the bridge. However, they continued to move slowly and finally crossed the bridge and casualties began to increase rapidly. In the 20 minutes it took to secure the bridge, the 1st Battalion suffered 78 casualties. Company C suffered 7 killed and 36 wounded; Company B suffered 1 killed and 25 wounded. Between the two companies, there were 9 minor wounds during the attack. Even though the steel and concrete structure of the bridge served as a somewhat protective shield, many of the brave troopers were wounded by ricocheted bullets.

In the meantime, the 2nd Battalion had remained on the east bank of the river, waiting for future and impending orders. Shortly after dark, the enemy launched a counter attack against the 1st Battalion. Orders were then issued for the 2nd Battalion to prepare for the bridge crossing and the 3rd Battalion would follow to protect the east bank.

Captain John Wadsworth, commanding officer of Company H, briefed all company officers on what our future objective would be after we crossed the bridge. From the map we were shown the battle plan that would move the 2nd Battalion through the 1st Battalion once the 1st Battalion secured the higher ground. The 2nd Battalion would then make a spearhead drive northward and seize the town of Paekch'on. He also informed us that this attack would take us

Thousands of North Korean soldiers surrendered near the 38th Parallel as they attempted to flee northward. By November 3, 1950, more than 135,000 enemy soldiers had surrendered. (Army)

House in the village of Naede, where North Korean soldiers committed atrocities on October 13, 1950. Later called Naede Murders. (U.S. Army photo; courtesy of Fred Herrmann)

Wounded North Koreean soldier who was identified as one of those involved in the Naede Murders. The officer is Major Brown of G-2 Intelligence, 1st Cavalry Division. (U.S. Army photo; courtesy of Fred Herrmann)

across the 38th Parallel into North Korea.

Then Captain Wadsworths' eyes focused on mine as he said; "Lieutenant Daily, you and I and the 1st Platoon will move across the bridge with the three rifle companies to give them support as directed. As it stands at this time, we should behind Company G".

Due to the circumstances that our particular company was heavy weapons, mobility of such prevented the entire company from crossing together because of the bridge weakness. These weapons and equipment would follow-up later in the attack, once the 8th Combat Engineers authorized their safe passage over the bridge. Miraculously, the 8th Combat Engineers repaired the bridge during the night and early morning hours, and at times under heavy enemy fire. The re-

maining elements of the 2nd Battalion completed the bridge crossing at daybreak of October 10.

During the entire night, Battery B of the 77th Field Artillery sent a withering barrage into enemy positions on the west bank. At approximately 0100 hours, and behind Company G, Captain Wadsworth, myself and the 1st Platoon of Company H made fast pursuit across the bridge.

The fanatical enemy continued to send a relentless concentration of mortar, small arms, and automatic weapons fire into our advancing column. Upon reaching the west bank, we immediately moved into position on the left flank of Company G. I then ordered my platoon to give the necessary fire support to elements of Company G.

As the 2nd Battalion attempted to secure positions along the road, they were met with stiff enemy resistance. Several enemy counterattacks were repelled and Lieutenant Colonel Gilman A. Huff, 2nd Battalion Commander, was slightly wounded in the chest by enemy small arms fire. After he was evacuated to the rear, Major John W. Callaway again assumed command of the Battalion.

Without hesitation, the 2nd Battalion, now under the leadership of Major John W. Callaway, continued its attack and broke through the enemy defense positions along the road. The enemy was now confused as they made their hasty retreat and the battalion moved northward toward the town of Paekch'on. The 2nd Battalion, now receiving little enemy resistance, arrived in Paekch'on around noon on October 10. The town was rapidly cleared of enemy troops and I was ordered by Captain Wadsworth to take my platoon along with other elements of the battalion and secure the high terrain northwest of the town.

The advance elements during this successful attack were from Company F and were under the leadership of 1st Lt. John C. Lippincott. His Award of the Silver Star Medal is in part and is as follows:

First Lieutenant JOHN C. LIPPINCOTT, United States Army, Company F, 7th Cavalry Regiment, 1st Cavalry Division, for gallantry in action against the enemy on 10 October 1950 near Paekch'on, Korea. When his company had been given the mission of battalion advance guard in an attack on Paekch'on, Lieutenant LIPPINCOTT, company executive officer, went forward to the assault line just as his men were engaged in attacking the firmly entrenched enemy positions. His unit was suddenly met by heavy enemy fire, and the advance slowed down. Immediately sizing up the situation, Lieutenant LIPPINCOTT rushed into the blistering fire and, with complete disregard for his personal safety took over the lead platoon. By displaying calm, forceful leadership, he inspired his men to move forward, ignoring the hail of fire, and close with the enemy. The foe became thoroughly disorganized at the determined advance and fled from their positions. Lieutenant LIPPINCOTT swiftly took note of their confused state, rallied his exhausted men and led them in pursuit of the enemy, continuously keeping pressure upon the fleeing troops. Through his courageous and inspirational leadership, the enemy was never given a chance to regroup and the battalion's mission was successfully completed. Lieutenant LIPPINCOTT's gallantry and conspicuous devotion to duty reflect great credit on himself and the military service..

Lieutenant John "Jack" Lippincott continued his military career and he retired from the United States Army as a full colonel on March 31, 1979.

We passed scenes along the road of total devastation-dead enemy soldiers, burned-out tanks, dead and bloating animals, artillery pieces pushed off the road into ditches, and tons of abandoned ammunition. Complete units of the enemy now fell pray to panic and virtually disintegrated.

At daybreak hours of October 11, all company officers were informed by Captain

Wadsworth that our present location, was approximately 25-30 miles behind enemy lines. He also gave us congratulations from Major John W. Callaway, our 2nd Battalion Commander, on our excellent battle performances at the Yesong River site and our drive northward to seize and secure the town of Paekch'on. There were many rumors that Lt. Col. William (Wild Bill) Harris, our 7th Cavalry Regimental Commander, even had a hot shower the previous night in the town of Paekch'on. Morale within our company was extremely high and complete defeat of the entire North Korean Army looked very immineny.

Orders then were received on October 11, at approximately 0900 hours, to immediately move out and proceed northward to the Hanpori-Kumchon area, to link up with the 3rd Battalion. Captain Wadsworth explained that our objective now was to establish a perimeter and cut off enemy troops as they attempted to escape northward. We were also informed that two enemy divisions were operating in that particular vicinity. The entire 1st Cavalry Division was now in quick pursuit to complete the encirclement of this enemy operation and retreat.

The 2nd Battalion was engaged in numerous battles at road blocks and various ambushes during October 12-13. In their attempt to escape, hundreds of North Korean soldiers were killed, wounded or captured on the rough, narrow winding roads. Many of the enemy straggled through the hills, broken, demoralized, shoeless and hungry. We overran their light defensive line of guns, vehicles and heavy equipment. At the 7th Cavalry Regiment roadblock at Hanpori bridge, an estimated 500 enemy was killed and 201 captured.

Enemy groups escaping from the Kumchon trap established many ambushes along the rough narrow roads. One such ambush took place as supply personnel were returning from Hanpori to Paekch'on for supplies. The 2nd Battalion would make a startling, agonizing revelation that would show the murderous caliber of the enemy they were fighting. One officer and four troopers lived through the ordeal and brought the tragic testimony to their comrades.

The following is an account of the north Korean atrocities on October 13, 1950, from Sergeant First Class Frederick C. Herrmann, Motor Pool Sergeant, Service Company, 2nd Battalion, 7th Cavalry Regiment.

In the early morning of October 13, 1950, many of the Service Company truck drivers were tired and exhausted from driving many long hours without getting the proper sleep. So I volunteered to drive a truck in the next supply convoy from our present location in the town of Paekch'on to the town of Hanpori. The rifle companies of the 2nd Battalion were located in that vicinity, which was our frontline.

However, within our area it was estimated that two North Korean divisions were cut off and might be attempting to flee or escape northward. At this particular time the 2nd Battalion had the enemy on the run and it was extremely difficult

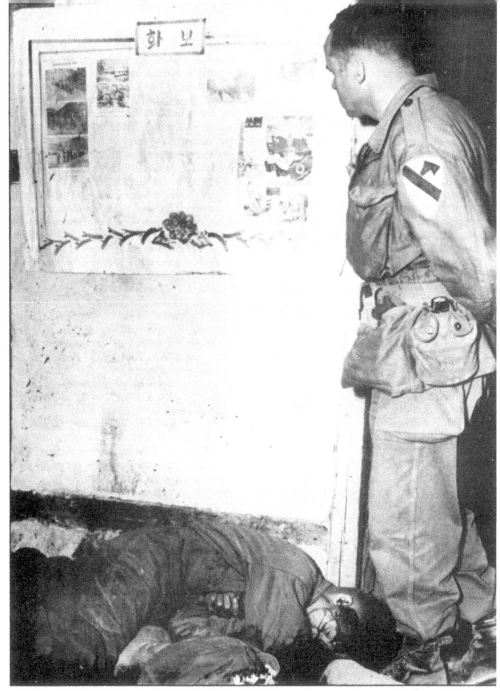

Major Brown of G-2 Intelligence, 1st Cavalry Division, as he investigates the Naede Murders. Note the spattered blood on the wall under the bulletin board. (U.S. Army photo; courtesy of Fred Herrmann)

for our supply trains to keep up with their constant movement. The roads throughout the area were rough, narrow and sometimes very congested due to the large numbers of destroyed enemy vehicles.

Our convoy trip to Hanpori went very well and all supply trucks arrived on schedule. It didn't take long for the trucks to be unloaded as Captain John Brewer, 2nd Battalion S-4, ordered us to return to the town of Paekch'on.

During the return trip, I had just made a comment to the gunner of the .50 caliber machine gun mounted on our truck, that it didn't seem like a war was going on in the area. Suddenly, enemy mortar rounds started landing on and near the road directly in front of us. Then North Korean soldiers appeared all over the place as we attempted to run the fire block. However, we were very soon forced to stop our trucks, and were immediately taken prisoner.

The enemy took our group of thirteen men,

including Captain Brewer, to a house for the evening. The enemy seemed to be very apprehensive of the situation. Just prior to dark, they started to talk with each other. I couldn't understand their language, but I would soon learn what they were talking about. They started shooting their automatic weapons as I saw one of my fellow comrades hit and fall near me. I immediately turned and dove under a nearby table for protection. I felt the pain as the bullets ripped through both of my legs. Many shots were fired as I lay there on the floor praying for my life.

Soon the North Koreans left the house, but I was afraid to say anything as I thought they might hear me and return. Throughout the night I lay on the floor just praying to God to help me get out of this horrible ordeal.

The next morning I soon discovered that the North Koreans had withdrawn during the night or early morning. Then I found out that five of us, including Captain Brewer, had miraculously survived the enemy atrocities. However, the eight others never survived and lay there in cold blood. Actually the enemy had left all of us for dead.

Captured enemy documents revealed that on October 14, the North Korean Premier and Commander in Chief, Kim Il Sung, issued an order to all troops of the North Korea Peoples' Army explaining the reasons for the army's defeat and outlining harsh measures for future army discipline. Alluding to the recent reverses, Kim Il Sung said; "Some of our officers have been cast into utter confusion by the new situation and have thrown away their weapons and left their positions without orders." He commanded; "Do not retreat one step further. Now we have no space in which to fall back." He further directed that all agitators and deserters be executed on the spot, irrespective of their positions in the Army. To carry out this order, he directed that division and unit commanders organize, by the following day, a special group, which he termed the "Supervising Army", its men to be recruited from those who had distinguished themselves in battle.

Then on October 14, an operations order was issued to the 7th Cavalry Regiment, which brought forth many cheers from everyone in Company H. Captain Wadsworth informed all company officers and enlisted men that the 2nd Battalion was selected to lead off the initial attack to seize the North Korean Captial — Pyongyang. To every officer and enlisted man within the 7th Cavalry Regiment, this particular mission was accepted as a great honor.

The following is an account of certain movements and various actions of the 2nd Battalion from October 2-15, from Sergeant Donald D. Down, assistant squad leader from the 3rd Platoon, Company F.

We were alerted on October 2, that the 2nd Battalion was going to be air lifted to the town of Suwon, to rejoin the rest of the 7th Cavalry Regiment. This air maneuver was accomplished on C119 transport planes, which were called "flying box cars".

After departing Teagu airport and once in the air, I had an opportunity to look down at the ground. Everything resembled the patch work of a quilt with many shapes and colors. The air trip didn't take too long and even the landing was pretty smooth. Upon leaving the plane, we quickly moved into an assembly area to wait for trucks and further orders. It didn't take the trucks too long to arrive to transport us to rejoin our regiment which was located near the town of Osan.

After a couple of days of cleaning weapons and rechecking equipment, we were ordered to saddle up and move out for the front line. As our convoy passed the capital city of Seoul, South Korea, it virtually lay in ruins from air strikes and artillery barrages. Near the outskirts of the city, I noticed two T-34 Russian tanks located on a very steep ridge overlooking the road. Both had been destroyed, but as we passed, I began to wonder how in the hell did the enemy get them into that totally impossible location.

Our truck convoy finally reached the Han River, but we eventually came to a stand still. We had to wait for a truck convoy of Marines who

were moving southward over the river on the pontoon bridge. Somehow certain comments betwen the Marines and our 2nd Battalion troopers got out of hand. At this point, a fist fight almost prevailed as Marine and 2nd Battalion officers moved up and down the convoy to stop the ridiculous arguing. Finally, terms were reached that each division was here to fight North Koreans and not each other. Myself, I thought it was pretty hilarious as our convoy started to move slowly across the pontoon bridge.

Our battalion was moved from an area near Kaesong on October 8 and ordered to proceed westward to the Yesong River. On October 9-10, we experienced extremely heavy fighting when we assaulted and crossed the partially destroyed bridge that spanned the Yesong River. Our objective was to secure the high ground and road on the west bank. This was the start of our drive to seize the town of Paekch'on.

At daybreak of October 10, we broke through the enemy blocking positions along the road leading to the town. With our fast sweeping movement and attack, the town of Paekch'on was secured around noon time by the 2nd Battalion. This northward drive would eventually take us across the 38th Parallel, and we all knew the North Koreans were in total defeat.

We had experienced a battle victory, but I was sort of depressed because in this drive my good friend and squad leader Sergeant Richard Cole, was killed. This vacant position moved me up to take over as squad leader. Seeing a close friend wounded you knew there was the possibility of seeing him again, once he recovered from his wounds. But in the case of one being killed in action, you knew then that you would never see them again. "Cole" was such a great person and soldier, and I knew that I would never see him again. However, such was the way and experiences of a combat trooper.

On October 11th, we continued to push across the 38th Parallel in pursuit of the enemy. From some of the small villages came North Korean stragglers as they attempted to surrender. Enemy defenses on the narrow road were light as our attack moved quickly through their positions. Around midnight we stopped to take up positions near a railroad station which was near the road. It was a restless night as the North Korean rearguard sent mortar barrages into our location.

The next morning we continued our northward attack for several days, cutting off the enemy soldiers as they tried to flee the encirclement of the 7th Cavalry Regiment. Hundreds of North Korean soldiers were killed or captured in our vicious assault on their positions. Word was passed on to everyone in Company F that the 2nd Battalion would continue their attack and seize the North Korean captial of Pyongyang. However, I would miss this part of the future attack and action, and the honor and glory of seeing the enemy defeated in their own captial city. I would receive wounds on October 15, which necessitated my evacuation and absence from the frontline for approximately ten days.

All company officers reviewed a map with Captain Wadsworth and our objective was to seize and secure the town of Namchonjon.

Then the 3rd Battalion would rapidly move through the 2nd Battalion, and continue northward to the town of Hwangju. However, as the 2nd Battalion attempted to advance and attack the town of Namchonjon from the south, fanatical enemy troops hit the advance column with heavy concentrations of mortar, automatic weapons, small arms and sniper fire. After several hours of intense fighting, we were ordered to hold back for the night and resume the attack the next morning. Sporadic enemy fire continued throughout the entire night.

Daybreak of October 15 brought forth air strikes of rockets and napalm bombs on enemy defensive positions near and in the town of Namchonjon. At approximately 0700 hours, the 2nd Battalion began their attack on the town from the south. After heavy fighting, the 2nd Battalion entered and secured the town prior to 1300 hours. The 2nd Battalion then continued its attack to secure the high terrain northwest of town. The 3rd Battalion quickly moved through the town, followed by the 1st Battalion and other units of the 7th Cavalry Regiment. In this attack on Namchonjon, the 2nd Battalion sustained 30 wounded and 10 killed.

Several North Korean prisoners who were interrogated said that the air strikes on Namchonjon during the morning had destroyed the 19th North Korean Division command post and killed the division Chief of Staff.

Every unit of the 2nd Battalion, combat and support alike, would know its moment of danger, of fear and death and glory. All would suffer more than others; but what each company, each platoon suffered, is a story in itself.

Men of the 2nd Battalion smiled and cheered as in any battle victory. You could see the individual determination of every officer and enlisted man to force himself on the enemy, and to punish the enemy for the crime of aggression and for starting the Korean War. Failure to let the 1st Cavalry Division cross the 38th Parallel no doubt would have made every officer and enlisted man within the division feel cheated. It was a feeling of revenge by chasing and killing an enemy that had chased and killed them earlier.

Now more than ever, I was extremely complacent that I had made the decision to return to my previous platoon and Company and to be an active participant in the military operations to completely annihilate the North Korean Army.

Meanwhile, on Sunday, October 15, when the Korean War looked very near the end, a group conferred on Wake Island. The conference was high level as President Harry Truman and General MacArthur discussed the rehibilitation of South and North Korea, both of which lay in ruins.

MacArthur told Truman that he expected an end to the Korean War around Thanksgiving. Truman then asked MacArthur, "What are the chances for Chinese or Soviet interventions?" MacArthur quickly replied, "Very little. And we are no longer fearful of their intervention. We no longer stand with hat in hand. The Chinese have no air force. If the Chinese try to get down to Pyongyong, there will be the greatest slaughter."

However, he went on to mention that the Chinese had 300,000 men in Manchuria, of which not more than 200,000 were along the Yalu River. Of these, not more than 60,000 could get across. But it was not what was said, but what was left unsaid that would change the course of the entire Korean War.

For the next couple of days, the 2nd Battalion continued on its northward objective to seize the capital city of Pyongyang. A link up was made with the 3rd Battalion near the town of Hwangju, as both battalions continued their attack toward the town of Hukkyori. Overall resistance from the enemy was light with sporadic sniper fire from enemy positions along the narrow road, which somewhat hampered the forward progress. Suddenly, from the outskirts of Hukkyori, enemy tank fire was received which put a halt to the forward elements of the 2nd Battalion.

During the evening darkness, various reports were being received over the SCR-300 radio from other elements of the 7th Cavalry Regiment. One such report indicated that between 2000 and 2500 North Korean soldiers were taken prisoner by the regiment. This encouraging news definitely helped the ego and morale of every trooper within the 2nd Battalion.

The rugged terrain of North Korea was actually no different than that of South Korea. The little roads around the area of Hwangju and Hukkyori in many instances resembled a cowpath. Men who have never walked the hills of Korea will never adequately understand that they were high and sometimes endless. In many circumstances there were no side roads, and no flat places anywhere where command posts, medical aid stations or anything else could be set up. The hills ran into each other; they overlapped; they blocked vision and hearing in every direction.

The weather in North Korea was getting cold and the rivers and creeks were half frozen. There was even light snow on the ground and the entire 1st Cavalry Division had yet to receive the appropriate winter clothing. In the coming weeks, the severe cold winter weather would take its toll on the United Nations Forces.

Yet morale in the 1st Cavalry Division was high. Most of the officers and enlisted men had heard rumors which were passed on that the city of Pyongyang was their final objective in the Korean War. Once the city was taken, the entire division would leave Korea. Practically everyone expected to eat Thanksgiving Dinner in Japan.

Daybreak of October 18 brought air strikes and artillery barrages on the enemy strongpoint at Hukkyori. The enemy positions were heavily defended with tanks, self-propelled guns and anti-aircraft weapons. However, when the 2nd Battalion attempted to resume its attack, the advance columns again experienced fierce enemy resistance. The air strikes and artillery barrages failed to dislodge the enemy from their positions.

In the late afternoon, Captain Wadsworth informed all company officers and squad leaders of the future plan of attack, which would include my platoon. However, due to the rugged terrain, the balance of Company H would remain in its present position. This decision was prompted because of the existing heavy weapons within our company. My platoon would move by foot with Companies E, F and G in a coordinated attack to outflank the strong enemy defenses during the night darkness. Our objective was to hit the enemy from the west flank and open the main road leading into Pyongyang.

Our discipline that had to be constantly enforced was overseeing the possibility of men discarding their equipment. In these very difficult and rugged hills, many men preferred to go light as possible. Proper discipline meant keeping a full bandoleer, a full canteen and extra hand grenades at all times. However, many men would discard their discipline and had to learn the hard way. All realized that if caught, there could be the possibility of a court-martial.

Many replacements had no stomach for Korea, either south or north. The older combat veteran had learned the hard way but many of them were gone. The law of combat is the disintegration and replacement of rifle companies and the pool from which replacements came from was the same that had furnished the first soldiers into Korea.

In the cold evening darkness of October 18, and 2nd Battalion began the forward attack with Companies E, F & G, and the 1st Platoon of Company H. As we departed from the assembly area, Captain Wadsworth came over to my platoon and said; "See you in Pyongyang, Lt. Daily!" I quickly replied; "Yes sir Captain, I'll be waiting for you!"

Again our objective was to outflank the enemy positions and seize the main road to Pyongyang. This attack was coordinated with the Regimental I & R Platoon, which had preceded us in the attack. Our movement was extremely difficult in the darkness and particularly over the endless rugged terrain. Several times we had to stop to recheck our compasses and map locations to verify the proper direction. This particular maneuver would take up approximately 10-15 miles through enemy-held territory.

Fortunately, very little enemy contact was made as we eventually came to a small stream. Small thin layers of ice had formed near the water's edge. Then word was received that the enemy was spotted across the stream and was in the process of digging in. According to scouts from the I & R Platoon, the enemy was estimated to be in full company strength. Orders were then passed on that we would quietly move away from this particular location and proceed back up stream. One important reason, we were told, was that the stream was too deep to cross in this area. Strangely, the enemy remained busy fortifying their defenses across the stream and never heard our movement to and from the area.

Moving back up stream, we came into contact with another scout from the I & R

Platoon. We were then told that a location was found where we could easily cross the stream with very little difficulty. Upon entering the stream we quickly discovered the water to be extremely cold, and the depth to be above our waist. Reaching the other side we immediately assembled and prepared for an attack. Again, scouts from the I & R Platoon notified us that an undetermined strength of enemy troops were dug in on the hill directly in front of us. On the other side of the hill was the main road leading into Pyongyang.

Company G was selected to make the assault and attack on the hill. I was ordered to take two squads from my platoon to support the rifle company attack. In this particular support attack, my two squads consisted of .30 caliber light machine guns. Suddenly and surprisingly, as Company G started its initial attack with fixed bayonets, the men began calling and screaming "GAR-RYOWEN", as they charged the hill. The enemy, being so surprised themselves, began to leave their positions and weapons and ran up and over the hill. Company G in hot pursuit, pushed forward to secure the hill as other elements supported the attack and continued on toward the main road to Pyongyang.

Through this dauntless display of bravery and successful attack, my two squads never had the opportunity to fire a single shot. Also in this brief skirmish with the enemy, there were no casualties within the battalion.

During the night and early morning hours, the 2nd Battalion, using an indirect route, had gone through approximately 12-14 miles of enemy held territory. Daylight was rapidly approaching as we proceeded to advance forward to secure the main road leading into Pyongyang.

Small pockets of enemy resistance were met as our battalion broke through their weak defenses along the main road. At daybreak we were informed to hold up on our advance and wait for further orders. At this time, I assembled my platoon adjacent to an apple orchard which ran parallel to the west side of the road. We would stay in this location and wait for Captain Wadsworth and the remainder of Company H to rejoin the regiment. A short distance up the road was our objective, the North Korean capital of Pyongyang.

From out of nowhere and from within the apple orchard, enemy stragglers, men, women, and children came running to us to hand over rifles, hand grenades, ammunition and other types of military equipment. I was completely astonished by this particular military and civilian behavior and could hardly believe my eyes. Just a couple of months prior, when I was a North Korean captive, I had remembered an extremely disciplined and devoted enemy soldier. Now I was witnessing a demoralized and defeated enemy soldier, with no pride or respect to fight any longer. To see this enemy defeat and surrender brought forth a feeling of satisfaction within my mind and soul.

Several of the enemy stragglers were shot

One of the finest hours as General Douglas MacArthur watches the invasion of Inchon from the bridge of the USS Mount McKinley. He is flanked by (from left) Vice Admiral A.D. Struble, Major General E.K. Wright, and Major General Edward M. Almond, X Corps Commander. September 15, 1950. (U.S. Navy photo)

down before actual identification could be made. Many troopers were not trigger happy, but had not forgotten the enemy and refugee problems that plagued the ranks during the previous hot summer battles in the vicinity of the Naktong River.

After leading the attack the majority of the way from Seoul, troopers of the 2nd Battalion watched in dismay as elements of the 1st Cavalry Division in a convoy of dusty tanks, trucks and jeeps went grinding by.

It didn't take long for the outcry of questions to come from the ranks of my platoon. "Lieutenant, what in the hell is going on here? Why did they hold up our battalion in the attack on Pyongyang? This is a damn bunch of bullshit!" Being somewhat puzzled myself, I didn't have an exact answer. Everyone in my platoon and I knew this included the entire battalion, that each trooper had prepared himself mentally not only for the attack, but the honor and glory of being first in Pyongyang. And I know this sentiment echoed throughout the entire 2nd Battalion.

Nevertheless, it would be another first for the 1st Cavalry Division as elements from Company F, 2nd Battalion, 5th Cavalry Regiment, under the leadership of 1st Lt. James H. Bell, entered the city of Pyongyang just after 11:00 hours on October 19.

With other elements from the 5th Cavalry Regiment, 7th Cavalry Regiment, Task Force Indianhead from the 2nd Infantry Division, and various other units, the city was finally under control of the United Nations Forces on October 20.

At daybreak on October 21, the 2nd Battalion, being held in reserve in the vicinity of Hukkyori, was alerted to saddle up and prepare to move out. Orders were issued to recheck all weapons, ammunition, and equipment for combat readiness. Captain Wadsworth informed all officers of Company H that we were going to the North Korean capital of Pyongyang to link up with other units of the regiment.

Near the outskirts of the city of Pyongyang, both sides of the rough dusty road were cluttered with destroyed enemy tanks and various pieces of military equipment. Several tanks were still smoldering inwardly and were discolored from heat and smoke. Numerous bloated bodies of dead enemy soldiers lay near the road side. Off to the right of the road I noticed three dead enemy soldiers still sitting upright in their heavy machine gun emplacement. Their lifeless bodies were bloated and their skin had turned a dark blue. Strangely, they appeared to be still alive and devotedly watching their rearguard position.

Arriving in Pyongyang our battalion went directly into an assembly area to receive further orders. I briefly looked at the partially devastated city, but from our location it appeared to me that many buildings were still standing and weren't totally destroyed by our air force.

In the assembly area all Company H officers and squad leaders were immediately informed and briefed on our future mission. Captain Wadsworth pointed out on a map that our next objective today would be the port city of Chinnampo. This city was located 35 miles southwest of Pyongyang and served as the port for the North Korean capital. He also told us that intelligence could not verify the estimated enemy strength defending the city.

Then Captain Wadsworth told us that the attack would be a fast movement assault on the main road leading into the city. He then informed us that we were being organized into a Battalion Combat Team (A Battalion or Regimental Combat Team is a temporary grouping of supporting forces of tanks, artillery, etc., with a battalion or regiment to accomplish a specific mission). In support of

the rifle companies, the majority of our company jeeps were equipped with .30 caliber light machine guns and 75-mm Recoiless Rifles.

By early afternoon, the 2nd Battalion Combat Team departed Pyongyang on its mission. In our rapid road movement only slight enemy resistance was received from futile rearguard action near the town of Kangso. After that brief skirmish, there was no further opposition from the enemy. As darkness fell upon us, orders were issued to turn on our vehicle headlights and proceed as fast as possible.

I personally rode in a jeep that had a .30 caliber machine gun mounted on a center support post. My first gunner was Corporal Robert Barnes, who really didn't have to fire a single shot. This of course, was my fastest trip through enemy held territory. We entered Chinnampo at 0130 hours as hundreds of cheering North Koreans lined each side of the road. Surprisingly, they were waving small South Korean flags and they seemed to be extremely happy to see us American soldiers. I still couldn't understand this type of civilian and military behavior in North Korea.

We quickly moved into an assembly area and I attempted to organize my platoon. Orders were issued for 100% alert within the battalion. Numerous men in the company were now complaining of being very cold. The North Korean weather was now going below the freezing level during the night. We still hadn't received the proper winter clothing yet.

By daybreak the rest of the regiment arrived to support the seize and search of Chinnampo for enemy stragglers, buildings and various other installations. In many of the buildings we found pictures of Stalin hanging on the walls and various articles and literature on communism. Hundreds of enemy soldiers came forward to surrender. Many began abandoning their equipment and running and others fled so fast they left hot food in headquarters buildings. Hundreds of the enemy had shucked their uniforms and tried to mingle within the general population only to fight later as guerrillas.

Our battalion moved to the outskirts of Chinnampo and October was coming to a close. We were being kept busy clearing the area of stragglers or groups of enemy soldiers and civilian sympathizers. Some elements of our regiment also assisted the Navy in clearing the harbor of mines.

The following is a brief story during the month of October 1950, from Sergeant First Class Harold Blanc, Communications Sergeant, Company H, 2nd Battalion, 7th Cavalry Regiment.

From one of the summer battles on the Naktong River, I had found a .45 caliber Thompson submachine gun on a dead North Korean soldier. At that time, the weapon was full of maggots from the decomposed body. However, with some hard work the weapon cleaned up very well and I was proud of my accomplishment.

After we secured the port city of Chinnampo, North Korea, our 2nd Battalion was placed in

Eighth Army reserve. One day, 2nd Lt. Ed Daily, approached me and asked to see my Thompson sub-machine gun. I could see from the look on his face that he really admired the weapon.

Then he looked at me and said; "Sergeant Blanc, this weapon isn't Army issue or regulation and furthermore you will have to turn it over to me." I quickly replied; "No way lieutenant am I turning this sub-machine gun over to you or anyone else! Major Mel Chandler gave me authorization a couple of months ago to keep the weapon. If you have any questions, it would be best that you see Major Chandler."

You could see that Lt. Daily didn't like my comments concerning the weapon. Then he said; "Okay Sergeant Blanc, for the time being you can keep the weapon, but I'm going to talk to Major Chandler about it." Then Lt. Daily and I saluted each other and he turned and headed for the 2nd Battalion Headquarters.

I saw Major Chandler the following day and I told him about Lt. Daily wanting my Thompson sub-machine gun. It was my understanding that Major Chandler told Lt. Daily that if he desired an automatic weapon like mine he would have to find one somewhere else.

Prior to my departure from Korea, Lt. Daily and I saw each other many times. Also, we continued to remain friends. However, there were no comments made in regard to my weapon. I know that Lt. Daily never did find a Thompson sub-machine gun, before he departed Korea.

Sergeant First Class Harold Blanc never remained in the Army and was honorably discharged in April 1952. Also, he had attained the rank of Master Sergeant and was one of the third youngest non-commissioned officers within the Army to hold such a rank.

Hot showers and food were frequent and most of us enjoyed the opportunity to rest and get a complete night of sleep. The rumors continued about the 1st Cavalry Division being pulled out of Korea and returned to duty in Tokyo. The end of the Korean War seemed very near and many within the 2nd Battalion thought for certain that we would have our Thanksgiving Dinner in Japan.

Early one afternoon, Major Chandler, the 2nd Battalion executive officer, was in our company area. We immediately saluted each other, then we shook each other's hand. He quickly asked me, "How are you doing, Lt. Daily?" I replied, "Fine sir." He then said, "You know what Lt. Daily, we have almost won this war and we're going to have one hell of a parade in Tokyo." I answered, "Yes sir, you're damn right we will." We saluted each other and he turned and departed or company area. However, little did each of us know at this particular time, that within a couple of days, the Chinese Communist Forces would eliminate this dream.

We were notified that Bob Hope, Jerry Calona, Marilyn Maxwell, Les Brown band and many others, were coming to Pyongyang to do a show for the Eighth Army troopers. I was very fortunate to attend along with many others from the 2nd Battalion. The show was excellent and was enjoyed by all. Everywhere I looked there were American soldiers, even on top of buildings and the high concrete fence that partially surrounded the complex. To all of us who saw the Bob Hope show that cold sunny day in late October, 1950, it was no doubt the greatest morale booster of all.

The Eighth Army operations in Korea looked excellent when Commanding General Walker, on October 25, was quoted as saying; "Everything is going just fine." Even in the United States the New York Times probably expressed the prevailing opinion there at this stage of the war when it stated editorially; "Except for unexpected developments along the frontiers of the penisula, we can now be easy in our minds as to the military outcome."

The successful attack of Task Force 777 and the drive northward from the Naktong River to the seizure of the North Korean capital of Pyongyang, brought great recognition to our regimental commander, Lt. Colonel William A. Harris. He had proven himself to be an excellent leader of the 7th Cavalry Regiment and the GARRYOWEN troopers. With an overcoat draped across his erect shoulders, a yellow scarf knotted around his neck and a walnut cane in his hand, he soon became a familiar figure on the frontlines. He even mounted a western horse saddle on the hood of his jeep, and from then on he was "Wild Bill" to his GARRYOWEN troopers.

Even though "Wild Bill" was known for his leadership and combat exploits, he was very considerate of his men. He called his troopers "son" and his officers by their first names. He fought the higher brass for everything he thought his men deserved — cigarettes, hot water, writing materials and various other supplies. When he came across the body of a GARRYOWEN trooper killed in combat, he was seen to weep openly and unashamed. He personally wrote a letter to the next of kin for each of his fellow troopers. Soon he would be facing the beginning of a new war which would be more tiring and vicious than the one supposedly just won.

All of us in the 2nd Battalion had high hopes that the full scale retreat of the North Korean People's Army would end the war. The final days of October were spent doing police call exercises, care and cleaning of equipment, and various other details, that in part were almost like garrison duty. The most popular assumption held within the 1st Cavalry Division was the capture of Pyongyang and Chinnampo. The rumor prevailed that these major assignments were the last for the Division and would be released from commitment in Korea. Also, the victorious troopers of the 1st Cavalry Division would have a "home coming" parade in Tokyo. This would be highlighted by everyone having a tailored OD uniform with gleaming Cavalry golden scarves. However, such was not to be the case.

On October 31, reports were circulated within our battalion that elements of the 1st Battalion, 7th Cavalry Regiment, were sent to assist units of the 5th Cavalry Regiment that met with unexpected strong enemy resistance. Further reports indicated they were engaged in combat with Chinese Communist Forces who had crossed the Yalu River into North Korea. Our morale was now being somewhat overshawdowed by such reports, but hopes of forthcoming peace still existed in our minds.

The following brief but somewhat humorous story, is from Colonel John W. Callaway, Commander, 2nd Battalion, 7th Cavalry Regiment.

After our race into North Korea in October 1950, the 2nd Battalion, 7th Cavalry Regiment found itself occupying the port of Chinnampo, North Korea. The Bank of Chosen building was selected as the 2nd Battalion Command Post. The vault in the bank was locked and we were intrigued as to what might be in that vault. Word was sent out through the companies to find out if there was someone who knew how to open safes. The response was negative, so we had to look for other alternatives.

When we were alerted to move to the north on the following day, we decided it was time for action. We had one of the men bring over a recoilless weapon and we fired it into the wall where the vault was located. The blast knocked out all of the glass windows in the building and did knock a small hole in the vault. We then had a few men with hammers and chisels enlarge the hole enough for a small man to climb through. Unfortunately, only seven telephones were found in the vault. I did hear later that US Navy units, which relieved us, did find a number of gold bars near Chinnampo in a cave overlooking the ocean.

The following is an account of the last few days of October, from Sergeant Donald D. Down, assistant squad leader from the 3rd Platoon, Company F.

On October 15th, when I was wounded in the vicinity of Hanpori - Namchonjon, I was sent to the evacuation hospital in Ascom City. After four days there, I was transferred to a hospital in Pusan, South Korea. Spending a brief seven days there, and being recovered from my wounds, I was released to return to my previous unit.

Prior to leaving Pusan, my old buddy, Sergeant Ralph Bernotas showed up and he had just returned from a hospital in Japan where he had recovered from previous wounds. He also was returning to his old unit, Company F. We left early that morning with a supply truck convoy which was going to the frontline area.

While riding on one of the trucks, I started to wonder what was in the bags that we were sitting on. A quick look revealed the newest type mountain sleeping bag. What a surprise! Needless to say, we kept warm the rest of the trip north. When we reached our destination, Bernotas and I made damn sure that each of us had a new sleeping bag before we departed the truck.

The next day, a group of soldiers were talking about going to see the Bob Hope show that was being held in Pyongyang. So Bernotas and I asked if we could go with them when they were ready to leave. Of course they welcomed us aboard, so within a short time we were on our way to Pyongyang.

When we arrived in Pyongyang, I never saw so many soldiers waiting to see the Bob Hope show. They were on top of buildings, trucks and various other vehicles, so they could see over the top of the large crowd. We mingled our way to a couple hundred feet from the stage. We even saw our Supply Sergeant, who had come to Pyongyang for supplies. In seeing the show and not reporting to Company F, we were actually A.W.O.L. Anyway, we really enjoyed the show and it helped our morale..

Well, we finally got back to Company F, and our platoon leader, 1st Lt. Joe Hickey, welcomed us back to the platoon and company. We were informed that we were in the port city of Chinnampo. Some of the men told me that they were on a detail with the Navy in removing sea mines from the harbor. There was the constant talk of our division being sent back to Japan. It was such a happy reunion being back with Company F, and throughout the 2nd Battalion, the morale was extremely high. However, this would be short lived a rumors on October 31st indicated that the Chinese Communist Forces had attacked units of the 5th Cavalry Regiment. This would eliminate our hopes of an early return to Japan. Also, this would mean the start of a new war and a different style of combat fighting.

The 2nd Battalion air transportability exercise to Sendai, Japan on February 22, 1950. This three day exercise proved to be valuable a few months later in the Korean War. (L. to r.) Brumagen, Cossich and Conlan. Both Cossich and Conlan were wounded in action on August 13, 1950. Brumagen was killed in action on September 6, 1950. (Courtesy of Don Down)

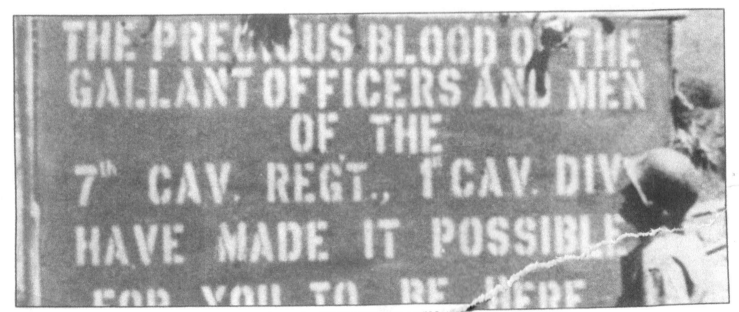

THE PRECIOUS BLOOD OF THE GALLANT OFFICERS AND MEN OF THE 7th CAV. REGT., 1 CAV. DIV. HAVE MADE IT POSSIBLE FOR YOU TO BE HERE

Compliments of the GARRYOWEN Regiment (U.S. Army photo)

Bob Hope and Marilyn Maxwell, doing a show for the Eighth Army Troops in the North Korean capital of Pyongyang on October 29, 1950. (Photo courtesy of Jim Harris, 70th Tank Battalion)

CHAPTER VIII
CHINESE INTERVENTION

...Water shapes its course according to the ground over which it flows; the soldier works out his victory in relation to the foe whom he is facing. Therefore just as water retains no constant shape, so in warfare there are no constant conditions...

Sun Tzu, The Art of War
(C.400-320 B.C.)

The beginning of a new war changed the future outlook of every man in the 1st Cavalry Division. Their jubilant expectations of a return to Japan would never come to reality. Many new handicaps would face the United Nations Forces, and winter clothing was not yet available. An overcast sky and occasional showers combined with freezing temperatures added to their discomfort. In the future days, weeks and months, many tough and bitter battles would have to be fought.

Just when and how did the Chinese Communist Forces come to Korea? The Chinese suddenly appeared in the Korean fighting near the end of October 1950. They had crossed the Yalu River from Manchuria during the period of October 13th to 20th. Keeping out of sight from aerial observation during the day and marching at night, they had reached their chosen positions approximately 50 air miles south of the Yalu River. Their line extended some 60 air miles from near Huich'on on the east to westward through Onjong and Unsan.

The Chinese had come into North Korea well fed and well clothed, and prepared to fight a winter war. The basic Chinese uniform was heavily quilted cotton usually of a mustard brown color that blended with the bleak North Korean landscape. The officers' uniforms differed only by the presence of vertical red piping on the trousers, on the left side of the jacket, around the collar, and diagonally across the sleeve cuff. Warm in dry weather, the quilted uniforms were impossible to dry when soaked. Beneath them the Chinese wore summer uniforms and any other clothing they happened to own. The cloth shoes were laceless and with rubber soles. Some also wore fur lined boots.

Forward elements of the 1st Cavalry Division had penetrated to within 35 miles of the Yalu River. The land of Korea is not sheltered by surrounding seas from the cold that sweeps the northern land mass of Asia. Korea is arctic when winter comes. In November 1950, the winter came early, blowing and screaming off the frozen Yalu River and Manchuria. The worst winter the land had seen in a decade.

On November 1st, Captain Wadsworth notified all Company H officers and squad leaders that we were going to be organized into a 2nd Battalion Combat Team. This operation would be called Task Force Allen - under the command of Brigadier General, Frank A. Allen, the assistant division com-

Refugee being searched and screened for safe passage. (Courtesy of Bob Mauger)

mander of the 1st Cavalry Division. Also we would be relieved of our duties at Chinnampo, by elements of the 187th Regimental Combat Team. By late afternoon, elements of our combat team departed Chinnampo.

This order definitely lowered the morale of many within the ranks of the 2nd Battalion. Every trooper sensed that the so-called Chinese Volunteer Forces were more than the remaining elements of the defeated North Korean People's Army.

Our 2nd Battalion Combat Team continued on northward, and we crossed the Chongch'on River early in the evening. At this point, we stopped to recheck our maps and to establish our actual location. Radio contact with other elements of Task Force Allen then clarified that we were to proceed further north to the town of Pakch'on. Once there, we would wait for further orders.

Still there were no actual reports concerning the Chinese or what was the outcome of their attack on the 5th Cavalry Regiment the previous day. As far as we knew, the 8th Cavalry Regiment was still in the vicinity of Unsan. So far, the advance elements of our combat team had made no contact with the enemy.

However, other disquieting events had already taken place in the afternoon of November 1st, in an area south of Unsan, and behind the 8th Cavalry Regiment. A combat patrol from Companies A and B, 1st Battalion, 5th Cavalry Regiment, had made contact with Chinese forces that held a position on the ridge extending across the road just south of the Turtle Head Bend of the Kuryong River. Therefore, the Chinese had set the stage for an attack that night against the 8th Cavalry Regiment in Unsan, and the ROK 15th Regiment, located northeast of the town.

Even though this book is primarily about the 2nd Battalion, 7th Cavalry Regiment, the author has included a brief story concerning the 5th Cavalry Regiment. The battle of "Bugle Hill" against Chinese Communist Forces, was located south of the Turtle Head Bend of the Kuryong River. This afternoon battle would be followed in the evening darkness by a massive Chinese assault and

eventual massacre of the 8th Cavalry Regiment, in the vicinity of Unsan.

The following is an account of the action of "Bugle Hill," from 2nd Lieutenant Alvin Storm, 1st Platoon Leader, Company B, 5th Cavalry Regiment. As previously mentioned in Chapter V of this book, Lieutenant Storm and the author were Battlefield Commissioned to 2nd Lieutenant, on August 10, 1950.

In the early afternoon of November 1st, Companies A & B, of the 5th Cavalry Regiment were ordered by Colonel Harold K. Johnson, 1st Battalion Commander, to send a combat patrol in search of the enemy. Also, we were supposed to make contact with elements of the 3rd Battalion, 8th Cavalry Regiment, which were positioned in the vicinity of Unsan.

I was the leader of the 1st Platoon, Company B, and I was ordered to be the point platoon. I directed a scout patrol squad to act as our platoon point. The rest of Companies A & B would follow our scouting mission.

After experiencing extremely rough terrain, we finally reached our destination at approximately 1500 hours. This was on a ridge just west of the Kuryong River. We stopped briefly to take a rest beak. At this particular time, we had made no contact with the enemy.

Completing our rest break, I then ordered my men to saddle up and proceed forward to the crest of the ridge. Previous orders still existed that Company A would move into position on our right flank and to the east of us, and Company B, to our left flank which was to the west of our location.

As my point squad started to move upward, I suddenly spotted movement on the ridge to the east. I could see numerous troops positioning machine guns. I quickly commented to the point squad leader, "How in the hell did Company A get ahead of us?" At that very moment automatic weapons and machine gun fire ripped into the entire platoon.

Now I could see vast numbers of troops moving across the entire skyline of the ridge, and the hail of fire seemed to be coming from all sides. Men were jumping and diving for possible concealment along the trees and in the shallow crevices of the ridge. Everyone continued to shout; "We're Company B! We're Company B!" Hold

Enemy soldier who died with his boots on. (Courtesy of Bob Mauger)

Chinese prisoners of war waiting for interrogation. (Courtesy of Bob Mauger)

your fire!" We still believed that Company A had erroneously moved ahead of our platoon.

Realizing that the fire was coming from enemy soldiers, I directed my radioman to immediately contact other elements of Companies A & B and inform them that we were under a severe attack. Casualties were depleting my platoon as we attempted to organize and return fire at the enemy. The overwhelming enemy fire was now forcing us to withdraw down the ridge.

Our withdrawal was not orderly as men were becoming scattered, and very few voices were answering. Some moved in groups of two or three as others retreated the best they could.

I moved with some of my men to a small draw for protection. Then suddenly, I saw Whitey, our company runner, and two other men move into our location. What a relief to my mind as I looked at Whitey, because I knew the rest of Company B had to be near. However, as I attempted to ask Whitey of our company location, he quickly replied, "Lieutenant sir, we've been hit by a massive attack from what they're saying is Chinese! Everyone had better shut up and prepare to pull back." As Whitey took off running, those of us remaining eventually worked our way down the ridge.

Moving to a nearby rice paddy, I attempted to organize the stragglers from my platoon. Of the wounded that were left behind, there was no way that I could possibly help them. Let alone even

reach them under the intensive fire from the enemy. Now with the few men left in my platoon, I knew that it was going to be a difficult task to set up defensive positions along the rice paddy dykes.

As darkness fell, the loud noise from the Chinese bugles and whistles echoed within the night. Enemy small arms, automatic weapons and mortars were devastating to our troops. Heavy fighting now existed within all ranks of Companies A & B.

Various colored flares lit up the dark night, as enemy mortar fire continued to hit our positions. Suddenly, I lost consciousness from a mortar round that landed very near my position. When I awoke, I was bleeding from a head wound, and I found myself in the hands of the Chinese.

Being a prisoner of war of the Chinese was a horrible experience. Each day I received a dirty ball of rice which they didn't want, and a little water that wasn't fit to drink. They attempted to indoctrinate us with Communist propaganda which I couldn't comprehend. Each day my health continued to fail because none of us received the proper medical treatment.

Then with the help and support of God, I was rescued in February 1951, by elements of Company B, 187th Regimental Combat Team. This elite unit made a successful parachute landing behind enemy lines and secured the compound where we were being kept prisoner. This unit was commanded by Major Mike (Iron Mike) Holland

and 1st Lieutenant Henry Franklin. Of the 26 prisoners who had been held, 21 were rescued by the combat team. Several days previously, five had escaped from the compound.

I never learned the fate of the other brave troopers in the battle of "Bugle Hill." After recuperating in a hospital in Japan, I volunteered to return to Company B, 5th Cavalry Regiment. Upon my arrival at my old unit in Korea, I quickly realized that I knew no one in Company B, or the 1st Platoon.

Later on in September 1951, I was seriously wounded in both of my legs from a Chinese hand grenade. After my evacuation, I was eventually transferred to the United States and medically discharged.

The early morning of November 2nd, our 2nd Battalion Combat Team was ordered to proceed northward to Yongsan-Dong. Our objective was to establish rear positions to cover the withdrawal of the 1st Cavalry Division. As we progressed on the rough, dusty road, we had no contact with the enemy. However, by afternoon the road became congested and clogged with vehicles from the 24th Infantry Division, which were traveling in the opposite direction. As we waited for the appropriate road clearance, rumors were being passed on to us that the 8th Cavalry Regiment was engaged in extremely heavy combat with Chinese Communist Forces. The majority in our combat team thought we would receive orders at any given time to rush to their support. However, those orders were never issued.

Through this congested mess on the road, and at times a very confusing operation, we didn't reach Yongsan-Dong until the early morning hours of November 3rd. By daybreak our combat team had arranged positions as directed for the withdrawal of the 1st Cavalry Division. Needless to say, these orders were to be changed the same day, and we would begin a withdrawal through Pakch'on to reestablish defensive rearguard positions. Now the rumors had it that the entire 8th Cavalry Regiment was completely surrounded by Chinese forces, and they had also suffered heavy casualties. These very grim reports were devastating to many of us. Just a few days prior, all of us thought the war was actually coming to a close.

The town of "Unsan" was destined to take its place in military records. As Colonel George A. Custer had met his defeat at the battle of the Little Big Horn, it had become a legend to the 7th Cavalry Regiment. Now the massacre of the 8th Cavalry Regiment at Unsan would become recorded in the history of the 1st Cavalry Division.

During this bitter and ferocious battle at Unsan from November 1st - 4th, the author cannot compute an accurate survey from records of this particular action. (However, a total of 1,481 personnel, of which over 1,000 were from the 8th Cavalry Regiment.) An actual breakdown of those wounded, killed or captured is not possible. Enemy sources indicated the Chinese captured between 200-300 men at Unsan. The principle officer casualties of the regiment included a battalion commander and most of his staff, five company commanders, two medical officers and one chaplain. Equipment losses were high, which included; 95 one-quarter ton trucks; 35 three-quarter ton trucks; 7 two and one-half ton trucks; 12 105-mm howitzers; 12 75-mm recoilless rifles and 11 tanks.

On November 3rd, the 8th Cavalry Regiment reported that it had only 45 percent of its authorized strength. The division G-4 considered the regiment inoperable until troops and equipment losses could be replaced. The Eighth Army Headquarters announced on November 5th that the 1st Cavalry Division would receive all the new replacements until further notice. For the next 12 days, the Eighth Army assigned 22 officers and 616 enlisted men as replacements to the 1st Cavalry Division. Most of them went to the 8th Cavalry Regiment.

The Chinese force that brought disaster to the 8th Cavalry Regiment at Unsan was the 116th Division of the Chinese 39th Army. Nevertheless, the tragedy at Unsan would have a great impact on every officer and enlisted man within the 1st Cavalry Division.

The 66th Army of the Chinese Peoples' Volunteer Army published a pamphlet entitled, "Primary Conclusions of Battle Experiences at Unsan." This captured enemy document was published approximately three weeks after the Unsan battle. It was taken from a Chinese prisoner by elements of the ROK 1st Division, on November 26th.

It revealed what the Chinese considered the strengths and weaknesses of the American forces based on their experience with the 8th Cavalry Regiment. The pamphlet said, "American soldiers when cut off from the rear ... abandon all their heavy weapons, leaving them all over the place and play opossum ... Their infantrymen are weak, afraid to die, and haven't the courage to attack or defend. They depend on their planes, tanks, and artillery. At the time, they are afraid of our fire power. They will cringe when, if on the advance, they hear firing. They are afraid to advance farther ... They specialize in day fighting. They are not familiar with night fighting or hand to hand combat ... If defeated, they have no orderly formation. Without the use of their mortars,

they become completely lost. They become dazed and completely demoralized...At Unsan they were surrounded for several days yet they did nothing. They are afraid when the rear is cut off. When transportation comes to a stand-still, the infantry loses the will to fight."

However, on the favorable side of the pamphlet it described in some detail the American method of making an attack and said:

"The coordinated action for mortars and tanks is an important factor ... Their firing instruments are highly powerful. Their artillery is very active ... Aircraft strafing and bombing of our transportation have become a great hazard to us ... Their transportation system is great ... Their infantry rate of fire is great and the long range of fire is still greater."

After analyzing the American's strengths and weaknesses, the Chinese set forth certain principles for future operations:

"As a main objective, one of the units must fight its way rapidly around the enemy and cut off their rear ... Route of attack must avoid highways and flat terrain in order to keep tanks and artillery from hindering the attack operations ... Night warfare in mountainous terrain must have a definite plan and liaison between platoon commands. Small leading patrol groups attack and then sound the bugle. A large number will at that time follow in column."

The Chinese summed up their viewpoint on the first phase of their intervention:

"Our 39th Army was the first expeditionary force ordered to hurry to the I-Ung-pong area of Unsan to relieve the North Korean Army and intercept the enemy advancing northwards at Unsan. We deployed our main force to encircle and annihilate the enemy, at Huich-on, Onjong and Chosan. At that time, we did not fully comprehend the tactical characteristics and combat strength of the enemy, and we lacked experience in mountain warfare. Moreover, we engaged the enemy (first in form of interdiction, then in that of attack) without sufficient preparation; yet the result was satisfactory."

The Chinese admitted they did not have an effective weapon against the American

tank, but said that 20-pound TNT charges placed on the tracks or under the tank would disable it. Anti-tank sections consisted of four men carrying two 20-pound and two 5-pound charges.

Undoubtedly, the Chinese were brave, tough and excellent soldiers, who followed a simple tactical doctrine which was expressed thus: "If the enemy attacks we defend. If his attack is too strong we withdraw. When he is tired, we attack. When he withdraws, we pursue and kill."

On November 4th, we had established a defensive rear guard position near the town of Yongbong-ni with orders to move within an hour's notice. Our 2nd Battalion Combat Team still had no contact with enemy forces. Orders were issued in the careful screening of all refugees that were attempting to flee southward. Various reports from within the regiment indicated that numerous captured Chinese prisoners were wearing fur lined boots. To many of us, there was no question that the Chinese were well prepared for a winter war.

For the next several days, we continued to withdraw and finally established defensive positions on the south bank of the Chong-chon River. Our 2nd Battalion Combat Team reverted back to the control of the 7th Cavalry Regiment. A new term on orders had emerged from the Eighth Army, which was classified as "Strategic Withdrawal." To many of us in the 2nd Battalion, this new term wasn't totally understood. Some thought we were being defeated by the Chinese, while others thought we were establishing positions that were advantageous to the 1st Cavalry Division.

Combat patrols from our company and battalion were sent daily across the river and proceeded northward into enemy territory approximately two to three miles. Troopers from the 8th Cavalry Regiment were still being encountered as they attempted to reach positions of the 7th Cavalry Regiment. All were suffering from exposure, lack of food and water and requiring immediate medical attention. Many civilians within the small villages were reporting that a group of Chinese horse cavalry were seen and possibly operating in the area.

During an afternoon combat patrol on November 9th, we had just recently entered a small village to seek and search, and possibly obtain information. With a usual interpreter we were able to converse with several friendly civilians and were assured of no enemy troops within the immediate area. However, Sergeant Tom Simmons, a squad leader from my platoon said that a particular civilian with an A-frame on his back was acting sort of strange. As Sergeant Simmons pointed to him he suddenly turned and started walking northward down the road. The interpreter then called to him to stop, but he quickly broke-out in a run. Sergeant Simmons, the interpreter and myself rapidly brought our M-1 rifles up in position to fire. Firing our weapons almost simultaneously, we dropped the civilian in his tracks.

Upon investigation of the civilian, he was

Roads were always clogged with refugees. (Courtesy of Bob Mauger)

found to have two wooden box type land mines strapped on the A-frame. According to the interpreter, the papers that he was carrying indicated that he was a North Korean soldier working with the Chinese forces. The interpreter then looked at us briefly and each of us acknowledged how lucky we were that we didn't hit one of the land mines on the A-frame, which no doubt would have triggered a dual explosion.

During the evening of November 10th, Captain Wadsworth had just returned from Headquarters, 2nd Battalion. Immediately, all company officers were briefed on the future plan of attack on the 7th Cavalry Regiment. Again the 2nd Battalion was selected to lead the attack across the river and proceed northward toward the town of Yongbyon. This town was approximately eight miles from our present location, and it was classified as the "walled city."

The morning of November 11th, we departed our positions on the Chongchon River to begin our attack to the north. For the next several days, our battalion virtually had no contact with the enemy. Our radio contact with other elements of the 7th Cavalry Regiment somewhat indicated that the Chinese forces had withdrawn to the Yalu River.

However, some of our patrols were receiving reports from various civilians in some of the villages that American prisoners had been there just a few hours earlier. Needless to say, this sad and unfortunate news revealed that they were held by Chinese forces, and they had been taken north toward the Yalu River. We assumed that many of the prisoners were from the 8th Cavalry Regiment.

The temperature was making it almost impossible to dig a foxhole, because the ground was frozen 12 to 18 inches down. To dig a hole was prolonged agony with numb hands. Nonetheless, each man had to dig his shelter and then lie shivering in it while waiting for an enemy attack. Feet and hands quickly turned white with frostbite. We carried dry socks next to our bellies to keep them warm and dry. Everyone was instructed to try and remember to change them every few hours. Water froze solid in canteens and our c-rations froze in their cans. Some men attempted to eat the frozen food only later to discover severe stomach pain from gastrointestinal distress. Many ate snow for moisture.

The temperature also created a severe problem with vehicles and equipment. Once a vehicle stopped it would hardly run again. To prevent vehicle gasoline lines and carburetors from freezing it was necessary to mix alcohol or alcohol-base antifreeze with gasoline. The heavy water-cooled .30 caliber machine guns in my platoon, required an alcohol-base antifreeze to prevent a frozen water jacket. The use of oil on weapons had to be carefully watched because many automatic weapons would fire but one shot at a time.

On November 14th, elements of the 3rd Battalion, 7th Cavalry Regiment, secured the town of Yongbyon and our 2nd Battalion consolidated to the left flank of the town and of the regiment. On the six foot concrete wall which surrounded the town of Yongbyon, we couldn't miss seeing the large white lettering that had been painted by the Chinese forces, which read in part, "Yankee go home, why fight this war for the Wall Street war mongers."

During the entire next week, patrolling continued northward and small groups of enemy were met and quickly overcome. Within the week of combat patrols, I had noticed from the observation with my binoculars that the enemy was building up a line and a screen of outposts in an area approximately five miles north of Yongbyon. However, interrogation of prisoners could not confirm a massive buildup, but reports did stipulate that Chinese forces were still coming into North Korea from Manchuria. The expected large enemy attack after the Unsan massacre did not come against the 1st Cavalry Division.

Late in the evening of November 20th, I was ordered by Captain Wadsworth to quickly assemble a light machine gun section from my platoon. Also, I was directed to take a 75-mm recoilless rifle section from the 2nd platoon, along on the combat patrol. The objective of this reinforced combat patrol was to give withdrawal support for elements of Companies L and M of the 3rd Battalion, 7th Cavalry Regiment. They were under heavy fire from the enemy, but of unknown strength.

Reaching our objective, we immediately employed light machine gun and 75-mm recoilless rifle fire against the enemy. I estimated the enemy to be of patrol size which quickly dispersed and fled from their positions. Securing a rearguard position for the elements of the 3rd Battalion, we remained as guard of the point area for the balance of the night. Our reinforced combat patrol suffered no casualties during this brief skirmish with the enemy.

During November 20 - 22nd, the 7th Cavalry Regiment had secured all of the surrounding high ground north of Yongbyon. Within this period many stragglers from the 8th Cavalry Regiment ambush at Unsan came into the regimental perimeter. Many were released by the Chinese as a propaganda gesture. Our extended patrolling greatly assisted these fortunate returnees. The constant fluid situation of patrolling and occasional light contacts with the enemy remained during our stay in this particular area.

Elements of the 25th Infantry Division took over our positions, and the 1st Cavalry Division went into Eighth Army reserve. It was difficult to realize that through various events, Thanksgiving Day was at hand. The many cooks within the 2nd Battalion were busy with Quartermaster personnel planning and preparing for the traditional big meal. The beautiful and delicious Thanksgiving meal with all the trimmings was enjoyed by all units of the 7th Cavalry Regiment. Also Colonel William Harris, the regimental commander, visited each company to extend his personal Thanksgiving Day greetings.

The 7th Cavalry Regiment was assembled in the vicinity of Kunu-ri, and had established a blocking position as a reserve area mission. During this reserve period, the long awaited winter clothes were distributed. Each man in the 2nd Battalion took heart to the much needed clothing, and they also knew they would be better prepared for the severest part of the winter.

On November 26, a regimental review was held for the purpose of awarding decorations for valor, and a special remembrance of those who had given their lives in Korea. Since our arrival in Korea, this was the first such awards ceremony. Each man that was to receive an award was given a yellow scarf prior to the ceremony to wear around his neck. This definitely highlighted the occasion. It gave Colonel William Harris, regimental commander of the 7th Cavalry Regiment, the first opportunity to speak and pay tribute to all GARRYOWEN troopers.

The awards were made by Major General Hobart Gay, commanding general of the 1st Cavalry Division. It was an extremely proud moment for me as I was awarded the Distinguished Service Cross for extraordinary heroism and the Bronze Star for valor. The Chaplain read the Twenty Third Psalm, followed

Homeless Orphans. (Courtesy of Bob Mauger)

by a brief period of silence for the honored dead. The same Psalm, which as a prisoner of the North Koreans during the past summer, I could only remember, "The Lord is my shepherd, I shall not want." I could not hold back the tears flowing from my eyes as I personally thanked God for his support and guidance within my military life.

I noticed many troopers within the ranks, their bodies began to shake or quiver as the monotones of taps from the bugler echoed throughout the North Korean hills; and as the Chaplain read the names of the men receiving posthumous awards. Many of us had brief thoughts and memories of those comrades and friends who were killed in previous battles.

After the awards ceremony concluded, we returned to our individual units. However, we were quickly informed to saddle up and the 2nd Battalion moved to the vicinity of Pukchang-ni. This was to guard the east flank of the Eighth Army and maintain close contact with the 6th ROK Division. I remember this particular South Korean division during our previous summer battles near the Naktong River. At that time, they were an excellent fighting unit. However, radio contact revealed that they were disorganized due to continuous heavy enemy attacks. We established road blocks for an orderly withdrawal of this particular division, including all refugees.

Early on the morning of November 29th, the defense perimeter of the 2nd Battalion came under attack. The Chinese Communist Forces were attempting to push through the gap left vacant by the disorganized 6th ROK Division. The conglomeration of ROK soldiers, refugees and enemy soldiers posing as refugees further added to the confusion of the total 7th Cavalry Regiment perimeter. Further confusing the situation, other enemy elements were approaching from the flanks.

Very near the road block, I had a machine gun section from my platoon which had established .30 cal., light machine positions along both sides of the road. Suddenly within the movement of the refugees and elements of the 6th ROK Division, a fire fight devel-

oped. It was difficult to issue a fire order due to the massive confusion as the 2nd Battalion troopers came under attack. Within two hours the attack was repulsed, and proper order was restored with reorganizing troops of the 6th ROK Division and sending refugees to the rear. During this brief attack, 1st Lt. John E. Sheehan, commanding Company E, was killed by a refugee who carried a rifle under his loose civilian clothing. Also, five other troopers were wounded by enemy small arms fire in this attempted road block break through.

In the early afternoon, orders were received from Headquarters, 7th Cavalry Regiment, that the 2nd Battalion had to establish a blocking position on the main road leading into the town of Sinchang-ni. According to our company commander Captain John Wadsworth, elements of the 19th Regiment, 6th ROK Division were supposed to withdraw through our sector of the road block.

After reaching our designated area, Captain Wadsworth immediately issued orders to me that a section of light and heavy machine guns from my platoon would give support to Company F. Also I was to contact Captain Arthur Truxall, commanding officer of Company F.

Company F had established a roadblock position on the main road and their line of defense extended further to the left flank. Extending further to the left flank with defensive positions were Companies E & G. The Command Post of Company F was located to the right of the main road. Also, to the right flank of the main road was Company C, 1st Battalion, 7th Cavalry Regiment.

Just prior to dark, Sergeant Tom Simmons assured me that appropriate machine gun emplacements had been established at a forward outpost and at the main blocking position on the road. This information was passed on to the Command Post of Company F, and their commanding officer, Captain Arthur Truxall. The captain and I saluted each other as I quickly departed the tent, to report to the command post of Company H.

The command post of Company H was

located just off the main road and north of Sinchang-ni. Upon my arrival, I greeted Captain Wadsworth with a quick hand salute. His face expressed a sad and worried look. He spoke very quickly, "Ed, we have been informed that a Chinese Communist division has moved southward and is located in the vicinity of our battalion. A large scale enemy attack is imminent and we must do everything possible to hold our positions! Whatever you do, keep in close radio contact with me and other elements of our battalion! Yes sir"! I gave Captain Wadsworth a hand salute, then I turned and left the tent.

Waiting outside of Company H Command Post tent was an assigned driver and jeep which had an SCR-300 radio mounted in the rear of the vehicle. This particular type radio was excellent for communications within our company and other support units of the 2nd Battalion. With no headlights turned on the jeep, the moonlit night however did give enough light to see as we drove slowly on the road to return to the established blocking position.

I was starting to feel apprehensive to the future attack by the so-called Chinese Communist Forces. Previous rumors indicated they were an excellent fighting soldier. From our brief skirmish earlier in the morning, it really didn't give me an exact opinion of their fighting ability. Nevertheless, what they did to the 8th Cavalry Regiment during the Unsan battle of November 1-4 still plagued the mind of every trooper in the 7th Cavalry.

The officers and troopers of the 7th Cavalry Regiment were tough minded because our discipline was extremely tight. Many had experienced fierce battles which had given them that indefinable emotions of a fighting man for his company, battalion and regiment. Again the story of one platoon, one company and one regiment, tells the story of all. Before the night passed, the entire 7th Cavalry Regiment would be deep in crisis.

Just prior to stopping at the road blocking position, sporadic small arms fire was starting to come from our forward outpost position. I informed the driver to stop the jeep very near the left edge of the road.

First Chinese prisoners. Some of them were possibly within the attacking enemy forces that brought devastation to the 8th Cavalry Regiment during the Unsan battle on November 1-4, 1950. (U.S. Army photo)

1st Cavalry Division trooper looking at dead Chinese soldier who was carrying an American novel, "Died in the Wool." (U.S. Army photo)

Suddenly eerie sounds echoed within the night darkness and North Korean hills. Sounds which I had never heard before. Bugles racketed along with the eerie sounds of whistles. Purple flares roared high in the sky and then popped. Then green tracers from enemy weapons zigged within the various hill sides. Enemy mortars fell and were bursting among our various defensive positions. The Chinese did not scream or shout like the North Korean soldiers.

I quickly exited the jeep to use the radio which was mounted at the rear of the vehicle. My radio contact was brief with our forward elements and outpost. They indicated that Chinese troops were seen on the road, and they were now penetrating our right flank. It was approximately 2100 hours, and the fierce battle began to rage on the ourskirts of Sinchang-ni. Radio reports indicated that some of the Chinese were speaking English.

As I attempted to clarify a somewhat confusing report, an enemy mortar round exploded on the road, very near the rear of the jeep where I was standing. The explosion blew me into the frozen ditch along the road side.

Shaken up from concussion, shrapnel wounds and a fractured left forearm, I managed to move back to the edge of the road. The driver of the jeep was laying on the road, very near the jeep. I ran to his aid, but he was already dead from a severe shrapnel wound. The rear of his skull had been practically blown away by the mortar explosion. I looked around for my rifle, but I couldn't find it. Then a quick check of the SCR-300 radio also revealed that it had been damaged by the mortar explosion.

My left forearm was afire with pain. I carried my .45 caliber pistol in my right hand. I now managed to move along the ditch toward one of my light machine gun emplacements near the road. Within the confusion, many troopers were firing at moving shadows to the right flank. Sometimes there was silhouetting, but there wasn't enough light to reveal the Chinese movement.

Suddenly I came into contact with First Sergeant Bob Earley of Company H. He informed me that Captain Wadsworth was trying to contact me by radio for machine gun support, which at the time was desperately needed. He then told me that possibly an entire Chinese division had us surrounded, and they were attacking the town of Sinchang-ni which was located directly down the road behind us.

Sergeant Earley and I managed to move along the frozen ditch toward our light machine gun emplacements. Our objective was to reorganize the machine gun section, and attempt to consolidate the perimeter and our right flank. Then we came into contact with Corporal Mack Bentley, a .30 caliber machine gunner from my platoon and we directed him to give fire support to the right flank.

The Chinese in their quilted jackets overran our forward outpost position, and they deeply penetrated our right flank. Now close-in fighting raged all over the road and nearby hills. The Chinese were stumbling over their own dead as they continued their attack.

It was now 2200 hours as we attempted to give machine gun fire support to elements of Company C, 1st Battalion. Their withdrawal of the right flank was in a desperate attempt to establish a defensive line. Shortly after this brief order, all radio communication within the 2nd Battalion was lost.

After a listless day of combat, every officer and trooper within the 7th Cavalry Regiment was tired, frozen and weakened from the severe cold. Now my left forearm was giving me severe pain, as First Sergeant Bob Earley commented that I should seek immediate medical attention. However, it was now questionable between the two of us, if I could even make it back to the 2nd Battalion medical aid station. It was then decided that he would take charge of my platoon, and he would also notify Captain Wadsworth of the situation. As I departed, Sergeant Earley and myself wished each other the very best.

I could not believe what my eyes were seeing as I continued to move along the edge of the road toward Sinchang-ni. Dead and wounded Chinese soldiers were scattered like dominoes along the road side. Within the darkness, I could hear the outcry of the enemy wounded.

From the sporadic small arms and automatic weapons fire that was coming from all directions, I started to become somewhat frightened. Not of being shot or killed, but the possibility of being captured by Chinese Communist Forces. I definitely made up my mind that this wouldn't happen to me again. I firmly clutched the .45 caliber pistol in my right hand, as I moved forward and toward the 2nd Battalion aid station.

Reaching the 2nd Battalion medical aid station, I was quickly processed by Captain John C. Rourke, 2nd Battalion Surgeon. However, my left forearm wasn't set or put in a cast at this particular time. This was because the battle was being fought very near and even in the street. An orderly attempt was being made to evacuate the entire medical aid station. Under the existing circumstances of an on-going fierce battle, the brave officers and troopers of the 2nd Battalion Medical Aid Company performed admirably.

Many of the wounded, including myself, were loaded on a 2-1/2 ton truck and transported to the 121st Evacuation Hospital in Ascom City. The truck ride was rough, dusty and dirty. This particular hospital was located very near the capital city of Seoul, South Korea. Immediately numerous x-rays were taken, and finally my left forearm was set and put in a cast.

The following day, I was then taken with many others to a railroad station where we were put on a special personnel train for the wounded and transported south to the port city of Pusan. Once there, I would receive treatment and care at a Swedish Hospital which had been established under provisions of the United Nations Forces. The nurses were beautiful, and they did an excellent job in attending to all of the wounded personnel. For the next five weeks, I would remain there recuperating from my wounds.

American and United Nations troops recently captured, begin their long journey into North Korea and to the Prisoner of War camps. Many would end up in Death Valley, where hundreds would die from starvation and exposure to the extreme cold weather conditions. (Chinese People's Committee for World Peace)

Li Chiang-yuan of the Chinese People's Volunteers, studies orders on the treatment of war prisoners. (Chinese People's Committee for World Peace)

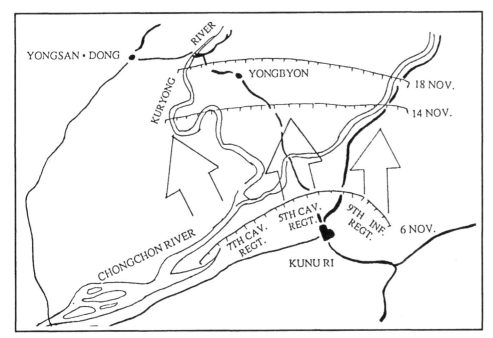

The Chongchon River Line - When the Reds failed to follow up their overwhelming attack against the 8th Cavalry Regiment, the 1st Cavalry Division occupied a defense line behind the Chongchon River. In mid-November, the Division advanced northward as far as Yongbyon meeting very little enemy opposition.

The following is an account of the action of Sinchang-ni on November 29th-30th from Colonel (then Lt. Colonel), John W. Callaway, Battalion Commander, 2nd Battalion, 7th Cavalry Regiment.

In the year that I spent in Korea, August, 1950 - July, 1951, the second most strategic battle in which the 2nd Battalion, 7th Cavalry was engaged was a defensive one at Sinchang-ni, North Korea. The massive Chinese offensive into North Korea had overrun Eighth Army's east flank and the Chinese forces were moving rapidly down the center of the peninsula having moved south of Eighth Army forces and threatened to trap the Army. At this time, the 7th Cavalry Regiment which was in reserve was ordered to move Southeast to block the Chinese forces at Sinchang-ni, a critical road junction, to permit the withdrawal of Eighth Army. The 2nd Battalion was ordered to defend the main avenue of approach. The front line companies were on a small ridge with F Company extending across the road leading from Pukchang-ni to Sinchang-ni, tying its right flank to the left flank of Company C on the side of a hill where Company C had its defensive position.

During the afternoon, word was received from observation aircraft of thousands of enemy troops moving into an assembly area a few miles northeast of our positions. I have often wondered why our combat aircraft did not engage these columns. An explanation was that all available aircraft were striking targets elsewhere. One of the mistakes we made here was moving our platoon of tanks up with F Company. In those days, tanks were very vulnerable at night in the front lines. That night two of our tanks were knocked out.

Shortly after dark, the enemy struck the 1st Battalion on our right. When word was received of the enemy attacks, we began firing all division artillery and walking it from our front lines up the valley along the road to its maximum range. VT fuses were used which accounted for many additional enemy casualties. The artillery fired throughout the night. Word was received from

Company F that the enemy had attacked. No word was heard from the company after that. Our Command Post was in a cottage in the northern edge of the village about 1000 yards behind the front lines. The 2nd Battalion Aid Station with Captain John Rourke in charge was in another cottage next to the CP.

Realizing that F Company had been overrun, I began organizing a second line of defense about 100 yards north of the Battalion CP. A tank that had come to the rear was turned around to assist in the defense. Several machine guns were added to this line and stragglers plus men from the 2nd Battalion headquarters company formed this line.

Suddenly we saw a column of men walking down the road about a hundred yards away. I ordered one of the men next to me to challenge the column. He called out, "Are you GI?" With that a bugle from the column sounded. This was a signal for our troops to commence fire. After a few seconds I ordered "Cease fire," and there was a not a sound from this enemy column.

Since we had a rather strong position, we simply remained where we were. Word came from regiment to move the CP and the aid station to the rear. I went into the aid station which was full of casualties and told Captain Rourke that he needed to move the aid station to the rear. I shall never forget that confrontation. He was angry and frustrated and told me in no uncertain terms that he did not intend to leave the wounded behind. He was able, through a great deal of initiative, to get the wounded to the rear and move his aid station back.

About this time, I received a call from the regiment to counterattack and return to the front lines where F Company had been. This didn't make sense to me so I explained that we were in a strong defensive position and should remain where we were. The regimental S-3 hung up the phone and soon it rang again. Colonel Harris, the regimental commander, ordered me to counterattack. He stated that the 1st Battalion CP had been overrun, and he had lost contact with the Battal-

ion Commander. He wanted us to get back to the original front lines so he could find out what had happened to the 1st Battalion Commander.

Leaving the tank and heavy machine guns behind, I ordered the foot soldiers to counterattack by conducting marching fire and return to the F Company positions. There was little opposition, and we moved back to the original front lines and remained there until daylight. This was probably the first counterattack against the Chinese since they had come into the war.

The enemy had been stopped cold and had suffered heavy casualties. The number of enemy dead in the column which we fired on was 76. Incidentally, one of the men picked up the bugle that was blown that night and gave it to me as a souvenir. Known enemy casualties within the regimental perimeter were 350. Air observers estimated that enemy casualties killed by artillery fire outside the perimeter numbered more than 1250. General Walker, Commanding General, Eighth Army, later stated that this action by the regiment not only inflicted severe casualties on the enemy, but gained Eighth Army at least four days of valuable time and was a major factor in preventing the encirclement of United Nations Forces. The losses suffered by the 7th Cavalry Regiment were 38 killed, 107 wounded and 11 missing in action. Of the missing in action from F Company, three were captured by the enemy and returned home after the war.

The following is an account of the action of Sinchang-ni on November 19th-30th, 1950, from Captain John C. Rourke, Battalion Surgeon for the 2nd Battalion, 7th Cavalry Regiment.

My memory of that night is vivid and enduring. The time element between 2100 hours of November 29 through 0400 hours on November 30 was some of the most intensely busy and frantic hours of my military service as a Battalion Surgeon.

The Chinese Communists attacked in force at 2100 hours and very quickly proceeded to overrun the 1st Battalion Command Post and Aid Station. My 2nd Battalion Aid Station was located in a small house on the edge of town and very near the enemy assault. It was an actual collecting point for all wounded personnel from both battalions.

Because of the rapid advances of the forward elements of the enemy assault, we were being endangered with the possibility of the enemy overrunning our aid station. We were quickly overwhelmed with a number of wounded, and many of them were very serious. The Chinese attack penetrated to within the edge of the town and only yards away from my aid station.

Fortunately the 2nd Battalion Headquarters Company under the direction of Lt. Colonel John W. Callaway, 2nd Battalion Commander, expediently set-up an interior defense line at the edge of the town to repel the attacking enemy forces.

Many personnel were directed to immediately establish defensive positions very near my aid station. A heavy .50 caliber machine gun and two other .30 caliber light machine guns were deployed to stop the advance of the enemy column. The Chinese trust was stopped and most of their forward point elements were destroyed. However, intense firing from the interior block by the 2nd Battalion forces continued for many hours.

Sporadic small arms fire from within the town of Sinchang-ni could be heard throughout the night. This indicated that small numbers of the Chinese had actually reached the town.

Immediate organizational plans for operating the aid station was to receive and examine and decide on urgency of treatment of each wounded as he arrived at the front door of the small house. The doors and windows of the house had been covered with Army blankets to black out the inside. There was no furniture, no electric lights or lanterns so we had to make use of hand held flashlights. Many numbers of the seriously wounded were treated with control of external bleeding and given morphine for the relief of pain as necessary. They were then bundled in blankets on a stretcher to keep them as warm as possible. They were immediately transferred to the back rooms of the house for further processing.

Fortunately the house was as warm as toast because of its design, where a fire in the ground level of the kitchen had converted hot heat beneath the floor of the house for warmth. This was a very useful thing because it prevented shock patients from getting worse by chilling.

The outside temperature was bitter cold and estimated to be about zero degrees. The night was unusually bright and clear with little wind blowing. There was a very bright moonlight that enabled us to see better than normal at this particular time and hour.

Those wounded who might be called "walking wounded" or "ambulatory" with wounds in the extremities or wounds that allowed them to get out on their own, were treated as quickly as possible with appropriate dressings and immobilization of the wounded part. However, it was decided not to give them much for relief of pain in order not to convert an ambulatory soldier into a drugged or sleeping one who would then be incapable of moving on his own accord. The prime reason for this was just in case the aid station was overrun.

As the numbers mounted, my aid station team was divided into an ambulatory group to take the numerous walking wounded out into a deep frozen ditch, which was located behind the house and ran parallel to the road. This task was done after the necessary treatment was completed by the doctor. This was necessary because there was not enough space in the small house, and we could disburse the wounded in the event of mortar fire. Furthermore, it allowed them the opportunity to take care of themselves in the event we were overwhelmed by the enemy.

One of the biggest problems was the lack of transportation because the aid station was supplied with four jeeps, and each one was equipped with two litters to carry the more seriously wounded to the rear area. These rapidly filled vehicles, sometimes had the ambulatory wounded riding the hood or holding on anyway possible to accompany the seriously wounded for further medical treatment.

It was not known at the time if any enemy roadblocks or patrols existed at the rear where the jeeps had to travel. Our medical clearing station was approximately two or three miles to the rear. The many trips that were required to transport the wounded became extremely long after the first rush. The vehicle shortage became critical and soon there were no jeeps available from my aid

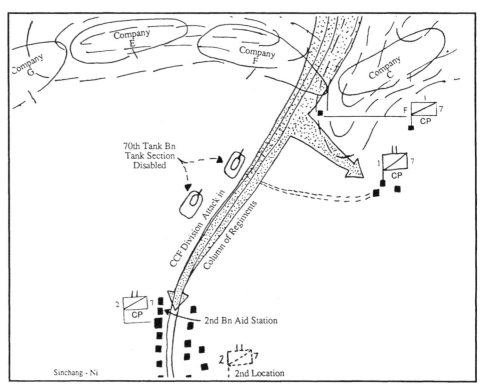

Battle at Sinchang-Ni, Night of November 29-30, 1950

station to transport the seriously wounded.

By midnight there were 27 or 28 seriously wounded laying on stretchers on the floor of the aid station. Most of them were sleeping because of the morphine, and many were on the verge of surgical shock. There was little or nothing to treat this specific problem. The only intravenous fluids available were two units of plasma. These units consisted of two glass bottles with dry plasma in one and the other contained sterile salt water solution to reconstitute the dry material into usable form. However, both of the liquid containers were frozen solid and could not be thawed, due the the extremely cold weather.

At approximately 0100 hours we still had the 27 or 28 seriously wounded, but we also had 30 or 40 ambulatory wounded in the large ditch at the rear of the aid station. By this time, I had already received three direct orders to move the aid station out of this forward and dangerous location. However, I could not do so because of the inability to move the wounded personnel.

Finally, between 0100 and 0200 hours, the nearby situation became clarified when Lt. Colonel John W. Callaway, 2nd Battalion Commander, stopped by to see me. He recognized the predicament and arranged through other sources to have four or five 2-1/2 ton trucks dispatched immediately from our supporting artillery units. These trucks had previously carried artillery ammunition but were very quickly unloaded and then rushed to our situation to help evacuate the wounded.

Once this was accomplished, and I don't know how many trucks were used, but we were eventually able to get all of the stretchers and ambulatory wounded evacuated to the rear area. By 0300 hours, we were then able to move the aid station and its personnel further to the rear, which was a school house that was located next to the 2nd Battalion Headquarters. Throughout the early morning, the wounded personnel were continued

to be brought in, but nothing like the first hour of battle.

From the book "Of GARRYOWEN And Glory," by Melbourne C. Chandler, it is recorded that the casualties of Sinchang-ni were, 38 killed in action; 107 wounded in action; and 11 missing in action. Some of the missing turned out to be prisoners of war of the Chinese Communists. Corporal Carl J. Bafs, a combat aidman from my aid station had been assigned as an outpost guard to the aid station during the battle. The other two were Master Sergeant Earl Early and Sergeant Glen Bumgarner from the Weapons Platoon of Company F.

After daybreak, the area of battle was carefully screened which revealed more wounded and dead who were brought to the collecting point near the aid station. By midmorning, I was able to accompany Lt. Colonel John W. Callaway, 2nd Battalion Commander, on a reconnaissance back to the roadway north of my aid station and up the road to the open field where the enemy assault was stopped.

There were hundreds of dead Chinese laying on the road between the aid station area and the northward perimeter line where Companies C and F were previously located. We did not go further north of this point, but we were informed that beyond the outer perimeter of the 7th Cavalry Regiment, there were over 1200 enemy dead. These enemy soldiers had been caught or trapped by our extensive artillery barrages as they attempted to flee northward. This was an example of how valuable the field artillery can be when effectively used.

In summary, the aid station personnel were able to perform well and adequately under very dangerous circumstances. The greatest problem confronting us that very hectic night may be listed as follows: first, the 374th Regiment, 125th Chinese Division of the 42nd Chinese Communist Army, in their desperate attempt to destroy

A Chinese soldier stands on top of a knocked out American M-26 tank of the 70th Tank Battalion, 1st Cavalry Division at the battle of Unsan. This particular tank (B-23 of Company B) was supporting elements of the 8th Cavalry Regiment, during November 1-4, 1950. (Eastfoto)

Chinese soldiers cover American soldiers emerging from a cave to surrender. Many American troopers from the 8th Cavalry Regiment, 1st Cavalry Division, were captured during the battle of Unsan on November 1-4, 1950. (Eastfoto)

the 7th Cavalry Regiment defenses; secondly, the extremely cold and below freezing temperatures were seriously injurious to the wounded personnel and immobilized very many; thirdly, the difficulties with coordinating the need for transportation to serve the overwhelming flood of wounded during the early part of the battle.

I'm very proud of what the regiment was able to accomplish and I'm very honored to have been a part of that service. There are many who deserve credit for our victorious outcome that night and early morning battle at Sinchang-ni on November 29th-30th, 1950.

First, of course, was the excellent leadership in the regiment and battalions and their ability to quickly and effectively respond to a very dangerous situation. I commend the many brave troopers that fought bitterly and to those that made the ultimate sacrifice; and finally I recall the great

effort that was put forth by the many aidmen and stretcher bearers who are the very frontline of medical care in combat. Many times they are unsung heroes, but are the angels of mercy dressed in khaki.

Captain John C. Rourke never continued his military career and was honorably discharged on June 1, 1952. After his discharge he then studied and trained for three years in Hospital Specialty Techniques, to improve his knowledge as a doctor. Then he established his own private practice and maintained the same office for thirty years. He retired from the medical profession in 1985.

No nation, no culture has an unblemished record in what is merely a part of the long story of man's inhumanity to man. History dictates it has often been better for men to die fighting than to be taken by the enemy.

During World War II, it was found that

the Geneva Conventions did not adequately cover the subject on prisoners of war. Nor was the subject properly covered during the Korean War. At the time, Western Civilization had tended to grow more humane in the treatment of its prisoners of all kinds, but the balance of the world had not.

For many years, the Army, as well as the government and society, knew of the Asian Communist culture and their methods of indoctrinating prisoners of war. Survivors had written of the unmistakable brutality by Communist soldiers and guards, and the degradation and death in Communist prison camps.

In the bleak and dreary prison camps of North Korea, it was no more than a continuation of a Communist power of a different culture and lesser standards of humanity.

Almost all of the American and United Nations Forces who were prisoners of war were captured during the first six months of the Korean War. Many experienced the snow-covered buildings of the old bauxite mining camp that was called Death Valley. In this area, many men died from battle wounds, infection, pneumonia, dysentery, and in many cases, malnutrition was the contributing factor.

During the battle of Sinchang-ni on November 29th-30th, several troopers of the 2nd Battalion were captured by Chinese Communist Forces. Each has expressed his own personal experiences during his 33-35 months as a prisoner of war in North Korea. Although each explanation may be brief or in detail, nevertheless, what each trooper experienced is a story of its own.

The following is an account of the action of November 29, 1950, from Master Sergeant Earl Early, Weapons Platoon Sergeant of Company F, 2nd Battalion, 7th Cavalry Regiment.

During the late evening of November 29, 1950, Company F was located to the left flank of the 1st Battalion, and the main road leading into the town of Sinchang-ni. The Chinese Communists penetrated our right flank and the 1st Battalion positions near the road. The enemy managed to fight their way behind positions that were held by the 2nd Platoon of Company F.

I received word that the platoon leader of the 2nd Platoon was new, and the platoon sergeant was previously wounded and had been evacuated earlier in the morning. So I thought that I could possibly be of some help or assistance to the platoon. When I reached the 2nd Platoon sector, it was an extremely chaotic and confusing mess. I was immediately captured by a Chinese soldier. Within a few minutes, they also captured the 2nd Platoon Leader, Lieutenant Soriano and Sergeant Glen Bumgarner, who was a squad leader from the light machine gun section. We were immediately taken away from the battle area.

I remained a prisoner of war of the Chinese Communists until September 1953. After my release, I was told later on that our commanding officer of Company F, Captain Arthur Truxall, was killed in action during the late evening battle of November 29, 1950.

As for other details of my prisoner of war or combat experiences, my memory is foggy at best, and as far as I am concerned, best forgotten.

Sergeant Early continued his military career and retired from the Army in 1963. His reason for not giving further statements is an example of so many like himself who previously experienced fierce combat or were prisoners of war.

The following is an account of the action of November 29th-30th, 1950, from Corporal Carl J. Bafs, combat aid man from the Medical Company, 2nd Battalion, 7th Cavalry Regiment.

The evening of November 29th was very cold and the temperature was near zero. There were rumors that the Chinese Peoples Volunteers had crossed the Yalu River and were fighting within our sector of the 2nd Battalion. The battalion aid station was located just off the main road in the town of Sinchang-ni.

Our 2nd Battalion aid station was filled with wounded, and many couldn't be moved. Sergeant Alvin C. Fuller and myself were ordered to help defend the aid station. It was very hard to dig a slit trench in the frozen ground, but somehow we managed. At approximately 2100 hours all hell broke loose as the fire fight seemed to be coming from all directions within the 2nd Battalion sector. The Chinese bugles and whistles sounded loud within the dark night.

From our slit trench we could see the movement of many Chinese troops crossing the frozen fields within the moonlit night. Leading the enemy troops was a Chinese officer who was riding a white Mongolian pony.

It didn't take long for Sergeant Fuller and me to use up our ammunition as the enemy continued to close in. Captain John C. Rourke, our 2nd Battalion Surgeon continued to operate and treat the wounded as the battle was now being fought all along the road and battalion sector.

Finally, the last of the aid station was evacuated and someone shouted for Sergeant Fuller and me to jump on a 3/4 ton truck which had a trailer hitched to the rear of it. Dead and wounded Chinese were laying on both sides of the road as we attempted to proceed southward. We traveled only 1/2 mile, when suddenly Chinese troops appeared in the middle of the road and fired their weapons directly into the front of the truck. The truck driver was hit in the face and head and died instantly. The truck then went off the road and jackknifed in the ditch. Everyone within the rear of the truck panicked and attempted to go out the rear of it. The waiting Chinese troops killed each one as they exited the rear of the truck.

By luck, a South Korean interpreter who was riding the truck with us cut a hole in the canvas top with his bayonet. Escaping through the hole in the canvas, the two of us proceeded to run up the edge of the hill. However, we were met by a Chinese soldier who stuck a bayonet in my ribs. Actually we were defenseless because we had no ammunition, and we were completely exhausted.

Being that we were from a medical company, the South Korean interpreter was told by the Chinese soldier to take him back to the battalion

The Marines claimed all of their dead on the retreat from Changjin Reservoir. Chinese soldiers stripped clothing from many of the bodies. (U.S. Marine Corps photo)

Frozen bodies of American Marines in November 1950. The winter was very severe during their withdrawal. British commandos and South Korean soldiers are gathered for group burial at Koto-ri. (U.S. Marine Corps photo)

aid station for penicillin. Shortly, we reached the battalion aid station tent, and I went inside to try and locate the penicillin. Inside was Sergeant Sweetwood and a couple of medical officers with their heads blown off. I quickly located the penicillin and gave it to the Chinese soldier.

Shortly they took our combat boots and gave us a pair of tennis shoes in exchange. From here they took us approximately two miles to the north where a creek crossed the road. Here we joined 28 American and ROK soldiers, which made our total 30. Then we continued to proceed on northward through mountain passages and always during the night. This was to avoid the American fighter planes during the daytime hours.

After approximately 30 days of marching at night we finally reached the town of Anju. North Korean guards locked all of us in a 12 foot by 12

foot room. Within one week, 22 American and South Korean soldiers died from starvation and diarrhea. During our stay in this room, the enemy gave us no food or water. Also we became infected with body lice.

One evening, a Chinese officer arrived and questioned us about the last time we were given food. We immediately told him around five weeks ago. He told us a truck would arrive the following night to haul eight of us to Chang-song where the prisoner of war camps one and three were located.

The following evening, the truck arrived and as scheduled to take us to camps 1 and 3 at Chang-song. The truck was partially loaded with straw rice bags and we were ordered to lay flat on our stomachs. However, before we left, the Chinese officer ordered the four North Korean guards who were in charge of us to be immediately blind-

Actual enemy photo of the Chinese Communist Forces attacking the defensive positions of the United Nations Forces. (Photo courtesy of John Cauley)

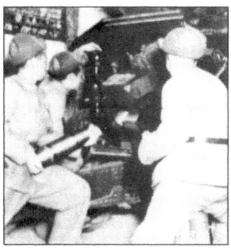

Actual enemy photo of Chinese Communist Forces artillery, firing on positions of the United Nations Forces. (Photo courtesy of John Cauley)

folded. They were quickly executed by being shot in the back of their heads.

We arrived in Chang-song in the early morning just prior to daylight. I would remain here as a prisoner of war until August 21, 1953. During this particular time, I estimate that over 500 Americans died from malnutrition, starvation and various other diseases.

During my 33 months as a prisoner of war, I would also witness many captured Air Force personnel that were tied to ox carts and paraded up and down the roads. Then they were hauled to Manchuria and never seen again.

I thank God for sparing my life and for granting me the opportunity to return to America and to my family and loved ones. However, the horrible experiences of combat and the agony of suffering as a prisoner of war will remain with me forever until the day I die..

The following is an account of the action of November 29, 1950, from Sergeant Glen G. Bumgarner, Squad Leader, Weapons Platoon of Company F, 2nd Battalion, 7th Cavalry Regiment.

How well do I remember the night of 29 Nov 1950? I have relived that night countless times in my dreams and daydreams. As I sit here and write, names and places flash through my mind, and I am again carried back through time to that night that changed my life and transferred me from a carefree young man into a God-fearing man. A person who transferred his values of life from care-free fun loving to survival. Time and places slip by ever so fast until something grabs you, shakes you and refuses to let go. That thing which grabbed me was the night of November 29, 1950.

Our mission on this night, along with Company A, 1st. Bn., 7th Cavalry Regiment, was to act as a buffer between the approaching enemy and the rest of the regiment. There had been reports all day that a large force was approaching our selected positions, and we were to hold the line while a South Korean Unit withdrew through us. Anyway, we had a road block with Bazookas and machine guns with a large rice paddy to the left of the road block with riflemen and automatic weapons. About 9:00 p.m. or 2100 hours, there was movement to our front. The night was crystal clear with a moon as only can be seen in Korea. Visibility was a good 1000 yards down the road

and all suddenly there were Chinese everywhere. The road, rice paddies, and hills to our left were full of Chinese.

We opened fire all along our line simultaneously. I remember quite well that suddenly only my section was still firing. (I've since found out 38 years later an order had been given to withdraw). I had a machine gun section and a rifle squad, and it didn't take long for the Chinese to overrun us and keep going on. The first Chinese forces to hit us that night were armed with Thompson sub-machine guns and potato smashers. The second wave had rifles and regular machine guns. We were firing in all directions, and seeing we were exposed from all sides, I attempted to move the rifle squad to a ditch part way to the road. We got to the ditch, and all we had were riflemen and about as much chance as a snowball in Hell in getting out. That's when my lights went out. I've always thought it was a mortar round or a potato smasher, but anyway, when I woke up I was laying in a creek bed with ice forming on the water. You might say I was iced away. Along with myself, there was 2nd Lt. Soriano, my Platoon leader of only a few days and my 1st Sergeant Earl Early, and a medic attached to our Platoon, Carl Baffs, and two men from Company A, 8th Combat Engineers. I believe their names were Young and Huff.

I was tied up with communication wire with my hands behind my back and some of the others were also tied. From looking at the moon, I would say the battle we were in lasted only an hour, but the battle with the rest of the Regiment was still going on. All I could see were tracers and exploding white phosphorus.

These Chinese troops were front line fighting troops and none spoke English. When they wanted us to move, they poked a bayonette at you. All night we moved like this, up and down the front line. That's when I really got respect for white phosphorus. I found out that they didn't like it. There were bodies laying in the road with heads missing where white phosphorus had hit them and still burning. Their combat uniform consisted of a padded suit of cotton cloth, filled with cotton, padded hat, rubber shoes, padded in winter, and armed with either a Thompson sub machine gun or Russian rifles with a supply of potato smashers. Their rations they carried with them consisted of a slim roll of rice or soy beans

shaped in a roll, slung around the shoulders. Only rear, I mean way back troops had field kitchens. They were expected to live off the land.

The following morning, after daybreak, they moved us off the front line and marched us up and down several valleys until we came to a small village with two or three houses still standing. A Chinese officer kept jabbering to us as if he expected us to understand him, and the more he talked to us the madder he became, and the guards got into it. Any time one of us would try to say anything, one of the guards would act like he was trying to shoot us. This went along for some time until American F-51's came over. Then they rushed us onto the side of a hill.

The hill was bare of vegetation and no cover what-so-ever. The airplanes made run after run up and down the valley, sometimes flying beneath us, machine gunning everything in sight. After the airplanes left, the Chinese took us back down into the valley and made us squat down. We were in this position until nearly noon, when we were again taken back up on the hill and remained until dark.

When it was fully dark, we came down from the hill and started marching in a northwesterly direction. To the best of my knowledge, the closest big towns from from where I was captured were Sunch-on and Singyong about 30 miles distance from Pyongyang. We walked all night, and the following morning we were huddled together again on a hillside. Most of us had wounds, but the Chinese weren't interested in treating them or feeding us. Again we stayed on the hillside until night and again started walking. This went on for several days and the nights were all below zero. Our clothing at the time consisted of regular fatigues, jacket and boots, and no hats. The Chinese didn't like the people wearing helmets so they threw them away (the helmets, I mean).

In about a week or maybe longer, a few other prisoners joined us. I'll speak more on them later on. That brought our total to 12, and we proceeded north (we thought). We later discovered we had been walking up one valley and down another in an area no more than 30 miles. When they did decide to feed us, it was not enough to keep a cat alive. After about a week to 10 days, your body starts downhill without the proper food. We all were so tired after each night's march, we would drop in our tracks when we stopped; and without proper clothing or lodging, freezing became another enemy.

Finally, we did start in a northerly direction as if they had a destination in mind. We walked another week, and one night they threw us on top of some trucks heading north. I well remember the truck we were on for it had bundles of crackers on it and the seven of us on that truck ate as much as we thought we could get away with.

The following morning, just before daylight, the trucks stopped at a group of small houses, and we were told to get off. They took us inside for the first time. Inside we were in a room with three American Navy flyers who had bailed out after being hit over HamHung. That led us to believe they were taking us to the coast. The North Koreans had the Navy flyers. One was a Commander and two were Lt. Commanders. The Koreans had them for about five days when we arrived.

The Chinese were trying to take the Navy men

and the Koreans wouldn't give them up. We almost had a full war right there in the room, but the Koreans kept the Navy men and after spending the day we were on our way North again that night.

The reason we moved at night was because the American Air Force would shoot at anything moving during the day.

Again we were on trucks, but all of us were piled atop a truck with sacks to sit on. Just before daylight we were off loaded in a town which was much larger than any of the other towns we had seen up to this time. This time we were herded into one room about 10 x 10, all 12 of us, and that is where the list of twelve was formed. We were turned over to the North Koreans who I consider to be barbarians. They enjoy hurting people. We were kept in this room I would say close to 30-35 days. The place was full of straw lice, the blood sucker type. What a job that was to try to keep our own blood rather than seeing those little suckers running around with it. The people who were together, known as the list of 12 were really 15. Three departed sometime during the day we spent with the North Koreans. Here I would like to give that list in case we could get together again: Soriano; Early Earl; Bumgarner; Baffs; Rogers; McLain; Sourbeer; Englehart; Huff; Young; Le Desmo; Glasgow George; Mowr; Snyder Jesse; LeVallie.

Our days were twofold, one trying to get outside to the toilet, and two keeping those lice off us. There wasn't room for us to lay anyway we wanted, so we would lay side by side and when one wanted to turn, we would all turn. The Koreans would feed us once a day, and the meal was approximately one teacup of boiled corn. That was our diet, and the reason for the many trips to the toilet. The Koreans kept the door locked all the time with a guard just outside the door, and you couldn't go to the toilet after dark. Can you imagine 15 men with dysentery and nowhere to go?

We had previously figured we were near the coast, and daily visits by Navy jets confirmed this. As I said earlier, this was a much larger town and had a rail head and the airplanes were regular visitors. Each time the planes would come over, the Koreans would head for bunkers they had dug in front of the building and leave us locked up. We had many close calls during this stay. But finally our stay was over with the Koreans and I for one would not book this lodging anymore.

We started marching north once more, and the Winter of '50-'51 was the coldest in Korea in 50 years. With our weak systems and lack of clothing, it took about all we had to survive. Our nightly marches continued through about one and a half weeks and our daily stopping places were caves, barns, and once a vacant house. We finally came to a long valley with houses scattered up and down each side. We were put into one of the bigger ones for the day, and the following day an interpreter came in and told us we would be staying in one of the houses and should respect the Korean people for being so good to us, and we shouldn't try to escape because a guard would always be outside. Ten of us moved the same day into a room about 12 x 12. A Korean family lived in the other part of the house. There was no connecting door.

We were again visited by the interpreter, and

he informed us we would be going to a meeting the following day where there would be many more Americans to hear a speech by the Camp Commander. We were not aware that we were in a camp, but the following day we were taken to a large barn-type structure, bare except for a small stage. There were about 150 Americans there all right, and they looked about as bad as we did. Anyway, this commander was a Chinese officer, and he had the same interpreter with him who had been to see us the previous day. He would talk and talk for five minutes, and then the interpreter would spend about one minute to tell us what he said. He said the Chinese Army had liberated us, and the Chinese people were our friends, and they would show us our wrong and teach us to be good people. He said all the Chinese soldiers in Korea were volunteers and came on their own to liberate the loving Korean people from the war monger Americans. Well, this went on for a good three hours, and the temperature was below zero. Finally it ended and we were marched back to our room. We did notice the others were marched off in all directions so we figured they also, like us, lived in one room in the houses scattered up and down the valley.

We were later to learn the Commander just wasn't whistling Dixie. We were subjected to many, many hours in that cold barn to lectures by the Camp Commander on subjects like the American cannon fodders sending its young men 10,000 miles from home to fight the peace-loving Koreans, and how the American-backed South Koreans had attacked the North. Subjects included how we treated the Indians and the Blacks, Marx, Lenin, the great Russian people, and again the rich war mongers back in the United States making all the money as long as the war went on.

We were always broken down into squads, so they decided we should study. They selected a squad leader, and he was supposed to supervise our study period. Our literature was mainly taken out of the *Daily News* which is a communist newspaper, and mimeographed sheets of front line news and how many Americans had been killed or captured.

Our food during this period consisted of two small bowls of rice soup or sorghum, once in the morning and once in the evening. Sometimes you might have a piece of fish in the soup or the bowl of sorghum. If they thought we weren't studying, we would only get one bowl a day. They were using food to get to our brain.

In the spring, they decided it was time for another walk. We did not know where the valley they had been holding us was, but we figured it wasn't too far south of the Yalu River. We departed heading in a northwesterly direction. We marched for about 10 days and came to a town called Kanggye, where we stayed about a month. Then we were off again along the Yalu River west to Wiwon where we again stayed several days. Every time we stopped there would be more Americans added. We were also getting some British and Turks.

We finally stopped in another long flat valley in a village either deserted or the Chinese ran them off, for we were becoming a large group, probably several hundred. We were put into houses, about 12 to 15 per house. At this village, the Chinese decided we should have our own cooks, so cooks were appointed. In our section of

about 200 we had Charlie Hrobak, Oliver Haney and Douglas Dugger. We had one more but I can't recall his name. I like to think it was a marine named Brill.

The food was mostly rotten, or every now and then we would have plain rice - which was considered a delicacy. Our bodies by this time had lost all fat, and we were skin and bones. During our stay here, we lost during some periods, 10 to 15 people per day. When a person sinks to a certain low, the mind gives up, and not long after that the body yields up. I know for I have been there. When a person got so sick he could not look after himself any longer, the Chinese would move him to a house set aside. We called it the death house. Very few people came out of the death house alive. The most able men were picked for burial details, and with the ground frozen, you couldn't put them too far under. About all we could do was to put them under a few inches and say a prayer. We lost so many good young men during our stay - a lot of people called it Death Valley. Some people ask me what did I learn from being there? My S.O.P. answer is that I learned to pray a alot. I would say "God, thank you for another day, and if you've a mind to, see me through this ordeal, and I promise I will never forget you." He didn't forget me, but I'm afraid we forget too fast.

We stayed here until the spring, and what was left of us started marching again. We were on the road this time probably six to eight days and came to a town by the name of Chosan. All these towns were along the Yalu River. In this town, again the Koreans had either left or run off. Prior to this move, all ranks were together, but during the first day here they took the officers and moved them to the other side of the village. A road separated us from them. At night B-26's, which we called "Bed check Charlie" came over nightly, dropping flares and machine gunning. If they started a fire, they would always come back and bomb.

One day after a bombing from the B-26's, the Chinese showed up with movie cameras to take pictures of the damage by the airplanes. They wanted the P.O.W.'s to lay around the holes as if

Actual enemy photo of an American liasion plane that was shot down by Chinese Communist Forces. Note the American pilot in upper right of photo (Photo courtesy of John Cauley)

Actual enemy photo of the first Chinese Communist Forces crossing the Yalu River in early October 1950. (Photo courtesy of John Cauley)

Actual enemy photo of a Chinese Communist tank. Very few tanks were used by the Chinese Communist Forces during the Korean War. (Photo courtesy of John Cauley)

Actual enemy photo of the United Nations Forces attacking a defensive position of the Chinese Communist Forces. Note torn enemy Guidon! (Photo courtesy of John Cauley)

they had been the victims of the bombing. No one would do it, so the Chinese took dummies and laid them around the holes and took pictures of them. Later I learned that two prisoners did pose for the pictures.

Our days in this camp were much like the days in other camps, all except that we were required to carry our own wood for cooking. I don't know how they figured out how much wood each person was to carry, but the smaller men had a higher quota. They would march us out in the morning heading for the mountains. Sometimes it would be a matter of a few miles and other times, five to eight miles. By this time, our clothing and foot-wear had worn out, and we were given Chinese clothing, blue in color and rubber footwear. I know I was required to carry 150 to 175 caddies per day. A caddy is a little more than a pound.

I had malaria really bad. One day I couldn't go on the wood detail so the men in the squad told me to hide out and they would cover for me, so I did. After the wood party got back, a Chinese came straight to where I was hiding and took me before the camp commander. I knew right away someone had turned me in. Later I found out who it was, and a black eye was followed shortly afterward. Also at this camp I saw one of the strangest things I have ever seen. One day several of us were standing out behind our building and off in the distance of about 1,000 yards was a very steep mountain. Along the bottom of the mountain was a fence of maybe three or four feet. Up on the side of the mountain two cows were grazing. As we were watching them, one lost its balance and fell down the mountain and over the fence. Now tell me, how many people ever saw a cow fall over a fence?

Our food at this camp was the same-bad. But every now and again we would have rice, and the cook would have a rice crust, and we would always try to get a little piece of this. By this time, everyone was beginning to wonder if the war would ever end and what would happen to us. Every bright day you could look into the skies and see Russian Migs coming south from China and American planes coming from the south. They would mix it up for 10 to 15 minutes and separate to go their respective ways. Each time a plane was shot down, we would follow it down and try to see if it was a Mig or one of ours. Each time we would see it was a Mig we would cheer, and you can imagine how the Chinese guards felt about this. No, they didn't like it, and they let us know it. One day, about mid-morning, we heard far away noises like a swarm of bees, closer and closer they came, and we could detect the roar of engines far off to our right. The sky was full of airplanes of all descriptions. Higher up you could the heavy bombers and at lower elevations were the fighters and dive bombers. Soon they were over us also. The sky was full of planes. Later on, after I came home, I read the history of the Air War of Korea, and I found out it was the biggest raid conducted during the Korean War on bridges and power plants along the Yalu River and Sinui-ju. If I remember the phrase, the commander of the flight said, "It was a beautiful day and a beautiful target, and we clobbered them."

You know, without humor I don't think some of us would have made it. It takes a great man to be going down for the third time and laugh about it, but we had people who were hurting as much

as we were, and they could still find time to crack a joke and bring a little sunshine into someone's life. One man immediately comes to mind, Oliver P. Haney, a tall old boy from Missouri. You might remember I mentioned his name once before, he was one of our cooks.

Just about this time during our stay at this camp, a platoon of British showed up. I would say probably 20, mostly sergeants, and they had a sense of humor all their own. The most foul-speaking people I have ever met. Every other word was F— this and F— that. I think they took to being prisoners quite well. Like all prisoners, a well-worn subject was food. Men would sit around and dream up all the different foods they were going to eat if they got home. It seems like the British were quite fond of some kind of meat pudding. They talked on it for hours. One of the things the British brought with them was homemade cards, and I became a close friend to one bloke who taught me to play Bridge. When the Chinese weren't harassing us, we would hide away in a corner and play Bridge - four of us.

I met a little Spanish guy along about this time, and he became my best friend. We played Bridge together, and we would sit around for hours trying to figure how to cheat so we could beat the British at Bridge. We had all types of hand signals and eye movements to help one another during our bidding. We were very raw at the game and much later, when we knew the game better, we realized the signals weren't needed for that was what bidding was all about. From this time on, any time you saw me, Liola, my Spanish buddy, would be with me.

I believe it was early '52, the Chinese decided we had stayed long enough in this place, so we started walking again. We walked several days and came to another town on the Yalu called Pyoktong. We didn't know at the time, but this was to be our home until we started our last journey towards the 38th parallel.

At this camp, the Chinese separated all the N.C.O.'s from the rest of the men along with all the blacks. They moved them about a mile away from us and across a small river.

I feel they finally realized they couldn't teach N.C.O.'s anything so they separated us from the rest.

There were about 200 to 300 N.C.O.'s split up into two companies with a high fence separating the two. All the British and Turks ended up in the company across the fence along with my old 1st Sgt. Earl Early. All Blacks and corporals and below, down across the river.

Life went on as usual here in this camp, and it was given the number of four. We did regular wood details and constructed a high mud and rock fence to keep the peace-loving Koreans from getting at us.

Here at this camp a favorite subject was escape. Several tried but no one ever made if from Camp Four. Many things were against us. One - food, two - condition of our bodies, and three - Americans are much bigger than Chinese or Koreans, and we were white. The plan talked about most was to get a boat or raft and float down the Yalu River to the Yellow Sea, there to be picked up by a patrolling Navy ship. Only thing escape ever got anyone was a few months in the turnip bin.

Capture - during my stay with the Chinese People's Liberation Army you hear of some very

American field-grade officers in a North Korean POW camp (Eastfoto)

Turkish soldiers in a North Korean POW camp. They were tough and their record proved it. (Eastfoto)

serious ways people get captured, but some are funny. Four cases come to mind, two funny and two by circumstances. The first one is about Bill Taylor from one of the Infantry Divisions. We called him Waddy. Anyway, the way he tells it, his unit was pulling back from the front line and he was in a sleeping bag on the back of a 2-1/2 ton truck. As the truck was going up a steep hill, Chinese ran up behind the truck and grabbed the end of the sleeping bag and pulled him and bag out. Thus, Waddy was a prisoner. Second was an Air Force radar operator stationed on a B-29 Base off Japan. Being a radar operator became boring so he hitched a ride on a B-29 for what they called a milk run over North Korea. The plane was hit over North Korea, and the crew bailed out along with our adventurous radar operator who became a prisoner - long range. Third was a radio operator aboard a B-26, flying a harassment mission over North Korea between the 38th parallel and the North Korean capitol of Pyongyang. The plane was hit in one engine south of Pyongyang but still flying. The pilot informed the crew one engine was hit but it was still flyable, and he would tell the crew when it was okay to bail out. The plane flew along for five to ten minutes before the pilot announced okay so the radio operator thought it was okay to bail out so he jumped. When he hit the ground, he looked up and the plane was flying smoothly south. Thus another prisoner for the Koreans.

The fourth parallels two individuals with us, one Air Force and one Marine. One an Air Force gunner aboard a B-29 over North Korea was jumped by Migs, and the plane caught fire and exploded. The next thing the Air Force sergeant knew he woke up on the ground not knowing how he got there. He didn't know how his chute opened and didn't remember being blown out of the plane. Another thing about him, he was also blown out of a B-17 over Germany and was a guest of the Germans for 18 months. Now our Marine sergeant at the time, I knew him already 18 years of service and was captured just below the Yalu River at one of the reservoirs and was being held prisoner with us just across the river from Manchuria where in WWII he was a prisoner of the Japanese for three years. In keeping with humor, I remember one day after Bed Check Charlie had dropped some Butterfly bombs, and the casing of the bombs was lying in a field next

to our camp. The Chinese arrived on the scene, masks covering their mouth and nose and wearing white gloves. Each was equipped with a long bag and a pair of tweezers. Apparently, one of the casings fell on an anthill and the Chinese told us that the United States was using germ warfare.

But it was quite a sight seeing those Chinese running around picking up piss ants with tweezers and putting them in a large bag.

Early '53 we knew something was going on for the Chinese marked our P.O.W. camp. Prior to that we were as big a target as they were. We also started getting rice, turnips and a little fish. We also got a little pork as rank as it was g-o-o-d. Later we found out the peace talks had started in Panmunjom. Our conditions improved quite a bit and in April '53 "Operation Little Switch" took place. In this switch, all wounded, missing limbs, mangled bodies were swapped. We had quite a few N.C.O.'s to make it out on this swap. We knew of a large valley about three miles from our camp which was full of storage sheds, and shortly after little switch, the Air Force paid the valley a visit and good-bye supplies. We had a ring side seat, and it was beautiful.

The planes paid us several visits after that, but only flyovers by mostly F-86 Saber jets.

In August of '53 we knew something big was up for we received new blue uniforms and were visited by a group of Swedish representatives who looked us over. Later, we boarded trucks and started our journey south. We knew something was up for we were riding this time. Our journey south lasted two days to "tent city" we called it. It was a large encampment in a clear valley with no village or houses in view.

We were there several days when then the Chinese informed us we were being swapped for Chinese troops, only a few hundred at a time. I remember most of the days were wet and there was a lot of mud, but we didn't care because we were so happy. It felt like we were so close, but yet so far away. Each day our little group got smaller, and I knew my name started with a B - yet when September rolled around, I was the only one left in the tent. They were small, 10-men tents, so I moved next door where there were two more sergeants. Finally my day came on the 5th of September, 1950, I too went across Freedom Bridge, and it was one of the happiest days of my life. It's something words cannot tell, of all the

beautiful words in the dictionary, thrilled, elated, overcome, joy, cloud nine, put them all together and it still couldn't describe how I felt.

After welcoming us home, a representative from the 7th Cavalry Regiment gave me a set of GARRYOWENS, then we were put into a vacant tent where we were sprayed with D.D.T., then into a shower with plenty of hot water and soap. After that we were given a medical exam.

I had my first American cigarette, and I got so dizzy I couldn't stand up. They were afraid to feed us too much, but they gave us plain mashed potatoes, plain roast beef, coffee and milk and some ice cream. It was a great time to be alive.

That afternoon we were taken by choppers to Seoul. The following day we were de-briefed and shown a thick book with thousands of names of Americans missing in action for identification. Each name that we knew and were a witness or were present when he died, we had to write down, along with where, when and how? This was a long process taking several days.

Anyway, I was put on a ship with several hundred other P.O.W.'s and headed home. I arrived home just before my birthday on the 20th of September, 1953.

I went on and spent 26 years and 27 days in the service, and yes, I did go back to Korea. I made up my mind that if I were to stay in the service, I had a better get the monkey off of my back.

In conclusion, I don't want to leave you with the thought that being a P.O.W., was only a waiting game. Our days were trying to survive to the next one as I spent 35 months as a P.O.W.

Purposely, I did not include the horror of the initial shock of becoming a P.O.W. which in itself is beyond literature.

Nights without numbers I have dreamed of that night back in November 1950, even after 35 years. If you have never experienced it, then there is no way I can explain it. I only wish I possessed the writing skills to explain the feeling.

Korea is a hard country. Koreans are hard people. Korea is the land of the midnight sun and the morning calm. But to many like myself, Korea is hell.

When that day comes, and we must account for ourselves to the Great One, I only hope he remembers we have already spent our time in hell.

A bondage thicker than blood was made during our long days in North Korea, and we still

North Korean Prisoner of War Camp #5, Pyoktong, North Korea. Located on the Yalu River. Many prisoners who died were buried in the adjacent hills. (Photo Courtesy of Lloyd Cornwell)

have a yearly reunion where today we can enjoy each other's company more as the years go by.

The 7th Cavalry Regiment survived the battle of Sinchang-ni on November 29th-30th. By 0700 hours on the 30th, the regimental perimeter was restored. Regimental casualties during this particular action were 38 killed, 107 wounded and 11 missing in action. However, the enemy would suffer dearly, as known casualties exceeded 1600 killed in action.

At dawn of November 30th, 1st Cavalry Division Headquarters sent up a light plane for radio relay. Some of the GARRYOWEN troopers were able to hear the plane's crew on their radios, but could not communicate with them. At one point, the observer in the plane spotted many Chinese bodies on the ground and was heard to say: "My God, the 7th Cavalry has been annihilated again!"

Even though the Chinese spearhead had been stopped, the proud GARRYOWEN troopers were eventually forced to yield hard-won real estate. Strategic withdrawals allowed time for the rear echelon to rebuild supplies, while at the same time it prevented the Chinese from developing its full force. The constantly shifting line was actually trading space for time.

By December 12th - 16th, the 7th Cavalry Regiment had taken up positions just east of Seoul, South Korea. This was well below the 38th Parallel. For the remainder of the month, defensive positions were prepared for the enemy movement and attack.

Just prior to Christmas, a parcel package of food and goodies from my mother and Uncle Omer had found its way to the hospital. It didn't take long for the entire box of food to completely disappear as everyone in the medical ward had a bite to eat.

Then on Christmas Day, we were served a hot turkey dinner with all the trimmings. There was a brief visit from a small group of South Korean children, who attempted to sing a few Christmas carols in English. Under the circumstances, all of us enjoyed the brief program.

As the last days of 1950 came to a close, various rumors and even the Stars & Stripes newspaper indicated a renewed enemy assault against the United Nations Forces. The newspaper reported that the U.S. 5th Air Force was not only destroying vast enemy supply lines, but they were killing Chinese soldiers by the thousands. Even though these numbers were high, it didn't seem however, to be stopping the Chinese movement and onslaught.

The true extent of the enemy buildup had become clear because they had at least 20 divisions poised for the drive on Seoul. Almost a million and a half Chinese and North Korean soldiers were on the Korean peninsula or ready to move in from Manchuria. The United Nations command had less than 250,000 soldiers.

With the new year approaching, for some unknown reason, as my left forearm improved, I was becoming anxious to return to Company H and the GARRYOWEN troopers of the 7th Cavalry Regiment. Within a couple of weeks, these thoughts would become a reality.

The following is a brief and amusing incident within the capital city of Seoul, South Korea, in late December, 1950, from Colonel John W. Callaway, Commander, 2nd Battalion, 7th Cavalry Regiment.

I have always maintained that the ingenuity of the American soldier is indeed remarkable. This story is a good example. In late December, 1950, the 2nd Battalion, 7th Cavalry Regiment, was protecting the northern outskirts of the city of Seoul, as Eighth Army troops evacuated to the south. On this particular evening, my communications officer came to me and suggested that we make a number of calls to the United States. He was a "ham" operator and could get the calls through from the Seoul telephone exchange. We sent word out for several men from each company who needed to phone home. We went into Seoul with my jeep and a 2-1/2 ton truck. The city was dark and small arms fire could be heard.

We found the Seoul communications center which was dark and abandoned except for a Korean who was sitting on the front steps of the building. When asked by one of our Korean interpreters where the generator was, he explained that it was several miles away. We sent this man with our interpreter in my jeep to crank up the generator. Once the electricity was on, our communications officer wasted no time in contacting the Oakland, California operator. He explained

that we wanted to place a number of calls in the US and would pay for them in Seoul. As each person's name was called, he went to a phone. When my call came through, my wife, Lynn, was on the other end of the line. It was 8:30 in the morning at Cape Cod, Mass., where she and our children were living at the time. After exchanging a few words, she asked me where I was calling from. I told her Seoul, Korea. She gasped and said that she had just heard the morning news and that Seoul, had fallen to the Chinese. I explained that I was in the middle of Seoul and I could assure her that it had not fallen to the Chinese, no one had told us. The following evening our Battalion went south through Seoul, and the city was turned over to the Chinese. I do not know to this day who paid for those calls.

The following is an account of action during November-December, 1950, from Sergeant First Class Donald D. Down, squad leader from the 3rd Platoon, Company F, 2nd Battalion, 7th Cavalry Regiment.

We were still in reserve in the port city of Chinnampo which was very near the capitol city of Pyongyang. Rumors were being circulated that thousands of Chinese Communist soldiers had crossed the frozen Yalu River and assaulted various units of the United Nations Forces. Most of us knew the North Korean Army was wiped out, and rumors continued that we would soon be returned to Japan. However, this would not be the case as orders were received on November 1st for us to saddle up and move out toward the north. For us in the 7th Cavalry Regiment, this would be our beginning of a new and totally different kind of warfare against the Chinese Communist Forces.

The weather was extremely cold, and we hadn't been issued our winter clothing yet. We were finding it difficult to even dig a foxhole because the ground was so frozen. It seemed that we had to keep moving around so we wouldn't freeze to death.

We continued to move in various positions along the front with our combat patrols. We were still finding troopers from the 8th Cavalry Regiment who were fortunate enough to escape the massacre at Unsan. All of us were saddened from the information that the entire regiment was annihilated in the battle by the full Chinese Division.

A new method of fighting had been developed which was now being called "strategic withdrawal." It was difficult to understand because most of us realized by rumors that the Chinese were good soldiers, and they were clobbering the United Nations Forces. Our movement was being shifted from one position to another to establish blocking positions to permit various elements of United Nations Forces to withdraw through us.

Everyone now realized that we wouldn't be back in Japan for Thanksgiving. We were also accepting the fact that we would probably spend our Christmas in Korea. Nevertheless, we tried to keep our faith in God, and we prayed that the war would soon come to an end.

Our combat patrols had made very little or no contact at all with the enemy. So far the Chinese had not moved their troops within our general area and things were pretty quite. I remember the town of Yongbyon and a large long stone wall which surrounded it. On this almost 6 foot high stone wall, the Chinese had written the words;

"Yankee go home - why fight this war for the Wall Street war mongers." At the time all of us in the company just laughed at the Communist propaganda.

From this town we were ordered to proceed about a mile, and if no contact was made with the Chinese, then we would return to the town and take up our old positions. Our platoon was the lead platoon and my squad was the lead squad, as we proceeded to move on the left side of the road.

At this particular time our company commander was new, and we all called him a "green horn." He was even walking right up front with us and down the center of the road. Finally, our platoon leader took corrective measures and ordered some point men out in front of us. Strangely, by the end of the month, this same company commander would be killed in action.

We proceeded slowly down the road for one mile when I spotted a civilian walking with something on his back. I called to him to stop as I started to move toward him. Suddenly, he dropped what he was carrying and broke out in a run. I immediately shot him down, and I walked over to see what he had dropped. When I opened up the bag, I could see that it contained enough explosives to blow a tank apart.

Then the new company commander began to yell and give me all kinds of hell for killing a poor defenseless civilian. I showed him the bag of explosives which seemed to surprise him, and he quickly changed his mind about the situation. I also told him that it was an old North Korean trick that was used very often. Our combat patrol returned to Yongbyon without any further problems.

On November 29th, we were shifted from one blocking position to establish another road block to permit the withdrawal of elements from the 6th Republic of Korea Division. They had been severely assaulted by Chinese forces and were now a somewhat disorganized unit. The careful screening of refugees also complicated the confusing situation.

Just prior to darkness, we established an outpost position near the road with a 57mm recoilless rifle team. Of Company F, one platoon was deployed across the small valley, one platoon on the hill to the right and my platoon the 3rd, was positioned on the hill to the left of the road. Also we had a platoon of South Korean soldiers assigned to our company and they were on the small hill directly in front of us. Several tanks were positioned within the small valley.

The night was clear, and the cold weather was almost unbearable. A commotion was coming from the road block so I sent my B.A.R. man, Private First Class Tom Boyd down to see what was going on. Within a short time he returned and said that South Korean soldiers were coming through our road block, and their outfit had been badly mauled by the Chinese.

Things sort of got quiet within the sector, and everyone was pretty well settled in for the night. I don't know what time that it was, but all hell broke loose as sounds of bugles and whistles echoed within the darkness. Firing was coming from the road block and throughout the entire small valley.

The platoon in the valley and the one across the road were now under a severe Chinese attack. Very shortly the South Korean platoon that was

Singing Christmas carols during December 1951, at Camp #5, Pyoktong, North Korea. Note Christmas tree and many American black prisoners of war. (Photo courtesy of Lloyd Cornwell, ex-Prisoner of War.)

in front of us came scrambling within our platoon sector because the Chinese had broken through their defenses. Our platoon leader immediately ordered us to pull back to the hill directly behind us which was approximately 100 yards away.

Once on the hill, we reestablished our positions and waited for the Chinese to continue their attack. The Chinese had concentrated their assault to the right of the road, and they successfully made a breakthrough between our company and Company C, of the 1st Battalion.

Our platoon never really got into the fight because the Chinese didn't continue their assault against our position. Sergeant Ralph Bernotas and myself kept walking the line to keep everyone alert just in case there was a change in their attack plans. Some of the company personnel complained about being so cold that they would rather lay there and die instead of trying to fight. Even for myself it seemed to be the longest and coldest day since my arrival in Korea.

It was approximately 0300 hours when elements from the 3rd Battalion arrived to assist our 2nd Battalion. By daybreak the Chinese assault had been stopped, and they were starting to retreat from their positions. Heavy artillery barrages were landing within their ranks as they attempted to flee northward.

Our company was relieved by another company and we made our way off of the hill and down to the road. We could easily see many dead Chinese in the open fields and along the road and ditch. When we reached the road, dead Chinese bodies were so close together that it looked as though they were laying head to toe. The Chinese had paid one hell of a price in their attempt to break through the GARRYOWEN defenses on November 29th - 30th, 1950.

December brought more cold weather and snow. The Chinese onslaught continued as we moved from various blocking positions in our strategic withdrawals toward the south.

Before the middle of December, our positions were being established below the 38th Parallel. We were now passing landmarks that only a few weeks earlier we had fought so hard to win from the North Koreans. Our retreat and march was long and slow as the vehicles on the road were bumper to bumper.

One night we kept moving south by foot, and we came upon an area that looked like the wide

open spaces. We were then ordered to walk single file toward the frozen river as most of us wondered if the ice could support our weight or not. The river we crossed was the Han River which was located near the capital city of Seoul, South Korea. After the river crossing, our battalion established defensive positions in an attempt to stop the Chinese onslaught.

On Christmas Day, all GARRYOWEN troopers were served hot turkey with all the trimmings. I know that everyone in Company F, really enjoyed this wonderful hot meal. But still there was the apprehension of the advancing Chinese Army. If our defenses could hold the relentless enemy attacks or not, only time would tell as the year of 1950 was coming to an end.

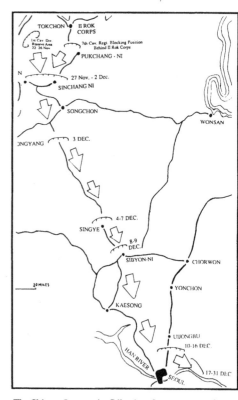

The Chinese Communist Offensive - In response to a limited United Nations offensive, the Chinese Reds launched their first full-scale attack on 26 November, and quickly shattered the II ROK Corps in the center of the line. United Nations forces then began a series of withdrawals that carried them below the 38th parallel before the end of 1950.

CHAPTER IX

WINTER COUNTER OFFENSIVE

He who supposes all men to be brave at all times ... does not realize that the courage of troops must be reborn daily, that nothing is so changeable, that the true skill of a general consists of knowing how to guarantee it by positions, dispositions, and those traits of genius that characterize great captains. — From the French of Maurice de Saxe, Reveries on The Art of War.

Prior to the close of 1950, Lieutenant General Matthew Ridgeway would assume command of the Eighth Army on December 26th. The previous commander Lieutenant General Walton Walker, while riding in his jeep with its handrail and autoloading shotgun, was spilled and killed in a collision on a dusty Korean road.

General Ridgeway's first task was to put heart in the Eighth Army. The American troops who were now veterans had risen from their own ashes of despair. Many were now knowledgeable and disciplined into a hard and tough fighting soldier. But many troopers still questioned the fact as to why in the hell were they in this godforsaken country of Korea.

General Matt Ridgeway knew this, and with a firm new hand, the Eighth Army gradually found itself. The line had to be held and the country of South Korea had to be protected. Before spring arrived, it was the Chinese who melted away into the snow-draped mountains, leaving their dead behind. But the Chinese retained the will to fight, and the assault northward did not come easy.

During the bitter cold months of December and January, there was a lull in the overall frontline activity. According to a brief history of the 1st Cavalry Division by the 14th Military History Detachment, "Four planned withdrawals were carried out. While supplies and reinforcements were massed in the rear, a fluid, yielding United Nations' line screened major movements, inflicted casualties, and prevented an actual breakthrough. Space was traded for time. The 1st Cavalry Division crossed the 38th Parallel on December 11th and 12th, and began to construct a defense in depth along the Han River in the vicinity of Seoul, South Korea."

Also air strikes by fighters and B-29 bombers were carried out in record numbers from the 38th Parallel to the Manchurian border. Even General MacArthur estimated that the Communists so far had suffered ten times as many casualties as the United Nations forces.

Despite these incredible losses, the communists began massing men and supplies in Yongchon, just above the 38th Parallel, as early as December 13th, for a knockout blow at Seoul. However, by December 28th, the

General Charles D. Palmer receiving his second star from General Bryant E. Moore, Commanding General of IX Corps. General Palmer then became Commanding Officer of the 1st Cavalry Division, February 1951. (U.S. Army photo)

7th Cavalry 1/4 ton jeep, which is stuck in the mud. The severe winter of 1950-51 brought many hardships to the American and United Nations troops. (U.S. Army photo)

7th Cavalry 2 -1/2 ton truck crossing a partially constructed bridge, near Uijongbu. (U.S. Army photo)

true extent of the enemy buildup had become clear. At least 20 divisions of Chinese and North Korean soldiers were ready for the drive on South Korea.

New Year's Eve began quietly as expected, as the 1st Cavalry Division with their weapons in defensive positions, waited in the extreme bitter cold weather. Within the first

minutes of 1951, and with no surprise, heavy barrages of Chinese artillery began pounding the United Nations forward units which were located at the 38th Parallel.

Following the artillery barrage all along the line, enemy soldiers struck southward in great force. Though the Eighth Army fought hard, it could not hold the advance.

The 14th Military History Detachment's account continues. "Crossing the frozen Imjin River, (which is located a few miles south of the demarcation line) and ignoring heavy losses, the Chinese Communist troops forced their way through minefields and barbed wire. The United Nations Forces fell back to their second line of defense on the Han River, abandoning Seoul. The city was evacuated on January 3, and more than a million refugees began the freezing trek south. But the enemy drive began to lose momentum when it crossed the Han River. After the fall of Seoul on January 4, a lull fell over the entire frontline in January 1951."

The 1st Cavalry Division pulled back to their sectors along the "Bridgehead Defensive Positions," south of the Han River. However, still north of the river, the 7th Cavalry Regiment moved to a new area closer to Seoul. This was in the vicinity of the hard-pressed 24th Infantry Division which stood directly in the path of the main Communist drive.

By January 4th, South Korean government officials and the United Nation troops pulled out of Seoul as the points of enemy soldiers entered it from the north. That night huge clouds of black smoke billowed up into the bleak winter sky as Seoul changed hands for the third time in a little more than six months.

For Seoul itself, the 24th Infantry Division and the 7th Cavalry Regiment had completed their crossing of the Han River early on the morning of January 4th. By January 5th, the exhausted troops of the 1st Cavalry Division had reached its new assembly areas west of the city of Chungju. These defensive positions would become the main delaying line. On January 8th, the 7th Cavalry Regiment was ordered to remain in position west of Chungju, where it would become a mobile reserve for the IX Corps.

The 1st Cavalry Division was plagued by many other problems. The harsh and severe Korean winter during January would see the early morning temperatures drop as low as 20 to 30 degrees below zero. The Division's vehicles had to be started as least every hour and moved regularly to free frozen brakes. Anti-freeze became a very serious and critical item. It was extremely hazardous for vehicles to travel on the icy narrow roads.

Endless streams of refugees flooded the roads and railways leading south. Some of the refugees carried only bundles, others dragged rude carts loaded with household possessions, and still others had only the clothes on their backs. Many died of exposure and starvation. Families became separated as children wandered, and their frantic parents sought them among the milling throngs. Crying babies were taken from the backs of their dead mothers. Many old people gave up hope and squatted beside the roads waiting for death. Civil assistance authorities did their best to help, and provided food, clothing and shelter of a sort for a large number; but there were too many to care for them all, and great numbers of innocent victims perished.

Meanwhile, Far East Supreme Commander Douglas MacArthur continued to feel the agony and frustration of the Korean War. General MacArthur, one of the most brilliant military minds America, has yet produced, graduated from West Point at the turn of the century. He stemmed from a distinguished military family; his father was a Lieutenant General and proconsul of the Philippines in his own right.

MacArthur had a profound hatred of war, but any war upon which he embarked must henceforth be a crusade. In no other way could the suffering be justified. He thought that any war was to be entered upon with sadness, with regret, but also with great ferocity.

In the Korean War he wanted a large-scale reinforcement of United Nations troops and retalitory measures against Red China, such as bombardment of Manchurian bases, naval blockage, or the use of Nationalist Chinese Forces.

Previously on December 29, 1950, MacArthur sent a message to the Joint Chiefs, as he had before, that he desired permission to blockade the China coast and attack air fields in Manchuria.

He stated he did not fear the Chinese would be provoked - MacArthur considered the United States already at war with China. He also stated that if his wishes were not granted, the Korean peninsula should be evacuated.

However, on January 13, 1951, President Harry Truman wired to MacArthur:

"I want you to know that the situation in Korea is receiving the utmost attention here, and that our efforts are concentrated upon finding the right decisions on this matter of the gravest importance to the future of America and to the survival of free peoples everywhere.

"I wish in this telegram to let you have my views as to our basic national and international purposes in continuing the resistance to aggression in Korea. We need your judgement as to the maximum effort which could reasonably be expected from the United Nations Forces under your command to support the resistance to aggression which we are trying rapidly to organize on a worldwide basis. This present telegram is not to be taken in any sense as a directive. Its purpose is to give you something of what is in our minds regarding the political factors.

"1. A successful resistance in Korea would serve the following important purposes:

"(a) to demonstrate that aggression will not be accepted by us or by the United Nations and to provide a rallying point around which the spirits and energies of the free world can be mobilized to meet the world-wide threat which the Soviet Union now poses.

"(b) To deflate the dangerously exaggerated political and military prestige to Communist China which now threatens to undermine the resistance of non-Communist Asia and to consolidate the hold of Communism on China itself.

"(c) To afford more time for and to

A wounded trooper from the Canadian Princess Light Infantry. They were a tough fighting and disiplined unit. (U.S. Army via United Nations)

Trooper carrying .30 caliber light machine gun during snow storm. (U.S. Army photo)

give direct assistance to the organization of non-Communist in Asia, both outside and inside China.

"(d) To carry out our commitments of honor to the South Koreans and to demonstrate to the world that the friendship of the United States is of inestimable value in time of adversity.

"(e) To make possible a more satisfactory peace settlement for Japan and to contribute greatly to the post-treaty security position of Japan in relation to the continent.

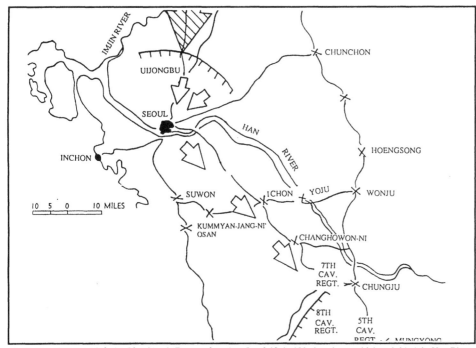

In the face of an overwhelming New Year's Eve attack against Seoul, United Nations forces withdrew behind the Han River early in January, 1951. The 1st Cavalry Division set up defensive positions in the vicinity of Chungju, south-east of Seoul.

"(f) To lend resolution to many countries not only in Asia but also in Europe and the Middle East who are now living within the shadow of Communist power and to let them know that they need not now rush to come to terms with Communism on whatever terms they can get, meaning complete submission.

"(g) To inspire those who may be called upon to fight against great odds if subjected to a sudden onslaught by the Soviet Union or by Communist China.

"(h) To lend point and urgency to the rapid built-up of the defenses of the western world.

"(i) To bring the United Nations through its first great effort on collective security and to produce a free-world coalition of incalculable value to the national security interests of the United States.

"(j) To alert the peoples behind the Iron Curtain that their masters are bent upon wars of aggression, and that this crime will be resisted by the free world.

"2. Our course of action at this time should be such as to consolidate the great majority of the United Nations. This majority is not merely part of an organization but is also the nations whom we would desperately need to count on as allies in the event the Soviet Union moves against us. Further, pending build-up of our national strength, we must act with great prudence in so far as extending the area of hostilities is concerned. Steps which might in themselves be fully justified and which might lend some assistance to the campaign in Korea would not be beneficial if they thereby involved Japan or Western Europe in large-scale hostilities.

"3. We recognize, of course, that continued resistance might not be militarily possible with the limited forces with which you are being called upon to meet large Chinese armies. Further, in the present world situa-tion, your forces must be preserved as an effective instrument for the defense of Japan and elsewhere. However, some of the important purposes mentioned above might be supported, if you should think is practicable and advisable, by continued resistance from off-shore islands of Korea, particularly from Cheju-do, if it becomes impracticable to hold an important portion of Korea itself. In the worst case, it would be important that if we must withdraw from Korea, it would be clear to the world that that course is forced upon us by military necessity, and that we shall not accept the result politically or militarily until the aggression has been rectified.

"4. In reaching a final decision about Korea, I shall have to give constant thought to the main threat from the Soviet Union and to the need for a rapid expansion of our armed forces to meet this great danger.

"5. I am encouraged to believe that the free world is getting a much clearer and realistic picture of the dangers before us and that the necessary courage and energy will be forthcoming. Recent proceedings in the United Nations have disclosed a certain amount of confusion and wishful thinking, but I believe that most members have been actuated by a desire to be absolutely sure that all possible avenues to peaceful settlement have been fully explored. I believe that the great majority is now rapidly consolidating and that the result will be an encouraging and formidable combination in defense of freedom.

"6. The entire nation is grateful for your splendid leadership in the difficult struggle in Korea and for the superb performance of your forces under the most difficult circumstances."

"[S] Harry S. Truman"

MacArthur might disagree with such a policy - but he could hardly fail to get the message. MacArthur was told to hold the frontier so that the tribes of the interior could continue to organize and to forget about carrying the war to the barbarians.

During the second week of January, the cast on my left forearm was finally removed. After a brief medical examination, I was given the okay to return to my old unit. Before departing the Swedish hospital, I made a personal round of the medical building to say good-by to medical officers and personnel whom I had met and made friends with during my brief stay. Medical care at the Swedish hospital was excellent, and I know that many other wounded soldiers shared the same sentiment.

Again I found it difficult to obtain a free ride north to reach the 1st Cavalry Division and the frontline. It seemed that supplies or ammunition being transported northward were going to various other divisions or units. I was finally informed by a master sergeant of that particular transportation company, that C-4 rations destined for the 15th Quartermaster, 1st Cavalry Division, were being loaded for immediate shipment.

Within a short time, the South Korean civilians had the trucks loaded with C-4 rations. As the small truck convoy departed

L. to R. Captain Crawford "Buck" Buchanan and Captain Herman K. Vester, Commander, Headquarters Company, 2nd Battalion, 7th Cavalry Regiment, February 1951. (Courtesy of Crawford Buchanan)

the supply area and warehouse, I found myself in the front seat of 2-1/2 ton truck riding as shotgun escort.

Attempting to get out of the city of Pusan was a task in itself, due to the small streets and narrow roads. The shifting masses were endangering military operations. Refugees had always presented a problem, but now the homeless wanderers trying to reach Pusan had every vital highway and railroad jammed and clogged. Various military units had extreme difficulty with their control points in keeping key roads and rail junctions clear and open.

After a rather bumpy and complicated ride on the narrow icy mountain roads, we finally reached the 15th Quartermaster supply point for the 1st Cavalry Division. I was very quickly informed that the 7th Cavalry Regimental Headquarters were approximately 80 miles further north.

From this point, I would now have to find some other unit to hitch a ride with. In a certain way, I was finding it somewhat ridiculous and difficult to reach the 7th Cavalry Regiment and the main line of resistance. However, due to the circumstances of the very bitter cold, and other underlying conditions within the entire Eighth Army, I had no other choice but to accept the overall facts.

Finally, after a more than brief search, I was fortunate enough to hitch another ride on a 2-1/2 ton truck with a group of new replacements who were assigned to the 24th Infantry Division. It was my understanding at the time that the 1st Cavalry Division was in reserve and located very near this particular Division.

By now I was extremely tired from a lengthy and disgusting ride to reach the 7th Cavalry Regiment. At approximately 2100 hours, I finally arrived at the reserve area and the command post of regimental headquarters. After a brief report and talk with the Regimental Sergeant Major, it was then decided that I would remain here for the night. I was temporarily issued a cot to sleep on, and I slipped into my sleeping bag, and within a few minutes I fell asleep.

After a good night of sleep, all of us were awakened within the tent to then receive a hot breakfast. During this meal, I would

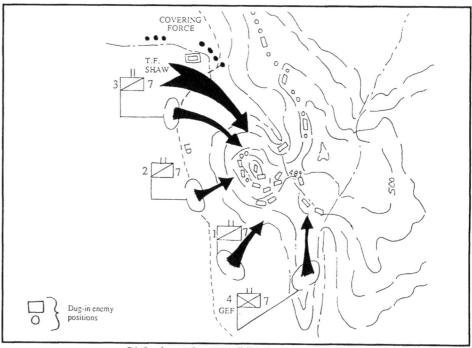

7th Cavalry attack against Hill 578 12-13 February, 1951

have the opportunity to personally meet and briefly talk with Colonel William A. Harris, Regimental Commander of the 7th Cavalry Regiment. I considered this a great honor because not only myself, but every officer and trooper within the regiment had very high respect and admiration for this very dedicated Colonel.

Even though I had seen Colonel Harris numerous times within the combat areas of our regiment, this brief personal talk was very special to me. He emphasized a hearty welcome of my return from the hospital and to the regiment. Also he stressed the need of my continued dedication and devotion to the 2nd Battalion and the 7th Cavalry Regiment. We both acknowledged the fact that of the original GARRYOWEN troopers from Japan, only a few still remained with the regiment.

Our brief conversation ended as we saluted each other, and he climbed aboard his awaiting jeep that had a horse saddle mounted on the hood. A true sight of inspiration to every GARRYOWEN officer and trooper.

Shortly, I was informed that a jeep was ready to drive me to the command post of Company H. I very soon discovered that our company location was south of the Han River and southeast of the city of Seoul, South Korea. In my mind, I thought back to just a few months earlier we had experienced the bloody battles of the Naktong River. The 7th Cavalry Regiment had led the drive into North Korea which was the longest drive in the shortest period of time in the history of the United States Army. Needless to say, our positions now were well below the 38th Parallel.

Upon entering the command post tent of Company H, I immediately received a welcome back greeting from company commander, Captain John Wadsworth. It was great to see the Captain again and to be back with Company H. The Captain quickly replied, "Lieutenant Daily, the 1st Platoon is still yours!" I answered, "Yes sir! I'm ready!"

Captain Wadsworth then explained briefly the future counterattack plans against the Chinese as we reviewed several terrain maps. A special emphasis on appropriate training was stressed and would be conducted by every officer and trooper in the company.

The Captain also expressed the fact that the Greek Expeditionary Forces (GEF), were now assigned to the 7th Cavalry Regiment, and had become the 4th Battalion. Many of the Greek soldiers were combat veterans, having fought the German Nazi in their native country of Greece during World War II. In the forthcoming weeks, they would prove themselves to be an excellent combat fighter against the Chinese Communist Forces.

By afternoon, I had gradually worked my way within the 1st Platoon. Everyone welcomed me back and overall personnel replacements had changed but very little since my absence from the platoon. However, everyone was complaining about the miserable and bitter cold weather, and many troop-

Attacking with the support of tanks from the 70th Tank Battalion. (U.S. Army photo)

Inside of a Mobile Army Surgical Hospital, which was normally equipped with 60 beds, 11 doctors and some 100 personnel in total. (Postoperative ward NorMash, Dr. Odd Oyen)

ers had already experienced frost bite.

During the battle lull of January, we continued to train and assisted various combat patrol missions. For some unknown reason, the enemy did not continue their assault south of the Han River. Various reports had it that the Chinese were retreating due to severe blows against their troops and supply lines by the American Air Force.

By the end of January, the 7th Cavalry Regiment was ordered to methodically move northward in a limited offensive. This was due to the absence of a large scale enemy resistance. Nevertheless, all combat patrols were painstaking as caution was emphasized to prevent possible bypassing of any hostile enemy troops. It was understood at the time that no enemy troops would be left behind that could possibly jeopardize the safety of other advancing units.

The following is an account of the wounded evacuation on January 30, 1951, from 1st Lieutenant, Mell S. Pelot, assistant to the Medical Officer, 2nd Battalion Aid Station, 7th Cavalry Regiment.

Medical support for the 2nd Battalion, 7th Cavalry Regiment in Korea was organically identical to that of any similar unit in an Infantry Division. Basically it consisted of the attachment of a Medical Platoon from the Regimental Medical Company to an Infantry Battalion. When attached, the platoon became known as the "Battalion Aid Station," and thus provided the second echelon of medical support following the assistance initially rendered to a casualty by the aid man attached to each platoon at the company level.

As the assistant to the Medical Officer, 2nd Battalion Aid Station, how well I recall my initiation to combat in Korea. In late January, 1951, an urgent radio call came into Battalion Headquarters requesting assistance in evacuating several casualties in the forward area. Having arrived at the Aid Station only a few days previously, and

perhaps wanting to prove my "mettle," I violated every Army axiom that states one should never volunteer for anything, and promptly volunteered "to go bring the wounded boys back." There was one major catch — the request to the Aid Station failed to mention that the casualties were members of a platoon pinned down by enemy fire!

The site of the pinned downed unit was in a frozen stream bed in a valley flanked by three hills with an open approach toward friendly lines.

Upon arriving at the site in a litter jeep with several medical aid men, we were approached by a rifleman who advised us where the casualties were and provided the cheerful news that they were pinned down and cut off.

Something had to be done and soon as the time was late and darkness would soon be upon us. I told the aid men to come with me but to remain very low. We started out and suddenly a machine gun opened fire, and we all virtually bore ourselves into the ground with hand made fox holes. An experienced rifleman was accompanying us on our approach to the casualties, and after chiding us for halting, he made an open dash for the casualties in an endeavor to spur us on. The machine gun opened up on him, and he too hastily dove for lower ground.

Fortunately, someone in the area made a radio call to our supporting artillery for smoke. I am sure that the smoke rounds that came in very soon and most accurately were heaven sent and guided by Providence. They landed forward, placed the casualties on litters, and hurried toward the opening to the rear.

The enemy troops were no fools — they seem never to be. They had leveled their weapons and zeroed in to fire through the smoke towards our escape route. I have never heard heavier "incoming mail." About this time, Lt. Charlie Coin, MSC, of the Regimental Medical Company, an experienced combat veteran, arrived on the scene. He apparently had heard the initial radio call for assistance and came forward to help. I yelled for

everyone to get lower, the incoming fire was so low. At that moment, a rifleman immediately beside me dropped, yelling "Medic." We immediately placed him on a litter and continued our rapid retrograde movement. (Not a retreat!)

As we reached the opening to make good our escape, a tank appeared - a most welcome addition to our meager forces. We placed the casualties on the litter jeep and the tank when suddenly automatic weapons fire opened up against us from the hill to our immediate right. The enemy had charged across the area we had just evacuated and were firing down on us.

The tank crew slammed the hatch on the turret and the machine gunner yelled to the commander, "I'll cover the hill, Sir, while you back us away." The tank fire was totally effective, completely silencing the incoming fire. From that point on we safely made our way back to the Aid Station with me squatted firmly down behind the tank turret, arriving just before dusk.

In recounting battle experiences, we almost inevitably inject a certain amount of humor and to a certain degree, some light humor has been inserted into this narrative. However, upon our return to the Aid Station and after the evening meal, I looked down and noticed four round, neat bullet holes through my field jacket just under my right arm. Only then did I realize how close that initial round of machine gun fire had come to making me a "statistic" rather than a fortunate survivor of the Korean War.

For his heroic achievement in the military operation against the enemy, 1st Lt. Mell S. Pelot was awarded the Bronze Star Medal with "V" Device. It reads as follows:

First Lieutenant Mell S. Pelot Medical Service Corps, United States Army, Medical Company, 7th Cavalry Regiment, 1st Cavalry Division for heroism in action against the enemy on 30 January 1951, near Nogong-ni, Korea. When an infantry platoon was on patrol and suffered four casualties from an encounter with the enemy, Lieutenant Pelot, hearing a radio call for medical aid support, immediately set out with a group of volunteer litter bearers. Due to intense hostile fire, the men were unable to reach the wounded soldiers by a direct route. Lieutenant Pelot then led his companions over several hills and down a forward slope in the face of enemy fire until he reached the injured men. While the Chinese concentrated on the only path leading from the area, Lieutenant Pelot courageously directed the evacuation of the casualties over 100 yards of bullet swept ground to cover. His actions undoubtedly saved his comrades from further injury or possible death. Lieutenant Pelot's heroism reflects great credit on himself and the military service.

Lieutenant Mell S. Pelot continued his military career in the Army and retired as a Lt. Colonel in 1966.

Also at the end of January, I was informed by Captain Wadsworth that my name was selected for the 5 day "R & R" leave in Tokyo. I really enjoyed the few days rest and rehabilitation and the opportunity to eat some delicious food and do some sightseeing in Tokyo. This particular program was established by the Eighth Army, and it was joyfully accepted by every officer and trooper in the entire command.

After returning from Tokyo on February

3rd, I soon discovered that prior to my arrival, the 2nd Battalion had launched an attack at approximately 0700 hours. Upon leaving the command post of Company H, I found myself in the midst of a bitter battle to secure Hills 481 and 512.

I talked to Captain Wadsworth, and he gave me a brief explanation of our attack plans. Then I went to see 1st Lt. Bruinooge who had temporary leadership of my platoon. He informed me of the location of the section of light machine guns which were assigned as support elements to Companies E and F.

The enemy had heavily fortified both of these particular hills. Extremely close air support was used in the coordinated attack plans. The fight for control of both hills were bitter as the concealed enemy waited in ambush for the 2nd Battalion troopers to approach within grenade range below them.

However, the ambush tactics were discovered by a Mosquito (T6), 5th Air Force observation aircraft. This information was quickly transmitted to F-51 Mustang fighter aircraft directly overhead. One particular F-51 aircraft came in at tree-top level through a hail of enemy machine gun and small arms fire, to drop a napalm bomb on the key position within fifty yards of our own assault troops.

This extremely close air support made it possible for the 2nd Battalion to secure their objectives. The dedicated fighting spirit of the 2nd Battalion troopers were the actual elements in defending and holding these important hill positions. The Chinese had launched three successive counterattacks against the GARRYOWEN troopers. But they failed in each of their attempts. At the end of the day's fighting, 105 enemy dead were counted in the surrounding positions.

The following is a brief story of a successful attack of Hill 481 on February 3rd-4th, 1950, from 2nd Lt. John Matthews, 3rd Platoon Leader, Company E, 2nd Battalion, 7th Cavalry Regiment.

Company E Commander, 1st Lt. Albert Moses, ordered my platoon to make the initial attack on Hill 481. We had just recently relieved elements of the Greek Expeditionary Forces (GEF), who previously held positions within this area.

Orders actually emphasized a fast assault on the hill. As we attempted to attack the hill, I moved with the point squad and a couple of scouts on the ridge to the right of our objective. The terrain wasn't that rough which enabled us to make forward progress a little easier. This also helped to get my scouts ahead of the platoon so they could possibly observe or spot any enemy movement and give us an early warning.

Shortly, one of the scouts informed me that he spotted enemy movement and at this time, we were approximately 100 yards from the top of the hill. Then all hell started to break out as we received automatic weapons fire from several enemy concealed positions. I ordered the platoon to fix bayonets and prepare to attack.

Then I received field phone contact from Lt. Al Moses, and he told me that a (T6) Mosquito observation plane had spotted enemy movement on the reverse slope of the hill. He further indi-

Move up that 3.5 Rocket Team (Bazooka) for support. Note enemy automatic rifle laying in foreground. (U.S. Army Photo)

cated that they could be regrouping for an apparent counterattack. He also stated that an air strike had been ordered to drop napalm bombs and strafe with their machine guns, the entire peak of the hill.

By now we were receiving machine gun crossfire from heavily fortified enemy positions. We desperately fought our way to within 50 yards of the hill peak. Then I ordered the air panel markers to be properly displayed for the air force.

Suddenly, F-51 Mustangs appeared as they strafed and dropped napalm bombs at an extremely close range to our forward elements. One fighter plane came in so close that I thought it was going to drop the napalm bomb directly on our platoon. However, the bomb cleared my platoon and landed on key enemy positions. This was my first experience with air support being so close to an attack. I know that everyone in the platoon had the hell scared out of them, including myself.

The artillery immediately followed with their constant barrages on the hill peak and reverse slope. This also inflicted heavy casualties to the enemy as they attempted to counterattack several times. We continued to attack and progressed forward under stubborn enemy resistance. By late afternoon, we finally secured our objective and Hill 481.

We continued to hold our positions, and throughout the night our support artillery sent endless barrages into enemy positions. Some of the support artillery was firing heavy 240-mm projectiles on enemy positions within Hill 512. The Chinese continued to blow their bugles throughout the night and early morning darkness.

With daybreak, we were informed that the enemy had withdrawn from their positions. Also, Lt. Colonel John Callaway, 2nd Battalion Commander, personally came up on the hill and gave congratulations to me and the entire platoon for a successful attack. He also emphasized that the overall attack was perfectly coordinated with support from the Air Force and artillery units.

The enemy suffered severely with approximately 150 casualties either killed, wounded or

captured. My platoon experienced seven casualties, with one killed and six wounded.

Within a few weeks, Company G would experience heavy casualties, and Lt. Al Moses would become Commander of Company G, and I would assume leadership of another platoon. However, this was a typical movement of officers in an infantry battalion and was expected and accepted within the conditions of combat.

2nd Lt. John Matthews continued his military career and attained the rank of Lt. Colonel. He retired from the Army in 1966.

After our successful attack during the day, and repelling three Chinese counterattacks, the 2nd Battalion by late afternoon closed in a tight perimeter. An immediate 100 percent alert throughout the night was ordered.

From my platoon, I ordered a .30 caliber light machine gun team to establish an outpost position. However, I was short an ammo bearer for the machine gun team. I talked briefly with Sergeant First Class Donald Down, from the 3rd Platoon, Company F, and he decided to loan me two troopers for the outpost position.

At daybreak, I was immediately informed that I had better investigate the possibility of several troopers from my platoon being killed sometime during the night. This report seemed strange because I knew of no enemy attack within the entire night.

Arriving at the outpost position, a medic was starting to check the lifeless bodies of the troopers. It was quickly and definitely concluded that all four troopers had been bayoneted in their sleep by a probing Chinese patrol. As much as it had been stressed and emphasized about falling asleep, the brave troopers of Companies F and H had somehow failed in their self discipline. The news of this very tragic incident, rapidly circulated throughout the 2nd Battalion.

Of the many disciplines that a combat trooper learns from his battle experiences, one is to avoid falling asleep while on a night position or outpost. This is regardless of how

Major General Hobart Gay salutes the 1st Cavalry Division as he prepares to depart Korea in February 1951. (U.S. Army photo)

Colonel William "Wild Bill" Harris, Commander 7th Cavalry Regiment, looks at confiscated Chinese Bugle. (Army photo)

tired and exhausted he may be or feel. This very serious discipline that a trooper learns, not only is to protect his own life, but the lives of his comrades within the squad, platoon, company and battalion.

Actually, this discipline is emphasized and taught in the very early stages of a soldier's basic training. During the training, all soldiers are taught to learn and remember the Army General Orders. Article No. 11 of the General Orders is as follows: "To be especially watchful at night and during the time for challenging, to challenge all persons on or near my post, and to allow no one to pass without proper authority."

The loss of a Corporal and a Private First Class from my platoon had put me in a very depressed mood. Particularly the way and manner in which they were killed. Both were excellent troopers and were seasoned combat fighters. It was a very difficult task for me to report the casualties to Captain Wadsworth. However, being the excellent company commander that he was, he accepted the sad and tragic casualty report as one of the unfortunate circumstances within the conditions of combat.

During the next several days, our regimental positions were consolidated as rumors indicted the enemy was in apparent celebration of the Chinese New Year. Radio contact with a particular combat patrol revealed that the enemy could be heard talking, laughing and singing at a particular villagew. The patrol stated that they were withdrawing and further requested that the artillery should immediately place a battalion Time on Target (TOT), concentration on the areas. (Time on Target is a concentration of artillery rounds fired from several different units so as to land on the target simultaneously).

The next morning, on February 6th, the 2nd Battalion saddled up and moved out to seize the high ground in the vicinity of Hill

231. No enemy contact was made, however, according to civilian refugees interrogated, the Time on Target concentration the previous day had successfully inflicted heavy enemy casualties.

The early morning of February 7th, the 2nd Battalion attacked Hill 243, and we were now experiencing enemy positions that were heavily reinforced with machine guns. We were encountering enemy troops that were using reverse slope tactics. The rough mountain terrain had endless trenches dug throughout the steep ridges and many continued to the rear or reverse slope of the hill. While an artillery barrage was being fired on the front side of a particular hill, the enemy could seek safety from the shelling by moving to the reverse slope. This enemy resistance slowed our attack, but we continued our assault and secured the hill by early afternoon.

The following morning, on February 8th, numerous combat patrols were sent out to make contact with the Chinese. We experienced extreme difficulty in the rugged terrain, and a different type of warfare existed. We discovered that during the battle lull of January, the Chinese had wasted no time in digging the endless trenches; and many with extremely heavy fortifications.

The point squad from the rifle platoon continued to move slowly with caution to closely observe any enemy movement within the vast hill trenches. The light machine gun section from my platoon was assigned as a support element to the rifle platoon of Company E. Observation with my binoculars failed to reveal any enemy activity as we proceeded forward. Finally, in the late afternoon, the point squad made contact with the enemy. We engaged with the enemy in an exchange of automatic and small arms fire. With the support of the light machine guns from my platoon, we attempted an orderly withdrawal to our 2nd Battalion perimeter.

A quick conversation with 1st Lt. Rod Confer, commanding officer of Company E, reveale l there were no casualties, and the enemy to be of a patrol size.

During the evening my platoon was established into a tight defensive position. Word was then received that our 2nd Battalion Commander, Lt. Colonel John W. Callaway had issued orders for 100 percent alert within the battalion. I had the personal feeling that something major was about to happen.

At approximately 0330 hours in the early morning of February 9th, units of the 2nd Battalion began assembling for this attack. We were issued illuminous buttons to fasten on our webbed belts to identify officers and non-commissioned officers of the assaulting units during the night attack.

At this particular time, it was not known what unit the elements from my platoon would support in the initial attack. We moved behind elements of Companies F and G, and we secured an assembly area at the base of Hill 202, at 0430 hours.

Company G made the initial attack just prior to daybreak, and I had assigned one squad from my platoon as an element of support with .30 caliber light machine guns. Squad leader, Sergeant First Class Tom Simmons, complained to me that he didn't believe the reports that the Chinese had withdrawn from the hill. I had the personal feeling that he could be right.

Shortly after they moved out in their attack, all hell broke loose as machine gun fire came from the top of the ridge and the flanks. From reports, the point squad had made contact with a Chinese outpost, which triggered the alarm. Under withering small arms and machine gun fire, Company G was forced to withdraw from their attack.

At 0600 hours, Company F reported by radio that they had made no contact with the enemy and had secured their objective.

L. to R. General Matt Ridgeway, Commander, Eighth Army; Major General Charles Palmer, Commander 1st Cavalry Division; Colonel WilliamHarris, Commander 7th Cavalry; Colonel John Daskalopoules, Commander Greek Battalion, attached to the 7th Cavalry. February 23, 1951 (Army Photo)

Lt.Colonel John W. Callaway, Commander, 2nd Battalion, 7th Cavalry, discusses with General of the Army Douglas MacArthur the tactical situation north of Chipyong, Korea 1951. (Army photo)

Shortly after this report, the Chinese from their well-concealed bunkers sent withering machine gun fire into the troopers of Company F.

Then it became necessary for Company G to reorganize and immediately move to the west flank of Company F. I quickly issued orders to Sergeant First Class Tom Simmons to move his squad as support element to the attacking rifle platoons. This attack was also reinforced with .30 caliber light machine guns from the 2nd squad of my platoon.

The assault on Hill 202 was slow and difficult, and it was clear that the Chinese had prepared to make a desperate fight. The enemy and our attacking units became heavily engaged in a dual exchange of machine gun fire. Even support elements from the 70th Tank Battalion with direct cannon fire could not dislodge the enemy from their fortified positions. With constant enemy counterattacks, both Companies F and G were forced to withdraw prior to midnight. Orders were then issued for the 2nd Battalion to revert to regimental reserve.

The following is an account of the action on Hill 202 from Corporal Herb Phillips, 2nd Platoon, Company F, 2nd Battalion, 7th Cavalry Regiment.

We started our objective for Hill 202 at 0300 hours in the morning. It was very cold attempting to cross the river as many troopers were slipping on the rocks that were covered with a thin layer of ice.

I was in the 2nd Platoon, and we were assigned to lead the attack. We were suppose to secure the ridge at the high point, then the rest of the company was to move up through us to secure the balance of the ridgeline. The overall terrain was extremely rough with many sharp and steep edges along the hillside.

Another ridge to our left was very dark and

sort of spooky, and we kept looking to possibly see some enemy activity. Then suddenly we could see Chinese soldiers silhouetted within the ridgeline. They had not seen our forward elements so far.

Then word was passed on to us that some Chinese soldiers were wanting to surrender. It was decided that a patrol would be sent forward to attempt to negotiate with the enemy, but it really turned out to be a real dumb move.

Suddenly the enemy started firing automatic weapons almost down our throats. We were on the reverse slope that had a small saddle approximately 35 yards away from us. Very soon we were experiencing casualties from an enemy heavy machine gun emplacement.

We couldn't throw a grenade that far, and we didn't have a grenade launcher with us. Our .60-mm mortar squads were now positioned and were sending a deadly blow upon the enemy. Then I noticed the 1st Platoon, making a maneuver around our left flank.

I was a radioman on a 536 walkie talkie radio, and someone started asking, "What's holding you up, what's holding you up?" I quickly replied that we were pinned down and unable to progress forward. Then I told them that we desperately needed litters and litter bearers for our wounded.

Our support artillery was now sending a heavy barrage into the entire hillside. Then the unexpected happened as two short artillery rounds landed within our platoon. Oh God, did we experience a lot of casualties from the explosions.

Several of us got up to move to another position because of our fear of the short artillery rounds. Corporal Bowman and myself went to a small saddle of the ridge to seek appropriate cover. Without hesitation, the enemy immediately started raking over us with their machine guns. Suddenly, Bowman and I both were wounded by a deadly hail of fire.

The bullet tore through my leg, and soon the

medic gave me the necessary medical attention. A team of refugees who were being used as litter bearers, arrived to remove me from the hill. However, the enemy continued to fire down our throats and I had to lay for a while in an open area before I was actually taken off of Hill 202.

I was put in a litter jeep and taken to the 2nd Battalion aid station. From there I was processed through a collecting station and then transferred to a regular MASH unit. There was a tremendous amount of casualties, and I would have to remain here for a day and a half, because chest and belly wounds were preference over leg wounds.

Here I would also see our mail clerk as he had been wounded trying to deliver mail to the troopers of Company F. As I continued to look around, I started to realize that I was still alive and hadn't died and went to a so-called heaven or hell.

Corporal Herb Phillips would spend many months in hospitals in the United States recuperating from his wounds. Eventually, he was honorably discharged from the Army.

From the few captured Chinese troops it was apparent that the age old scourge of armies was taking its toll within enemy ranks, and many were suffering from frostbite, trench foot and typhus. Moreover, the Chinese did not have by Western standards, proper medical facilities. The Chinese were now fighting 260 miles south of the Manchurian border, which was quite different from that in November when they had their bases to their immediate rear.

On February 10th, while in regimental reserve, information was received that elements from the 4th Battalion (GEF), assaulted Hill 202 using fixed bayonets, grenades and flame throwers. Again the enemy counterattacked, forcing the brave Greek soldiers to withdraw from part of the dominating terrain just north of Hill 202. However, this resistance was finally overcome by a coordinated attack with support elements from the 3rd Battalion. On the previous day, the 2nd Battalion had taken the same knoll three separate times.

The courageous Greek soldiers, under the leadership of Lieutenant Colonel D. Arbouzis, Commander, 4th Battalion (GEF), had established their fighting reputation in Korea. In a previous battle on January 30th, the enemy lost an estimated 800 killed in their struggle to gain control of Hill 381. The (GEF) had earned high respect from all of the officers and troopers of GARRYOWEN.

The early morning of February 11th, the 2nd Battalion was ordered to saddle up and move out for an attack on Hills 229 and 277. Captain Wadsworth ordered me to contact 1st Lt. Rod Confer, Commander, Company E. After talking to Lt. Confer about the planned attack on Hill 229, it was decided that a light .30 caliber machine gun section from my platoon would give the necessary fire support to elements of the rifle platoons of Company E. In this coordinated attack, Companies F and G were ordered to attempt a sweeping flank movement, and their objective was to seize Hill 277.

Our advance on Hill 229 was quickly met with fierce enemy resistance. However, elements from the rifle platoons with 57-mm recoilless rifles and 75-mm recoilless rifles from the 2nd Platoon, Company H, zeroed in on the enemy machine gun bunkers with extreme accuracy. The 2nd Battalion attack was successful, and by early afternoon the enemy attempted to withdraw, and we caught them in a withering cross fire with our small arms, automatic weapons, machine gun, artillery, mortar and tank cannon. By late afternoon, we had established a tight perimeter within the 2nd Battalion.

The troopers of the 2nd Battalion for the most part were seasoned fighters and knew what the soldiers' trade was all about. They had learned how it is in combat, and how it must always be. Many realized and accepted the fact that they had to become a soldier, or they would die.

Many brave men existed in the ranks, but they were learning that bravery of itself has little to do with success in battle. On the frontline, most normal men are afraid, have been afraid, or will be afraid. Only when disciplined to obey orders quickly and willingly, can such fear be controlled. Properly conditioned against the shattering experience of war, only knowing almost from rote what to do, can men carry out their tasks, come what may. Knowing they are disciplined, trained, and conditioned, brings pride to men — pride in their own ability; and this pride will hold them true when all else fails.

It had become apparent that we would not remain in temporary regimental reserve. One very difficult mission remained to be completed by the 7th Cavalry Regiment. We were alerted that our future attack plans would be against the enemy strongpoint on Hill 578.

On the morning of February 12th, I was notified along with other officers of Company H, to report to Captain Wadsworth for a briefing. After listening to the Captain explain our future attack plans on Hill 578, it was obvious from the briefing that it would be a difficult task to seize our objective. You could see from the contour intervals on the terrain map, the possibility of many heavily dug-in enemy positions.

Reports were filtered back to Company H that numerous combat patrols probing the surrounding hill mass from all sides had met stiff enemy resistance. By the late afternoon of February 12th, my platoon had finished cleaning their weapons, and resupplies of food and ammunition had been properly distributed. We were now prepared to attack and anxiously awaited for orders to be issued.

However, Captain Wadsworth again notified all Company H officers to report for a briefing. He had recently returned from 2nd Battalion headquarters where he had met with other battalion officers, and the battalion commander, Lt. Colonel John Callaway. Their prime discussion was the future status of Hill 578.

According to the Captain, the future attack would not be attempted until softening up of the hill mass by artillery and air strikes were completed. He then emphasized that the entire crest of the hill mass had been assigned to the 2nd Battalion. However, a certain area north of the crest, which was to our left flank, was tentatively assigned to the 3rd Battalion. The 1st Battalion and the 4th Battalion (GEF), were to our right flank and would cover the southern and eastern portions of the hill mass.

The Captain further briefed us on the decision of the 2nd and 3rd Battalion Commanders to have a 24-hour period of artillery and air strike preparation on the hill mass objective. This would commence on February 13th, but the attack plans would not be initiated until the following morning. The attacking rifle companies of the 2nd Battalion and the support elements from Company H, were tentatively scheduled for attack at 0900 hours on February 14th. It was also emphasized within the 2nd Battalion, that every trooper should attempt to get as much rest as possible prior to this scheduled assault.

The 7th Cavalry had to accomplish its mission under extremely difficult and hazardous conditions. The strongly defended enemy positions continued within the steep approaches and to the very crest of the hill. The enemy was exerting a determined effort to defend the adjacent ridges and knolls surrounding the crest of the hill.

During the night of February 12th - 13th, the 77th Field Artillery supported by other units of the Division Artillery, commenced firing TOT concentrations on the hill mass. In conjunction with this, fire from the heavy mortar company was directed on known enemy targets within the ridge line.

On February 13th, available air support strafed and bombed the entire hill mass. Also, direct cannon fire from tanks of the 70th Tank Battalion attempted to destroy enemy fortifications or dug-in positions along

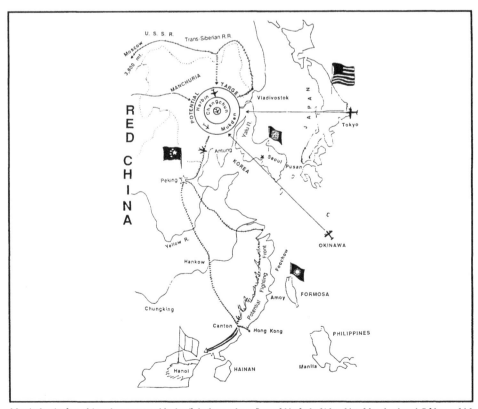

MacArthur's plan, although never stated in detail, is shown above. It would include: 1) bombing Manchurian airfields on which enemy planes are now massing; 2) blockading the coast of China; 3) bombing Chinese supply centers; 4) helping the Chinese Nationalists to build up anti-Communist resistance in South China. These actions, together with an advance by the United Nation Forces in Korea, might endanger the Chinese Red regime, forcing them to end the war. Truman, however, feared that attacking the Chinese anywhere outside the Korean peninsula would provoke the Russians into entering the war.

the ridge line leading to the crest of the hill.

The early morning of February 14th, troopers of the 2nd Battalion were ready for the initial assault on Hill 578. It was anticipated that the softening up preparation from the artillery units, and the air strikes, had been effective in destroying many of the enemy positions and fortifications. However, discouraging information was received that we would not have any air support or preparation from napalm bombs just prior to our actual jump off time. (We were told later on that all available air support was desperately needed for the 2nd Infantry Division. Certain elements of the division had been surrounded by Chinese Communist Forces).

The 2nd Battalion had been assigned the ridge line from the western side and the very crest of the hill mass. Company G crossed the line of departure shortly after 0900 hours, which was almost on schedule. It didn't take long for their point patrol squad to make contact with the enemy.

Heavy mortar, small arms and automatic weapons fire from enemy positions continued with increased intensity. I could easily see with my binoculars that Company G was making slow progress up the ridge line and toward the crest of the hill.

Support elements from my platoon were not assigned with the initial assault company. It was now early afternoon, and it became apparent that Company G was having extreme difficulty in reaching the hill crest objective. The enemy was determined to defend and hold the hill regardless of the circumstances. These well trained and battle-hardened veterans of the China held iron control.

Prior to darkness and beset by the crisis within the 2nd Battalion, orders were finally issued by Captain Wadsworth that elements from my platoon would give the necessary support to Company E. From the briefing, our maneuver would be to the left flank of Company G and a further attempt to link up with Company L, 3rd Battalion.

Within the area to the left flank of Company G, the enemy had five machine guns emplacements on the hill. These fortified positions had excellent fields of fire and were sweeping the entire area with cross fire.

Just prior to our arrival to the left flank of Company G, a flame thrower operator from that company successfully knocked out one of the enemy machine gun emplacements. Since my arrival in Korea, it was the first time that I had seen this type of weapon used in combat. It was my understanding that the weapon was extremely heavy and cumbersome for mountain fighting.

Floundering about in a morass of uncertainty within the darkness, we slowly progressed to the left flank of Company G. As we moved into position, we were caught in withering machine gun fire, and showered with enemy hand grenades. Many of the hand grenades were exploding as they bounced down the hillside. In the darkness, it gave me a strange feeling of insecurity in not being able to see them; or even know where in the hell they were falling or landing.

We quickly searched for concealment to establish appropriate firing positions. Very soon the machine guns of Companies E and H became engaged in a dual exchange of fire with the enemy. The hill mass exposed a panoramic view from the zigzagging of green tracers from enemy machine guns, and the pinkish tracers from the machine guns of the GARRYOWEN troopers.

The enemy hand grenades and machine gun fire were inflicting wounds to numerous troopers of Company E. It seemed that every time the rifle platoons advanced, the Chinese would immediately counterattack. After several hours of maneuvering our positions, elements of Company E finally reached the top portion of the ridge.

The brave troopers of Company E, in their advance to reach their objective had destroyed two machine gun nests. However, two enemy machine guns still remained in position and continued to operate. At this particular time, no physical contact had been made with Company L, 3rd Battalion.

Reestablishing our positions within the higher portion of the ridge, it then gave us an advantage in holding the ground which we had gained. However, Company E continued to suffer casualties, and the shout for "medic" was repeated many times, and echoed within the night darkness. The combat aidman had his hands full, and the litter bearers had extreme difficulty in getting the wounded down the steep hillside.

At daybreak, we continued our attack toward our objective to seize the crest of the hill. The enemy hastily counterattacked, but failed in their desperate attempt to force us to withdraw. This unsuccessful counter-attack by the enemy definitely proved to be their last effort in defending Hill 578.

As I attempted to move forward on the ridge line to direct several ammo bearers from my platoon, I came eyeball to eyeball with an enemy soldier as he was attempting to throw a hand grenade. After he released the grenade, he quickly turned and started running within the passage of a long trench. I immediately took aim with my rifle and rapidly fired five shots as he tried to escape.

Suddenly his body fell forward to the floor of the trench. I moved cautiously toward the body to see if he was possibly alive or not. Upon my investigation, I soon discovered that he was dead, and he was a Chinese officer. Of the five shots that I had fired, three had ripped through his back.

I then noticed that he was carrying a strange looking pistol which I quickly removed from the side of his body. Then I placed the pistol and holster into my field jacket to keep for my own personal possession. Later on I was told that the pistol was a Japanese Nambu and was carried by officers during World War II. I assumed that the pistol was obtained from the Japanese at the end of World War II by Chinese Nationalists.

Not wasting anymore valuable time, I then directed the ammo bearers to continue to follow me to one of my light machine gun positions. The enemy continued to fight hard to hold their defensive positions, and they were moving from one position to another in

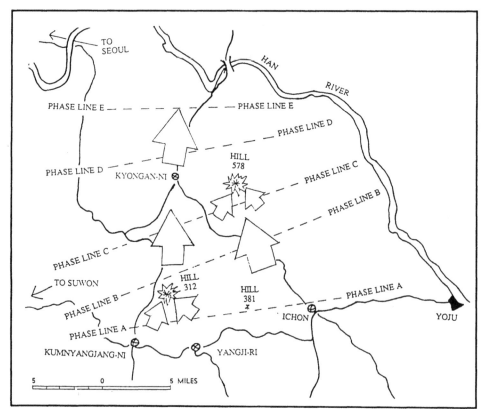

When the Chinese failed to follow up their all-out attack on Seoul, the Eighth Army began probing northward again. On 25 January, in the IX Corps sector, the 1st Cav. undertook a reconnanissance in force. Due to the absense of large-scale enemy resistance, this soon developed into a limited offensive which carried methodically northward across a series of phase line (A-E) until the Division was relieved in mid-February.

Thousands of refugees perished during the severe cold weather of 1950-51. Here a Korean mother and her two children, found frozen in a ditch at Osan, February 1951. (Irwin Tress-INP UPI)

Corporals Seebold and Suey Lee of the 3rd Platoon, Company F, 2nd Bn., 7th Cavalry, look over two dead Chinese on Hill 578 in February 1951. Enemy soldiers were probably killed by artillery fire or air strikes. (Courtesy of Suey Lee)

the various trenches that were deeply dug throughout the slopes and ridges. The determined enemy resistance was so severe that actual hand-to-hand fighting existed in the attacking rifle platoons of Company E.

Between 0800-0900 hours, the enemy resistance finally broke, and we continued to attack to secure our objective. The enemy was now fleeing down the reverse slope of the hill and were actually caught in the direct tank cannon fire, from the 70th Tank Battalion.

All companies of the 2nd Battalion established a perimeter, and we made our physical contact with Company L, 3rd Battalion. Previous contact with the company was impossible because we had been separated by a half-moon formation on the reverse slope of the hill.

Immediately, various patrol squads were ordered to make a complete sweeping movement of the area to clear the approaches and slopes to the hill. This completed the seizure of Hill 578.

Even though the attack on Hill 578 was regarded as extremely successful, the GAR-RYOWEN victory was still costly. The total casualty list of the 7th Cavalry Regiment, was 16 killed and 137 wounded.

By 1300 hours, my platoon was relieved by elements from the 27th Infantry Regiment, 25th Infantry Division. After the exhausted troops moved off of the hill, we were then ordered to proceed to a temporary assembly area. Once there, all of us settled down to a much needed rest.

The next morning, on February 16th, the entire regiment was ordered to saddle up and move out to a new assembly area which was located very near the town of Changkow-ni. After our arrival we would have our hot showers, a replacement of clean fatigue uniforms, and most importantly, hot chow.

Various combat stories of Hill 578 were circulated within the 2nd Battalion, and one was about its commanding officer, Lt. Colonel John W. Callaway. On February 14th, at 1735 hours, he had gone personally up the hill to the vicinity of the attacking rifle platoons of Company G. He had reported that the battalion's position was untenable, and requested permission to withdraw, reorga-

nize and begin the attack, the next day; however, he was directed to storm the hill regardless of the costs, and to capture the objective. As directed, the brave officers and troopers of the 7th Cavalry continued their attack and successfully accomplished their mission and objective. GARRYOWEN!

This successful operation on Hill 578 by the 7th Cavalry Regiment brought forth a letter of commendation from the division commander. The letter is as follows:

HEADQUARTERS 1ST CAVALRY
DIVISION
OFFICE OF THE COMMANDING
GENERAL
APO 201

17 February 1951
SUBJECT: Commendation
TO: Commanding Officer
7th Cavalry Regiment, APO 201

Through you, I wish to commend all elements of the command which constituted the Seventh Regimental Combat Team during the period of offensive action from 24 January 1951 to 15 February 1951.

During this period of three weeks, your command pressed continuous offensive action in which it was necessary to overcome not only a stubbornly resistive enemy but also many difficulties of terrain. This action was climaxed by an outstanding display of determination, leadership, courage and endurance in the successful assault of the determinedly held Hill 578.

The magnificent showing of the members of your command during this action, under your leadership and guidance, was representative of that courage, ability, and will to do which symbolizes the high traditions which have made American soldiery always successful in the ultimate.

[S] Charles D. Palmer
CHARLES D. PALMER
MAJOR GENERAL USA
COMMANDING

The following information concerning the combat battle report of the 7th Cavalry attack on Hill 578, is from Training Bulletin No. 1, dated 4 February 1952, Office Chief Army Field Forces, Fort Monroe, Virginia. (Reproduced by Headquarters Second Army, 18 February 1952.)

It became necessary for the 7th Cavalry Regiment to seize Hill 578, a heavily defended key terrain feature in the regimental zone. Plans and preparations for this attack were initiated on 12 February 1951 after an unsuccessful attempt was made to surround the hill and force its capitulation by use of maximum air and artillery, coupled with probing from all sides by strong combat patrols. The attempt to surround the hill was frustrated by the enemy defenses in depth located north of the town of Mugam-ni, which prevented the 3d Battalion from moving in rear of the hill. (See fold-over map on last page.)

The commanders of the 2d and 3d Battalions, who were to make the main effort, met with the regimental and battalion operations officers in the zone of the 3d Battalion, where excellent observation of the enemy position was available. Contemplated objectives were pointed out to both commanders, and zones or responsibility were agreed upon. It was decided that the very crest of the hill mass would be assigned to the 2d Battalion alone, and that certain key features north of the crest would be assigned to the 33d Battalion. This decision was necessary because of the length of the ridge line extending north and east from the crest. Both battalion commanders discussed with the regimental operations officer their planned route of approach to hill mass and the contemplated deployment of their units. They were assured that maximum available firepower would support the operation, that secondary attacks on the part of the 1st (7th Cavalry) and 4th (Greek) Battalions would assist in the seizure of the ridge, and that an air preparation would be requested on the objective.

Because of the time needed for coordination, planning, reconnaissance, and rest, it was determined that the operation should commence on the 24th of February. This would also provide a 24-hour period for softening up the area by artillery and air. It was estimated that movement to and closing of attacking elements on the ridge line would take from 2-1/2 to 3 hours even if there were no enemy on the hill. Both commanders agreed that for the attacking infantry battalions, 0900 hours was the most desirable "H" hour. This hour provided:

a. Sufficient time for organization and deployment of the attacking forces during daylight hours.

b. Sufficient time after crossing the line of departure to reach the objective and, under favorable conditions, to seize and organize it prior to darkness.

With minor modifications the plans were approved by the regimental commander. The regimental operations officer then contacted the Division G3 and advised him of these plans, and a request was made for the following:

a. An additional artillery battalion.

b. An additional company of tanks.

c. A 20-minute air preparation of Napalm and 1000-lb VT bombs on the crest of the ridge.

d. An air smoking mission on the high ground north of Mugamni.

e. An air strike every 30 minutes after 0900 hours. The Division G3 stated that the Division Artillery would support the operation, and he would check on the possible attachment of the Reconnaissance Platoon, 70th Tank Battalion, to the regiment. The Division Air Officer forwarded both air requests for approval.

The 1st and 4th Battalions as well as the artillery, heavy mortars, tanks, engineers, and regimental staff were advised of the approved attack plans, and the artillery and heavy mortar company in particular were given instructions to intensify their fires on

Dead Chinese soldier, still smoldering from napalm bomb. (U.S. Army photo)

The sheer ridges and the crest of Hill 578 contained many enemy machine gun positions. In the forground troopers of Company F, 2nd Bn., 7th Cavalry, take a breather. (Courtesy of Suey Lee)

the night of 23 February through 13 February. The tactical air control party was also briefed and all available air was placed on the crest of the ridge line and other known enemy targets on the hill mass.

During the night of 12 - 13 February, the 77th F A Battalion, supported by other units of Division Artillery, fired a number of TOT concentrations on the objective area. In conjunction with these TOT concentrations, a series of "Surrender Now" broadcasts in the 3d Battalion area were made over a loudspeaker system. In these broadcasts, the regular team was assisted by an enemy lieutenant colonel who had been captured in the 5th Cavalry area. Three (3) of the enemy surrendered on 13 February as a result of these broadcasts.

Three (3) final steps were taken in the fire support plan. One provided that the artillery would fire one round every five (5) seconds after 0900. This fire was intended to prevent the enemy from reinforcing, moving his reserves, and manning his positions at the tip of the ridge. It was to be lifted on request of

either of the leading company commanders. An emergency flare signal was established for lifting this fire in the event other communications were out. In addition, the 1st and 4th Battalions were directed to furnish support fire on the south and eastern portions of Hill 578, utilizing their own organic mortars to the maximum. The third step was the use of Co. C, 70th Tank Battalion, for direct supporting fire. Two (2) platoons of tanks were attached to the 2d Battalion for direct fire support of its assaulting units, and a platoon of tanks was attached to the 3d and 1st Battalions for the same purpose.

Further preparation for the operation included organization of Task Force Shaw, composed initially of the two (2) platoons of tanks supporting the 2d Battalion, whose fires would be masked as the 2d Battalion seized its objective. This Task Force was to move out when the assault units moved on to their objective areas, and proceed through the village of Magam-ni to a position in the rear of Hill 578 to direct fire into the reverse slope.

Mountainous Korea was the worst possible place to fight a war. (U.S. Army photo)

A Chinese attack at night with blazing gunfire and flares. (Warren Lee-UPI)

Hill 578 was devastated by air strikes and artillery fire. February 1951. (Courtesy of Suey Lee)

On request of the 1st Battalion commander, the original attack plans were modified to provide for seizure of the piece of ground immediately north of the 1st Battalion's position. This ground, which was known as the "Ice Cream Cone," dominated the 1st Battalion area, and was strongly held by the enemy. The change was made a part of the plan.

Following final coordination and the firming of "H" hour as 140900 February, it was requested that the 8th Cavalry launch an attack, in conjunction with the 7th Cavalry's effort, against the high ground northwest of Mugam-ni to divert enemy fire from the north flank of the 3d Battalion. The 8th Cavalry was involved in a number of mopping up operations at this time. However, the Commanding Officer, 8th Cavalry, agreed to send a company-strength unit, supported by a platoon of tanks, against the high ground. He stated they would not be able to attack with any larger force because of other commitments.

During the night of 13-14 February, it was learned that a heavy attack was being prepared by the enemy. Units of the 7th Cavalry were on an alert status for most of the night. The enemy actually hit the 8th Cavalry area, and elements of the 8th Cavalry were engaged until well after daylight. As a result, the 8th Cavalry, could not stage its diversionary attack against the high ground northwest of Mugam-ni. It was necessary to rearrange the regimental plan by placing one section of tanks, formerly supporting the 2d Battalion, plus the tank Reconnaissance Platoon, in positions on the north flank of the 3d Battalion to engage this area by fire during the attack.

The Regimental Commander and his Command Group, consisting of the Operations Officer, Artillery Liaison Officer, TACP, Heavy Mortar Liaison Officer, Tank Liaison Officer, a number of radiomen and an additional officer from the S3 Section plus a journal clerk, moved to Regimental OP at 0630, from which the leading elements of the 1st, 2d, and 3d Battalions could be observed. Wire and radio were available to all units and to Division Headquarters.

The initial artillery preparation of time and VT fire went off as planned, beginning at 0700 hours, over the forward slope of the hill mass, coupled with sporadic intense concentrations on suspected troop areas on the reverse slopes. At approximately 0820 hours, we were notified by Division Air Officer that no air would be available. Therefore, the artillery was requested to continue its preparation up to H-10 in lieu of the air preparation. (Note: Napalm would have been extremely effective against concentrations of enemy defenses on the tip of the ridge.)

Elements of K Company crossed the line of departure at 0900 hours. G Company crossed the line of departure on time, but utilized nearly twenty (20) minutes for reorganization prior to continuing up the hill. Division aircraft operating in the area began to report enemy mortar positions and camouflaged supplies. These enemy targets were taken under fire by the artillery. At 0934 hours, Air OP sighted two (2) enemy running down the reverse slope of 578. This was the first indication that the enemy was aware our forces had actually jumped off in the attack. By 0940 hours, the tank screening force of one section plus the Reconnaissance Platoon of the 70th Tank Battalion arrived in position on the north flank of the 3d Battalion and began the execution of its fire mission against known enemy positions on the high ground north of Mugam-ni. Aircraft reported five (5) more enemy moving on the trail on the reverse of 578 at 0942, and this group was taken under fire. At 1005 hours, sporadic small arms fire was received by K Company, and from this point forward, mortar and small arms fire continued with increased intensity.

It was reported at 1120 hours that the 1st Battalion had begun its attack and was receiving heavy mortar, small arms and automatic weapons fire.

G Company reported receiving white

phosphorus rounds and an immediate check was made to determine whether our artillery or mortars were falling short. None of our weapons were firing at this time, and it was determined that the white phosphorus was enemy fire. Our air OP was directed to determine the location of the enemy mortars.

As of 1155 hours, K Company was temporarily held up in its advance by heavy automatic weapons and small arms fire. At 1202 hours, both I and K Company was temporarily held up in its advance by heavy automatic weapons and small arms fire. At 1202 hours, both I and K Companies were receiving extremely heavy mortar fire. A number of reports of enemy recoilless rifle fire were received, but this fire later proved to be 2.36 rocket launchers being used as antipersonnel weapons.

At 1210 hours, Air Op had located two (2) mortars. These positions were taken under fire directed by the aircraft. Tanks screening the 3d Battalion left (north) flank were receiving heavy mortar fire at 1225 hours. At 1325, a report stated that K Company had reached its objective and was receiving heavy small arms and automatic weapons fire. L Company, following in the trace of K Company, dispatched one platoon to the right of K Company and above the objective area, and this platoon succeeded in getting above and behind the enemy forces defending the area. Suddenly finding themselves surrounded, fourteen (14) of the enemy surrendered and the rest were killed. During this action, there were numerous occasions in which enemy soldiers continued to fight until killed on the spot by the infuriated attacking infantrymen. At 1340 hours, Army aircraft reported forty-two (42) enemy moving east on the road out of Mugam-ni, apparently to reinforce the enemy position in the 578 area. Artillery fire was directed against these troops.

By 1345 hours, both of the attacking companies of the two (2) leading battalions were in assault positions. K Company had already secured its objective, and G Company was within twenty-five (25) yards of the crest. At this time, the 1st and 4th Battalions were ordered to begin their coordinated movement so that neither would be in advance of the other. At 1400 hours, Air OP reported fifteen (15) enemy lying in ambush immediately behind a position on the ridge which G Company was approaching at a distance of only fifteen (15) feet. This message was immediately flashed to G Company which shortly became hotly engaged with these and other enemy infantry. G Company troops moved up to the ridge line and were met by a shower of grenades from the enemy troops in the area. Machine guns on both flanks opened up, and the leading elements of the 2d Battalion withdrew approximately twenty-five (25) yards. G. Company battled the enemy along the ridge line using hand grenades and light mortars. The 3d Battalion was directed to move elements up the hill (to the south) from where it could support the 2d Battalion by firing on the reverse slope. K Company had an extremely difficult time in seizing its strongly defended objective which turned out to be the communications center for the entire hill mass and included the regimental CP, one battalion CP and several company CP's. The CP area was particularly well defended, and many enemy were killed in this area. It was necessary to pass L Company through K Company to continue the momentum of the attack at 1445 hours.

At 1440 hours, Task Force Shaw was ordered to proceed on its mission, and the tanks began moving out of their attack positions. The 4th Battalion reported that their lead elements, the 2d Company, had moved out at 1445 hours. By 1505 hours, they were receiving heavy fire. Instructions were issued to the 4th Battalion to have them block in their forward positions, taking the local enemy positions under fire until the ROK's had seized the dominating ground on the east. At 1525 hours, Task Force Shaw found that the road west of Mugam-ni had been mined, but the tanks promptly backed up and blew the mines out of the road with their tank cannon and proceeded on their mission. The Task Force shot up the town of Mugam-ni, but apparently all supplies, ammunition and enemy casualties had been removed. Leading elements of Task Force Shaw moved on through Mugam-ni to a point several hundred yards beyond where the road narrowed down to a trail. It was impassible for tanks. Several enemy were firing at the tanks with small arms, machine guns, and mortars, and these were taken under fire by the tanks. One of the tanks had a round jammed in the chamber and one of the crewmen, without hesitation, moved in front of the tank with a rammer to dislodge the jammed shell. In doing so he was wounded by mortar fire which had been falling sporadically in and around the tanks. The wounded man was placed on the back of one of the tanks and evacuated to the 3d Battalion Aid Station while the remainder of the task force continued to engage the enemy.

Elements of the 1st Battalion were heavily engaged, and B Company was stopped on the approaches to the objective. The 1st Battalion commander immediately committed elements of C Company around both flanks and pushed his attack successfully in overrunning the objective. Despite the difficult terrain, considerable enemy casualties were inflicted, enemy supplies were captured, and by 1600 hours the objective of the 1st Battalion was secured.

As of 1600 hours, the leading elements of the 2d Battalion were maneuvering on top of the ridge, still heavily engaged with the enemy. Also, L Company continued its move up the slope followed by K Company, under

Chinese prisoners captured by 1st Cavalry Division troopers during Operation Killer, February 27, 1951. (U.S. Army photo)

Strategic withdrawal south of Seoul on January 3, 1951. (U.S. Army photo)

fire by the enemy. However, in its attempt to outflank the enemy on the reverse slopes, L Company ran into an enemy strong point and was under grenade, machine gun, and mortar fire. By 1730 hours, L Company was pinned down. Elements of the 2d Battalion continued to maneuver, with the enemy "looking down their throat," in an attempt to outflank and overrun the enemy position. The 2d Battalion was receiving a number of casualties from mortar fire and was in an extremely exposed position.

At 1735, the Commanding Officer, 3d Battalion, who had moved up the hill to the vicinity of the assault company, reported that his position was not tenable and requested permission to withdraw, reorganize, and begin the attack the next day. Permission was refused by the Regimental Commander. The 2d Battalion commander was directed to take the hill. The 3d Battalion was notified of this order, and L Company was placed under operational control of the 2d Battalion pending seizure of the hill and under daylight next morning.

By 1755 hours, the fighting was still raging on the ridge line, but darkness had set in to the point where observation from the OP was not practical. The regimental command group departed for the regimental CP. The commanding officer stopped at the 2d Battalion CP enroute. The instructions concerning seizure of the ridge were re-emphasized, and a last minute report on the situation was secured.

Fighting continued throughout the night. The 2d Battalion commander, who had gone personally to the scene of action to direct his battalion, maneuvered F Company to the right. However, they were pinned down by fire and driven back. He then committed E Company to the left of G, so as to join physically with L Company which had reached the crest on the north and was firing into the northwestern portion of the reverse side of 578. It was impossible for L Company to fire into the southeast portion of the hill because of the terrain which consisted of two (2) half-moon formations on the reverse side of the hill. The enemy's strongest reinforcements were in the southeastern area. The Chinese had placed five (5) machine gun pillbox emplacements on the hill. These guns had excellent fields of fire and were able to sweep the entire area with cross fire. The majority of the time from the arrival of G Company to the time of darkness was used in attempting to maneuver a 75-mm recoilless rifle into position to knock out these machine guns. This was unsuccessful. A flame thrower operator from G Company finally pushed forward about 1700 hours and knocked out the machine gun position on the extreme northern flank. Shortly afterward the operator was driven back by enemy fire. His work enabled later capture of this end of the ridge by the 2d Battalion.

Reports from prisoners captured during the daylight fighting indicated as of 2045 hours that there were approximately twenty (20) enemy manning the topographical crest of the ridge. However, enemy in position behind the crest included a battalion plus two (2) platoons. These enemy reserves successfully counterattacked each time our forces succeeded in moving up on the ridge.

At 2330 hours the 2d Battalion reported that E Company, which had been committed on the left flank of G Company, had finally overrun the top of the ridge on the extreme northern portion of the position and had destroyed two (2) machine gun nests. Three (3) additional machine guns were still in position and operating, and both E Company and L Company, which were not yet in physical contact with each other, were pinned down by fire from these guns. It was suggested that marching fire be used, and the reply was, "There is no room to march."

At 0255 hours, it was reported that enemy resistance was slackening, and another attempt was being made to push over the ridge. Our own 60-mm mortars were being used effectively against the enemy by the leading companies. One of these, Company L, fired 300 rounds from one mortar. F Company continued to maneuver to the right flank and get behind the enemy, while E Company held on to the high ground which it had gained. During the period 0400 - 0600 hours, the 2d Battalion again assaulted the enemy positions and was in turn hit by a counterattack of approximately fifty (50) enemy in a desperate attempt to drive them off the position before daylight. However, this was unsuccessful and proved to be the enemy's last effort.

When the counterattack was first reported, air was urgently requested from division, and fighters began arriving shortly and were directed against the rear slope of the hill. By 0725 hours, it was reported that E Company had seized an additional portion of the ridge, and this portion was now held in strength.

Task Force Shaw was ordered to move out at 0735 hours to exploit the reverse slope of the hill. The 4th Battalion was ordered to move to an assembly area vicinity of the 3d Battalion CP, and to be prepared to relieve the 2d Battalion after seizure of the objective. The air controller reported that a number of enemy were withdrawing as of 0845 hours. Task Force Shaw was directed to take them under fire.

By 0900, the 2d Battalion reported the enemy was in flight, and the ridge line had been seized in a final period of hand-to-hand fighting. All companies of the 2d Battalion and L Company organized perimeters on the ridge line, and immediately sent patrols to clean out the general area and the approaches. The 1st Battalion was directed to send a patrol up from the south to the crest of 578. This completed the capture of the hill mass.

The enemy organization of the area placed the 2d Battalion, 336th Regiment on the west slope, north slope, and the peak proper. The 1st Battalion, 336th Regiment, reinforced by units from the 342d Regiment, occupied the south and east slopes. The 1st Battalion, in addition, covered the saddle between Hill 578 and Hill 489. The 3d Battalion of the 336th did not exist, having been annihilated on Hill 202 previously. Since all of these units had suffered a large number of casualties in previous fighting, the total strength holding the hill was not over 700. As the attack proceeded, it developed that the 3d Battalion objective was the location of the CP 2d Battalion, 336th Regiment. The enemy defended this position with small arms, automatic weapons, grenades, and mortars until it was apparent we were about to overrun it. At this time, CCF officers passed additional grenades to their men, instructed them to hold the line while they started to withdraw to the peak. They were caught in the open while in the middle of this move, and an undetermined number of them were shot down by our machine gun fire. The remaining defenders of the position resisted until their ammunition was expended and they were killed or captured. The remainder of the 3d Battalion, 336th had organized the peak of the hill with five (5) machine guns placed in mutually supporting positions. These guns, well dug-in and camouflaged, were positioned to cover the ridge line approaches to the hill from the west, south, and north. Our advance overran two (2) of these guns placed on the western slope, but was quickly repulsed and the gun positions remained. The enemy then resisted all attempts to advance through the cross fire from these weapons and from mortars, small arms and hand grenades.

The operation demonstrated that when the chips are down against determined resistance, that when our troops are within assaulting distance and supporting fires are lifted, the objective must be taken by prompt, aggressive assault, using marching fire, hand-to-hand fighting, and the determination and guts of the infantry. The enemy in small numbers can hold these mountain ridges against forces many times stronger unless our soldiers have the intestinal fortitude to move in and finish him off.

If we can train our soldiers to move more closely under their supporting fire and to assault quickly in that critical moment when fires are lifted, we shall have success with minimum casualties. Any delay after fires are lifted will tend to greatly magnify our casualties. Also along with the proper employment of supporting fires, the operation provided an excellent example of the full utilization of infantry weapons. Grenades, mortars, recoilless rifles, flame throwers, machine guns and individual weapons all played an important part in seizing the objectives.

Division aircraft were extremely valuable in bringing enemy positions under the fire of supporting arms, and in pointing out enemy troop locations to our assaulting infantry.

The assault and seizure of Hill 578, was definitely a successful operation. The Training Bulletin further emphasized that the 7th Cavalry Regiment used good battle technique, employed with courage and determination in all ranks, has turned the tide in many conflicts where the odds were otherwise stacked against the winner. GARRYOWEN!

The following account of January - February 1951, given by Sergeant First Class Donald D. Down, squad leader from the 3rd Platoon, Company F, 2nd Battalion, 7th Cavalry Regiment.

I remember the extreme cold weather of January 1951, and our established positions near the Han River. There seemed to be a lull in the Chinese movement and assault. We didn't know if it was the cold weather or the constant bombing of their supply lines and troop movement that was causing the enemy to hesitate in their continued assault on the United Nations Forces. Nevertheless, we continued to make combat patrol missions to seek and search for enemy positions and movement.

Near the middle of the month we were relieved of our positions and sent to Division reserve. This area was located in a flat valley and after two days there, we were ordered to dig foxholes. Needless to say, the ground was so frozen that we were given permission to burn pieces of tree branches in an attempt to thaw out the dirt so we could dig. Rumors had it that we might be hit with a Chinese air attack. After a lot of hell raising from the troops, we finally accomplished the job.

Very near this reserve area location were the Greek Expeditionary Forces which were now our 4th Battalion. Several of us went to visit them and thought maybe we could take advantage of them with some quick talk and possibly trade a few items of interest. However, I think it turned out the other way around. We very soon learned that the Greeks were not only excellent fighters, but were masters at the art of trading. Nevertheless, all of us in Company F welcomed them as part of the 7th Cavalry Regiment.

While in reserve, we were notified that we could receive our pay in either partial or full payment allowances. Many troopers decided to receive their pay, and it didn't take long to see card games and dice shooting within the company area. In a way, what else were they going to do with their money? After dark many continued their games in the cook's mess tent. As in any type of gambling there were some winners, and of course, some losers as well.

The supply lines were located many miles behind us, and the truck trains had extreme difficulty on the narrow icy roads. This necessitated an air drop of supplies which landed very near our reserve area. Many of us were given the detail of handling and loading the much needed supplies on our company trucks.

There were even 55 gallon drums of gasoline dropped into the area. They were heavy and difficult to handle. Later in the day our company cooks served us a delicious hot meal, which was enjoyed by all. Of course, the cigarette supply was great and well appreciated. Also throughout our location you could see the dim glow from the lighted cigarettes as we puffed away unconsciously in the evening darkness.

One day some troopers from the platoon found a cow, and it didn't take long for the animal to be butchered up. We had no frying pans or apparatus to place the meat on, so we just threw it into the open fire to cook. Needless to say, we had meat that was wood-charred fried. To eat the meat, we had to scrape the burnt crust off and then pull pieces apart that looked decent enough to eat. Later on some medics told us that the meat could

possibly be contaminated. Those of us who ate the meat never developed any health problems and actually enjoyed the taste; even though it had been burned in some cases to a crisp.

I remember in early February we were ordered to make a combat patrol mission to search for the enemy. Along with me was Sergeant First Class Ralph Bernotas, assistant platoon sergeant of the 3rd Platoon, and he carried a field telephone for communication purposes with the Company. In this particular combat patrol, there was a total of 10 troopers. Within this total was a three man (B.A.R.) team with automatic rifles. This gave us the added fire power within our patrol in case it was needed. We strung the necessary fire for the field phone, and we made our advance to more than 100 yards in front of the company position. Earlier reports indicated that the enemy had been seen in this particular area.

The mountain where we established our positions wasn't too high. However, it still gave us a commanding view of the road and open valley to the front of us. To our right flank was a saddle which linked up to a hill approximately 200 yards away. We finally settled down around midnight.

At 0130 hours we got hit by a Chinese patrol that was probing the area to locate our positions. Immediately we became engaged in an exchange of hand grenades, automatic and small arms fire. Sergeant Bernatos then called on the field phone to alert the Company that we were going to pull back. Word was then passed on to the patrol that we were going to withdraw.

As we attempted to move down the hill, grenades were exploding and bullets were cracking and snapping all around us. In the darkness, we were stumbling and falling down, and the enemy was right on our heels. The Chinese were playing their games with the eerie sounds and bugle calls.

Finally we reached the platoon sector and by now the whole battalion was under attack. We took a quick head count and discovered that one trooper was missing from our combat patrol.

Our artillery fire was exploding within the enemy ranks on the hill and throughout the valley. The barrage was coming in so close that you could have held up your hand with a kitchen match in it, and the projectiles could have lit it up for you. Word was then passed on that we would fix bayonets and be prepared for hand to hand combat when the artillery barrage stopped.

At daybreak the artillery barrage let up, and suddenly we saw a lone figure approaching us from the front. He was shouting that he was coming in and we soon found out that he was the one missing trooper from our combat patrol.

Somehow he had remained in a safe position during the artillery barrage. He said that the enemy had been all around him, and the artillery barrage had inflicted many casualties of dead and wounded.

The Chinese never continued their attack on our positions. At 0800 hours a combat patrol was sent out to investigate the enemy casualties, and to see if they had pulled back or not. Within the hour, the combat patrol returned and reported that they could not find any enemy wounded or dead. Also they made no contact at all with the enemy. It was assumed that the Chinese had picked up their wounded and dead after the artillery barrage had ended and then continued to flee northward.

One evening after we secured our objective in the vicinity of Hills 481 and 512, 2nd Lt. Edward Daily, a platoon leader from Company H, approached me and asked if he could borrow two men for an outpost position. Seeing no problem, I gave him the two men which were to be used as additional support for a machine gun outpost position.

During the night, the enemy didn't launch an attack as expected. However, the next morning I was informed that four troopers on an outpost position had been killed sometime during the night. Then I was further saddened by the report when I was told that two of the men were from Company F. It was the same two men that I had loaned to Company H, for their machine gun outpost position.

All four men had been bayoneted in their sleep by a probing Chinese patrol. I thought to myself, "what a way to die on the frontline." There should have been no reason for them to fall asleep, particularly with four men assigned to the outpost. I had to accept the fact that it was one of the mistakes in combat; however, this one cost the lives of four good men.

We moved into position which was a staging area, and we were informed that our next objective would be Hill 578. For three days, we would watch the artillery, and the fighter planes soften up the hill for our future attack.

On our second day there, we were served some hot chow, and we had our South Korean interpreter eating with us. Our platoon was positioned on and near the road, but we still hadn't receive any orders for the future attack.

Suddenly we noticed three strange looking South Korean soldiers that were sitting down, and they were wearing the old-style Army overcoats. However, we knew of no one being issued this type of overcoat in the 2nd Battalion. We told the South Korean interpreter that we should investigate the three strangers.

A couple of us and the interpreter went over to the strangers and questioned them. To our surprise we soon discovered that all three were Chinese, and they wanted to surrender; and they wanted something to eat. We immediately turned them over to the company commander. No doubt they supplied some valuable information about the enemy fortifications on Hill 578.

Finally in the early morning of February 14th, we were notified of the planned attack on the hill mass. Company G was selected to start the attack at 0900 hours and attempt to secure the very crest of the hill. Company F, was alerted to hold ready to move when notified to the right flank of Company G.

As we waited for our orders to attack, we could hear and see that Company G was having one hell of a battle with the enemy. They seemed to be pinned down by enemy machine gun fire that was coming from several directions at the top of the crest.

It was late afternoon when we received orders to move to the right flank of Company G. We fought our way to a small saddle between the halfway mark and the crest of the hill. The terrain was very rough with sharp ridges running up to the crest. The crest was heavily fortified with enemy machine gun nests and this fire power was making it almost impossible to proceed forward. Company F had temporarily come to a halt.

Just prior to dark, a flame thrower team made their way into position and successfully destroyed a pocket of enemy resistance. During all of my previous battle engagements in Korea, I had never seen a flame thrower used in combat. The flaming petroleum jelly really did a trick on the enemy position.

Then dark came, and the enemy machine gun tracers were coming from the top of the crest, and bullets were snapping all about us. Captain Harold Grey asked for 12 volunteers to go with him and attempt to fight their way up the ridge. He got his 12 volunteers, and then they disappeared into the darkness. They were quickly showered with enemy hand grenades and small arms fire.

The enemy was making a desperate fight to keep control of the hill mass. By daybreak, however, the enemy resistance had slackened off, and our 2nd Battalion had made slow progress in their attempt to seize the hill.

By midmorning the enemy had retreated, and we secured our objective. We patrolled the ridges to make sure that all of the pockets of enemy resistance were cleared out. We took only one prisoner on the hill, and he was a Chinese medic.

Then I could not believe my eyes as I looked around the hill at the complete devastation caused by the three previous days of constant artillery and fighter plane bombing. How did the enemy survive this to put up a vicious fight to keep control of the hill? Well, anyway, so ended another battle and the successful capture of Hill 578.

For the remainder of February, the GARRYOWEN troopers were assigned to Division Reserve. However, the 2nd Battalion continued to maintain aggressive combat patrols throughout the area.

The last week of February would bring unseasonal warm temperatures and torrential rains, creating floods that turned frozen ground into cold mud. In some areas the mud was almost two feet deep. The GARRYOWEN troopers were temporarily bogged down. Also the rain and overcast skies hampered air support.

During this particular time, word was received that our division commander, Major General Hobart Gay, was relieved of his duties. Major General Charles D. Palmer, immediately assumed command of the 1st Cavalry Division. Every officer and trooper of GARRYOWEN had high respect for General Gay; and now we welcomed General Palmer as our new Division Commander with the same respect and admiration. General Palmer was previously the commander of the 1st Cavalry Division Artillery.

The rain continued, and most of our bridges were wiped out due to the swollen streams. The situation was critical as the supply trains experienced difficulty in crossing the swollen streams. Our food supply was being depleted rapidly, so the entire 1st Cavalry Division was forced to begin two meals per day. Air drops had to be employed, particularly for the ammunition supply. However, this was limited because many other Divisions in the Eighth Army were in the same predicament.

The weather continued to warm up causing more thawing which resulted in nearly

L. to r. Lt. Jim Gorman, Captain Harold C/O, 1st Lt. John Potts and 1st. To, Kilduff, of Company F, 2nd Bn., 7th Cavalry, Hongchon Valley, March 1951. (Courtesy of Suey Lee)

Chinese soldier who surrendered. (Courtesy of Bob Mauger)

impassable roads in many area. Even the 8th Combat Engineers had built several ferries to be used to cross the river. Every possible method was used to alleviate the supply situation. Had IX Corps ordered the entire 1st Cavalry Division to proceed and attack the enemy, it could have done so only with very great hardship.

CHAPTER X

CHINESE SPRING OFFENSIVE

Man's greatest weakness is not money, or drugs, nor women, but his greatest weakness is that he forgets. . . . .

Apaxu Maiz
Navajo Indian (1988)

At the end of February, while still in Division reserve, the 7th Calvary Regiment had several new officers assigned within its ranks. In Company H, we expressed a hearty welcome to the new officers that were designated as platoon leaders. This also helped to boost our morale as various rumors throughout the entire battalion indicated that a future rotation back to the United States was forthcoming for many of us.

2nd Lt., John "Jack" Martinez was appointed 3rd Platoon Leader, which was our 81-mm mortar platoon. Then 2nd Lt. James Manns was appointed as 1st Platoon Leader, and was actually my replacement. However, I was directed to remain with the platoon as orders were pending for my possible transfer to the 2nd Battalion S-2 or S-3. Within a few days, the leadership of 2nd Lt. Manns of the 1st Platoon, would abruptly come to an end.

With the arrival of March, it brought forth renewed feelings of confidence within the ranks of all troopers of the 2nd Battalion. Many of the older combat veterans had alread experienced the 5 days R&R leave (rest and rehabilitation) in Japan. This particular plan was extremely successful and was recognized as a magnificent booster of morale.

Most of the troopers in my platoon felt considerable satisfaction as we talked about and looked back at the battles of January and February. We acknowledged the fact that the Chinese Communist Forces had been punished severely the previous two months; their losses, for the most, were staggering.

During the previous months, I had heard and noticed the various conversation between the troopers while in combat. One had become very typical and very common. First trooper (gazing and gaping at the oncoming attack by the enemy): "Jesus Christ, look at that!" Second trooper (would softly answer, almost reverently, as if in church): "Holy shit....."

The words "bug out" had become a common phrase that many troopers used in their conversations. Particularly, when using the term of orderly withdrawal or pulling back, in many instances would be replaced with "buggin' out." Or maybe they would occasionally use "movin' on." In either case, the phrases were somehow originated in the early stages of the Korean War.

Many tanks of the 70th Tank Battalion, were now painted with tiger heads showing their white teeth and various orange stripes to give the armored vehicle an extra psychol-

ogical advantage. Every GARRYOWEN trooper had high respect for the brave officers and soldiers of this outstanding armored unit. Since the previous summer battles on the Naktong River, Company C of the armored battalion had been assigned as a support unit to the 7th Cavalry Regiment.

The weather was improving each day, and the supply lines were now capable of reaching their designated areas. This very definitely helped the effort of the entire Eighth Army, and their Operation Ripper, which was instituted in late February.

All battalions within the 7th Cavalry Regiment were now using large loud speakers that were mounted on certain jeeps and 3/4 ton weapons carriers. Their sole purpose was to broadcast propaganda to the enemy in an attempt to encourage them to surrender. In some areas it was reported that certain individuals or small groups of the enemy actually surrendered prior to the battle.

We continued to remain in Division reserve; however, we still maintained our combat patrol missions against the enemy. The enemy constantly harassed the entire 7th Cavalry with their 75-mm artillery and heavy mortar fire.

Even though I still remained with the platoon, I was no longer the platoon leader. 2nd Lt. James Manns had replaced me as platoon leader, and I was waiting for further orders of a possible transfer within the battalion. Captain Wadsworth had directed me to give Lt. Manns all the possible help or assistance that he might need concerning any questions about heavy weapons or their particular deployment.

On March 5, Captain Wadsworth called all company officers and key sergeants for a special briefing. We were informed that the 7th Cavalry would continue a northward offensive in the central zones to seize the towns of Hongchon and Chunchon. This would be coordinated with the original plan of Operation Ripper.

We made a detailed study of the road nets and other terrain features of the area in which we were to advance or attack in the future days. Again, the purpose was to destroy enemy soldiers and equipment, and to use constant pressure to prevent the enemy from mounting a counteroffensive.

In the early morning of March 7th, the 2nd Battalion moved northward in a major attack against the enemy. However, within our area, little or no contact was made with the enemy forces. By dark, we had secured our initial objective and closed in a tight perimeter for the night.

During the early evening, plans were discussed about the attack on enemy positions at 0700 hours the following morning. The night passed with only an occasional shot being fired within the battalion perimeter.

This was Lt. Mann's first experience in combat as leader of his newly assigned platoon. I quickly observed that Lt. Manns was a fine officer, and he was in excellent physical condition. He experienced very little difficulty in adjusting to the rough mountain terrain of Korea.

However, Lt. Manns did receive a complaint from a couple of disgruntled troopers in the platoon. They had become provoked over his insistance to move more rapidly during the attack, earlier in the day. Then they told him that he wasn't considerate of the actual weight of a heavy machine gun, or just how cumbersome the weapon really was. Nevertheless, after a brief discussion, all parties involved came to a mutual understanding.

On March 9, the 2nd Battalion continued its attack at 0700 hours, with Company E leading the assault. After receiving sporadic small arms and automatic weapons fire, they secured Hill 285 and their objective by 0910 hours. Orders were then received to continue the northward attack without hesitation. However, by late afternoon enemy mortar and artillery fire temporarily halted the assault.

Combat screening patrols were then directed to seek and search for enemy positions and to estimate their possible strength. Some reports indicated an enemy battalion was operating within the area. A tight perimeter was established in the battalion for the remainder of the night.

During the evening, Captain Wadsworth held a briefing and it was determined that a section of light and heavy machine guns from the 1st Platoon would give support to the rifle platoons of Companies E and G. The attack was scheduled for 0700 hours, the following morning.

The scheduled attack at 0700 hours on the morning of March 10, was delayed approximately one half hour, due to the balance of the regiment moving up in full strength, and during the early morning they had experienced extremely congested traffic conditions on the road.

Without any further delays, Companies E and G finally started the attack on Hill 554, between 0700 and 0800 hours. From Company H, 2nd Lt. Manns had previously assigned a machine gun section as support elements to the attacking rifle platoons. Also assigned as support to our left flank on the hill mass were units from the 4th Battalion (GEF).

Lt. Manns and I moved with the support elements from our platoon, and directly behind the attacking rifle platoons of Company G. Along with us was 1st Lt. Albert Moses, commanding officer of Company G. Even from the previous summer and the early days of combat on the Naktong River, Lt. Moses had proven himself to be an excellent officer. Now as a company commander, his leadership abilities were regarded as the finest.

At first we received only sporadic small arms fire or an occasional shot from an enemy sniper. It soon became difficult to advance, due to the sheer and steep edges of the ridgeline. To reach the crest of the hill and our objective, it was necessary at times, to maneuver in a single file over the rough terrain.

After reaching an area approximately 100 yards from the very peak of the hill, the enemy started to sweep the advance elements of Company G with machine gun fire. Then small arms and automatic weapons fire started to come from the ridges to our right, and extreme right flank. The enemy cross fire had us temporarily pinned down, and we soon realized that the Chinese had placed three pill box type machine gun emplacements within the steep crest.

Shortly, Lt. Moses received word that his point squad was all safe and had pulled back and was waiting for further orders. It was then decided that Lt. Manns and I would accompany Lt. Moses to get a better look at the situation.

However, before leaving I suggested to Lt. Manns that we should take with us at least one .30 caliber light machine gun team, and an extra ammo bearer. He agreed and immediately directed the team and extra ammo bearer to follow us.

As our small group attempted to proceed foward, bullets were snapping and cracking loudly around us. Suddenly, the outcry of pain and the shout for "medic" came from behind me. I quickly turned and saw that the assistant machine gunner from our platoon had been hit by enemy small arms fire. Within a minute the combat aidman had arrived and very quickly administered the necessary medical aid.

I could easily see that the brave trooper was wounded in the right cheek of his buttocks. Surprisingly, the bullet didn't exit the flesh to cause further wound damage. I managed to say goodby to the wounded trooper, and wished him the very best of recovery from his sustained wound.

To avoid any further delay, I then picked up the light machine gun that the fallen trooper had been carrying. Again, our small group continued to proceed forward as quickly as possible.

Maneuvering our way through the deadly cross fire, we safely managed to reach the forward elements of Company G. I quickly placed the light machine gun on the tripod that the first gunner Corporal James "Buck" Buckley was carrying. I then directed him to establish a firing position, and to use the experienced ammo bearer as the replacement to the assistant gunner who was wounded earlier. The earlier decision to bring the extra ammo bearer really helped our particular situation.

To my immediate left was Lt. Moses, Lt. Manns and a radioman who had an SCR 300 radio strapped to his back. We were still pinned down by enemy fire, and we had to adjust our positions with extreme caution.

By radio contact, Lt. Moses directed fire support from his light 60-mm mortar, and requested further fire support from the heavy 81-mm mortars of the 3rd Platoon, Company H. Immediately, mortar fire hit the target area, and the dominating crest with the enemy machine gun emplacements. Also, the mortar fire hit into enemy positions along the ridges to the right, and the extreme right flank.

After the softening up of the objective with mortar fire, Lt. Moses then decided to

Shell torn earth within a fierce battle. (U.S. Army photo)

Combat screening patrol from the 2nd Battalion, 7th Cavalry in the Hongchon Valley - March 1951. (Courtesy of Bob Mauger)

Tank support from the 70th Tank Battalion, attached to the 7th Cavalry. (Courtesy of Bob Mauger)

send one squad to the east side of the crest to possibly maneuver its way around the rear. At this particular point, it was estimated that only a small enemy group remained in defense.

While the one squad was attempting their brave maneuver, it was further decided that we would try to keep the enemy engaged in an exchange of machine gun, automatic weapons and small arms fire. I directed Corporal Buckley to keep firing his light machine gun into the various openings of the enemy machine gun emplacement, or at any enemy movement on the crest of the hill.

Suddenly, Lt. Manns shouted for my attention, and I turned to my left to see what he wanted. "Look Ed, I can see the Chinese moving inside of the machine gun positions." I quickly looked up, and I also observed enemy movement and activity.

At this particular moment, Lt. Manns moved himself into a kneeling position to fire his .30 caliber carbine at the enemy movement. Suddenly, I felt moisture hit the left side of my face, and then I heard the sound of a helmet hit the ground.

Then I wiped the left side of my face with my left hand, and noticed blood on my finger tips. I didn't feel any pain, but I first thought that I had been wounded. Then I observed splattered blood on the left sleeve of my field jacket, and I knew that it wasn't mine.

I quickly turned and I didn't see Lt. Manns next to my left any longer. Turning further to my left and looking backward, I then saw Lt. Manns laying on his back and his helmet was missing. I immediately moved to give him medical aid, and to see how badly he was wounded. As I moved, I started to shout for a "medic".

Looking at his head wound, I could easily see that it was very serious, because he had been shot directly through the top center of his skull. His eyes were fixed and straring at the sky. His lips were quivering; however, he never uttered a word.

The combat aidman was quick to arrive and I helped him move Lt. Manns to a safer position. Without hesitation he applied a large white medical bandage onto the head wound. I knew from my experience that it was a very serious wound and could be fatal. Two litter bearers had now arrived and I helped them place the wounded body onto the stretcher. They quickly attempted to move Lt. Manns down the rough hill side.

Before I returned to my position, Lt. Moses informed me that he had Captain Wadsworth on the radio and he wanted to talk to me. Over the radio, I briefly told him of the situation and that I personally thought Lt. Manns wouldn't make it. The Captain then directed me to reassume leadership of the 1st Platoon, and to keep in close radio contact in regard to our attack and progress on the hill. I quickly answered with a, "Yes sir!" Then I handed the phone back to Lt. Moses.

I returned to the position next to Corporal "Buck" Buckley, and he was still firing relentlessly at the enemy concealments. He asked me how Lt. Manns looked and I told him that I didn't think he would survive the

wound because of its severity. I then told him that Captain Wadsworth had directed me to take leadership again of the 1st Platoon.

Suddenly, "Buck" stopped firing the machine gun, and he looked directly at me, and said; 'Hell Lieutenant, you didn't want a transfer anyway! You know damn well that your heart is right here with the 1st Platoon!" I really didn't have an answer and my reply was, "Yes Buck, I guess you're right!"

Shortly, we were notified that the very crest of the hill would be softened up by 105 mm howitzer fire from Battery B, 77th Field Artillery.

The squad that attempted to maneuver behind the steep crest couldn't reach its objective, and were forced to withdraw. The enemy had rolled hand grenades down the steep crest which exploded and inflicted numerous wounds to the brave troopers.

After the artillery bombardment on the hill crest, orders were then issued to the rifle platoon to fix bayonets and prepare to resume the attack. However, little enemy resistance was encountered and we soon discovered that the enemy had withdrawn from their positions and were sighted moving to the north. By 1400 hours the hill mass and objective were secured.

Before we closed in a tight perimeter for the night, I received word that Lt. Manns had died earlier from his head wound, before the litter bearers had reached the bottom of the hill. He was such a fine officer and even though I had only known him a very short time, we had grown to respect each other's friendship.

The 1st Cavalry Division had always been a segregated division prior to the Korean War. There had been rumors of the black soldiers' performance in the outbreak of the Korean War, during the summer of 1950. However, in March 1951, the division was finally integrated and much resentment existed within the entire command.

The American society had permitted Negroes little chance to develop pride. The American society tends to give its black segments an inferiority complex, almost from birth. In the military service at that time, placed solely among other black soldiers, there is developed not mass pride, but mass neurosis. Few black soldiers understandably felt the urge to prove themselves in front of other black soldiers.

The Eighth Army Headquarters Command recommended one black soldier per squad, or possibly two, but no more. It was believed that if the one soldier was guilty of malfeasance, the others would take charge of him.

In my particular platoon, the first four black soldier arrivals were assigned as one to each individual squad. Their designated positions were ammo bearers, which necessitated in them carrying two containers of .30 caliber machine gun ammunition.

Also, to arrive in early March was Private Eugene G. Thomas, who was assigned to my platoon. I soon discovered that he was from Fort Thomas, Kentucky. This particular city

was very near my home of Covington. I directed Private Thomas to become an ammo bearer in the 1st squad of by platoon, and within the forthcoming weeks I personally got to know him very well.

He ended up being the tallest trooper in the platoon. Many troopers jokingly made comments that he made a better target for the enemy. Nevertheless, Private Thomas became very adapted to the rigorous mountain terrain, and he eventually became very proficient with the use of a .30 caliber machine gun.

During the next several days, the 2nd Battalion continued its northward attack within the outlying mountains of the Hongchon Valley. As we moved toward the Hongchon River objective, enemy resistance at times was extremely heavy. Attempting to secure the dominating features of various ridgelines, it became very difficult not only because of the rough terrain, but small pockets of die-hard enemy soldiers who refused to yield.

Efforts from the 77th Field Artillery and air strikes, as our support units, were very limited on their success. The enemy had dug deep underground positions that were connected by long endless trenches. They had strongly entrenched pill-box and bunker type positions which required, in many instances, direct hits to eliminate them.

From our company briefings, the 7th Cavalry Regiment Intelligence reported that an enemy regiment was operating within the hills that dominated the Hongchon River Valley.

On March 16, I was directed to take a squad from my platoon to support a screening patrol from the I & R Platoon of Headquarters and Headquarters Company. Our objective was to patrol the ridgelines east of the positions established by the 1st Battalion. This was to determine enemy strength and their locations for the future attack plans to secure a bridgehead across the Hongchon River.

In our forward progress within the ridgelines, we encountered sporadic small arms and mortar fire from various enemy positions. Our patrol stopped briefly to take a rest break. I suddenly noticed to my left on the small open ridge, a lonely trooper staggering around with no helmet on; nor was he carrying his rifle. He was completely exposed to the enemy. I very soon recognized that he was an ammo bearer from my platoon.

As I shouted to him to return to his position, an enemy mortar round exploded very near him. Strangely, the explosion didn't seem to phase him in the least, and he never responded to my continued commands. I then took off running across the small saddle that linked together the ridgeline in an attempt to rescue the trooper before he was seriously wounded or killed. He was definitely oblivious to what was really happening.

However, I failed in my desperate attempt to reach him because a second mortar round exploded as I hit the dirt. After the dust and debris cleared, I looked up and observed the trooper's body laying off to the edge of the ridgeline. Then I noticed that I had been hit by a small piece of shrapnel in my left knee. Strangely, it was an extremely small piece of steel that was protruding from the flesh at the base of the left knee. There was only a trace of blood, and there was very little pain. God had looked out for me again.

Without further delay, I got up and ran to the fallen trooper's body to move it to an un-exposed and safe position. I definitely thought the enemy would continue to fire mortars into the immediate area, but for some reason they failed to do so.

I started shouting for a "medic," and very shortly one arrived to administer medical aid. However, the "medic" looked at me with a sad expression on his face, and said the fallen trooper was dead. Within the lifeless body I never saw any shrapnel wounds or a trace of blood. The "medic" then said that he thought the fallen trooper had died from concussion because there were no wounds.

Then I showed the "medic" my left knee, he quickly removed the small pieces of shrapnel; and applied the appropriate medical treatment and a bandage to the minor wound.

Now I had to find out what possibily caused the fallen trooper to act with com-plete and total disregard of his own personal safety while in combat.

I very soon found out from troopers of the 2nd squad that the fallen trooper was drunk, and he supposedly had gone to urinate during the time he was killed. Then they further told me that someone had given him Canadian Club Whiskey, which had been brought back from Japan during R&R leave. During my combat experiences in Korea so far, I had never seen any type of alchohol within the frontline action.

Needless to say, I didn't like the idea of re-porting such tragic information to Captain Wadsworth. Particularly the way and man-ner the combat casualty actually happened.

After our brief rest, and the tragic loss of one trooper from Company H, our patrol continued toward Hill masses 320-325 and 655. These particular hills dominated the Hongchon River valley. So far, resistance was light and we received only sporadic fire from the enemy.

Radio contact was made with a combat patrol from the 1st Battalion which indicated they were receiving heavy automatic and small arms fire, and were experiencing diffi-culty in their attempt to advance. They fur-ther reported that they had made contact with a combat patrol from the 4th Battalion (GEF) which also had met heavy enemy resistance, and were making plans to with-draw from Hill 325.

Then two scouts arrived from the I&R Pla-toon and reported that during their aggres-sive probing, they had discovered numer-ous heavily dug-in machine gun positions within the outlying mountains. Also they had observed heavy concentrations of en-emy troop activity in the adjacent hills and ridges to the east. It was estimated that an enemy battalion or possibly a regiment, was operating within the general area.

It was then decided that to proceed any further with our combat patrol mission, it would possibly jeopardize the lives of every trooper in our small group. Due to the en-emy strength, a hard fight was ahead if we attempted to advance. Furthermore, the I&R Platoon had already secured enough valu-able information concerning estimated en-emy strength and locations of their heavily defended positions.

Radio contact with the 2nd Battalion Head-quarters confirmed our decision, and or-dered our combat patrol to withdraw imme-diately. Again we made radio contact with the 1st Battalion combat patrol and they were also planning to withdraw.

After our arrival back to the battalion sec-tor, I reported to Captain Wadsworth to in-form him of the combat fatality from his company. I quickly discovered that he had already heard of the casualty through our battalion and company communications.

During our brief discussion we both ac-knowledged the fact that this was the first such case involving a trooper drinking alco-holic beverages during actual combat or frontline duty. He then asked me if I saw the whiskey bottle that the fallen trooper sup-posedly was drinking from. I answered that I did not.

The Captain sent the company clerk to bring back the several troopers and the squad leader from the 2nd squad, to question them about the incident. However, the Captain and I soon realized that certain secrecy pre-vailed during the brief questioning. Each trooper said that they knew he had a fifth of Canadian Club whiskey, but they didn't know who possibly gave it or sold it to the fallen trooper. Strangely, no one saw him actually drinking the whiskey.

Nevertheless, the Captain quickly re-sponded by his issuance of orders to all offi-cers, non-commissioned officers and troop-ers within the company. The consequences of any company personnel caught within their possession or consuming alcoholic beverages during frontline duty would be subject to an immediate court-martial.

After being served a hot meal, all officers and key sergeants were briefed on our future attack plans within the Hongchon Valley.

From the terrain map we could see that Phase Line Baker had been reached and se-cured. Now our advance would be toward Phase Line Buffalo, and the 7th Cavalry Regiment had been given the mission of attacking and securing Hill mass 655.

The plan to seize Hill 655 was as follows:

Phase I - the 4th Battalion (GEF) and the 1st Battalion were to attack at 0730 hours on March 17 to secure the bridgehead across the Hongchon River. The 4th Battalion (GEF) to seize Hill 325 and be prepared to continue the attack to Hill 655. The 1st Battalion to secure Hills 320 and 349.

Phase II - the 2nd Battalion was to be pre-pared to pass through the easter portion of the 1st Battalion and contine the attack upon seizure of the bridgehead.

The 3rd Battalion was to be in regimental reserve and to support the attack with 81-mm mortar fire, heavy machine gun fire and 75-mm recoiless rifle fire on the southern slopes of Hill mass 655.

An intense artillery and mortar prepara-tion was to be placed on the objective area during the night of March 16-17, and a gen-eral artillery preparation to be fired to and after H-hour. Air strikes were requested for March 17 with the first strike to begin at 0715 hours.

All 2nd Battalion troopers had cleaned their weapons, then issued the necessary ammunition; and were prepared for their next objective. However, the attacks on Hill mass 655 by 4th Battalion (GEF), and the 1st Battalion on March 17-18 were so successful against the enemy that our 2nd Battalion was not alerted to attack until two days later.

Finally, at 0700 hours on March 19, the 2nd Battalion saddled up to attack the en-emy. Company G, was ordered to lead the attack to our next designated phase line. As my platoon moved out as a support element, we actualy never experienced any direct fighting. The enemy continued their hasty retreat, and elements of Company G received only light small arms and automatic weap-ons fire. We experienced no combat casual-ties during this brief, but very fast battle ma-neuver.

By early afternoon the 2nd Battalion had secured Phase Line Red. Clearing the phase line in its zone without enemy resistance, the relief of the 7th Cavalry Regiment was com-pleted by late afternoon. The 2nd Battalion was assigned to Division reserve, and went to an assembly area near Hongchon.

Enough cannot be said about the success-ful attacks on Hills 320, 325 and 655, by the 4th Battalion (GEF), and the 1st Battalion. On Hills 325 and 655, the gallant Greek troopers killed 187 enemy soldiers and wounded an estimated 300. The Greek National Flag waved proudly on Hill 655. On Hill 320, the brave troopers from the 1st Battalion killed 96 enemy soldiers and wounded an esti-mated 200; also, 14 enemy prisoners were taken. "GARRYOWEN"!

From March 22-25, and within this period, we were not only being organized into more smaller combat patrols, but aggressive units with the support of tanks from Company C, 70th Tank Battalion. These tank reinforced combat patrols were to penetrate deeply into enemy territory in the vicinity of Chunchon.

It was reported to all 2nd Battalion per-sonnel that Major General Charles D. Palmer, Division Commander of the 1st Cavalry Divi-sion had his personal jeep stolen on March 24. We never heard of it actually being recov-ered. Strangely, of all the vehicles within the Division, who would really want the General's jeep?

Our combat patrols were probing deep into enemy territory with little opposition. Within this particular zone, the enemy was still continuing to withdraw northward. De-fensive positions by the 1st Cavalry Division were now being established along Phase Line Cairo.

On the afternoon of March 25th, I was no-tified by Captain Wadsworth that I would

The Hwach'on Reservoir Power House, along the Pukhan River. April 10, 1951. (Courtesy of Suey Lee)

Extremely sharp and razor-like ridges existed within the Hwach'on Reservoir. April 11, 1951. (Courtesy of Suey Lee)

have to attend the special Greek ceremonies the following day, on March 26th. He also told me that the 7th Calvary Regimental Color Guard and the 4th Battalion (GEF), would be involved with the presentation of awards to members of the Greek Battalion. Later on I would learn that the celebration also marked the 125th Anniversary of the Greek Independence.

A brief description of what transpired during the special festivities, is from the Command Reports of the 7th Cavalry Regiment, dated Mar. 26, 1951, and is as follows:

The 4th Battalion (GEF) remained in regimental reserve on March 26 to celebrate Greek Independence Day with a parade, review and other festivities. The celebration was attended by Lieutenant General Matthew Ridgway, Eighth Army Commander; Lieutenant General William M. Hoge, IX Corps Commander; Major General Charles D. Palmer, Commanding General of the First Cavalry Division; Colonel William A. Harris, Commanding Officer of the 7th Cavalry Regiment; Major General Athanasios Dascarolis, Commanding General, Greek Expeditionary Forces in Korea; Colonel John Daskslopoulos, Commander Greek Expeditionary Force; Lieutenant Colonel D. Arbouzis, Commander 4th Battalion (GEF); and other invited dignitaries.

The celebration was highlighted by a presentation of awards to members of the Greek Battalion and addresses commemorating Greek Independence Day. First Cavalry Division shoulder patches were presented to all members of the 4th Battalion (GEF) as Greek and American friendship was greatly enhanced during the festivities of the day.

During the ceremony, the following address was delivered by Major General Athanasios Dascarolis:

"The commander of the fighting Greek Battalion and the Commander of the Greek ground forces in Korea in their orders to their unit, praised the history and significance of our Independence Day.

"Now, permit me, the senior Greek officer, and the representative of Greece in the Far East, to express to you in a few words neither the fighting spirit nor the skill in the art of waging war of the Greek Expeditionary Forces, for that purpose you are more qualified than I, but to express to you the feeling of those Greek officers and men, your comrades in battle in this war against Communism in Korea.

"All the Greek soldiers, fighting under your command are not a select group among the Greek forces, but are a small unit of the Regular Greek Armed Forces, with the natural and acquired characteristics of the Hellenic people.

"We do not know if you gave much thought in attacking the Battalion to the 1st Calvary Division and to the 7th Cavalry Regiment, the famous GARRYOWEN, but we feel that you have captured 1,000 Greek hearts by doing so, and the leaders who win the hearts of soldiers can realize miracles and wonders.

"As soldiers we will do our best so that one day to hope that the future officers and men of the 7th Cavalry Regiment will remember in their songs our names as in the verse—

'Look at Cameron and O'Brien Sergeant Flynn With a smile they're fighting, dying Sergeant Flynn
Though not one will be alive
Still their spirits will survive
To sing the names and fame of dear old GARRYOWEN.'

"Greece through its long life three thousand years ago respecting the noble traditions and the human dignity, looks at all the facts in all their bleakness and nakedness with a manly optimism and dares to hope and remain alive."

During the festivities it gave me the personal feeling of pride and honor just to witness the ceremony and to see the overall dedication that existed within the ranks of every individual Greek officer and soldier. The Greek soldier had definitely proved his fight-

ing capabilities to every officer and trooper within the 7th Cavalry Regiment.

It was widely recognized that the Greek soldier knew hardships and he was proud of his manhood and his fighting ability. He knew that his ancestors from the Empire of Greece had their courage with cold steel, and had rarely been equaled. Into each battle in Korea, he carried with him that faith in heritage, tradition and courage.

Also during the ceremony, my company commander, Captain John B. Wadsworth, was awarded the Distinguished Service Medal of Greece. I could see from his eyes and the expression on his face, that this was a very overwhelming event in his military career. I shook his hand in congratulations on his achievement and heroic military decoration. Within the day I would have the gracious opportunity to shake the hands of many brave officers and troopers not only in the Greek Expeditionary Forcers, but the 7th Cavalry Regiment, and Eighth Army as well.

An everlasting bond of comradeship between the Greek Expediantory Forces, the 7th Cavalry Regiment, and the 1st Cavalry Division had now been established. This would be more expressed in General Orders No. 2, Department of the Army, Washington 25, D.C., 2 February 1956. The Bravery Gold Medal of Greece was awarded to the 1st Cavalry Division, and every unit within the Division Command.

No device is authorized to be worn for this award. The citations are as follows:

The Bravery Gold Medal of Greece (Chryssoun Aristion Andrias) which was awarded by Paul, The King of Greece in accordance with Royal Order dated 15 June 1955, is confirmed in accordance with AR 220—315.

In accordance with The Royal Order dated 15 June 1955, Chryssoun Aristion Andrias (Bravery Gold Medal) is awarded to the Colors of the 1st Cavalry Division U.S. Army because, during the long period of the war in

Private Lee of Company F, 2nd Bn., 7th Cavalry, was killed in action and his body is being evaculated by litter bearers. Captain Harold Gray, Commanding Officer of Company F, was also killed in action as he attempted to rescue the wounded trooper. Hwach'on Reservoir, April 11, 1951. (Courtesy of Suey Lee)

The call for "medic" as Corporal O'Neil of the 3rd Platoon, Company F., 2nd Bn., 7th Cavalry, was killed in action. Hongchon Valley, March 1951. (Courtesy of Suey Lee)

Korea, the above unit positioned together with the Greek Expeditionary Forces, with which the latter was assigned, took part in hard fought battles in which the fluidity and the maneuvers experienced by the American and Greek soldiers, who falling together in the field of honour, won battles and succeeded the final victory, defending their colors and the Freedom of Humanity. Garry Owen!

After adjusting and settling down from the festivities of the previous day, the 2nd Battalion was notified to saddle up on the morning of March 27. Now the objective was to continue our advance and secure defensive positions in the vicinity of Phase Line Benton. During this particular combat advance, we met very little enemy opposition.

As the month of March came to a close, the troopers of the 2nd Battalion remained very optimistic about the continued withdrawal of the Chinese Communist Forces.

Also, before March ended I would see our Company Commander, Captain John Wadsworth, transferred to regimental S-2. The majority of personnel in Company H hated to see the Captain leave, but they realized he still would be serving within the 7th Cavalry Regiment.

Major Mel Chandler, the Executive Officer of the 2nd Battalion, made it known that during the month of March, the 7th Cavalry Regiment had estimated enemy casualties with 3,500 killed in action, 7,522 wounded in action and 200 prisoners of war captured. GARRYOWEN!

Many survivors of the North Korean Army had turned to guerrillas and melted into the population of South Korea. Even during 1951 in many of the so-called peaceful valleys and hills, what seemed like normal peasantry and agriculturists by day, became armed marauders by night.

United Nations convoys continued to be

fired on; individual soldiers were wounded and sometimes killed. Troop and hospital trains running between Taegu and Pusan — in spite of frequent railside patrols, sentry posts, and flatcars filled with infantry on each train — were fired on almost daily, sometimes inflicting casualties.

One of the favorite tricks of the insurgents was to slip close to the rail line by night, set up a machine gun, then wait for a well-lighted hospital train with its passengers strapped helplessly in berths, to go puffing by. Then, in a matter of seconds the train could be sprayed with bullets, the gun dismantled, and the guerrillas in their white peasant clothing were gone into the night.

Many mountain villagers knew which men went on these nocturnal excursions, but it was no simple matter to make them talk. The Republic of Korea Government, with the advice of the American Military, tried to solve the problem. It was never completely resolved and did not affect the war — but it was a constant nuisance.

In Chapter V, the author had previously written about his combat and prisoner of war experiences with the North Korean 10th Division. However, the author cannot accurately determine after engaging in combat with this particular enemy division, that after being captured, if he remained with elements from this same enemy division. From all possible indications, those American or ROK soldiers that were captured on or prior to August 12, 1950, did not remain with the North Korean 10th Division. Nevertheless, in my particular case we can not rule out a very strong possibility.

Based upon records of the Far East Command, the United Nations Command, and the Eighth Army, the following is a brief story concerning the North Korean 10th Division:

One of the great mysteries of the Korean

War occurred with the North Korean 10th Division. Even though it had suffered severe losses August 12-14, 1950, it still remained almost 7000 strong. It was in position to move against the beleaguered United Nations Forces, and drive east toward Taegu. If the 10th Division had added its weight and continued the assault, the pressure might well have been more than the United Nations Forces could stand. But the 10th Division either through misunderstanding or ineptitude of its command did not continue to move against the Naktong River defense. However, remnants from the 10th Division would be organized into guerrilla activities which would bring havoc to the United Nations Forces during the bitter cold months of the 1950-51 winter. Furthermore, the Army Historian wrote, the 10th North Korean Division was not well-trained or battle-experienced. It was definitely saddled with "Inept" commanders.

In March 1951, as Operation Ripper ground slowly forward, General Ridgway ordered the ROK I Corps in the east to complete the destruction of remnants of the North Korean 10th Division in the Chungbong Mountains southwest of the coastal town of Parhani. This enemy division, currently harassing the South Korean forces engaged in Operation Ripper, had infiltrated southward in January through the mountains from the 38th Parallel to within twenty miles of Taegu. Relying on the countryside for food and clothing and on captured material for ammunition, it had been able to make itself the full-time concern of at least one United Nations division, plus ROK security forces. It had suffered constant attack and heavy losses. Because it had no medical supplies or facilities, only the fittest survived. Yet the North Korean 10th Division managed to maintain the form of a military organization. As early as March 13, what was left of the

Air strikes bombing the Hwach'on Reservoir dam. The dam actually contained eighteen sluice gates. (Army)

division had made its way as far north as the Chungbong Mountains, where the surviving elements continued their operations. During the next few days, four ROK regiments harried the North Koreans in an effort to wipe them out. Though the 10th Division casualties were high, many must have survived to escape: the major activity in the sectors of the ROK 3rd and 9th Divisions, on March 17th-18th, consisted of fighting enemy groups that entered United Nations area from the rear, fought their way through, and disappeared to the north.

Meanwhile, in Washington, President Truman had long understood that General MacArthur disagreed with him, but he had not understood the extent; nor could Truman really understand MacArthur. Truman could not be sure that the General was playing for the gallery, trying to embarrass the President, and as political leader of the nation, Truman found this intolerable. MacArthur was challenging traditional civilian supremacy in government, and Truman was not at all certain but that Caesar was speaking beyond the Rubicon.

However, McArthur was no Caesar with immense political ambitions. He was a servant of the Republic of America who felt so strongly that the course of the Administration, askewing triumph over the transgressor, was immoral that he had put himself into public opposition. Actually, he was trying to influence policy.

Under the Constitution of the United States, no soldier has that privilege.

For General of the Army, MacArthur, America's Supreme Commander in the field, in a statement almost unprecedented in American history, beat President Harry Truman to the punch.

On March 24, 1951, with no word first to Washington, he issued his own pronouncement from Tokyo:

"Operations continue according to schedule and plan. We have now substantially cleared South Korea of organized Communist forces. It is becoming increasingly evident that the heavy destruction along the enemy's line of supply, caused by our round-the-clock massive air and naval bombardment, has left his troops in the forward battle area deficient in requirements to sustain his operations...

"Of even greater significance that our tactical successes has been the clear revelation that this new enemy, Red China, of such exaggerated and vaunted military power, lacks the industrial capacity to provide. . . crucial items necessary to the conduct of modern war. He lacks the manufacturing base. . . he cannot provide . . . tanks, heavy artillery and other refinements science has introduced into the conduct of military campaigns. Formerly his great numerical potential might well have filled this gap, with the development of existing methods of mass destruction, numbers alone do not offset. . . such deficiencies. "These military weaknesses have been clearly and definitely revealed since Red China entered upon its undeclared war in Korea. Even under the inhibitions which now restrict the activity of the United Nations forces and the corresponding military advantages which accrue to Red China, it has shown its complete inability to accomplish by force of arms the conquest of Korea. The enemy therefore, must by now be painfully aware that a decision of the United Nations to depart from its tolerant effort to contain the war to the area of Korea, through an expansion of our military operations to its coastal areas and interior bases, would doom Red China to the risk of imminent military collapse. These basic facts being established, there should be no insuperable difficulty in arriving at decisions on the Korean problem if the issues are resolved on their own merits, without being burdened by extraneous matters not directly related to Korea. . .

"The Korean nation and people, which have been so cruelly ravaged, must not be sacrificed. This is a paramount concern...Within the area of my authority as the military commander, however, it would be needless to say that I stand ready at any time to confer in the field with the commander in chief of the enemy forces. . . to find. . . means whereby realization of the political objectives of the United Nations in Korea, to which no nation may justly take exceptions, might be accomplished without further bloodshed."

Right or wrong, this was a remarkable statement to have been issued by an American proconsul in the field. It was more than a statement of military policy; it was a political act. It disregarded Washington's instruction for FECOM to abstain from declarations on foreign policy. It flouted the announced policy of the United Nations.

MacArthur had delivered Red China an ultimatum. He had hinted that the full power of the United States and its allies might be brought to bear against the Chinese homeland; threat was redolent throughout the discussion of Chinese weakness; and it was a threat that MacArthur obviously relished.

When Truman read it, he went white. MacArthur's announcement was a challenge to the authority of the President, under the Constitution, to make foreign policy.

History has proven that military men who are willing to risk their lives have very little sympathy with anyone unwilling to risk his office. While politics may be the art of the possible, war is often the art of the impossible.

President Harry Truman, however, will be regarded in history as one of the most unpopular and unrespected of the Presidents. If the people and the Congress rose behind MacArthur, supported his particular views, Harry Truman and his Administration would have been in deep trouble.

With the arrival of April 1st, the 2nd Battalion was experiencing difficulty in their attempt to establish bridgeheads on the Soyang River. Even though enemy resistance continued to be light, the terrain within the area was devoid of roads. In some cases, only small trails existed to provide means of moving food and ammunition supplies.

On April 2nd, with the support from the 4th Battalion (GEF), two bridgeheads were finally established on the Soyang River. As we secured our objective, the combat screening patrol from a rifle platoon of Company G, had made no contact with the enemy. Orders from the 2nd Battalion Headquarters stipulated to close in a tight perimeter for the night.

I didn't like the idea of spending my birthday during frontline duty, but of course there was no other choice. Just prior to dark, I was contacted by the company clerk of Company H. He handed me a sealed envelope and said that Lieutenant Richard Gerrish informed him to tell me to read the letter as soon as possible. At first, I thought it might be some bad news from home. I carefully opened the envelope.

In the shadowy winter's light, I slowly began to read the letter. To my total surprise, it was a birthday greeting letter from the Commander of the 7th Cavalry Regiment, Colonel "Wild Bill" Harris. The letter really cheered me up, and I immediately passed it around for members of my platoon to read.

The letter contained the following birthday greeting:

HEADQUARTERS, 7TH CAVALRY REGIMENT
APO 201
2 APRIL 1951

LIEUTENANT EDWARD L. DAILY
COMPANY "H"
7TH CAVALRY REGIMENT
APO 201

DEAR LIEUTENANT DAILY:

AS RECORDS SHOW THAT YOU HAVE COME TO ANOTHER ANNIVERSARY MARKER IN YOUR LIFE, I WISH TO EXTEND YOU THE CONGRATULATIONS AND BEST WISHES OF THE OFFICERS AND MEN OF THE 7TH CAVALRY REGIMENT.

IN THESE CRUCIAL INSTANCES OF OUR LIVES WHILE AWAY FROM OUR DEAR ONES, AND WHERE WE FIGHT FOR THE PRESERVATION OF OUR BEAUTIFUL IDEALS, IT IS WITH PLEASURE THAT I EXPRESS AN EARNEST DESIRE FOR HAPPY RETURNS OF THE DAY, FOR YOUR CONTINUING SUCCESS AND FOR MANY HAPPIER OCCASIONS TO COME.

SINCERELY,
[S] W.A. HARRIS
W.A. HARRIS
COLONEL, ARTY
COMMANDING

Here in the midst of combat, a regimental commander had taken a few minutes of his precious time to send a birthday greeting letter to a platoon leader. Further, the letter was an example of the compassion and respect that the Colonel had for every officer and trooper within the GARRYOWEN regiment.

Orders were received in the early morning of April 3rd, from Lt. Colonel John W. Callaway, 2nd Battalion Commander, for the entire battalion to continue its northward advance and cross the 38th Parallel. I was directed by Lieutenant Richard Gerrish to take elements from my platoon to support the forward combat scout patrol platoon from Company E.

After experiencing extreme difficulty over the rough terrain, our scouting mission finally reached our objective by early afternoon. Surprisingly, during this advance we had encountered only sporadic sniper fire from the enemy; and we experienced no casualties.

Our location now was directly adjacent to Hill 785, and intelligence reported that the large hill was heavily fortified with enemy forces. As we secured our positions the enemy never attempted to fire on our location.

I received word that the platoon from Company E was going to be served some hot chow. Rumors prevailed that it was creamed chicken being served over hot biscuits. Now

that really started my mouth to drool, so I decided to take one squad at a time through the chow line of Company E.

At the time, the 82nd Field Artillery was firing 155-mm howitzer rounds on Hill 785. The echoes of the projectiles passing overhead had previously sounded normal. However, as I attempted to lead one squad toward the chow line, I noticed that the line had maintained a five yard interval between each trooper. Then the unexpected happened as I quickly observed the change in sound of the projectiles passing overhead. It sounded as an approaching freight train, and without hesitation I shouted, "Hit the dirt!"

The artillery round hit the side of the hill and within the chow line of Company E, with a tremendous explosion. It sent a spewing gout of greasy smoke and whinning shrapnel through the rolling dust and debris. The projectile had landed approximately 40-50 yards from me.

Then the cry of pain from the severely wounded and the shouts for "medic" quickly prevailed, as confused and shaken-up troopers attempted to help or assist the wounded.

The Forward Observer immediately sent a radio dispatch to the 82nd Field Artillery to cease fire and to hold all firing positions on each artillery weapon, pending an investigation.

One of the severely wounded troopers almost landed on top of me, as his body was hurled through the air by the force of the explosion. His right leg, between the knee and ankle, was practically torn away by shrapnel; only a small piece of tissue actually connected the lower part of his leg.

I attempted to administer medical aid to the severely wounded trooper. The "medic" gave him a shot of morphine to alleviate the pain, as I assisted in applying a tourniquet to his right leg. Shortly, the litter bearers arrived and Sergeant First Class Frank Almy, a

platoon sergeant from Company E, helped me place the wounded trooper on the stretcher.

Needless to say, the short artillery round ended our desire for hot chow, and my platoon and I appeased our appetites with the normal c-rations.

We received word from the 82nd Field Artillery that all firing positions on their artillery weapons were proper and acceptable. However, it was assumed that one of the powder charges was insufficient for the designated target range. I suppose that completed their investigation.

Nevertheless, it was a very tragic combat experience, and which our own weapon inflicted many fatal and wounded casualties within Company E.

The following is an account of the short artillery round on the afternoon of April 3rd, from Sergeant First Class Frank Almy, Platoon Sergeant, Company E, 2nd Battalion, 7th Cavalry Regiment.

I remember the 82nd Field Artillery was firing its 155-mm howitzers on the hill that was directly across from our positions. I just finished eating some delicious hot chow, which was chicken and homemade buns or biscuits. Suddenly, a short round landed about 50 yards from me and it sounded like a train before it hit. At the time, many troopers were either eating or waiting in the chow line to be served a hot meal.

After the explosion, much confusion existed as I tried to give medical aid and assistance to the many wounded troopers. I noticed one trooper who had the lower part of of his right leg almost blown off by the explosion. I assisted 2nd Lt. Edward Daily of Company H in placing the severely wounded trooper on a stretcher. I knew from my experience that he would definitely lose part of his leg; and hopefully God would spare his life.

That one short round was a horrible mistake on someone's part in the particular artillery crew. In

Tank Task Force of the 70th Tank Bn., and 3rd Platoon, Company F, 2nd Bn., 7th Cavalry. Hongchon Valley, March 1951. (Courtesy of Suey Lee)

Company E, we would have to accept the very hard facts of the casualties that existed because six were killed and 15 wounded. Many good troopers that experienced and survived the fierce battles in the previous months, had now either lost their lives or were crippled for life..

Sergeant First Class Frank Almy did not continue his military career and was honorably discharged on November 19, 1951.

Darkness arrived and a tight perimeter was secured due to the possibility of an enemy attack; and a 100 percent alert was ordered. Then during the night the Chinese continued to expose a small bright light. So far in Korea, I had never seen the enemy use this type of combat tactic. Orders were then issued to hold all fire!

The enemy would turn the light on for so many seconds, and then turn it off. This same procedure was repeated from various positions on the hill. We assumed it was only one light that was being manipulated by the enemy. There was no exchange of fire between us and the enemy.

Then at approximately 0100 hours, a loud mouth enemy soldier with a good pair of lungs and a voice box, started to shout; "Hey yankee, why don't you go home"! Surprisingly, his English was fairly good, but his voice box must have given out because he didn't repeat himself very long.

It seemed to have agitated a couple of troopers in my platoon, as one said to me "Hey, Lieutenant, I sure would like to take my foot and shove it right down his damn throat!" I quickly told first gunner, Corporal Bob Barnes, to shut up and keep quiet.

At 0400 hours the enemy ceased to expose their bright light trick. However, prior to daybreak some enemy noise and talk was observed coming from the hill. Still there was no exchange of fire with the enemy.

With the arrival of daybreak, plans were being discussed on the future attack of Hill 785. Word was being circulated that no enemy activity could be seen on the hill. I slowly observed the hill with my binoculars and I also couldn't see any enemy movement. However, I had seen this same situation before, wheareas the enemy was in concealment and quietly waited for the kill.

A point patrol squad was directed from a rifle platoon of Company E to seek and search the hill. With my binoculars, I carefully watched the riflemen and point man of the squad methodically move up the hill. Very fortunately, not one shot had to be fired because the enemy had already made their withdrawal from the hill earlier in the morning. Without any hesitation, the 2nd Battalion quickly secured Hill 758; another hill taken, and another waits ahead.

On April 5, the 2nd Battalion was relieved by the 4th Battalion, and we went into temporary Division reserve, just north of the 38th Parallel. Needless to say, we were all ready and anxious for a hot shower, hot chow and the change of clean fatigue clothing.

In the meantime, politics in Washington continued to heat up over General MacArthur and his military strategies in the Korean War. Sometime between March 24 and April 5, 1951, Harry Truman resolved to relieve MacArthur of his command. When the next evidence of MacArthur's insubordination arose, Truman's mind was already made up — but what occurred on April 5, 1951, in effect allowed Truman no other choice.

On that particular date, Joe Martin, the leader of the opposition in the House, rose and read a personal letter from MacArthur. Martin, of Massachusetts, had long been an isolationist, clinging beyond 1941 to the old school of American thought, much like Taft and Wherry in the Senate.

The old school of thought was honest and sincere, but contradictory. The old school was highly suspicious of the military, and preferred to cut arms spending to the bone.

Representative Joseph W. Martin, a sincere man, stood before the House on April 5, 1951. Previously, he had written MacArthur in early March, saying among other things, that he considered it sheer folly not to use Nationalist Chinese troops in Korea. He had asked for MacArthur's comments, and now he read them aloud:

'I am most grateful for your note of the eighth forwarding me a copy of your address of February 12 . . . .

'My views and recommendations with respect to the situation created by Red China's entry into war against us in Korea have been submitted to Washington in most complete detail. Generally these views are well known and understood, as they follow the conventional pattern of meeting force with maximum counterforce as we have never failed to do in the past. Your view with respect to the utilization of the Chinese forces on Formosa is in conflict with neither logic or this tradition.

"It seems strangely difficult for some to realize that here in Asia is where the Communist conspirators have elected to make their play for global conquest, and that we have joined the issue thus raised on the battlefield; that here we fight Europe's war with arms while the diplomats there still fight it with words; that if we lose this war to Communism in Asia the fall of Europe is inevitable, win it and Europe most probably would avoid war and yet preserve freedom. As you point out, we must win.

"There is no substitute for victory."

In 1951, defeat of Red China, whether it would have brought on a general war with Russia or not, would have alienated the whole world. However, a war can no more be successfully fought without political concerns for the future than an Army can fight without ammunition.

Nevertheless, wherever it lay, whoever was right, or who was wrong, MacArthur's letter to Joe Martin was insubordination.

President Truman hit the ceiling. He called a meeting with Acheson, Bradley, Marshall and Harriman. On April 6, he asked these men bluntly what they felt should be done. All were agreed that the Administration faced a serious threat.

Within an hour, each one expressed their feelings and decisions.

Overall, Harriman, head of the Mutual Security Agency, stated that MacArthur should have been relieved two years ago. Harriman was unhappy with MacArthur's handling of some occupation matters in Japan, where he had also opposed Washington policy.

Acheson, moustached and deliberative, said he believed that MacArthur had to be relieved but that he thought it should be done very carefully. "If you relieve MacArthur, you will have the biggest fight of your Administration," he said.

Omar Bradley, head of the Joint Chiefs of Staff, looked upon the question as a matter of military discipline. A true centurion, Bra-

Troopers of the 3rd Platoon, Company F, 2nd Bn., 7th Cavalry, in Hongchon Valley, March 1951. Platoon leader was 1st Lt. Jim Gorman. (Courtesy of Suey Lee)

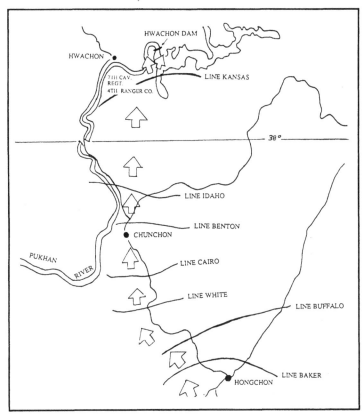

Commencing on 7 March, Cavalry units drove northeast to the Hongchon area, then turned north and continued through Chunchon to line Kansas, north of the 38th parallel. On 11 April elements of the 7th Cav. Regt. and the 4th Ranger Co. pushed on to the Hwachon reservoir. Their initial assault on the enemy defenses here was successful, but they were soon pinned down and received orders to pull back.

The Chinese spring offensive got under way on 22 April, and the 1st Cav. Div. was soon committed along line Golden in the defense of Seoul. When the Red drive had been stopped, United Nations forces began probing northward. During the latter part of May and early June, the Cavalry jumped off and pushed ahead to line Wyoming, which was to be its main line of resistance until October, 1951.

dley saw a clear case of insubordination; he felt MacArthur deserved relief.

George Marshall, Secretary of Defense, counseled caution. He was reluctant to discipline MacArthur; it might make trouble with Congress.

President Truman let these men talk, then and later. He did not advise them that he had already made up his mind and that the "ayes had it." MacArthur would be relieved. Truman advised Marshall to reread the file of communications between Tokyo and Washington.

On April 7, Marshall reported back to Blair House that he now felt MacArthur should have been fired long ago.

Then on April 8, the Joint Chief of Staff concurred.

On Monday, April 9, with everyone in agreement, Truman then told them that he made his decision after MacArthur's "pronunciamento" of March 24th. At 3:15 that afternoon, the President signed an order relieving MacArthur of all his several commands, and replaced him with Lieutenant General Matthew B. Ridgway.

Truman's intention was that this notice of relief be given MacArthur through Secretary of the Army Frank Pace, then in the Far East. Dean Acheson sent orders through Korean Ambassador Muccio, with instructions that Pace was to proceed immediately to Tokyo, to deliver them in person.

But Pace could not be reached; he was up near the Eighth Army front, firing a howitzer in the company of General Ridgway. One of the traditions of modern war that had grown up was that distinguished visitors be taken to a firing battery of heavy artillery, suitably behind the front, and there be allowed to fire "one at the enemy," which made for a good picture and gave a feeling of active participation, all without untidy risk.

Pace could not be reached, and the message was too hot to be bandied about in lesser hands.

Later, General Matt Ridgway, who had spent all afternoon in Frank Pace's company, without ever learning that he was already Supreme Commander, Far East, remarked that Mr. Pace had an odd sense of humor. It did not occur to General Ridgway that Mr. Pace was as ignorant of the fact as he.

President Truman then sent word to John Foster Dulles to go to Japan and inform the Japanese Yoshida Government that the change would affect them in no way. While Dulles prepared to emplane, Omar Bradley dashed into Blair House, visibly excited.

There had been a leak, Bradley said, and a Chicago newspaper was going to print the story of MacArthur's relief the next morning on April 11th.

A President - any President - hates to be scooped almost more than anything else. More than once such a fear has changed the course of history, and now Harry Truman decided that courtesy be damned, he could not wait until Frank Pace finished getting his kicks gallivanting around the frontline.

General MacArthur would get his notice over the wire, at the same time everyone else in the world got it. And so he did!

On April 11th, at 0100 in the morning, Truman's press Secretary gave a group of grousing, sleepy-eyed reporters a presidential release:

"With deep regret, I have concluded that General of the Army, Douglas MacArthur is unable to give his whole-hearted support to the policies of the United States Government and to the United Nations . . . I have, therefore, relieved General MacArthur of his commands and have designated Lieutenant General Matthew B. Ridgway as his successor.

"Full and vigorous debate on matters of national policy is a vital element in the constitutional system. . . It is fundamental, however, that military commander must be governed by the policies and directives issued to them...in time of crisis, the consideration in particularly compelling.

"General MacArthur's place in history as one of our greatest commanders is fully established. The Nation owes him a debt of gratitude for the distinguished and exceptional service he has rendered...For that reason I repeat my regret at the necessity for the action I feel compelled to take in his case."

General of the Army Douglas MacArthur took the news, which came to him as a slap in the face, calmly, and with good cheer. When General Matt Ridgeway reported to him at Dai Ichi in Tokyo on April 12, MacArthur was quiet, composed, and entirely helpful and friendly. Ridgway could ascertain no trace of bitterness. As a soldier, he did not question the President's right to do what he had done. But out of the loyalty he held in his heart for MacArthur, he was angry that the

L. to R. - 2nd Lt. Edward Daily, Leader 1st Platoon, Company H, 2nd Bn. 7th Cavalry, Corporals Barnes, Buckley and E. Thomas. Digging defensive positions on Phase Line Benton, March 31, 1951. (Courtesy of Margie Thomas)

The Greek Expeditionary Forces were disciplined and tough soldiers. (U.S. Army photo)

The "Glosters" of England in Korea, 1951. This famous regiment was attacked on April 22, 1951, in the Chinese Spring Offensive, and they held their position for four days. Only a hand full survived, but the Chinese suffered crippling losses. (United Nations)

the dismissal had been done so summarily.

The relief of General MacArthur was not a satisfying answer for the Truman Administration. Millions disliked or distrusted it, but could not put forth a better course. There was frustration and trauma.

The National Research Bureau, Inc., Chicago, Illinois, published a small book concerning General Douglas MacArthur. It contained the highlights of his career and his address to the joint session of Congress on April 19, 1951. His comments about the Korean Conflict during the historic address to Congress is in part, and is as follows:

With this brief insight into the surrounding areas, I now turn to the Korean Conflict.

While I was not consulted prior to the President's decision to intervene in support of the republic of Korea, that decision, from a military standpoint, proved a sound one. As I say, a brief and sound one, as we hurled back the invader and decimated his forces. Our victory was complete, and our objectives within reach when Red China intervened with numerically superior ground forces.

This created a new war and an entirely new situation, a situation not contemplated when our forces were committed against the North Korean invaders; a situation which called for new decisions in the diplomatic sphere to permit the realistic adjustment of military strategy. Such decisions have not been forthcoming.

While no man in his right mind would advocate sending our ground forces into continental China, and such was never given a thought, the new situation did urgently demand a drastic revision of strategic planning if our political aim was to defeat this new enemy as we had defeated the old.

Apart from the military need, as I saw it, to neutralize the sanctuary protection given the enemy north of the Yalu, I felt that military necessity in the conduct of the war made necessary,

(1) The intensification of our economic blockade against China;

(2) The imposition of a naval blockade against the China Coast;

(3) Removal of restrictions on air reconnaissance of China's coastal areas and of Manchuria;

(4) Removal of restrictions on the forces of the republic of China or Formosa, with logistical support to contribute to their effective operation against the Chinese mainland.

For entertaining these views, all professionally designed to support our forces in Korea and to bring hostilities to an end with the least possible delay and at a saving of countless American and Allied lives. I have been severely criticized in lay circles, principally abroad, despite my understanding that from a military standpoint, the above views have been fully shared in the past by practically every military leader concerned with the Korean campaign, including our own joint chiefs of staff.

I called for reinforcements, but was informed that reinforcements were not available. I made clear that if not permitted to destroy the enemy build-up bases north of the Yalu, if not permitted to utilize the friendly Chinese force of some 600,000

men on Formosa, if not permitted to blockade the China coast to prevent the Chinese Reds from getting succor from without, and if there were to be no hope of major reinforcements, the position of the command from the military standpoint forbade victory.

We could hold in Korea by constant maneuver and at an approximate area where our supply line advantages were in balance with the supply-line disadvantages of the enemy, but we could hope at best for only an indecisive campaign with its terrible and constant attrition upon our forces if the enemy utilized its full military potential.

I have constantly called for the new political decisions essential to a solution.

Efforts have made to distort my position. It has been said in effect that I was a warmonger. Nothing could be further from the truth.

I know war as few other men now living know it, and nothing to me - nothing to me - is more revolting. I have long advocated its complete abolition, as its very destructiveness on both friend and foe has rendered it useless as a means of settling international disputes.

Indeed, on the second of September, 1945, just following the surrender of the Japanese nation on the Battleship "Missouri", I formally cautioned as follows:

"Men since the beginning of time have sought peace. Various methods through the ages have been attempted to devise an international process to prevent or settle disputes between nations. From the very start, workable methods were found in so far as individual citizens were concerned, but the mechanics of an instrumentality of larger international scope have never been successful. Military alliances, balances of power, leagues of nations, all in turn failed, leaving the only path to be by way of the crucible of war. The utter destructiveness of war now blocks out this alternative. We have had our last chance. If we will not devise some greater and more equitable sytem, Armageddon will be at our door. The problem basically is theological and involves a spiritual recrudescence and improvement of human character that will synchronize with our almost matchless advances in science, art, literature, and all material and cultural developments of the past 2,000 years. It must be of the spirit if we are to save the flesh."

But once war is forced upon us, there is no other alternative than to apply every available means to bring it to a swift end. War's very object is victory, not prolonged indecision.

In war there is no substitute for victory.

There are some who for varying reasons would appease Red China. They are blind to history's clear lesson, for history teaches with unmistakable emphasis that appeasement but begets new and bloodier war. It points to no single instance where the end has justified the means, where appeasement has led to more than a shame peace. Like blackmail, it lays the basis for new and successively greater demands until, as in blackmail, violence becomes the only other alternative. Why, my soldiers asked of me, surrender military advantages to an enemy in the field? I could not answer.

Some may say to avoid spread of the conflict into an all-out war with China. Others, to avoid Soviet intervention. Neither explanation seems valid, for China is already engaging with the maximum power it can commit, and the Soviet will not necessarily mesh its actions with our moves. Like a cobra any new enemy will more likely strike whenever it feels that the relativity in military or other potential is in its favor on a world-wide basis.

The tragedy of Korea is further heightened by the fact that its military action is confined to its territorial limits. It condemns that nation, which is our purpose to save, to suffer the devastation impact of full naval and air bombardment while the enemy's santuaries are fully protected from such attack and devastation.

Of the nations of the world in Korea alone, up to now, is the sole on which has risked its all against Communism. The magnificence of the courage and fortitude of the Korean people defies description. They have chosen to risk death rather than slavery. Their last words to me were: "Don't scuttle the Pacific."

I have just left your fighting sons in Korea. They have met all tests there, and I can report to you without reservation that they are splendid in every way. It was my constant effort to preserve them and this savage conflict honorably and with the least loss of time and a minimum sacrifice of life. Its growing bloodshed has caused me the deepest anguish and anxiety. Those gallant men will remain often in my thoughts and in my prayers always.

I am closing my 52 years of military service. When I joined the Army, even before the turn of the century, it was my fulfillment of all of my boyish hopes and dreams. The world has turned over many times since I took the oath on the plain at West Point, and the hopes and dreams have long since vanished, but I still remember the refrain of one of the most popular barrack ballads of that day which proclaimed most proudly that old soldiers never die; they just fade away. And, like the old soldier of that ballad, I now close my military career and just fade away, an old soldier who tried to do his duty as God gave him the light to see that duty. Good-by.

On April 14, rotation back to the United States was started within the 7th Cavalry Regiment. This sort of news definitely boosted the morale of every officer and trooper in the 2nd Battalion. By the end of April, 12 officers and 193 enlisted men were rotated from the GARRYOWEN regiment.

However, rotation would bring forth new troopers and receiving new troopers in a platoon was sometimes difficult to accept in as much as it was losing troopers due to casualties. It was equally difficult to judge misfits who could not obey orders, any orders, and who could not stand immense and searing mental and physical pressure.

In Korea, for his own sake and for those around him, a combat trooper had to be prepared for the awful shrieking moment of truth when he realized that he was all alone on a hill thousands of miles away from home; and that he may be killed at any given moment.

This individual discipline was accepted by many; however, there were those certain few who had to be carefully watched and supervised by his fellow troopers in the platoon.

The warm spring sun and air were defi-nitely appreciated after a bitter cold and difficult winter. However, the melted ice and snow made many of the Korean roads deep with spongy mud. Nevertheless, a new spirit had blossomed within the ranks of every unit in the 1st Cavalry Division.

On April 10, all company officers and key sergeants were briefed on our future attack mission and seizure of the Hwach'on Reservoir.

Running along the commanding ground north of the 38th Parallel was the 10-mile water barrier of the Hwach'on Reservoir, which was Seoul's source of water and electric power. The dam itself was 275 feet high, and contained 18 sluice gates. The terrain within this area was extremely rough, nearly devoid of roads and therefore difficult for both United Nations and enemy forces.

This rugged terrain of the central sector hampered the overall movement of every supply route. On April 9, the enemy opened several sluice gates of the dam that controlled the water passing from the Hwach'on Reservoir into the lower Pukhan River. The Pukhan, originating in the mountainous country to the north, flowed south to the reservoir and thence southwest to its confluence with the Han River east of Seoul.

Within an hour the water level had risen over four feet; one engineer bridge was broken, and IX Corps Engineers were forced to swing a second one back to the banks. To prevent the enemy from opening all eighteen sluice gates and flooding Pukhan, a task force from the 2nd Battalion, 7th Cavalry Regiment and the 4th Ranger Company, were hastily organized.

The formation of Task Force Callaway — under the command of Lt. Colonel John W. Callaway, Commander of the 2nd Battalion, 7th Cavalry Regiment, quickly moved northward in an attempt to seize the dam, close the gates, and immobilize the gate-opening machinery. The 7th Cavalry Regiment historian wrote, "The regiment's rapid advance over the rugged terrain during the preceding few days, had placed them in an area where it was impossible for vehicles larger than a one-quarter ton jeep to travel due to poor roads." The division's three artillery battalions of 105-mm howitzers could not reach the dam area; only one battalion of 155-mm howitzers could just barely do so, providing only limited support.

Previously, General Matthew Ridgway had flown directly over the dam for an inspection. They circled low watching the outflow of water, which didn't appear to be as serious as the initial reports had indicated. General Ridgway returned to Chunchon to confer with General Bill Hoge, Commander IX Corps, and General Charles Palmer, Commander 1st Cavalry Division. Then Ridgway flew over the dam a second time in a helicopter. He confirmed that the flooding was not calamitous. It appeared that the Chinese had not opened the sluice gates all the way, or that the water pressure behind the dam was less than had been calculated. Nonetheless, the Hwach'on Dam remained, if not a serious threat, a very distinct annoy-ance.

After our morning briefing of April 10, we quickly saddled up and moved out for our assigned objective. I soon experienced some of the most difficult and rugged terrain since my arrival in Korea. By afternoon we came into contact with the enemy and met stubborn resistance from heavy machine gun and mortar fire.

Shortly, four Navy Corsairs (F4U) arrived and they strafed and dropped napalm bombs on the enemy positions along the ridgelines, and hill sides. Soon the Chinese started to withdraw and our forward elements methodically moved against the retreating enemy.

During the last strafing pass by the Corsairs, the forth one fired on the enemy positions, but failed to pull out of his dive. I surmise that it was hit by enemy fire which caused the fighter plane to take a sharp bank to the left, and then crash into a distant mountain. The pilot never ejected from his seat.

Our battalion continued to attack the stiff enemy resistance within the narrow neck of land between the Pukhan River and the reservoir. We couldn't dislodge the Chinese from their positions. Even air strikes could not drive the enemy from their heavily concealed entrenchments.

In the meantime, Colonel Harris had definitely decided to launch an amphibious assault. Further, he issued orders for motorboat mechanics or anyone who knew anything about motorboats to be sent to the dam as quickly as possible.

To further support the attack on the dam, the following equipment was received from the engineers: 35 assault boats, 20 outboard motors, 245 paddles, 160 life preservers, 1 demolition kit with detonators, 50 electric caps, 400 feet of primer cord, 386 lbs of TNT, 100 non-electric caps, 500 feet of time fuse, 45 fuse lighters, 20 adapters.

However, the water-borne attack did not wait for the motorboat mechanics. Elements of Company I, 3rd Battalion, 7th Cavalry Regiment and the 4th Ranger Company crossed the reservoir from the south and had initial success in securing the dam and the ground north of the dam. Overcoming small arms and automatic weapons fire, this assault in boats had embarked at 0345 hours and they had secured their objective by 0520 hours. By 1130 hours they were joined by more elements from Company I.

However, at 1330 hours an estimated enemy battalion counterattacked, viciously driving them back and prevented further gains. It was then determined that the attack could not advance any further and they were ordered to withdraw. This, of course, had to be accomplished by boat. Many of the plywood boats were smashed by mortar fire before they reached friendly shores. The withdrawal was finally completed at 0130 hours on April 12, and both companies had suffered severe casualties.

The following is a brief account of the battle at the Hwach'on Reservoir from Private First Class Jose Alva, a gunner on a 57-

mm recoilless rifle, of the weapons section of the 4th Platoon, Company I, 3rd Battalion, 7th Cavalry Regiment.

We were ordered to cross an area of water in the reservoir in small plywood boats to give support to the 4th Ranger Company. They had previously crossed the water in the same small boats, prior to daybreak on April 11, 1951.

After our boat reached the shore, I fired several shots from my weapon at enemy positions. Just how effective they were, I really don't know. Then we immediately moved forward into position to assault the enemy. We soon discovered that the enemy was heavily dug-in and refused to yield. The terrain within this area was the worst that I had ever experienced in Korea.

The Chinese Communists fought a fierce battle, but we finally reached our objective at 1130 hours and joined with elements of the 4th Ranger Company. We had success in securing the dam and some land just north of the dam. However, by 1300 hours the enemy started a vicious counterattack, forcing us to withdraw.

The 4th Ranger Company was permitted to withdraw first as we attempted to maintain rear guard positions for their orderly withdrawal. It was extremely difficult for them to withdraw across the water in the small plywood boats because the enemy was firing on them with their mortars. They accomplished their crossing prior to darkness and we established a perimeter near the water's edge.

Somewhere within the confusion of the battle, I lost my assistant gunner and three ammo bearers. To this day, I don't know what happened to them. It was very cumbersome for me to carry my weapon, plus I had the difficult task of dragging the bag of ammo with me. However, at this particular time I had only three rounds of WP (white phosphorus) left. A lieutenant directed me to fire them at particular enemy positions before darkness set in. This was to mark the positions so they could attempt to destroy them with 155-mm artillery howitzers. Also during the day my 57-mm rifle had fired right on target, because I had success in eliminating five to seven Chinese machine gun emplacements.

Shortly after midnight and within the cold spring night, we loaded up in Army "Duck" vehicles. We made it safely across the water, but our company had suffered severe casualties during this very tough and difficult battle.

Private First Class Jose Alva was wounded several times during his combat experiences in Korea. Also he never remained in the military and was honorably discharged on December 9, 1951. Nevertheless, for his very brave and heroic deeds during the Hwach'on Reservoir battle, he was awarded the Bronze Star Medal for Valor. The Citation is in part and is as follows:

Private First Class Jose Alva, Infantry, United States Army, Company I, 7th Cavalry Regiment, 1st Cavalry Division, for heroism in action against the enemy for 11 April 1951, near Hwachon, Korea. During the initial attack on the high ground surrounding the Hwachon reservoir, Private Alva displayed excellent marksmanship with his 57-mm recoilless rifle, as he succeeded in destroying four of the key hostile machine gun emplacements. When the advance squad became pinned down by extremely heavy mortar, au-

tomatic weapons and small arms fire, he unhesitantly moved forward over 100 yards of exposed terrain, carrying his weapon and ammunition in order to place the 57-mm rifle in closer support of the pinned down unit. Private Alva voluntarily assaulted and eliminated three more of the Chinese emplacements. After his supply of ammunition was exhausted, he quickly picked up a rifle and continued in the attack. His courageousness and aggressiveness were greatly responsible for the successful completion of the units' mission and were an inspiration to all the men of his company. Private Alvas' heroism and devotion to duty reflect great credit on himself and the military service..

The following is a brief story concerning the Hwachon Reservoir battle from Sergeant First Class James A. McClure, squad leader Intelligence Reconnaissance Platoon (I&R), 7th Cavalry Regiment, 1st Cavalry Divisions.

Since our arrival in Korea, the majority of my combat scout patrol missions were accomplished with the 2nd Battalion. On April 10, 1951, we were notified that our future orders would be the seizure of the Hwachon Reservoir and Dam. A 2nd Battalion Task Force was organized which was under the operational control of Lt. Colonel John Callaway, Commander, 2nd Battalion.

The terrain within the reservoir was extremely rough which made our forward progress the most difficult. And the Chinese had many heavily fortified machine gun positions throughout the ridge lines leading to the dam. And we were soon told that we had gone beyond the maximum range of our support artillery. We had placed ourselves in a very serious predicament.

On April 11, 1951, the 4th Ranger Company and Company I, 7th Cavalry Regiment, had made an amphibious landing across the reservoir to the northeast in an effort to capture the dam. We heard that both companies had met stiff enemy resistance in the early morning assault. However, by early afternoon we were notified that the enemy had made a counterattack and it was necessary for both companies to withdraw.

Prior to darkness, an officer whom I didn't know approached my squad and asked if any of us had previous experience with the operation of a 16-foot assault boat that was equipped with a 33 H.P. Evinrude motor. I immediately answered that we had used them the previous summer to cross the Naktong River to conduct combat scouting patrols in enemy held territory. I hesitated for a moment, then I told the officer that I would volunteer my services for whatever he needed.

The officer then informed me that the 4th Ranger Company had orders to withdraw and the 16 foot assault boats would be used to bring them back across the water of the Reservoir. Very quickly, myself and several others in their assault boats, were in the water heading across to the opposite side of the Reservoir. All of a sudden, enemy machine gun fire from the distance started to hit the water very near us.

Just prior to landing on the opposite s shore of the Reservoir, seven or eight Rangers attempted to walk into the water to meet our boats. However, an officer with the rank of Captain who was carrying a Thompson sub-machine gun ordered them out of the water. He then directed them to remain on the shore so everyone could attempt to withdraw together in an orderly fashion.

One must also realize that there were no neutral controls on a 33 H.P. Evinrude motor. Even on low idle, the motor continued to supply the boat with power, making it move about and making it difficult to load it with personnel. To shut off the motor gave everyone the fear that it might not start again. None of us were taking any chances!

We finally got the boats loaded with the brave troopers from the 4th Ranger Company and we proceeded to withdraw in an orderly manner across the water of the Reservoir. Actually we were almost like sitting ducks in a pond as enemy mortar rounds and machine gun fire hit the water all around us. I don't remember much after that, however, we did make a safe return to friendly lines. Nevertheless, I know that the 4th Ranger Company and Company I, suffered many casualties in their assault and withdrawal operations.

Sergeant First Class James A. McClure never continued his military career and he was honorably discharged in 1952.

Previously, on April 11th, the daybreak had brought forth an overcast sky and heavy fog within certain areas of the dam. Everyone realized now that there was no possible way of receiving air support because of the weather conditions. From the eyes of every trooper, you could see the dismal look of a tough battle ahead.

Near the edge of the dirt road I briefly talked to 2nd Lt. John Matthews who was platoon leader from Company G. A machine gun section from my platoon was assigned as a support element to his rifle platoon, which was scheduled for attack at 0730 hours.

Lt. Matthews expressed his personal feelings that we would have a hard battle coming up due to the tough enemy resistance. Further he added that we had no air support and we were limited on artillery support also. I shared his opinion and sentiment.

Within the hillside I heard a vehicle moving around, and closer observation revealed it was a jeep with a 75-mm recoilless rifle mounted on it. Then I looked through my binoculars and to my surprise it was Major Mel Chandler, our 2nd Battalion Executive Officer. There he was attempting to manipulate and maneuver the vehicle to fire on enemy positions. Everyone was wondering how in the hell did he ever get the jeep up on the hill.

Major Chandler hadn't changed from his normal persistent determination as he assisted the rifle team. Several shots were fired from the position, but just how effective it was on enemy positions was questionable. Nonetheless, it soon brought return fire from the enemy and shortly it was moved to another location.

After talking to Captain Albert Moses, company commander of Company G, it was decided that a machine gun section from my platoon would give support to elements of his company that were scheduled for an attack at 0730 hours. Our objective was the camel's nose within the narrow neck of land between the Pukhan River and the reservoir.

As I attempted to return to the location of my platoon, an explosion came from the small sloping ridge near the road. I soon realized that members of my platoon were at that same location. I started to run as fast as my legs could carry me. After my arrival I quickly discovered that five members of my platoon were killed in the one explosion and direct hit.

Again, it was one of the many mistakes that can happen within the conditions of combat. The enemy had taken advantage of the situation. Sergeant First Class Tom Simmons reported to me that the small group of troopers had decided to build a small fire to cook either coffee or hot chocolate. They had assumed that the heavy fog had given them protection from the sight of the enemy.

However, the enemy spotted the smoke from the fire and they zeroed-in a 75mm pack howitzer from the opposite hill. The projectile exploded within the small group. Killed in the group was Corporal Hank Wright, a first gunner from the state of West Virginia. Strangely, he was wearing the steel helmet that belonged to P.F.C. Eugene Thomas. Both were good friends; however, P.F.C. Thomas wasn't in the group. Also, during the previous day, Corporal Wright had given all of his personal money to P.F.C. Thomas to keep for him. At the time, he had told him that he had a strange feeling that something might happen.

I was mentally shaken from the loss of five men from my platoon. However, the battle raged on and now I had to make quick but temporary adjustments within my platoon.

At times Sergeant First Class Tom Simmons was almost like an extra right hand to me. With his help a fast manipulation of troopers between two squads of my platoon and we were now ready for the 0730 attack with Company G.

The attack went off as scheduled under heavy enemy machine gun and mortar fire. Captain Albert Moses had maneuvered some of his men within abandoned enemy trenches, which gave them a better view of the enemy positions.

One platoon had fought their way near the nose of the camel's head, but they got severely shot-up and had to withdraw under heavy enemy fire. However, one rifle squad of the platoon was unable to make the very chaotic withdrawal. A patrol got them out later, but they were all dead.

The Chinese refused to yield from their heavy fortified positions. Finally, at 1800 hours, all units were ordered to break contact with the enemy and return to previously occupied defensive positions.

During this battle, my company commander, Lieutenant, Richard Gerrish, was killed in action. He and the 2nd Battalion Commander, Lt. Colonel John W. Callaway were at an Observation Post and the enemy had fired a 75-mm pack howitzer almost directly into the position. With the grace of God, Lt. Colonel Callaway miraculously escaped injury.

Actually, I never got to know Lt. Gerrish that well because he was the Commander of Company H only a few weeks. Also during this battle, Lt. Von de Lieff, our 2nd Platoon Leader, sustained a foot wound. He was previously the 3rd Platoon Leader in Company F. 1st Lt. Robert Preslan our company executive officer, assumed temporary command of Company H. However he was replaced within 24 hours by 1st Lt. Richard Tobin.

Captain Harold Grey, Commander of Company F also was killed in action during the battle as he attempted to rescue Private Lee, a rifleman in his company, who had been seriously wounded. As he bravely and daringly lifted the body of the fallen trooper, a nearby enemy machine gun sent a withering hail of bullets that ripped through both of their bodies. Both lay dead!

I personally liked and admired Captain Grey as a fellow officer and he was an excellent company commander. I believe that every officer and trooper within the 2nd Battalion that knew Captain Grey expressed extreme anguish over the loss of this very popular officer and company commander.

Within this same period came a dramatic change in command. On April 11, after a series of public utterances revealed sharp differences over national policy and military strategy, President Truman relieved General MacArthur of all his commands and replaced him with General Ridgway. Lt. General James A. Van Fleet was dispatched posthaste from Washington to take command of the Eighth Army and attached forces. He arrived and assumed command on April 14.

As the battle raged on for seizure of the Hwach'on Reservoir on April 11, the message was never received within the 2nd Battalion that General MacArthur was relieved of his command. However, a violent storm broke over much of the frontline of Korea. It snowed, hailed and a howling wind blew stinging the eyes of every trooper within the 2nd Battalion. Was God perhaps expressing his anger over General MacArthur being sent back to the United States?

During the afternoon of April 12, word finally filtered about the news of General MacArthur being relieved of his command by General Matt Ridgway. For the most part, the news was accepted as a total shock. Within the hearts of every trooper there was a certain amount of loyalty and respect held for the old soldier, aristocrat, man of God, General of the Army, Douglas MacArthur. Many were angered at President Truman because the dismissal had been done in a succinct manner. Nevertheless, in the soggy, just turning-green hills of Korea, the war went on.

Elements of the South Korean Marines relieved our battalion during the early morning of April 12. We moved to an area just northeast of Seoul, and would remain in Eighth Army reserve for the next ten days. This rest and rehabilitation was enjoyed by all troopers, and it gave us the opportunity to clean and maintain our equipment. Also the entire battalion participated in various training exercises.

The following is an account of the action of the Hwach'on Reservoir during April 10-12, from Colonel (then Lt. Colonel), John W. Callaway, Battalion Commander, 2nd Battalion, 7th Cavalry Regiment.

As stated previously, this description of the operations in connection with Hwach'on Reservoir Dam represents my personal recollections as the Commander of the 2nd Battalion, 7th Cavalry Regiment. This operation was selected because it was unusual and demonstrates how some small mistakes can be costly.

This operation began on April 10, 1951 with the battalion conducting a reconnaissance in force toward the Hwanch'on Reservoir some ten miles away. Initially, the enemy resistance was not that bad in the extremely rugged terrain. As a matter of fact the terrain was such that it was impossible for vehicles to keep up. Companies F and G led the reconnaissance with E Company in reserve. I and my radio operator accompanied Company G. Shortly after noon we reached the reservoir and Company G followed a road northward along the bank of the lake. We soon were able to see the Hwanch'on Reservoir Dam. There was no enemy activity in front of Company G. At this time a message was received from an excited radio operator that F Company had been ambushed and that medics and stretchers were urgently needed. I took the radio from my operator and asked to speak to Captain Grey, the F Company commander. After a moment the company radio operator replied that Captain Grey had been killed. I asked if any other officers were in the vicinity. The answer was negative. I told the company radio operator to locate the company executive officer and have him taken charge of the company and I would join the company shortly. I ordered Companies G and E to halt, go into defensive positions and await further orders. According to the coordinates given me, Company F was about 700 yards west of my location. The terrain was extremely rugged but I felt I could reach the Company within an hour. After going over a number of rugged ridges, I realized that the coordinates furnished me were incorrect. I had no choice but to continue to the west to locate the company. Finally, after an hour and a half I located the company. To my amazement there were only two casualties, Captain Grey and the lead point man, both killed. I then gave instructions to the executive officer to go into defensive positions and await further instructions.

By the time I reached the ridge overlooking the reservoir, it was around 1700 hours. I saw that the gates on the Hwach'on Reservoir Dam were being opened. As I studied the terrain toward the dam, I could see that the peninsula formed by the reservoir and the Pukhan River on the west was about 300 yards wide with a knife ridge up its center. This peninsula was wide enough for only one company to attack. At I was sitting on this OP my S-3 came up with a strange message from higher headquarters. It read "Take the Hwach'on Reservoir Dam if possible, but don't get hurt."

G Company was selected to make the attack up the peninsula the following morning. Unfortunately, we had out-distanced our 105-mm direct support artillery.

The following day my artillery forward observer spent the day trying to zero in any heavy artillery which was available from the division 155-mm howitzers or Corps artillery. Because of the extreme range involved and the rugged ter-

rain, the forward observer was never able to adjust the artillery fire so we were without this critical support. My request for air strikes was denied because of the low ceiling. The only crew support weapons we had were our machine gun, mortars, and one 75-mm recoilless weapon on a jeep which Major Mel Chandler had managed to winch over a mountain to get it to us.

Captain Moses, the G Company commander used one of his platoons and his supporting weapons to lay down a base of fire. Using the limited width of the peninsula he tried to maneuver his other platoons around the flanks of the enemy on the ridge. The enemy had every avenue covered and was well dug in. I joined Company G in hopes that my presence might make a difference. It became clear that the enemy defenses were too strong and that we would receive too many casualties if we attempted to storm the enemy positions. With no air or artillery support, and

L. to R. - 1st Lt. Richard Tobin, Co. Commander, Co. H and 2nd Lt. Robt. Earley, 3rd Platoon Leader, Co. H, in 1951. 2nd Lt. Earley received a Field Commission in Apr. 1951

limited maneuver room, the dam could not be taken by going up to the peninsula in daylight.

Colonel Harris was advised of the situation and decided to obtain some pontoon motor boats to cross the lake the following morning and attack the enemy from that direction. During the first day there had been no enemy artillery or mortar fire. Because of this I and other members of my staff exposed ourselves on the Observation Post overlooking the action of Company G as it attacked the enemy up the peninsula. Suddenly, an enemy artillery shell landed within a few feet of us on the OP. I was knocked off my feet but was not hurt. I began to check the others near me. Only my heavy weapons company commander, Lt. Richard Gerrish, had been hit. He was killed instantly. Two of my company commanders had been killed in this operation!

My plan for the following morning was to have E Company conduct a night attack. I ordered the attack to commence at 0400 hours because I wanted to seize the objective just before daylight so that our troops could defend against a counterattack during daylight hours. For some reason the attack did <u>not</u> take place at 0400 hours. As a matter of fact it was daylight before the lead platoon crossed the line of departure. The enemy was awake and could see our troops approaching. The enemy opened fire and E Company was able to do no better than G Company the day before.

Company I and a Ranger Company attached to the 7th Cavalry Regiment crossed the reservoir in boats and landed without opposition; however, after moving a short distance toward the dam, the two companies ran into heavy enemy fire and were forced to withdraw.

Lieutenant John Matthews' platoon of Company G was ordered to provide security for the battalion CP. The platoon had moved along the road some 500 yards south of the peninsula when suddenly without warning an enemy mortar round landed on the platoon killing several of its members. These types of deaths don't make sense since the enemy mortar fire in this area had been practically non-existent.

We were unable to seize the Hwach'on Reservoir Dam. We withdrew and joined the division in reserve positions some miles to the south.

As I recall this operation, I wonder what would have happened if rather than halting G Company, I had continued with the G Company toward the dam the first after noon of the operation. We had surprised the enemy as evidence by his opening the dam gates. I am convinced that with air and artillery support we could have taken the Hwach'on Reservoir Dam. I also believe that if E Company had attacked at night as ordered, the company could have seized a foothold on the ridge along the peninsula and assisted Company I and the 4th Ranger Company in taking the dam.

Just prior to the departure of Lt. Colonel John W. Callaway, from Korea, he would receive another honor. His 2nd Battalion was selected by the Eighth Army Command to be the first to guard the Allied Peace Camp at Panmunjom in 1951. The Armistice Agreement with North Korea and China was eventually signed in this particular camp in July 1953.

Further, he had the honor to return to Korea in 1964-65, and become the Chief of Staff of the 1st Cavalry Division. He soon discovered that over the previous years, there had been very little change in the area since his departure in 1951.

He continued his military career and after almost 36 years of active duty, he retired a full Colonel on April 30, 1971.

The following is an account of the combat actions during March-April 1951, from Sergeant First Class Donald Down, Squad Leader, 3rd Platoon, Company F, 2nd Battalion, 7th Cavalry Regiment.

Sometime during the first week of March, Company F was ordered to conduct a combat patrol mission within the Hongchon Valley region. Our 3rd Platoon under the leadership of 2nd Lt. Vonderlee, was directed to move northward on a dirt road which had rice paddies on each side. One of the platoons within our company had moved with us, but they were probing the ridgelines and hills to our left flank.

We progressed down the dirt road when suddenly we could see a bridge in the distance. On both sides of the bridge, the sloping ridgelines extended directly down toward the rice paddies and dirt road. Very shortly, Platoon Sergeant Elzondo Berryman ordered us to hold our positions because enemy movement was sighted on the small ridgeline to our right flank. Many of us could see the enemy movement, but Lt. Von de Lieff insisted that he couldn't see the enemy activity, and ordered us to move out.

As we got to within 50 yards of the bridge a lonely enemy soldier appeared with his hands and arms above his head to surrender. At this particular time Lt. Von de Lieff was leading half of the platoon off of the dirt road and into the rice paddies on our right flank. I immediately shouted to Lt. Von de Lieff which alerted the entire platoon and stopped everyone right in their tracks.

Then Lt. Von de Lieff shouted to me to send one man from my squad to bring back the enemy prisoner. I really didn't have to say anything as one man from my squad volunteered to proceed to the bridge and bring back the enemy soldier who had surrendered.

Fix bayonets and prepared to attack. (U.S. Army photo)

Suddenly, a small observation plane from our support artillery was flying low overhead and very near the ridgelines where the enemy movement was seen earlier. The man that went to bring back the enemy prisoner had almost returned, when all hell started to break loose.

The enemy cross fire caught half of the platoon in the open rice paddies, as they attempted to seek shelter. There was a mud hut to the left side of the road and I directed my squad to follow me to that location. Very shortly many troopers from the open rice paddies made their way safely to this same position.

Even though the enemy small arms and machine gun fire had us pinned down, the man from my squad with the enemy prisoner finally arrived safely. By this time the good old Air Force was starting to clobber the enemy positions with their machine guns and napalm bombs. The enemy was well dug-in and every time we attempted to pull back they hit us with a cross fire from their machine gun positions.

Several of us squad leaders and the platoon sergeant talked over the critical situation. We decided that the safest and best route for our pull back would be the open ditch along each side of the dirt road.

We sent the machine gun squad back first so they could quickly establish positions to then give us fire coverage as we attempted withdraw. With our platoon being the point position, we were way out in front of our company sector. Being pinned down by a withering enemy cross fire, we all knew it would be a difficult task to safely withdraw.

Once we hit the open ditch we very soon discovered it was full of water and mud, which came halfway up to our knees. This made running that much more cumbersome. Enemy machine gun bullets were bouncing off of the road and all around us. This however, seemed to give everyone renewed leg strength and we started to move a lot faster.

Corporal O'Neil from my squad was close behind me when he was suddenly hit in the back and died instantly. I almost managed to crawl to a position by an old burned-out military truck. But the Chinese machine gun fire forced me to then follow a rice paddy dyke, which gave me good coverage until I reached a fork in the open ditch.

At first I thought I saw a Chinese soldier move in front of me, as my heart jumped up inside of my mouth. However, I soon found out that it was crazy Dave Prescott, the combat medic from our platoon. He and I continued to withdraw and within a short distance we came across five more men from our platoon who were sitting in a shell hole which was partially full of icy cold water.

After sitting in cold water for awhile, we all decided it was time to make another move. Some of our men had previously made their way to a hill which was only about 50 yards away. They had received only a few rounds of enemy mortar fire, so we decided to head for that position by sending two men at a time.

We safely made it to this position, and we were soon told that two squads from our platoon were still trapped where we had left them earlier.

It was late in the afternoon when several tanks from the 70th Tank Battalion arrived with troopers from one of our other platoons. Soon we headed back up the dirt road to rescue the other

two squads from our platoon. This time we felt a lot better with the tank support to our rifle platoon and with their capability of firing point blank into the enemy positions.

Very soon we made enemy contact and the tanks started firing into various enemy positions. The tanks destroyed numerous enemy machine gun emplacements and actually kept them pinned down as the troopers from the two squads made a hasty retreat down the dirt road. When they finally joined the rest of our platoon, it was a very happy moment for all of us.

We recovered the body of Corporal O'Neil, which was placed on the rear deck of our particular tank to be transported back to our battalion perimeter. Also during the day, Private First Class Robby Robinson was wounded in action. So ended another day of combat in Korea.

I remember the battle on April 10, at the Hwach'on Reservoir, and the very difficult terrain that surrounded the area. During this assault 2nd Lt. Robert E. Peardon was our 3rd Platoon Leader and Captain Harold Grey was our company commander. Also, the 4th Ranger Company was attached to our attacking forces and battalion.

We received heavy mortar fire from the hills directly in front of us, which prevented us from progressing forward. Very shortly Navy Corsairs flew in low and rocketed and machine gunned the enemy positions. As we attempted to maneuver across the road, Captain Harold Grey went to the aid of a wounded trooper by the name of Private Lee. When Captain Grey lifted up the wounded trooper, a blast from a nearby Chinese machine gun ripped through both of their bodies. Both were instantly killed. The word of the loss of Captain Grey soon reached every trooper within Company F. Everyone was devastated by the report, because he was highly respected as our commanding officer.

Von de Lieff of the 2nd Platoon, Company H, was wounded in the foot and had been evacuated to the battalion aid station. We had other casualties during the day.

The following morning we were briefed by our platoon leader. Rumors prevailed that Lt. Bill Hoffman had assumed command of Company F. We were informed that we had a new task and were moving closer to the banks of the reservoir. The whole area was covered with fog and misty rain.

Our platoon leader then told us that we were going to try to use small assault boats and land on the back side of the hill that jutted out into the reservoir. He then told us that we would probably have to jump off of the boats in four or five feet of water to reach firm ground. Needless to say, it was a very grim situation and we knew we would suffer numerous casualties. The purpose of this assault was actually to give some additional support to the 4th Ranger Company.

We knew the noise of the boat motors would give us away. For myself, I felt like it was my last

After General MacArthur, General Matt Ridgway became Commander-in-Chief of the UN Forces. With pearl handled pistol is General James A. Van Fleet, April 1951. (Army)

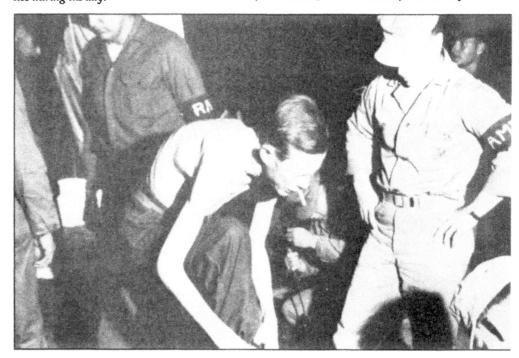

Emaciated and wounded American soldier receiving new clothing at Freedom Village, Panmanjom. (U.S. Army photo)

day on earth, because the boat assault was going to be a do or die situation. We also knew that the enemy had machine gun positions that were capable of showering us with bullets and we would be sitting ducks once we were in the water. All of us waited very silently and time seemed to stand still.

Between 1000 and 1100 hours, our platoon leader sent word for a briefing with all platoon sergeants and told that the boat assault had been called off, because the 4th Ranger Company had reached and secured their objective. It was great news for all of us and you could see the happy expression on the faces of every trooper in Company F.

On April 14th, Sergeant First Class Donald Down was within the first group of troopers of the 7th Cavalry Regiment to be rotated back to the United States. He continued his military career for a brief period of time until he was honorably discharged from the Army in 1952.

The following is an account at Hwach'on Reservoir on April 10th-12th, 1950, from Corporal Wong Suey Lee, Platoon Messenger, 3rd Platoon, Company F, 2nd Battalion, 7th Cavalry Regiment.

It was now early April and spring was in the air. The wakeness of that bitterly cold winter was now giving way to the warm rays of the sun and once again the evolution of plant life was repeating its natural cycle. It seemed so ironic that we were now involved in a destiny to destroy life at our next objective, the Hwach'on Reservoir.

Before the sunset on that beautiful day, we arrived at the south end of the Reservoir and moved up the hill to establish a defensive perimeter. The artillery continued to shell both of our flanks and in front of our positions.

To the north was the water's edge, and a long and low ridge line completely enveloped by smoke, which was probably caused by white phorphorous (WP), rounds from the artillery and mortar support units. As I looked west, the beautiful sunset made the terraced rice paddies look very peaceful.

When darkness came, we were notified to keep a 100 percent alert, just in case of an enemy counterattack. Our support artillery kept firing endless barrages on enemy counterattack. Our support artillery kept firing endless barrages on enemy positions throughout the night.

As morning came we were ordered to move out by our platoon leader, 2nd Lt. Robert E. Peardon. Our platoon sergeant was Sergeant First Class Elzondo Berryman, who was from Thacker Mines, West Virginia. We soon discovered that the terrain within this area was extremely rugged, but very scenic.

This high ground gave us a bird's eye view of the dam and the deserted power plant below us. The Pukhan River flowed north and then around a sharp bend to the south, then to the dam.

While enjoying the view, came the reality of war. The 1st Platoon of Company F, made contact with the enemy as firing became heavy and very erratic. I moved forward with Lt. Peardon, to get more visibility of the situation. From this forward position, I could see the Chinese moving about in their low trenches that connected a network of closed-in firing positions. Some were as close as seventy yards as I began to fire at them with my M-1 rifle. Several of the enemy dropped from being hit, but I don't know if it was from my fire, since there were others firing also.

Then came the bad news! Word was passed on that Captain Grey, our commanding officer, had been killed down by the road. At first I didn't want to believe it because he was a courageous soldier and an epitome in the leadership of men. I kept thinking that maybe he was only wounded and I wanted to go down there to help bring his body up, if he was actually dead.

Soon, Navy F4U Corsair fighter planes arrived and immediately began to rocket and napalm bomb the trenches that contained many enemy positions. They made a second strike, but it wasn't in the cards as daylight was leaving fast and darkness approached.

I witnessed four men in a litter team carrying a wounded trooper to the aid station. Later on I was told that his name was Private Lee and it was the same trooper that Captain Grey attempted to rescue and both were killed. Strangely, the young Private had the same last name as me. However, he was Caucasian and I was Chinese.

Shortly, all firing stopped as we pulled back to establish a defensive perimeter. Many of the men were openly cursing loudly as we kept trying to maneuver and maintain a foothold in the very rocky and steep terrain.

We got somewhat organized as a four man litter team carried the body of Captain Grey and laid him down about six feet from me. An Army blanket covered him up to his chest, but his face was exposed. His GI glasses had fallen off of one ear, while still attached to the other ear. I didn't adjust his glasses as I pulled the blanket over his face. Now, I finally realized that Captain Grey was definitely dead.

The remainder of the night was somewhat uneventful as the artillery fired flares within the enemy positions. However, we still maintained a 100 percent alert just in case the enemy attempted a counterattack. The weather had taken one of its unpredictable changes. It had turned colder with light hail and snow.

At daybreak we were informed that the 4th Ranger Company and Company I of the 3rd Battalion, 7th Cavalry Regiment had run into quite a bit of trouble in their engagement with the enemy. Also, we were informed that we had been selected to make a water borne assault to give aid and rescue to the beleaguered Rangers and troopers of Company I. Further, we were told that there would be no air support.

We moved down to the water's edge for further instructions and to board the assault wooden boats, powered by outward motors and no armament or fire power capability. By now the entire platoon had a sad look within its ranks, as everyone knew we would be sitting ducks once we were in the water.

While waiting to board the boats, we could see the enemy mortar rounds hitting the water near out position. Thoughts were going through my mind on how I could possibly survive the enemy shelling with all the weight from my equipment and avoid being drowned. I believe that everyone was praying to God for his support. To make things even worse, I couldn't swim.

Our prayers were answered as we were notified that our water borne assault had been cancelled. Then we were ordered to return to the hill and join the rest of Company F. We were eventually relieved by elements of the South Korean Marines and our 2nd Battalion was ordered to go into IX Corps reserves.

Once off this hill, we were served hot chow, our first in several days. I noticed the troopers who were serving the hot chow from thermal containers, were speechless and looking at me very strangely. I soon discovered that everyone thought that I was the Lee that was killed with Captain Grey. They had taken it for granted that it was me. Private Lee had been in Company F only a few days and perhaps personnel at the Company Command Post didn't realize that there were two of us.

Corporal Wong Suey Lee was seriously wounded on June 9, 1951, during the vicious battle of the "Iron Triangle." He never remained in the military and was released from the Army in 1951. After meeting his required reserve time, he finally received an honorable discharge several years later.

For several days, rumors had prevailed of a possible major enemy attack from three or four Chinese divisions. Then on April 21st, the entire 7th Cavalry Regiment was alerted for possible movement to the Uijongbu vicinity. Intelligence reported that a shift in enemy troops to that sector, could be the start of the Chinese spring offensive.

I had the personal feeling that I possibly wouldn't be rotated out of Korea as soon as expected. Also, I felt differently about the rumors of the pending Chinese attack, and our future combat engagement with them. I knew that God had looked-out for me over the previous months of combat and during my brief captivity with the enemy.

However, I had never been baptized, and I felt the desire and urgency to have it done before the next battle.

On the morning of April 22nd, I mentioned my intensions to many of the troopers within my platoon, to see if anyone else wanted to be baptized with me. Corporal Robert Barnes a first gunner, agreed to go with me to Headquarters and Headquarters Company to see the Chaplain.

Once there, we had the opportunity to meed Chaplains 1st Lt. Bruce A. Cumming, and Captain Andrew H. Beahm. It didn't take long for the Chaplains to baptize us and to reaffirm our faith in God during the brief ceremony. I know that Corporal Barnes and myself both left the Chaplain's tent feeling religiously enriched in our minds and souls.

During the evening we were alerted and

then briefed on our future regimental screening patrols which were to be conducted within the Uijongbu sector. Also, we were informed that the entire 7th Cavalry Regiment would be under the operational control of the 3rd Infantry Division.

Shortly, orders were issued for us to saddle up and move out for our designated objective. As we departed the area, the air was calm and cold; and the moon was full and extremely bright. A sight that I had seen many times before in Korea.

Following four hours of artillery bombardment in the clear cool evening of April 22nd, the Chinese struck the 17,000 yard front of the British defense. The enemy sounded their bugles and horns which echoed throughout the dark Korean hills. The enemy were now in their First Step, Fifth Phase Offensive. The enemy struck with six divisions, and more than fifty thousand men, and waiting for this enemy onslaught was the 29th British Brigade.

Within this elite fighting brigade was the 8th King's Royal Hussars, who had charged on horseback at Balaclava, but were now riding fifty-ton Centurion tanks in Korea. Also, there was the Gloucestershire Regiment "Glosters" — which dated back to 1694, and their battle streamers included the names of Waterloo, Quebec, and Gallipoli. A total of forty-four in all, and more than any regiment of the British Army. Each unit in the brigade was long known for its' history and steeped in glory.

During the next four days the unit of "Glosters", gallantly held its position even after it was isolated and virtually overrun. They fought with viciousness and determination. The Chinese very soon realized that their spring offensive was failing. The enemy suffered crippling losses in their attempt to crush the British defenses.

The famous Gloucestershire Regiment would very soon earn their forty-fifth battle honor, and an American citation for outstanding bravery. Only a handful of soldiers from the famous regiment were able to make their way back to the main United Nations line.

Also within the month of April, we would see the departure of our regimental commander, Colonel "Wild Bill" Harris. The majority of the officers and troopers of the 7th Cavalry Regiment hated to see its' famous commander leave. Under his leadership during the previous eight months, which was almost continuous combat action, we had seen the spirit of the Garry Owen regiment rise unquestionably to one of the best fighting units in Korea.

General Ridgway personally chose Harris's replacement, which was Lt. Colonel Dan Gilmer, a forty-one year old officer and West Pointer from the class of (1932). However, he is documented as being a total disaster and among the worst regimental commanders to serve in Korea. It became indisputably the "worst personnel mistake of Ridgeway's career".

Prior to Colonel Harris formally turning over the 7th Cavalry Regiment Command to Lt. Colonel Gilmer, there had been many rumors that eventually intensified. Colonel Harris sensed big trouble and he went directly to General Charles Palmer, the Division Commander.

He warned General Palmer that he thought a terrible mistake had been made and insisted that someone other than Lt. Colonel Gilmer be found to relieve him. But General Palmer could do nothing. Lt. Colonel Dan Gilmer was "Ridgeway's boy," in Korea at Ridgeway's specific request. Lt. Colonel Gilmer needed to "get his ticket punched," so he would be better qualified for promotion to Brigadier General and beyond. The so-called "up shot," was to be utter disaster for the crack 7th Cavalry Regiment.

Colonel Harris returned to the United States to enter the fall class of Army War College. Later he was promoted to Brigadier General and eventually rose to two stars of Major General before his retirement in 1966, due to a physical disability.

After Colonel Gilmer took command of the 7th Cavalry Regiment on April 20th, he had his jeep especially equipped with a round metal ring mount. This would enable him to stand up inside of the ring mount next to the driver and grasp his hands to the edge of the mount to avoid falling off the jeep. It was my understanding that the ring mount had actually come from the assembly of a .50 caliber machine gun, that was used on a 2-1/2 ton truck.

From a standing position, I suppose this gave the Colonel a better view while inspecting his troops. Nonetheless, he very soon acquired the nickname of "Ring Mount Dan," from the troopers within the 7th Cavalry Regiment. Prior to my departure from Korea, I never once had the opportunity to personally meet Colonel Dan Gilmer.

At the end of April, we were ordered to withdraw from established positions just northwest of the town of Uijongbu. It was raining extremely hard and overall visibility was poor due to the foggy weather conditions. A machine gun section from my platoon was directed to act as a rearguard assignment, as other elements from the 2nd Battalion attempt an orderly withdrawal.

Finally at 0130 hours, orders were received for us to withdraw and rejoin the other units within the battalion. The hill side was pitch dark and it was difficult to move down the ridgeline because we were walking in a spongy mud that was actually up to our ankles.

I reached for my compass to obtain a reading on our location and future direction. I very soon realized that my compass was missing, as I now began to feel in all of my pockets. My compass was definitely lost. Somehow and somewhere, I had lost a very important piece of my equipment.

I immediately questioned Sergeant First Class Tom Simmons to see if he was carrying a compass. Needless to say, I very soon discovered that no one in my platoon had this small but vital piece of equipment within their possession.

Now the troopers in my platoon were starting to mumble and complain about the weather and of Korea in general. The rain continued to pour down and the endless artillery barrages between the enemy and the United Nations Forces kept the night alive with panoramic views from the bright flashes fo the exploding projectiles.

We finally reached a small ridgeline and proceeded to withdraw from this position. Then we came into an open area that I thought would take us to elements of our battalion. As we continued to walk in the mud, I had a strange feeling that we were wandering in no man's land. So far we had not been challenged by any troopers from any command.

As daylight approached us, I very soon realized that we had actually spent several hours just walking in circles. It didn't take long for most of the troopers to become amused over the entire ordeal. With the rain beating upon our faces, each of us just kept looking at one another. Suddenly, all of us started laughing at each other over what had happened during the dark early morning hours of the day.

Strangely, not very far from this position were elements of a rifle platoon from Company F, 2nd Battalion.

During the month of April, the 7th Cavalry Regiment experienced 26 killed in action, 131 wounded in action and 149 non-battle casualties. Also, 235 new replacements and 217 hospital returnees were received during the month.

Also, by the end of April I would see many departures of personnel on rotation back to the United States. This gave me the renewed faith that future orders for me would be forthcoming very soon.

The first two weeks of May, the 7th Cavalry Regiment established patrol based in the vicinity of Uijongbu. Combat screening patrols were emphasized and dispatched on a daily basis.

Overall operations within the period of May 4th to the 20th revealed 383 enemy dead and 40 wounded. Also 187 enemy prisoners were taken and it was estimated that they suffered an additional 1,100 dead and 1,691 wounded.

In the late morning of May 10th, the long awaited orders finally reached me that indicated my rotation back to the United States. The company clerk said a jeep was waiting to take me to regimental headquarters to be processed.

Without hesitation I briefly said good-by to those members of my platoon that were with me at the frontline position in the vicinity of Hills 361, 158, 213, just north of Uijongbu. I never saw my replacement nor did I hear what his name was. Even my personal duffle bag was still at Headquarters - Headquarters Company which was located at the rear echelon area. At the particular time, I was anxious to leave Korea and I didn't care about leaving personal items behind.

Upon my return to the United states, I continued by military service until I was honorably discharged on May 27, 1952. Then I quickly mingled with and attempted to adjust myself as a civilian within the free and decent society of America. However, it was difficult to put Korea behind me, as the memory of misery and trauma continued to linger on.

The 7th Cavalry Regiment continued its assault on the enemy in the Uijongbu vicinity. From the period of May 20th to 31st, counted enemy casualties were two enemy dead with an additional estimated 215 dead and 257 wounded. Also, 26 enemy prisoners were captured.

During an attack on June 3rd, the 2nd Battalion advanced 5,000 yards against heavy small arms and automatic weapons fire. The enemy was also using larger amounts of artillery and mortar fire as the attack continued until June 9th, when Phase Line Wyoming was reached.

With Phase Line Wyoming being established, then 2nd Battalion advanced another 12 miles to maintain contact with the main enemy force. On June 15th, an advance patrol base was established to permit extended patrol activities.

Counted enemy casualties during June were 729 killed and 1 wounded with an additional estimated 1,286 killed and 1,810 wounded. A total of 251 enemy prisoners were captured.

On June 25th, a review attended by Major General Charles D. Palmer, 1st Cavalry Division Commander was held in commemoration of the 75th Anniversary of the Battle of the Little Big Horn.

Total casualties suffered by the regiment for the month of June were 25 killed and 290 wounded.

The 7th Cavalry Regiment continued to occupy defensive positions along Phase Line Wyoming and from the period of July 1st to 15th, a great number of enemy casualties were inflicted. Counted enemy killed were 86 with an estimated 263 killed. Also, 217 were estimated wounded and 9 enemy prisoners were captured.

During this period the entire 7th Cavalry Regiment with the exception of approximately four officers, consisted of all new personnel. All the experienced combat veterans that were with the regiment since the beginning of the Korean War had either become casualties or rotated from Korea.

On July 10th, peace talks began between the United Nations Command and the Communist Forces. The 2nd Battalion on July 14th which was now under the command of Major Melbourne C. Chandler, was selected from among all other Eighth Army units as the Honor Guard for the Peace Camp at Munsan-ni where the United Nations peace delegates were quartered. The 2nd Battalion was placed under the operational control of the Eighth Army for this duty. This assignment lasted until August 11th, at which time the battalion returned from the Peace Corps and then released to regimental control.

Before the close of August, 472 enlisted men and 34 officers were rotated from the 4th Battalion (GEF), to their homeland of Greece. This was the first rotation from this gallant Greek Battalion which had fought so bravely as an integral part of the 7th Cavalry Regiment.

Much of the activities of the 2nd Battalion during September consisted of preparing defensive positions along adjusted Wyoming Line and extensive combat screening patrols. Many of these patrols resulted in skirmishes with squad and company-size enemy units on key terrain features in the regimental sector. However, as early as September 24th, initial plans were published for this general advance of the I Corps lines. These plans had been revised by the end of the month and preparations were under way for their execution. The offensive was named "Operation Commando" and the third day of October was designated as "D Day".

Actually Operation Commando was part of an overall Eighth Army operation being carried out during the autumn months of 1951. Earlier, in late August, the truce talks had ground to a halt and only the sub-committee remained active, trying to devise ways of bringing about the resumption of full-scale negotiations.

To the east, "Heartbreak Ridge" changed hands repeatedly; each time at a great cost to both sides. Names such as "Bloody Ridge" and the "Punchbowl", appearing in news releases, reminded the American public that the Korean War had by no means faded as had the Peace talks.

The 1st Cavalry Division was designated Line Jamestown where the Chinese main line of resistance existed. It was clear that a strongly dug-in enemy held a commanding series of ridgelines entirely too close for comfort to the railroad that runs northward from Seoul, through Yonchon and Chorwon to Kumwha. This became known as the "Iron Triangle" and disruption of this railroad would have meant disruption of what became a main supply line to the west-central United Nations sector.

On D-Day October 3rd, the 7th Cavalry Regiment moved out at 0600 hours as Operation Commando began to assault its objective, Line Jamestown. Very soon all units ran into a wall of steel. The enemy had prepared their winter line with carefully made bunkers and trenches; and they were extremely deep.

The 2nd Battalion assaulted Hill 272 and made initial progress. However, the battalion could not maintain its position against half a dozen enemy counter attacks. In the regimental sector where the key stronghold on Hill 346 was located, hardly any progress was made.

The Greek Battalion (GEF) attached to the 7th Cavalry Regiment, moved to Hill 313 and soon became engaged in hand to hand combat. Extremely heavy casualties finally forced the Greeks to pull back for the night. Nevertheless, Hill 313 would eventually be seized and the Greek Battalion later received a Distinguished Unit Citation for their outstanding heroism and bravery during this vicious battle.

Enemy mortar and artillery rounds were fired at an unprecedented number and during one 24 hour period, it was reported that some 3300 rounds had fallen in the 7th Cavalry Regiment sector alone.

Vicious enemy counterattacks were launched by fresh troops that had been held behind their lines. It was extremely difficult for the 2nd Battalion to gain or hold positions against these repeated, desperate Chinese assaults.

Nevertheless, by the end of the third day the enemy main line of resistance had begun to crack in the 7th Cavalry Regimental sector to the north. Companies E, F and G of the 2nd Battalion had combined forces the previous day when the survivors of all three companies only totaled some 60 men; however, this small brave force assaulted and secured a hill to one side of Hill 418. GARRYOWEN!

During the period of October 6th to 11th, the 7th Cavalry Regiment although seriously depleted, continued to beat off numerous vicious enemy counterattacks and push forward. In some instances and despite the use of every weapon available, the attacking troopers could make only inch-by-inch progress in securing various objectives in Phase Line Jamestown.

By October 19th, Line Jamestown was secured and in friendly hands, thus successfully concluding Operation Commando. Only a few pockets of scattered enemy resistance remained in the vicinity. Operation Commando was costly to the Chinese Communists because they lost not only a carefully prepared winter line, but large numbers of soldiers as well. The once powerful 47th Chinese Communist Forces Army remained only a battered remnant. Those who survived had withdrawn to the northeast, where they were feverishly preparing positions, not knowing if the United Nations offensive would be continued or not.

The enemy had severely suffered 2,501 killed (with an estimated 616 additional killed), an estimated 8,787 wounded and 210 were taken prisoner.

During the sixteen days spent in taking Line Jamestown, the 7th Cavalry Regiment was engaged almost constantly in the most bitter and bloodiest fighting in the entire Korean campaign. Two-thirds of its rear area personnel had been sent up to frontline units to fill the gaps left by an unprecedented number of casualties. The regiment suffered 175 killed, 1,110 wounded and 70 missing in action, during the operation.

And it was clear to the flood of incoming replacements and who previously had only a hazy idea at best, that a struggle was going on as they passed through various stages of processing on their way to the frontline. At first some of the stories of the battles were discounted as they believed them to be the natural exaggerations of old veterans telling green replacements about the front.

Nonetheless, one look at "Old Baldy" was enough to convince them. That name had been given to Hill 346, the sheer, rock-like mountain that had become as its name indicated, completely bald, a mass of shattered rock and twisted charred stumps of trees.

By mid-November, certain units of the 1st Cavalry Division were experiencing short periods of reserve. The Division had been hard hit during Operation Commando. Other units that remained on the frontline, were placed under the operational control of the 3rd Infantry Division.

On November 21st, the 7th Cavalry Regiment was moved into division reserve status for the 3rd Infantry Division. This reserve area was located in the vicinity of Yonchon. Units not under the control of this particular division were moved south by truck to the 1st Cavalry Division's old reserve area, east of Uijongbu.

From November 1st to 21st, total casualties inflicted upon the enemy by the 7th Cavalry Regiment were 171 counted dead, 7 counted wounded, 11 prisoners and an estimated 403 killed and 310 wounded. Casualties suffered by the regiment during this same period were 23 killed, 303 wounded and 161 missing in action.

However, prior to midnight on November 20th, operations within the 1st Cavalry Division were suddenly and dramatically altered. Word received that night at Division Headquarters stipulated that the new mission for the division, was to return to the country it had left in the summer of 1950. There it would assume responsibility for the defense of the mountainous northern island of Hokkaido, Japan.

After seventeen months of continuous combat in the Korea War, the 7th Cavalry Regiment departed Korea on December 18, 1951. They were relieved by an advance party from the 179th Infantry Regiment, 45th Infantry Division. When the regiment arrived in Muroran, Hokkaido, on December 22nd, it was assigned to Camp Crawford with its steam heated red brick barracks, just outside the island's capital city of Sapporo.

Soon the regiment undertook a long range comprehensive training program in winter warfare. A 17-week intensive training cycle was initiated with emphasis on cold weather training including over snow mobility, arctic survival, skiing and snowshoeing.

After spending almost one year at Camp Crawford, the regiment was again called for service in Korea. The regiment sailed from Otaru, Japan on December 12, 1952 and arrived in Pusan, Korea on December 15, 1952. Soon the regiment would perform guard and security duties generally in the Pusan area and the small islands off the southern coast of Korea.

After three years, one month and two days of war with the North Korean Peoples Army and the Chinese Communist Forces, an Armistice Agreement was signed on July 27, 1953.

Lt. General William K. Harrison, Jr., the senior United Nations delegate to the armistice negotiations signed the armistice papers. At the same time the senior enemy delegate, General Nam II, placed his signature on the documents. The signing took place at this time to permit the armistice to go into effect at 2200 hours of the same day, as required by the agreement. Later General Clark for the United Nations, General Kim Il Sung, for North Korea, and General Peng Teh-Huai, for the Chinese forces on the peninsula, affixed their signatures.

The signing of the armistice brought an end to the shooting; it did not bring an end to the ideological war. President Dwight Eisenhower said as the Pannumjom negotiators reached agreement; "We have won an armistice on a single battleground, not peace in the world. We may not now relax our guard nor cease our quest."

The countries that fought under the flag of the United Nations to prevent the conquest of South Korea had demonstrated their ability to put aside differences and act in unison against a Communist enemy. That nations of highly diverse cultural, religious, and racial backgrounds were willing to place their forces under a single command, in this case the United States, was evidence that free men could rise above national pride in their never-ending fight to remain free.

The armistice terms provided, within ninety days of cease-fire, all prisoners of war had to be screened and repatriated, or otherwise disposed of. Of the 132,000 North Korean and Chinese military taken prisoner by the United Nations forces, fewer than 90,000 chose to return home. The North Koreans were settled in the Taehan Minkuk, and some 13,000 Chinese went singing and chanting to Taiwan.

Those North Korean or Chinese prisoners of war who refused repatriation were screened individually by a neutral commission at Freedom Village, Panmunjom, and his won people allowed to persuade him, while the Indian Army stood guard.

After watching the Communist tactics, the Indian Army became decidedly anti-Communist, regardless of the notions of its government. The Indians had to fly in and out of the Demilitarized zone, causing considerable difficulty to the United Nations Command. President Syngman Rhee refused to allow one Indian soldier to set foot on South Korean soil.

There were 474 North Korean female personnel among the thousands of Communist prisoners of war on the island of Koje-do. Also, these girls were among the worst of the lot, and they were put on a South Korean train and sent north to Freedom Village for repatriation. During the trip there, they revealed Communist flags, and screamed and shouted at the gaping South Koreans that stood along both sides of the tracks.

Prior to their arrival in Freedom Village, they began to tear off their capitalist-made and imperialist-issued clothing, so they could return home in Communist purity. They ripped and tore up the train seats, and even urinated on what they could not destroy. Many of them defecated in the train aisles. Strangely, the women had decided to come home in a different way, which shocked the United Nations Command.

Over 5.7 million American servicemen and women were involved directly or indirectly in the Korean War, inflicting 54,246 casualties. In addition, 103,284 Americans were wounded and 8,177 are still listed as missing or unaccounted for.

Of the 7,140 American prisoners of war captured, 4,418 were returned to U.S. Military control. A total of 3,745 were repatriated in two major operations. During "Little Switch", (April 21 - May 3, 1953), 149 seriously sick or wounded prisoners of war were released by the enemy. For most of the remaining 3,596 prisoners of war, they were released by the enemy during "Big Switch", (August 4 - September 6, 1953). The remaining 673 prisoners of war evaded or escaped prior to these two operations. Staggering were the facts that thousands of American prisoners died while in captivity.

The Korean War showed that a free government must be prepared to do unpopular things to gain success against communism. However, millions of Americans found no real meaning in any of it. The free and decent society of America attempted to control the military forces by their limited commitment to avoid an all out war with Communist China.

In Korea the United Nations Forces were willing to defend the free world by committing a quarter of a million ground troops in a skirmish with Communism. Their task was moral or immoral according to the orders that sent them forth to suffer and die in the midst of incredible hardships of combat.

It is possible that one or both segments of mankind will eventually embark upon what will be the last crusade. However, it is more likely that they will collide again on a lesser scale, as they have before. Nevertheless, even on a lesser scale the gam e will be won or lost, and with the sacrifice of thousands of human lives.

The lesson of the Korean War is that it happened, but it was the first war against communist aggression that had borne the priceless fruits of victory against all odds. Over the centuries man has learned from the experiences of battle or the history of war. However, many lessons were either ignored or completely forgotten; and in the case of Korea, it eventually became known as "The Forgotten War".

General Mark W. Clark, Far East Commander, signs the Korean Armistice Agreement on July 27, 1953, after two years of negotiation. (U.S. Navy photo)

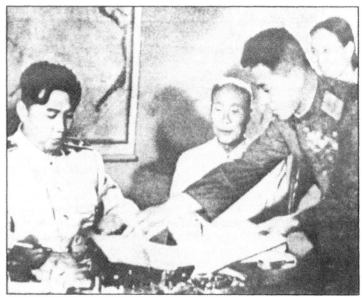

North Korean Premier Kim Il Sung prepares to sign Armistice document handed to him on July 27, 1953 by General Nam Il. (Eastfoto)

Enemy Delegation L. to R. - General Fang; General Hua, Chinese Army; General Nam Il, Delegate for the Communists, General Lee Snag Cho and General Chang Pyong San, North Korean Army. (U.S. Army photo)

UN Delegation L. to R. - General Craigie, USAF; General Yup, ROKI Corps; Vice Admiral Joy, Far East Naval Commander; General Hodes, 8th Army, Rear Admiral Burke, U.S. Navy. (U.S. Army photo)

The following statistical data concerning numbers captured, repatriated and still was reported by the American Ex-Prisoners of War on January 1, 1989:

KOREAN CONFLICT (a/b)

	Total	Army	Navy	Marine	Air Force
Captured and interned	7,140	6,656	35	225	224
Died While POW	2,701	2,662	4	31	4
Returned to U.S. Military Control	4,418	3,973	31	194	220
Refused Repatriation	21	21	–	–	–
Alive on Jan 1, 1982	3,770	3,390	26	166	188
Alive on Jan 1, 1989	3,394	3,050	22	151	171

a) This data indicates status through November 4, 1951. As of that date 24 were still missing. By September 15, 1955, fifteen of these men had been released and the other nine were declared dead.

b) Does not include eighty-one Navy personnel who were invloved in the Pueblo incident.

Acts of Valor
THE MEDAL of HONOR
The Korean War
1950-1953

Number of medals: 131

AIR FORCE: 4   ARMY: 78   MARINES: 42   NAVY: 7

AIR FORCE

*Davis, Maj. George A., Jr. (Sinuiju-Yalu River Area)
*Loring, Maj. Charles J., Jr. (Sniper Ridge, N. Korea)
*Sebille, Maj. Louis J. (Hanchang)
*Walmsley, Capt. John S., Jr. (Yangdok)

ARMY

 Adams, Sfc. Stanley T. (Sesim-ni)
*Barker, Pvt. Charles H. (Sokkogae)
*Bennett, Pfc. Emory L. (Sobangsan)
 Bleak, Sgt. David B. (Minari-gol)
*Brittin, Sfc. Nelson V. (Yonggong-ni)
*Brown, Pfc. Melvin L. (Kasan)
 Burke, 1st Lt. Lloyd L. (Chong-dong)
*Burris, Sfc. Tony K. (Mundung-ni)
*Charlton, Sgt. Cornelius H. (Chipo-ri)
*Collier, Cpl. Gilbert G. (Tutayon)
*Collier, Cpl. John W. (Chindong-ni)
*Coursen, 1st Lt. Samuel S. (Kaesong)
*Craig, Cpl. Gordon M. (Kasan)
 Crump, Cpl. Jerry K. (Chorwon)
 Dean, Maj. Gen. William F. (Taejon)
*Desiderio, Capt. Reginald B. (Ipsok)
 Dodd, 2d Lt. Carl H. (Subuk)
*Duke, Sfc. Ray E. (Mugok)
*Edwards, Sfc. Junior D. (Changbong-ni)
*Essebagger, Cpl. John, Jr. (Popsudong)
*Faith, Lt. Col. Don C., Jr. (Hagaru-ri)
*George, Pfc. Charles (Songnae-dong)
*Gilliland, Pfc. Charles L. (Tongmang-ni)
*Goodblood, Cpl. Clair (Popsudong)
*Hammond, Cpl. Lester, Jr. (Kumwha)
*Handrich, MSgt. Melvin O. (Sobuk San Mountain)
*Hanson, Pfc. Jack G. (Pachi-dong)
*Hartell, !st Lt., Lee R. (Kobangsan-ni)
 Harvey, Capt. Raymond (Taemi-Dong)
*Henry, 1st Lt. Frederick F. (Am-Dong)
 Hernandez, Cpl. Rodolfo P. (Wontong-ni)
 Ingman, Cpl. Einar H., Jr. (Maltari)
*Jecelin, Sgt. William R. (Saga)
*Jordan, Pfc. Mack A (Kumsong)
*Kanell, Pvt. Billie G. (Pyongyang)
*Kaufman, Sfc. Loren R. (Yongsan)
*Knight, Pfc. Noah O. (Kowang-San)
 Kouma, Sfc. Ernest R. (Agok)
*Krzyzowski, Capt. Edward C. (Tondul)
*Kyle, 2nd Lt. Darwin K. (Kamil-ni)
 Lee, MSgt. Hubert L. (Ip-o-ri)
*Libby, Sgt. George D. (Taejon)
*Long, Sgt. Charles R. (Hoeng-song)
*Lyell, Cpl. William F. (Chup'a-ri)
*McGovern, 1st Lt. Robert M. (Kamyangjan-ni)
*Martinez, Cpl. Benito (Satae-ri)
*Mendonca, Sgt. Leroy A. (Chich-on)
 Millett, Capt. Lewis L. (Soam-Ni)
 Miyamura, Cpl. Hiroshi H. (Taejon-ni)
 Mize, Sgt. Ola L. (Surang-ni)
 Moyer, Sfc. Donald R. (Seoul)
*Ouellette, Pfc. Joseph R. (Yongsan)
*Page, Lt. Col. John U. D. (Chosin Reservoir)

*Pendleton, Cpl. Charles F. (Choo Gung-Dong)
*Pililaau, Pfc. Herbert K. (Pia-ri)
 Pittman, Sgt. John A. (Kujang-dong)
*Pomeroy, Pfc. Ralph E. (Kumhwa)
*Porter, Sgt. Donn F. (Mundung-ni)
*Red Cloud, Cpl. Mitchell, Jr. (Chonghyon)
 Rodriguez, Pfc. Joseph C. (Munye-ri)
 Rosser, Cpl. Ronald E. (Ponggilli)
*Schoonover, Cpl. Dan D. (Sokkogae)
 Schowalter, 1st Lt. Edward R., Jr. (Kumhwa)
*Shea, 1st Lt. Richard T., Jr. (Sokkogae)
*Sitman, Sfc. William S. (Chipyong-ni)
*Smith, Pfc. David M. (Yongsan)
*Speicher, Cpl. Clifton T. (Minari-gol)
 Stone, 1st Lt. James L. (Sokkogae)
*Story, Pfc. Luther H. (Agok)
*Sudut, 2nd Lt. Jerome A. (Kumhwa)
*Thompson, Pfc. William (Haman)
*Turner, Sfc. Charles W. (Yongsan)
*Watkins, MSgt. Travis E. (Youngsan)
 West, Pfc. Ernest E. (Sataeri)
 Wilson, MSgt. Benjamin F. (Hwach'on-Myon)
*Wilson, Pfc. Richard G. (Opari)
*Womack, Pfc. Bryant H. (Sokso-ri)
*Young, Pfc. Robert H. (Kaesong)

MARINES

*Abrell, Cpl. Charles G. (Hangnyong)
 Barber, Capt. William E. (Chosin Reservoir)
*Baugh, Pfc. Willaim B. (Koto-ri ro Hagaru-ri)
 Cafferata, Pvt. Hector A., Jr. (Chosin Reservoir)
*Champagne, Cpl. David B. (Korea)
*Christianson, Pfc. Stanely (Seoul)
 Commiskey, 2d Lt. Henry A., Sr. (Yongdungp'o)
*Davenport, Cpl. Jack A. (Songnae-Dong)
 Davis, Lt. Col. Raymond G. (Hagaru-ri)
*Dewey, Cpl. Duane E. (Panmunjon)
*Garcia, Pfc. Ferndando L. (Korea)
*Gomez, Pfc. Edward (Hill 749)
*Guillen, SSgt. Ambrosio (Songuch-on)
*Johnson, Sgt. James E. (Yudam-ni)
*Kelly, Pfc. John D. (Korea)
*Kelso, Pfc. Jack W. (Korea)
 Kennemore, SSgt. Robert S. (Yudam-ni)
*Littleton, Pfc. Herbert A. (Chungchon)
*Lopez, 1st Lt. Baldomero (Inchon)
 McLaughlin, Pfc. Alford L. (Korea)
 Matthews, Sgt. Daniel P. (Vegas Hill)
*Mausert, Sgt. Frederick W., III (Songnap-yong)
*Mitchell, 1st Lt. Frank N. (Hansan-ni)
*Monegan, Pfc. Walter C., Jr. (Sosa-ri)
*Moreland, Pfc. Whitt L. (Kwagch'i-Dong)
 Murphy, 2nd Lt. Raymond G. (Korea)
 Myers, Maj. Reginald R. (Hagaru-ri)
*Obregon, Pfc. Eugene A. (Seoul)
 O'Brien, 2nd Lt. George H., Jr. (Korea)
*Phillips, Cpl. Lee H. (Korea)
*Poynter, Sgt. James I. (Sudong)
*Ramer, 2nd Lt. George H. (Korea)
*Reem, 2nd Lt. Robert D. (Chinhung-ni)
*Shuck, SSgt. William E., Jr. (Korea)
 Simanek, Pfc. Robert E. (Korea)
 Sitter, Capt. Carl L. (Hagaru-ri)
*Skinner, 2d Lt. Sherrod E., Jr. (Korea)
 Van Winkle, SSgt. Archie (Sudong)
*Vittori, Cpl. Joseph (Hill 749)
*Watkins, SSgt. Lewis G. (Korea)
 Wilson, TSgt. Harold E. (Korea)
*Windrich, SSgt. William G. (Yudam-ni)

NAVY

*Benford, Hospital Corpsman 3d Class Edward C. (Korea)
 Charette, Hospital Corpsman 3d Class William R. (Korea)
*Dewert, Hospital Corpsman Richard D. (Korea)
*Hammond, Hospital Corpsman Francis C. (Korea)
 Hudner, Lt. (j.g.) Thomas J., Jr. (Chosin Reservoir)
*Kilmer, Hospital Corpsman John E. (Korea)
*Koelsch, Lt. (j.g.) John K. (North Korea)

*Awarded Posthumously

ACKNOWLEDGEMENTS

By Edward Daily, author

I have tried to find as many various accounts as possible to tell the story as it was seen through the eyes of those who actually did the fighting. However, many discrepancies abounded. It was not easy to reconcile conflicting evidence to establish the actual account of a particular battle. The framework for map locations were taken from Command Reports, books, operations journals and periodic reports or various command echelons.

Nevertheless, a personal word of thanks is due to those who assisted the author along the way. To all of the former officers and enlisted men, my deepest thanks and appreciation for their generous help I have received in the preparation of this book. If there is not enough space here to thank each one separately, then it is hoped that this book will serve as their reward.

I wish also to acknowledge a special debt to Colonel (retired) John W. Callaway for his individual support and encouragement to complete the book project.

In honor to John W. Callaway, Colonel (retired), United States Army; former Battalion Commander, 1950-51, 2nd Battalion, 7th Cavalry Regiment, 1st Cavalry Division.

The following are from the 2nd Battalion, 7th Regiment, 1st Cavalry Division:

Robert G. Abarr
John Brewer
Crawford "Buck" Buchanan, Colonel (retired)
Robert M. Carroll, Lt. Colonel (retired)
Rodney R. Confer
Robert L. Earley, Lt. Colonel (retired)
John J. Fatum
James Gorman
Pennel "Joe" Hickey, Colonel (retired)
John G. Hill, Major General, (retired)
William H. Hoffman, Colonel (retired)
William Kaluf
Thomas Kilduf
John C. "Jack" Lippincott, Colonel (retired)
John "Jack" Martinez
John Matthews, Lt. Colonel (retired)
Richard L. Morton, Brig. General (retired)
Albert C. Moses
Robert E. Peardon, 1st Lieutenant (retired)
Mell S. Pelot, Lt. Colonel (retired)
John O. Potts, First Sergeant (retired)
Robert S. Preslan
Dr. John C. Rourke
Thomas H. Stone
Richard Tobin, Colonel (retired)
Herman K. Vester
Von de Lieff
William L. Webb
William O. Witherspoon

To the memory of those officers who had served with bravery and gallantry; and to those who made the supreme sacrifice. *Killed in Action

In memory of D. Arbouzis, Lt. Colonel, Greek Army; former Commander Greek Expeditionary Forces, (GEF), 4th Battalion, 7th Cavalry Regiment, 1st Cavalry Division.

In memory of Melbourne C. Chandler, Lt. Colonel, United States Army; former Executive Officer and Battalion Commander, (after Callaway), 2nd Battalion, 7th Cavalry Regiment, 1st Cavalry Division.

In memory of Athanasios 'Dascarolis, Major General, Greek Army; former Commanding Gen. Greek Expeditionary Forces, (GEF), in Korea.

In memory of John Daskslopoulos, Colonel, Greek Army; former Commander Greek Expeditionary Force, (GEF), attached to the 7th Cavalry Regiment, 1st Cavalry Division.

*In memory of Fred De Palma, Captain United States Army; former officer 2nd Battalion, 7th Cavalry Regiment, 1st Cavalry Division.

*In memory of Herschel "UG" Fuson, 1st Lieutenant, United States Army; former officer 2nd Battalion, 7th Cavalry Regiment, 1st Cavalry Division.

In memory of Hobart R. Gay, Major General (retired), United States Army; former Division Commander, 1st Cavalry Division.

*In memory of Richard Gerrish, 1st Lieutenant, United States Army; former officer 2nd Battalion, 7th Cavalry Regiment, 1st Cavalry Division.

*In memory of Marvin Goulding, 1st Lieutenant, United States Army; former officer 2nd Battalion, 7th Cavalry Regiment, 1st Cavalry Division.

*In memory of Harold Grey, Captain, United States Army; former officer 2nd Battalion, 7th Cavalry Regiment, 1st Cavalry Division.

In memory of William H. Harris, Major General, (retired), United States Army; former Regimental Commander, 1950-1951, 7th Cavalry Regiment, 1st Cavalry Division.

*In memory of Omar Hitchner, Major, United States Army; former Battalion Commander, 2nd Battalion, 7th Cavalry Regiment, 1st Cavalry Division.

In memory of Douglas MacArthur, General of the Army, United States Army, former Allied Supreme Commander, Far East Command.

*In memory of James Manns, 2nd Lieutenant, United States Army; former officer 2nd Battalion, 7th Cavalry Regiment, 1st Cavalry Division.

*In memory of James T. Milam, Captain, United States Army; former officer 2nd Battalion, 7th Cavalry Regiment, 1st Cavalry Division.

In memory of Charles D. Palmer, Major General, (retired), United States Army; former Division Commander (after Major General Hobart R. Gay), 1st Cavalry Division.

**In memory of Alan F. Plummer, 2nd Lieutenant, United States Army; former officer 2nd Battalion, 7th Cavalry Regiment, 1st Cavalry Division.

**First Officer killed in action from the 2nd Battalion.

*In memory of Radcliff, 2nd Lieutenant, United States Army; former officer 2nd Battalion, 7th Cavalry Regiment, 1st Cavalry Division.

*In memory of John E. Sheehan, 1st Lieutenant, United States Army; former officer 2nd Battalion, 7th Cavalry Regiment, 1st Cavalry Division.

In memory of John B. Wadsworth, Colonel (retired), United States Army; former officer 2nd Battalion, 7th Cavalry Regiment, 1st Cavalry Division.

*In memory of Arthur Truxall, Captain, United States Army; former officer 2nd Battalion, 7th Cavalry Regiment, 1st Cavalry Division.

In memory of Herman L. West, Captain, United States Army; former officer 2nd Battalion, 7th Cavalry Regiment, 1st Cavalry Division.

*In memory of Robert Wood, 2nd Lieutenant, United States Army; former officer 2nd Battalion, 7th Cavalry Regiment, 1st Cavalry Division.

To the enlisted men and non-commissioned officers that served with relentless courage and dauntless bravery. And to those who made the supreme sacrifice—their names are not listed due to limits of space in this book. However, this book is a tribute to them and their families.

Former Troopers, 1st Battalion, 7th Cavalry Regiment, 1st Cavalry Division

Robert Bloss
Bobby D. Chapin
James Coogan
James Crowley
Richard Dowell
John C. Howell
Charles M. Kennemore, Jr.
Bill Kesterson
Reuben Kvidt
George Lewis
James Lowry
Warren J. Maledy
Homer McNamara
Norval M. Miner
Billy R. Ross
Charles Shipman
Ted Short
Jack Smith
Elsie Tyree
Roy Wolgamott

Former Troopers, 2nd Battalion, 7th Cavalry Regiment, 1st Cavalry Division

Robert Alicia
Roy E. Allen
Frank Almy
Carl J. Bafs
Mack Bentley
Ralph G. Bernotas
Elzondo Berryman
Harold Blanc
Royal Bollinger
Tom Boyd
William Brown
Glen G. Bumgarner
Guy R. Calhoun
Donald Carlson
Donald D. Down
Earl Early
Larry Girard
Millard G. Gray
Curtis E. Harry
Frederick C. Herrmann
Robert Kinler
Al Klein
Robert Larson

Bill R. Laws
Homer K. Leacock, Sr.
Wong Suey Lee
Henry N. Matthias
Daniel P. Mancini (HQ. & HQ. Company)
Robert Mauger
James McClure
Russ McKinley
Dale H. Miller
William Montgomery
William T. Mooney
Fred Palmer
Thomas L. Palmer
Herb D. Phillips
Ecton J. Plaisance
Walter Raisner
Raymond Scarberry
Harry Shappell
Thomas C. Simmons
Barton M. Smith
J. P. "Smitty" Smith
William D. Smith
Eugene Thomas (In Memory)
Norman Tinkler
Noe Trevino
George C. Vernon
Former Troopers, 3rd Battalion, 7th Cavalry
Regiment, 1st Cavalry Division
John P. Abbey
James R. Abshear
Jose Alva
James J. Brennan
Eligah F. Burdich
John "Jack" Cauley
William Garber
Charles Horn
William Houston
John A. Johnson, Jr.
John Kosinsky
Robert Miller
John Mexin
Lewis O'Neal
Pete Samaniego
J. Edward Tichenor
James D. Williams

Special Recognition
Peter J. Visclosky, Congressman, 1st District
of Indiana; his wife Anne Marie O'Keefe and son
John Daniel
Larry E. Dickey, Caseworker Supervisor for
the office of Congressman Peter J. Visclosky, 1st
District of Indiana.
Matthew Ridgway, General (retired), United
States Army; to one of the Army's finest gen-
eral's, former Commander-in-Chief of the United
Nations Forces during the Korean War.
Harold (Hal) Moore, Lt. General (retired)
United States Army; thanks for your support and
encouragement to write my manuscript.
Peter (Pete) D. Clainos, Colonel (retired),
United States Army; former Battalion Com-
mander, 1st Battalion, 7th Cavalry Regiment,
1st Cavalry Division.
Bob Hope; what can I say about a truly great
person and individual who had dedicated his
entire life to the world of entertainment — espe-

cially to the Military of the United Stated Armed
Forces — thanks for the memories!
Robert F. Litle, Jr., Colonel (retired), United
States Army; former Battalion Commander, 2nd
Battalion (Vietnam), 7th Cavalry Regiment, 1st
Cavalry Division; presently Executive Director,
1st Cavalry Division Association.
Michael P. Bellafaire, Director, 1st Cavalry
Division Museum, Fort Hood, Texas.
Alvin A. Storm, United States Army; former
officer, 1st Battalion, 5th Cavalry Regiment, 1st
Cavalry Division.
Kathy and Tom Spencer; a special thanks
Kathy for the support and diligent work on you
part in typing my manuscript, which was in-
serted into the computer.
Greg Bittle, VA Counseling, Psychologist and
the entire Counseling Staff, VA Regional Office,
Indianapolis, Indiana.
Mr. Vera Chandler, (widow of Melbourne C.
Chandler); associate member, 7th U.S. Calvary
Regiment.
James Chandler, (son of the late Melbourne C.
Chandler); his wife, Suzanne, and son, Christo-
pher.
Mrs. Barbara Nelson, (former widow of the
late John B. Wadsworth); her sons, John III and
Todd, and their families; and the Mary Hope Luke
family.
Mrs. Margie Thomas, (widow of the late Eu-
gene Thomas), who was a former trooper, 2nd
Battalion, 7th Cavalry Regiment, 1st Cavalry
Division.
Mrs. Zelma McNabb Daily, my wonderful
mother.
Mrs. Hilda C. Daily, my wife who tolerated me
for over 37 years; and to the entire Reis family.
Edward L. Daily, Jr., my terrific son, and to his
wife Mary; and my lovely grandchildren, Eddie
III, Patrick and Julie; and to the entire Nacarato
family.
Omer and Wanda McNabb, my uncle and
aunt; and to the entire McNabb and Kroger fami-
lies.
Fred and Lois Carlen, Carlen's free-lance pho-
tography-thanks for the excellent photo service.
Richard Jerome, Private, RA 13333318, United
States Army; Former Trooper, Company H, 2nd
Battalion, 7th Cavalry Regiment, 1st Cavalry
Division. His name is on the list of 389 Prisoners
of War that are unaccounted for in North Korea.
The only name shown from the 2nd Battalion, 7th
Cavalry Regiment.

In Recognition of
Legion of Valor
American Ex-Prisoners of War
Association of Ex-Prisoners of War of the
Korean War, Inc.
Military Order of the Purple Heart
National Order of Battlefield Commissions
Disabled American Veterans
Veterans of Foreign Wars
American Legion
Korean War Veterans Association
1st Cavalry Division Association
7th U.S. Cavalry Association

SOURCES

The 1st Cavalry Division
Korea, June 1950 - January 1952
Albert Love Enterprises, Publishers
Atlanta, Georgia

At War in Korea (1985 edition)
George Forty, author
Bonanza Books, Publishers
Distributed by Crown Publishers, Inc.
225 Park Avenue South
New York, New York 10003

The Korean War - History and Tactics
David Rees, Consultant Editor
Cresent Books, Publishers
Distributed by Crown Publishers, Inc.
225 Park Avenue South
New York, New York 10003

South to the Naktong - North to the Yalu
Roy E. Appleman, author
United States Army in the Korean War
Office of the Chief of Military History
Department of the Army
Washington, D.C.

Korea, 1950
Copyright 1952 by Orlando Ward
The Chief of Military History
Department of the Army
Washington, D.C.

Korea, 1951-53
By John Miller, Jr., Owen Jr. Carroll, Major
U.S. Army and Margaret E. Tackley
The Chief of Military History
Department of the Army
Washington, D.C.

This Kind of War
By T.R. Fehrenbach, author 1963
The Macmillian Company
New York, New York

The Forgotten War
Clay Blair, author
Times Books, a division of Random House of
Canada Limited, Toronto

General MacArthurs' Address to Congress
Joint Session of Congress, April 19, 1951
National Research Bureau, Inc.
Chicago, Illinois

National Military Archives
Richard Boylan
Assistant Chief
Washington, D.C. 20409

UNITED NATIONS CASUALTIES IN THE KOREAN WAR

Along with American servicemen and women, medical units from Sweden and India, and allied combat contingents from the countries listed below, were the "First United Nations Army." All of these countries responded to the U.N. appeal to support the Republic of Korea in confronting Communist aggression. We honor them in their commitment to the cause of freedom.

Country	Dead	Wounded	Missing	Captured	Total
Austria	291	1,240	39	21	1,591
Belgium	97	350	5	1	453
Luxembourg					
Canada	291	1,072	65	12	1,396
Colombia	140	452	65	29	686
Ethiopia	120	536			656
France	288	818	18	11	1,135
Great Britain	710	2,278	1,263	766	5,017
Greece	169	543	2	1	715
Netherlands	111	589	4		704
New Zealand	34	80		1	115
Phillipines	92	299	57	40	488
South Africa	20		16	6	42
Thailand	114	794	5		913
Turkey	717	2,246	107	219	3,349
United States	54,246	103,284	8,177	2,000	172,707
Korea (Military & Non-Military)	392,000	230,000	330,000	85,000	1,037,000

Source: World Almanac & Korean Overseas Information Service
The Korean War showed that a multi-national army can function effectively in spite of differences in language and military doctrine

CHAPLAINS WHO DIED IN THE LINE OF DUTY DURING THE KOREAN CAMPAIGN:

Lawrence F. Brunnert
Wayne H. Burdue
James W. Conner
Francis X. Coppens
Leo P. Craig

*Robert M. Crane
Herman G. Felthoelter
Kenneth C. Hyslop
**Emil J. Kapaun
Bryron D. Lee

Samuel R. Simpson

*Episcopal Chaplain Robert M. Crane was the last U.S. Army Chaplain to be killed in action in Korea, while serving with the 40th Infantry Division.

**Died as a prisoner of war in the North Korean prison camp.

MILITARY SYMBOLS

UNIT SIZE AND IDENTITY
(THESE ARE APPROVED UNITED STATES MILITARY SYMBOLS)

Examples, as used in book:

Infantry Unit	E Company, U.S. 7th Cavalry Regiment	
Artillery Unit	203rd Regiment, N.K. 105th Armored Brigade	
Armored Unit	3rd Regiment, N.K. 4th Division	
Army Group	2nd Battalion, U.S. 7th Cavalry	
Army	9th Regiment, 2nd Infantry Division	
Corps	3rd Border Constabulary Brigade	
Division	N.K. 105th Armored Brigade (less some units)	
Brigade	1st Battalion, U.S. 32nd Infantry Regiment (plus attached units)	
Regiment	1st U.S. Cavalry Division	
Battalion	19th Infantry, U.S. 24th Division	
Company, Battery	Command Post, U.S. 19th Infantry Regiment	
Platoon	A Battery, U.S. 77th Field Artillery Battery	
Command Post		
Howitzer or mortars		
Gun		
Machine Gun		

Unit symbols, as given above, are presumed to be U.S. Marine Corps or U.S. Army unless underneath the symbol appears "KMC" (Korean Marine Corps), "ROK" (Republic of Korea Army), or "NK" (North Korea Peoples Army). An Arabic numeral on the right side of a unit symbol is the number of the division or regiment depicted (or, if the unit is smaller than the regiment, the number of the parent regiment). On the left of the block, an Arabic numeral signifies which battalion of the given regiment is indicated; a letter, which company (or, for headquarters and service company, "H & S;" for weapons company, "Wpns").

GLOSSARY OF PRINCIPLE WEAPONS

During the Korean War all combatants chose to fight largely with surplus weapons from World War II. The United States made innovations and great improvements in logistical techniques, cold-weather clothing, and medical services. However, no startling developments, either in weaponry or tactics, came out of the conflict. One of the only new developments was the use of helicopters for reconnaissance, transport, and evacuation on a large scale, and the employment of the jet aircraft in combat. The most modern jet at that particular time was the F-86 Sabre, which was thrown into the aerial war when the Communist forces introduced a first-rate aircraft, the MIG-15, as a field test.

Although newer series of weapons, radios, and vehicles were developed and available on both sides, the entire course of the Korean War remained of World War II vintage. Also withheld were the use of nuclear weapons. One great weakness at the beginning was caused by the failure of the United States to procure modern weaponry for ground warfare following World War II. However, the Communist forces had followed the same course by employing only old or obsolescent weaponry.

The principal infantry weapons used in the Korean War were the following, and the majority of which are now obsolete. (Exception for British issue to Commonwealth forces).

U.S. RIFLE CALIBER .30 M-1 (Garand): The basic shoulder weapon of United States, ROK, and many other U.N. rifle regiments. A vintage of the mid-1930's, it was gas-operated and semiautomatic, fired an 8-round clip, and weighed 9.5 pounds, 10.5 with bayonet. Its effective range was about 500 yards, and its rate of fire up to approximately 30 rounds per minute.

U.S. CARBINE CALIBER .30: Produced as both semiautomatic and full-automatic weapon, it fired a lighter bullet than the M-1 Rifle, with correspondingly less range, accuracy, and killing power. Fitted with a 15-round magazine, or 30-round or so-called "banana magazine"; gas-operated, it was carried principally by company-grade officers, NCO's, clerks, and the like. Weight, 6 pounds. Developed during World War II from Garand principle.

PISTOL, CALIBER .45 M-1911 A-1: The standard United States side arm, a large semi-automatic pistol, with great stopping power and an effective range of some 25 yards. Developed and issued prior to World War I, it was carried by field-grade officers, signal linemen, gun crews, tankers, and men whose duties or other burdens precluded carrying of rifle or carbine.

BROWNING AUTOMATIC RIFLE, or **BAR:** Firing the same cartridge as the Rifle, M-1, either semi- or full automatic, the BAR could be operated either as a shoulder weapon or from a bipod. With a rate of fire of almost 500 rounds per minute, it was the principal automatic weapon of the rifle companies, one or more being issued to each rifle squad. Weighing 16 pounds, it was developed from Browning's principle during World War I.

U.S. MACHINE GUN, CALIBER .30, M-1919 A-4 (light machine gun, or LMB): An air-cooled, 32 pounds fully automatic machine gun, with bipod and shoulder rest; recoil-operated on the Browning principle, capable of sustained fire of 450-500 rounds per minute. Firing the same cartridge as the Rifle, M-1 and BAR, it was the infantry platoon machine gun. Developed in World War I.

U.S. MACHINE GUN, CALIBER .30, M-1917 A-1 (Heavy Machine Gun, or HMG): A heavier version of the above, water-cooled and tripod mounted, and thus capable of both a greater, longer, and more accurate rate of fire. Issued to the Weapons Company of the infantry battalion. There were approximately 500 machine guns of both types in the U.S. infantry division.

U.S. MACHINE GUN, CALIBER .50, BROWNING: Weighing 82 pounds, this large-caliber machine gun was mounted on trucks, tanks, and other vehicles, and not carried into close infantry combat. Air-cooled, but with a heavy barrel, the .50-caliber machine gun fired approximately 575 rounds per minute, to a range of 2,000 yards. Approximately 350 scattered throughout the infantry division.

ROCKET LAUNCHER, 3.5-INCH OR 2.36-INCH (Bazooka): Rocket launchers, developed during World War II, fire a hollow shaped charge capable of penetrating thick armor plate. The 3.5, which replaced the obsolete 2.36 in 1950, weighing 15 pounds and fired an 8.5-pound charge. There were some 600 bazookas in the Korean infantry division. Characterized by a large and distinct backblast, the aluminum tube generally was not effective beyond 75 yards against medium armor. Widely issued as infantry antitank weapon.

THE 57MM, 75MM, AND 105 MM RECOILLESS RIFLES: Infantry-carried artillery. They develop high blast from escaping gases on discharge, but no recoil, as with howitzers or cannon. The obsolescent 57mm could be shoulder-fired, while the newer and heavier guns were crew-served, firing from tripods. Effective against infantry and fortifications, such as bunkers, they fire regu-

larly shells with a flat trajectory over long ranges. The 105mm was developed during Korea.

INFANTRY MORTARS, 60MM, 81MM, 4.2-INCH: Mortars are primarily antipersonnel weapons, consisting of simple, sealed-breech tubes and base plates, which throw high explosive shells at a high angle, capable of reaching into valleys, trenches, and into defilade impervious to direct fire. The 60mm mortars were carried into position with the rifle companies; the 81mm's were handled by the weapons companies, and the 4.2-inch fired by a special mortar company within the regiment. The 81mm, with an effective range of 4.000 yards, to 1,800 for the 60mm, weighs more than 100 pounds and is not easily transportable in rough terrain by foot troops. The 4.2-inch, virtually an artillery weapon, is normally vehicle mounted.

THE QUAD .50: This was a half-tracked vehicle of World War II vintage, mounting four .50 machine guns capable of being fired as a unit. Developed as an antiaircraft weapon, with the advent of fast jet craft it became an antipersonnel weapon capable of hurling an immense amount of fire into hillsides and valleys against advancing infantry, or of throwing long-range harassing small-arms fire against enemy routes by night. Firing as many as 100,000 rounds per day, the Quad .50 could go over hills like a vacuum cleaner, sucking them devoid of life.

THE DUAL 40: Also developed as an AA weapon, the Dual 40 was a fully tracked vehicle with a tanklike silhouette mounting twin Bofors 40mm antiaircraft automatic cannon. It was also used to support the infantry line, in the same manner as the Quad .50.

THE ARTILLERY WEAPONS: During Korean operations, the standard U.S. artillery of World War II, the 105mm, 155mm, and 8-inch howitzers and rifles were employed in tremendous quantity. Developments were made in directions, spotting, and radar-sensing. Toward the end of the conflict, Korea was primarily an artillery war, with both sides dug in and cannonading each other rather than employing maneuver.

ARMOR: At the onset of the fighting, to its tremendous disadvantage, the United States had no tank in the Far East capable of engaging the obsolescent Russian T-34. The light M-24, primarily a reconnaissance vehicle with thin armor plate and light 75mm cannon, was augmented during August and September, 1950, with various U.S. interim model medium tanks, such as the M-26 Pershing, mounting a 90mm gun. Gradually, the old M4A3E8, the World War II workhorse, the Sherman, fitted with a newer high-velocity 76mm gun, became the principal Korea battle tank. It had a high silhouette, light armor, and an inadequate gun, but it was more maneuverable in the alternately steep and boggy Korean terrain than more modern tanks, such as the heavy-armor, heavy-gun British Centurion III. Failure to mass-produce a good main battle tank was one of the Army's principal weaknesses during the period; the concentration was more on seeking an effective antitank weapon than relying on the more expensive tank itself.

THE COMMUNIST NATIONS

Throughout the fighting, the enemy was adept at capturing and employing U.S. weapons and equipment. During the first ninety days, the North Korean People's Army secured enough equipment from ROK and U.S. divisions to outfit several of their own; and the Chinese Communist Forces, on entrance, were in many cases equipped with U.S. arms shipped to the Nationalist Government both during and after World War II, all of which had fallen into Communist hands. The Chinese (as the ROK's) also had a considerable quantity of surrendered Japanese arms and ammunition, from rifles to field guns. The principal source of armament for both North Koreans and Chinese, however, was Soviet Russia. Just as the Unites States provided 90 percent of all munitions used in the United Nations forces, the Russians designed, mass-produced, and delivered the bulk of all Communist weapons.

As with American arms, the majority of Russian equipment was of World War II vintage.

Russian weaponry, as Russian equipment in general, has one marked characteristic: it is extremely rugged, of the simplest design consistent with efficiency, and very easy to maintain, making it in many cases more suitable for the equipping of peasant armies than the more sophisticated U.S. arms. Despite its simplicity and lack of refinement, it is good.

INFANTRY RIFLES. The Communist forces were equipped with a miscellany of shoulder weapons, from the Russian 7.62mm carbine, a bolt-action rifle of 1944 vintage, to Japanese 7.7mm Imperial Army rifles, taken by the Soviets from the Kwantung Army in 1945 and turned over to the CCF. The tendency in Communist armies had been to discard the rifle in favor of the submachine gun, less accurate, bu table to throw much higher volume of fire in the hands of unskilled personnel.

THE SUBMACHINE GUN 7.62MM PPSh 41 (Burp Gun): Designed during World War II, the PPSh 41 submachine gun indicated the Soviet belief that highly accurate small arms were wasted in the hands of ground troops, while a large volume of fire was a requisite. Cheap to make, simple to operate, and thoroughly dependable under any battlefield conditions, the Soviet submachine gun was the best of its class during World War II. Fired either full or semiautomatic, it held a magazine of 72 rounds, with a cyclic rate of 100 per minute. Inaccurate except at close ranges. Toward the end of the war, Chinese infantry carried submachine guns or grenades almost exclusively while on the offensive.

THE TOKAREV 7.62MM SEMIAUTOMATIC RIFLE: This rifle, fitted with flash hider and bipod, served a purpose similar to that of the U.S. BAR.

THE DEGTYAREV 14.5MM ANTITANK RIFLE, PTRD-19411: This extremely long, ungainly weapon was designed against armor of the early World War II type. With the advent of thicker plate it became an antivehicular rifle, and was used for long-range sniping against personnel. Each NKPA division carried 36 of these, called by Americans the "elephant" or "buffalo" gun.

THE MACHINE GUNS: Several varieties of light machine guns were used by the NKPA and CCF, together with the Coryunov heavy machine gun, which was wheel-mounted. Russian machine guns were generally 7.62mm, an excellent military cartridge.

THE MORTARS: While as with other arms, a miscellany of calibers and types was found in Communist armies, the standard Russian makes predominated. Because of its ready transportability by hand and its cheapness of manufacture, the mortar was a favorite weapon of both the NKPA and CCF. An NKPA regiment contained six 120mm mortars; each of its three battalions had nine 82mm's; and the smaller 61mm was found at company level. The smaller Soviet mortars had an added advantage of being able to fire U.S. 60mm and 81mm mortar ammunition, of which the Communists captured great stores. The American tubes, unfortunately, could not reciprocate. Other infantry support weapons, such as rocket launchers and recoilless rifles, were not standard enemy issue; the were employed only when captured.

ARTILLERY: The artillery support of NKPA and CCF divisions closely followed that of the World War II Soviet division, though initially the CCF left most of its heavy artillery behind on crossing the Yalu. A division contained twelve 122mm howitzers, twenty-four 76mm field guns, twelve SU-76mm self-propelled guns on the T-34 chassis, and twelve 45mm antitank guns. In addition, each of the division's three regiments had four organic 76mm howitzers. The 122mm rifle was also furnished by the Soviets. With the exception of a few Japanese pieces, Communist artillery was Soviet-made, and during the later stages of the fighting appeared in quantities reminiscent of the Soviet massed artillery used in front of Berlin in 1945. Larger, long-range artillery, such as the 152mm gun, were used sparingly, in contrast with U.S. employment of medium artillery (155mm) in great quantities; the CCF had a marked reluctance to fire on targets they could not observe.

ARMOR: The Russian T-34/85, the Soviet main battle tank of World War II, which appeared in final form during the winter of 1943-1944, remained the Communist battle tank throughout. The T-34, weighing 35 tons and capable of 34 miles per hour, had excellent traction and was admirably suited to the terrain of Korea, where heavier American tanks such as the Patton found rough going. The T-34, mounting an 85mm gun and two 7.62mm machine guns, was considered by the Soviets an obsolescent tank in 1950. Their heavier, more modern tanks, such as the Josef Stalin III, were never furnished to satellite or auxiliary armies. In the first weeks, 150 T-34's, spearheading the NKPA attack, raised havoc with both ROK and U.S. forces. Later, both preponderance of American armor and airpower reduced Communist armor to a minor role; it was carefully concealed and hoarded, and rarely employed.

Since both combatants tended to use old and obsolescent armament—such as the T-34/85 and the Sherman M4A3E8, or the 1944 7.62mm rifle and the pre-World War II M-1—no comparison of weaponry is particularly significant or valid in the Korean War. In general, Communist equipment proved adequate, and in its class comparable in performance to American.

The city of Waegwan was almost completely destroyed. (U.S. Army photo)

Roster of the 7th U.S. Cavalry Association

Richard Abel
James R. "Jim" Abshear
Warren E. Adams
William A. Adams
William Alexander
Robert Alicea
Roy E. Allen
Frank H. Almy
Jose "Joe" Alva
Terry Ammons
Ashley C. Anderson
James A. Anderson
Robert J. Anderson
Robert P. Anderson, Jr.
Robert V. Anderson
Robert "Bob" Arbasetki
Edward Cross Armstrong
James Daniel Back
Wendy Mae Back
Ralph Baer
Robert R. Balicki
Thomas A. Balish
Jesse B. Ball
Henry E. Ballard, Jr.
Stephen T. Banko, III
Joseph S. Barca
John Richard Beard
Hall Bearden
Virgil H. Becker
Edwin Bell
Urcel L. Bell
Edmond B. Benn
Mack Bentley, Jr.
Michael D. Benton
Ronald H. Benton
Ralph G. Bernotas
Guy F. Bess
Harold Blanc
Willaim Blanc
Robert W. Bloss
Mike Bodnar
Gordon Bennie Boles, Jr.
Royal D. Bollinger
Thomas E. Bookwalter
Donald John Bosse
Arnold Jimmy Bowman
Margaret Ann Boyd
Richard T. Boyd
Thomas E. Boyd
Richard E. Bradbury
Ralph E. Braunstein
Joseph B. Breen
Charles L. "Chuck" Bremer
Donna L. Brennan
Michael Brennan, M.D.
Richard T. "Dick" Britton
Paul E. Brooks
Tim Brosius
Vincent G Bruner, Sr.
Crawford Buchanan
Billy N. Bullington
Glen G.. Bumgarner
Elijah F. Burditt
Billy D. Burns
Jonathan R. Burton
Milton Byron
Dennis J. Calabrese
Guy R. Calhoun
John W. Callaway
James Campbell
Peter V. Cangro
Donald T. Carlson
Douglas E. Carnahan
John Carroll
Robert M. Carroll
Joseph L. Chacon
Bobby D. Chafin
Rayford E. "Ray" Chance

Harold J. Clark
Orval D. Clark
John J. Cloeter
Robert E. Clutts
Richard L. Coblentz
Allen Coffman
Peter C. Cole
William T. Collins
John J. Conlon, Jr.
Lawrence E. Connors
Robert M. Cooper
Everett L. Copeland
C.L. Copello
Mauricio F. Cordero, Jr.
Jack L. Couch
James V. "Jim" Court
Daniel J. Cox, Jr.
George T. Creamer
Dominick Creazzo
Joseph H. Cross, Jr.
John F. Crowley
Noel F. Croy
Frank J. Culley
Harriet Culley
Donavan A. Cullings
Elliott R. Cumbow
James F. Cummings
James W. "Jim" Curram
Glen E. "Slim" Curran, Jr.
Edward L. Daily
James E. Daly
James R. Daly
Kevin M.. Dandy
Matthew W. Dandy
Marvin C. Daniel
Francis "Pancho" Daughterty
Donald Daujatas
Robert M. "Bob" Davie
Claude L. Davis
James C. Davis, Jr.
Dennis J. Deal
Stephen Robert Deal
John Della Ripa
Vincent M. Dempewolf
Philip Dempsey
James J. Dennigan
Allen E. Dewitt
William A. Deyoe
Justo M. Diaz
John C. Doherty
David A. Donnelly
Donald R. Donnelly
Robert E. "Bob" Doran
John M. Doughterty
John J. Dowd
Richard K. Dowell
Donlad D. Down
Edna Down
David P. Duff
Robert L. Dunaway
Jonathan K. Dunkleberger
John H. Dutram
Chirls S. "Charly" Duty
Johnnie M. Dyson
Earl Early
Kenneth G. Eastham
Michael G. Echert
Woodrow P. Edwards
James Elkins
Ester H. Ellis
Lance English
Thomas J. Evans
Erwin D. Fahrnow
Sam P. Fantino
James E. "Jim" Farrell
Peter T. Farelly
Eugene Fels
Ron Ferraro

Victor L. Fox
Ellen R. Finch
Sherman C. Flanders
Russell C. Fonder
Buford W. Ford
Leland C. Foster
Allen G. Fox
Robert Frisbie
Robert S. Frix
Lawrence A.Frost
Joseph L. Gallaway
Joseph G. Gange
Homer Garcia
Paul Gargis
Martin T. Gavin
Bernard N. "Barry" Gemelli
Mrs. Marilyn Genz
Lyle R. Gibbs
Robert E. "Bob" Gibson
Francis V. Gigandet
Lawrence R. Gilbert
Terrance P. Girard
Frank D. Gish
Anthony D. Glasco
Michael B. Glenn
Conrad "Duke" Glodowski
James T. Godfrrey
Horace T. Goodrich
Daniel F. Gourley
John F. Graham
Otto G. Graumann
Millard G. Gray
Jesse L. Green
Charles E. Griffin
Don Griffiths
John Grisius
Karl J. Grocott
Albert Guarnieri, Jr.
James F. "Jim" Hackett
Sherman P. Haight
Stephen D. Hale
Dillard R. Hall
Kerry D. Hall
Virginia G. Halladay-Pierce
John C. Hanell
Douglas C. Hardy
Lawrence E. Hargrove
Charles W. Harman
Charles M. Harris
James Harris
Curtis E. Harry
Thomas E. Hartin
John "Jack" Haskell
Alain Victor M Hasson
Gardner Hatch
Douglea Hayes
Robert D. Hazen
L. Wesley Hedges
William Hedley
Nancy Bernice Heltsley
Larry P. Henry
Gilberto A. Herrera, Jr.
Fred Herrmann
Jacque Hill
Thomas Hill
Samuel R. "Richard" Hillegas
John T. Hindman
Michael C. Hobbs
William H. Hoffmann
Theron Holland
Charles R. "Chuck" Horn
John M. Howden
George Hudson
Richard G.. Hughes
Thomas Edward Hughes
Mark Hume
Frank Lee Hutson
Scott W. Hyatt

Thomas R. Illing
Dennis Inka
John M. Jackson, M.D.
William W. "Bill" Jean
Roy W. Jerome
Kenneth D. Johnson
Alzalkie C. Jones
Douglas W. Keeton
Ronald Kencke
Charles M. Kennemore, Jr.
William J. Kesterson
John D. Kieslar
Gerald R. Kietzman
Charles E. "Bob" Kincaid
Robert E. Kinder
C. King
Robert R. Kinler
Harry W.O. Kinnard
Michael L. Kinney
Alfred A. Klein
Gunther Klincke
Matilda Klincke
E. Kent Kluever
Patty Kluever
Julius Korry
John E. Kosinki
Roger W. Krachinski
Willian H. "Bill" Kreischer
Richard T. Kruske
Rueben D. Kvidt
Richard S. Lacey
Willian J. Lacey
Tim Landis
John R. "Bob" Lane
Rorik W. Larson
Bill R. Laws
Homer K. Leacock
Edgar J. Lee
Jesse F. Lee
W. Suey Lee
Elzie G.W. Lemmons
Timothy N. Lenihan
Thomas D. Lent
Lewis T. Lepre
George Lewis
John C. Lippincott
Robert F. "Bob" Litle, Jr.
Little Big Horn Assoc..
Nicholas G. Lorris
William C. "Bill" Lovell
James M. "Jim" Lowry
Velmer R. Lucas
Richard L. Lucero
Tammy J. Ludke
Frank J. Lukes
Roger Luta
Herman A. Mace
James C. Madigan
Daniel P. Mancini
Peter J. "Pete" Mariotti
Randall D. Martin
John Maruhnich
Gary L. Massey
Charles A. Mateya
William Matichak
Charles W. Mattes
James Mattes
Henry N. Matthias
Robert N. Mauger
Richard E. Maybury
Jack H. Mayse
Emilio A. Mazza
Charles MaAleer
Joseph "Joe" McAnany
Jack E. McBride
John McCamley
James A. McClure
Clyde W. "Mac" McComas
George J. McDonald, Jr.

Paul McElhannon
Grover C. McGraw
Thomas L. McKeon
Russell "Russ" McKinley
Thomas L. McKnight
William N. "Bill" McKown
Carmen S. Miceli
Ronald J. Migut
Tim Millar
Dall H. Miller
Hank Milum
Norval M. Miner
Walter D,. Minnick
Saluatore Mione
E.A. Mike Molloy
Wm. T. "Bill" Mooney
Harold G. "Hal" Moore
James R. Moore
William F. Moore
James Morelli
Claude B. Morrison
Richard L. Morton
Rodger L. Mumby
Charles U. Murphy
George N. Murphy
Thomas L. Murphy
Jacob C. Myres
Albert Nacke
Ramon A. "Tony"Nadal, II
Alice Nemec
Gregory P. Nonweiler
George J. Nye
Gary A. Oakes
Lewis John Oneal
Andrew Oresick
George M. Osborn
Norman R. Osterby
Peggy Osterby
Joseph K. Owen
John O'Brien
"Mike" Milton L. ODea
Fred L. Palmer
Jackson F. "Jack" Palmer
Ernest Paolone

Larry B. Parker
John J. Parle
Joey N. Parton
Connie Passos
Ignacio "Nash" Passos
Howard D. Patterson
Henry John Pauley, Sr.
Mrs. Nadean Ross
Marvin Rottenberg
John C. Rourke, M.D.
Dr. E.H. Royan
Myron D. Runyon
Frank L. Ryan
James M. Sales
Pedro "Pete" Samaniego, Jr.
Kenneth R. Sammons
Robert B. Sammons
Fred Schaaff
Jim Schild
C.R. Schleusner
Gregroy A. Schlieve
James Schneider
Raymond J. Schooner
Eldon D. Screws
David C. Sebranek
Michael L. Serge
Domenico P. Serri
John I. Setelin
Gordon J. Severson
Robert A. Shannon
Daniel Sheehan
Charles C. Shipman
John Shingler
Lawrence J. Short
Ted Short
Richard L. Siegreen
Carl H. Silber, III
Harry G. Simmeth
Milton E. Simmons
Nena Singer
Ronald G. Sleeis
Arlo C. Smith
Barton M. Smith
James C. Smith

John P. "Jack" Smith
Joseph M. Smith
William D. Smith
John A. Smythe
Jo Sowder
Tom W. Spalding
James A. Sparrow
Stephen P. Spencer
Robert D. St. Martin
Arthur J. Stanley, Jr.
Jan P. Steffen
Roy Stern
Randall R. Stevens
Carlos J. "Jay" Stockton
Thomas H. Stone, Jr.
Fredersick A. Stoutland
Jack Stowe
Carrol D. Stripling
Vallie H. Stump
Kenneth G. Sullivan
Charles K. Sutton
John Swahn
Richard A. Swain
William H. "Bill" Swan
Jose M. Talavera-Toso, III
Howard G. Tallau
Robert L. Templeton
Angelo L. Thompson
Jamie Campbell Thompson, III
Richard E. Tobin
Robert H. "Bob" Toberg
William R. Tompkins
Robert L. Towles
Noe S. Trevino
Dave Turner
Elzie Tyree
Peter J. Valenti
Sherman M. Van Dyke
Mike A. Velarde
Edward J. Villacres
Mrs. Margarete Von Ruedgisch
Leonard F. "Bud" Vosmier
E.L. "Chip" Votaw
Edward Wagnild

William C. Wallace
Jon W. Wallenius
William J. Walsh
Richard J. Ward
Albert A. Webster
Charles Alfred Welch
Craig W. Wenger
Merrill Wernsing
Robert D. West
William W. West
Richard White
William J. White
John A. Wickham, Jr.
Harold M. Wigant
Herman D. Williams
James D. Williams
Nevin R. Williams
Nevin R. "Pete" Williams, II
Barry L. Williamson
James A. Wilson
Clifford R. "Bucky" Wiltshire
Franklin F. Wing, Jr.
Peter J. Winter
James Wood
Clinton A. Woodley
Ms. Kathleen Cronan Wyosnick
Chester D. "Chet" Young
Edwin William Younger
Felix E. Ysais
Jerald D. "Jack" Zallen

"Poor Guy, Hell! He's Just Comin' Back From R&R Leave."

"Well, Our Goose Is Cooked. . !."

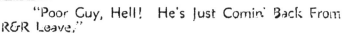

From the Stars and Stripes Newspaper, 1950-51. (Courtesy of Ed Daily)

REMEMBER

It is a fact that prisoners of war have offered their best in the service of their country. The only difference between them and those who have so gallantly died in so doing is that the enemy did not choose to kill them when they were overpowered.

If you are close enough to the enemy to be captured, you are close enough to be shot or bayoneted.

Let no man believe there is a stigma attached to having been honorably captured in battle. Only the fighting man gets close enough to the enemy for that to happen. That he is not listed with the slain is due to the infinite care of Providence.

Be proud that you carried yourselves as men in battle and adversity. You will be enriched thereby.

Let us, anew, pledge ourselves, that we may return to our place in the American life better fitted to carry on the duty assigned to us and none the worse for the inevitable role we have carried for so long.

> Thomas D. Drake, Colonel U.S.A.
> Senior Officer, OFLAG 64
> Ex-POW, Germany World War II

THE KOREAN WAR
Our Finest Hour

In the macabre march of military history, every nation has one finest hour. It comes when the weapons of war cannot bring victory and only the character of the warrior can prevent defeat.

For free nations, that hour came in Korea. But few were aware. Obsessed with the ideal of total victory, we had come to view anything less as total defeat. Arrogance, born of past successes, led to ignorance of the challenges we faced. And ignorance, born of past excesses, led to arrogance of our capabilities to meet them. So our finest hour came and went, and the nations never knew it.

But the hour shone brightly on those who bore the brunt of battle. For, at the height of their life-or-death struggle, courage triumphed over cowardice; patriotism over cruelty; sacrifice over self-preservation and integrity over self-interest. In a savage hell of untold misery, they stood, fought and died as principled men in an unprincipled realm.

Proudly, Korea was our finest hour. Sadly, only those who served, sacrificed and survived, shared the moment.

> Brigadier General E. M. Lynch
> United States Army, Retired

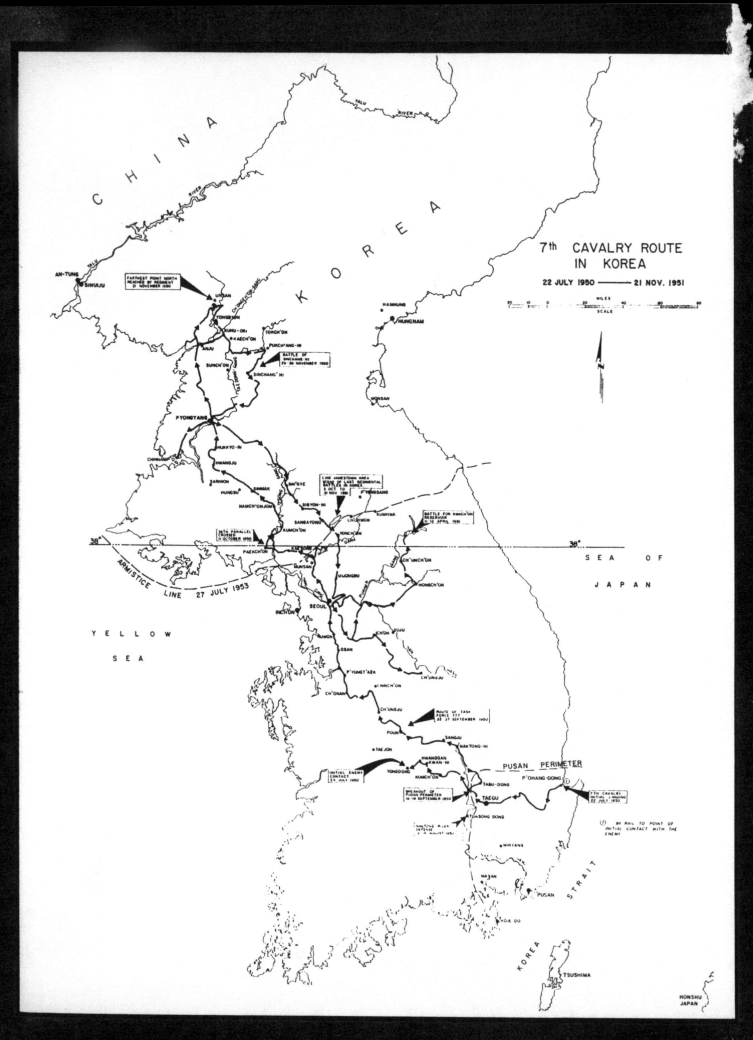

Camp McNair training base for the 1st Cavalry Division, 1949 -- Note Mt. Fuji in the background. (Courtesy of Ed Daily)Below: A temporary grave site in Taegu, South Korea, 1950, "In sacred memory of these brave American and United Nations soldiers who gave their lives during the Korean War, 1950-53." (U.S. Army)

Right: Major General William M. Hoge, Commander IX Corps, decorates Lt. Colonel D. Arbouzis, Commander 4th Battalion (GEF), and other officers of the Greek Battalion, attached to the 7th Cavalry, April 1951. (United Nations photo). Below: The courtesy speaks for itself. "GARRYOWEN' From Of GARRYOWEN and Glory'. Below center: High dug in position with a .30 caliber light machine gun. (U.S. Army photo) Bottom: An attacking rifle squad with fixed bayonets. (U.S. Army photo) Next page - Top: Preparing to move out from trench positions. (U.S. Army photo) . Bottom left: 1st Cavalry Division troopers looking at where two bullet holes almost went through the same hole in his helmet. (U.S. Army photo) Bottom right: Another rugged hill secured. (U.S. Army photo)

Printed in the USA
CPSIA information can be obtained
at www.ICGtesting.com
JSHW060055150824
68134JS00032B/2737